T0134668

Computer Communications and Networks

Series editor
A.J. Sammes,
Centre for Forensic Computing
Cranfield University, Shrivenham Campus
Swindon, UK

The **Computer Communications and Networks** series is a range of textbooks, monographs and handbooks. It sets out to provide students, researchers, and non-specialists alike with a sure grounding in current knowledge, together with comprehensible access to the latest developments in computer communications and networking.

Emphasis is placed on clear and explanatory styles that support a tutorial approach, so that even the most complex of topics is presented in a lucid and intelligible manner.

More information about this series at http://www.springer.com/series/4198

Pethuru Raj • Anupama Raman
Dhivya Nagaraj • Siddhartha Duggirala

High-Performance Big-Data Analytics

Computing Systems and Approaches

 Springer

Pethuru Raj
IBM India
Bangalore, India

Anupama Raman
IBM India
Bangalore, India

Dhivya Nagaraj
IBM India
Bangalore, India

Siddhartha Duggirala
Indian Institute of Technology
Indore, MP, India

ISSN 1617-7975   ISSN 2197-8433 (electronic)
Computer Communications and Networks
ISBN 978-3-319-36324-0   ISBN 978-3-319-20744-5 (eBook)
DOI 10.1007/978-3-319-20744-5

Printed on acid-free paper

Springer International Publishing AG Switzerland is part of Springer Science+Business Media
(www.springer.com)

Foreword

In the recent past, the data growth has been unbelievably phenomenal due to a plethora of converging technologies (digitization, connectivity, integration, perception, miniaturization, consumerization, commoditization, orchestration of knowledge discovery and dissemination, etc.). In short, every common and casual thing in our personal as well as professional environments gets connected with one another and service-enabled to innately enable them to participate seamlessly and sagaciously in the mainstream computing. The device landscape is also going through a variety of innovations and improvisations in the recent past. Precisely speaking, the deeper and extreme connectivity among all kinds of digitized artifacts and devices is primarily responsible for the massive amounts of data.

This brewing trend and transformation brings forth a variety of challenges as well as opportunities not only for IT professionals but also for data scientists. The discipline of data analytics is bound to grow in multiple dimensions and directions. Newer types of data analytics (generic as well as specific) are bound to emerge and evolve fast. The compute, storage, and network challenges are also destined to become severe. With the ever-increasing data size, structure, scope, speed, and value, the biggest challenge for any enterprise and its IT team is how to flawlessly capture and process data and extract actionable insights in time. Each type of data emanating internally as well as externally provides hidden insights in the form of usable patterns, fruitful associations, timely alerts, fresh possibilities, and opportunities.

In this book, the authors have passionately explained why big and fast data analytics need high-performance infrastructures (server machines, storage appliances, and network connectivity solutions) to do justice for the next-generation data analytic solutions. With the sole aim of conveying the nitty-gritty of the state-of-the-art technologies and tools which are emerging and evolving in the high-performance big data analytics domain, authors have consciously focused on the various types of enabling IT infrastructures and platforms for the same.

Data Analytics: The Process Steps It is a well-known fact that typically there are three major phases/stages in any data analytics task:

1. *Data capture* through data virtualization platforms
2. *Data processing/interpretation* platforms for knowledge discovery
3. *Knowledge dissemination* through a host of data visualization platforms

The Emerging Analytics Types With the ever-increasing data volume, velocity, variety, variability, viscosity, and veracity, a bevy of powerful analytics (generic as well as specific) use cases is getting unearthed. All kinds of business verticals and industry segments are employing different types of analytics to squeeze out actionable insights from their data. The generic/horizontal analytic types include:

- Sensor analytics
- Machine analytics
- Operational analytics
- Real-time analytics
- High-performance analytics

The domain-specific analytic types include social media and network analytics, customer sentiment analytics, brand optimization analytics, financial trading and trending analytics, retail analytics, energy analytics, medical analytics, and utility analytics.

Emerging IT Infrastructures and Platforms IT infrastructures are increasingly becoming converged, centralized, federated, pre-integrated, optimized, and organized in an attempt to evolve into a right and relevant option for futuristic businesses. Analytical platforms are hitting the market like never before. Having understood the significance of carefully and cognitively doing analytics on every form of data to be competitive in their business operations, enterprises across the globe are eagerly looking out for high-performing IT infrastructures and platforms to run big and fast data analytical applications in an effective and efficient manner.

The authors have extensively written about the existing and emerging high-performance IT infrastructures and platforms for efficiently accomplishing flexible data analytics. The prominent IT infrastructures which are discussed in this book include:

1. Mainframes
2. Parallel and supercomputing systems
3. Peer-to-peer, cluster, and grid computing systems
4. Appliances (data warehouse and Hadoop-specific)
5. Expertly integrated and specially engineered systems
6. Real-time systems
7. Cloud infrastructures

The authors have consciously brought forth all the value-adding information on next-generation IT infrastructures and platforms for big and fast data analytics in this book. This book will be highly beneficial for technical experts, consultants, evangelists, and exponents apart from business executives, decision-makers, and other stakeholders. I am doubly sure that software engineers, solution architects, cloud professionals, and big data scientists across the world will find this book informative, interesting, and inspiring to deeply understand how data analytics will emerge as a common service and play an indispensable role in shaping up the world towards becoming rewardingly smart.

IBM Analytics, Orange County, CA, USA
TBDI, Orange County, CA, USA

Sushil Pramanick, FCA, PMP

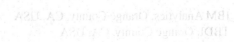

Preface

Several industry trends and a host of powerful technologies and tools in a synchronized fashion undoubtedly lead to the massive data explosion. Incidentally data is overwhelmingly acquiring the status of a strategic asset across industry verticals. The prominent foundations for the unprecedented data include the following noteworthy transitions: the device ecosystem expands continuously as per the widely changing peoples' imaginations, machines are becoming intelligent with smart instrumentation and interconnectivity generating data in the range of petabytes and exabytes, personal and professional applications are meticulously service-enabled to be interoperable for beneficial data sharing, everyday social networking sites are producing terabytes of data, ordinary objects in and around us are minutely digitized generating a lot of multi-structured data at different velocities, etc. On the other hand, ICT infrastructures and platforms are highly optimized and organized for effective data storage and processing and analytics, adaptive WAN technologies are being formulated to accelerate data transfer securely, newer architectural patterns are assimilated, processes are systematically made nimble, etc. to make sense out of data.

This data when analyzed carefully can provide a wealth of information which can revolutionize all facets of our life. This idea has evolved to be a game changer in the present day IT domain and is widely referred to as big data analytics. Considering the data size, speed, scope, and structure, the compute, storage, and networking infrastructures need to be immaculately efficient. Primarily the big data world brings forth three crucial challenges for the IT world: big data storage and management, big data analytics, and producing sophisticated applications leveraging analytics. Precisely speaking big data analytics (BDA) is quickly turning out to be the next-generation high-performance computing discipline for our students, scholars, and scientists to unearth competent algorithms, patterns, methodologies, best practices, key guidelines, evaluation metrics, etc.

This book is a humble attempt to provide a bird's eye view of those techniques. A sincere and serious attempt is made to analyze the network and storage infrastructure optimizations which are the need of the hour in order to capture, ingest, crunch, and handle big data efficiently for knowledge discovery and dissemination. Some use cases of big data analytics in various industry sectors are also included in this book to let you know the heightening importance of data analytics in a simplified and streamlined manner.

Chapter 1: *The Brewing Trends and Transformations in the IT Landscape*—This chapter, being the first chapter for the book, lists out the emerging transitions in the IT arena especially in the context for the big and fast data world. The promising and potential technologies and tools in the ICT domain are being given prime importance in this chapter in order to give an indication of what is in store for the readers in this book.

Chapter 2: *The High-Performance Technologies for Big and Fast Data Analytics*—This chapter has categorized the most visible technologies for high-performance big and fast data analytics.

Chapter 3: *Big and Fast Data Analytics Yearning for High-Performance Computing*—We have explained the nitty-gritty of big and fast data analytics here as a precursor for conveying the significance of high-performance computing needs for productively extracting actionable insights out of data heaps.

Chapter 4: *Network Infrastructure for High-Performance Big Data Analytics*—This chapter summarizes the network infrastructure requirements for effective transfer of big data. In order to transfer big data efficiently through the networks, it is necessary to perform some modifications to the existing network infrastructure. Some of the techniques which could be used are network virtualization, software-defined networks (SDN), two-tier leaf spine architecture, and network functions virtualization. Each of these techniques is explained in detail in this chapter. It is also necessary to optimize the existing Wide Area Network infrastructure so that it can transfer big data efficiently. A novel approach for transfer of big data efficiently using TCP/IP protocol using a technology called FASP is also discussed in this chapter. Some of the implementation aspects of FASP are also included in the discussion of this chapter.

Chapter 5: *Storage Infrastructures for High-Performance Big Data Analytics*—This chapter summarizes the storage infrastructure requirements of applications which generate big data. Present-day storage infrastructures are not optimized to store and handle big data. The main concern with the existing storage techniques is their lack of scalability. Hence it is the need of the day to devise new storage techniques which can handle big data efficiently. In this chapter, we are adopting a multifaceted approach: at first we discuss the existing storage infrastructure and their suitability to handle big data. Later on we discuss some platforms and file systems which are designed only for handling big data like PANASAS file system, Lustre file system, GFS, and HDFS.

Chapter 6: *Real-Time Analytics Using High-Performance Computing*—This chapter talks about analytics in the real-time environment. It covers all recent real-time analytics solutions like machine data analytics and operational analytics. This is an eye opener on how data can be handled in real time and the value that it adds in changing our lives for a better tomorrow.

Chapter 7: *High-Performance Computing (HPC) Paradigms*—This chapter covers in detail the reasons behind the evolution of high-performance computing over the years in mainframe. A few years ago, the world came to a conclusion that mainframes are going to be extinct with the evolving technology. But organizations like IBM have proved that mainframes are not going to be extinct but have come back with a bang providing solutions that were once assumed completely impossible.

Chapter 8: *In-Database Processing and In-Memory Analytics*—This chapter is for elucidating the in-database analytics techniques and in-memory analytics techniques. When the business systems run at large scale, moving data in and out of the data store can be really daunting and expensive. While moving the processing near to the data, the data processing is done in the data store itself; by doing this we can reduce the data movement costs and use much larger data sets to mine the data. While the businesses are moving, the speed has become crucial. This is where real-time databases come into the picture. This chapter covers all aspects pertaining to in-database and in-memory analytics techniques with appropriate examples.

Chapter 9: *High-Performance Integrated Systems, Databases, and Warehouses for Big and Fast Data Analytics*—For the ensuing big data era, there is a distinctive need for newer kinds of data management systems. We have clearly catalogued and written about the emerging clustered SQL, NoSQL, and NewSQL databases. There is an explanation on big data-specific data warehouses.

Chapter 10: *High-Performance Grids and Clusters*—This chapter is for elucidating the techniques and software tools available to enable big data analytics and high data-intensive processing. Businesses around the globe are under pressure to reduce the TCO of analytical platforms and yet quite ably perform at the required level. Using these versatile high-performance systems, businesses are able to meet the performance demands that are put forward to them. This chapter explains the different use cases about the usage of cluster and grid computing systems in the realm of big data analytics.

Chapter 11: *High-Performance Peer-to-Peer Systems*—This chapter is for elucidating the peer-to-peer techniques and tools that are used in big data analytics domain. Due to the large-scale nature of the data stores or analytical systems typically have master-slave relationship between servers. This helps in parallelizing the application, but a problem arises when the master fails. Then no request will be replied back. In these scenarios, if the software structure is decentralized, meaning no master servers, then there would be no single point of failure. Hence the entire request will be answered. This chapter explains the different use cases about the usage of high-performance peer-to-peer systems.

Chapter 12: *Visualization Dimensions for High-Performance Big Data Analytics—This chapter* is for elucidating the visualization techniques and tools. As the data size increases and complexity of the data increases, it becomes difficult to comprehend the meaning of the data and the analysis which is uncovered. If the data or analytical output is displayed in some visual format instead as simple numbers, users can easily grab the meaning and work on it accordingly. This chapter explains the different use cases about the usage of information visualization techniques which are prominently used in the big data analytics field.

Chapter 13: *Social Media Analytics for Organization Empowerment*—This chapter highlights social media analytics which is one of the prominent technology use cases of big data analytics. One of the major drivers for big data is the huge amount of unstructured data which is generated by the social media networks. This has led to the evolution of a new stream of analytics which is called social media analytics. This chapter discusses the various drivers for the evolution of social media analytics. The various use cases which depict the usage of social media analytics for the transformation of organizations are discussed at length in this chapter. The content metrics which are used to track the impact of social media for organizations are also discussed at length in this chapter. Some key predictive analytic techniques which are used for social media analytics are network analysis and sentiment analysis using text mining. These two techniques are discussed in this chapter. Some of the tools which are used for social media analytics are also discussed in this chapter.

Chapter 14: *Big Data Analytics for Healthcare*—This chapter explains the primary importance of analytics in the healthcare sector. It is rightly said that the future of healthcare is the future for all of us. This chapter covers important driving factors for analytics in healthcare and the use cases for big data analytics in healthcare. The chapter sets an example on how data that got unnoticed in the past has proven to be a ray of hope to deliver quality care to patients in a cost-effective manner.

Disclaimer: The book and its contents are intended to convey the views of the authors and not their organizations.

Acknowledgment

The Acknowledgment (Pethuru Raj)

I express my sincere gratitude to Mr. **Simon Rees**, Springer, Associate Editor, Computer Science, for immensely helping us from the conceptualization to the completion of this book. I wholeheartedly acknowledge the fruitful suggestions and pragmatic contributions of my esteemed colleagues Anupama, Siddardh, and Dhivya. I need to remember my supervisors Prof. Ponnammal Natarajan, Anna University, Chennai; the late Prof. Priti Shankar, Computer Science and Automation (CSA) Department, Indian Institute of Science (IISc), Bangalore; Prof. Naohiro Ishii, Department of Intelligence and Computer Science, Nagoya Institute of Technology; and Prof. Kazuo Iwama, School of Informatics, Kyoto University, Japan, for shaping my research life. I wholeheartedly thank my managers at IBM in extending their moral support all along this book journey.

I, at this point of time, recollect and reflect on the selfless sacrifices made by my parents in shaping me up to this level. I would expressly like to thank my wife (Sweetlin Reena) and sons (Darren Samuel and Darresh Bernie) for their perseverance. I give all the glory and honor to my Lord and Savior Jesus Christ for His grace and guidance.

The Acknowledgment (Anupama Raman)

At the outset, I would like to express my heartfelt thanks to Mr. Simon Rees, Wayne Wheeler, and the Springer publishing team for their wholehearted support. My special thanks to Dr. Pethuru Raj for his constant support, guidance, and insights which helped me in crafting various chapters of this book. I would like to thank IBM management for their wholehearted support in the successful completion of this book project. At this stage I would also like to sincerely acknowledge the sacrifice of my

parents which made me what I am today. A special note of thanks to my husband
(R. Murali Krishnan) and daughter (Aparna) for their constant support and motivation. I would also like to acknowledge the support given to me by my parents-in-
law, my sisters, and their family. I thank all my friends who have constantly helped
and supported me to complete the book successfully.

The Acknowledgment (Dhivya Nagaraj)

I would like to express my thanks to the editors and the publishing team of Springer
Publications for their support. I cannot express enough my sincere appreciation
to my mentor Anupama Murali for her majestic professional help in shaping the
contents of this book and also to Dr. Pethuru Raj for all the encouragement and
moral support.

I would like to extend my heartfelt thanks to my managers Sandip Singha and
Prasenjit Bandhopadhyay and also the IBM management for being with me throughout this journey and helping me to aid the successful completion of the book. It is
difficult to meet success without the support from our dear ones. This would be the
right opportunity to thank my dear husband (Dr. Sudeep Gowda) and my parents
for the unequaled and exceptional support in this travel. A special thanks to my
daughter without whose support this wouldn't have been achievable and to all
my dear friends for all their prayers.

The Acknowledgment (Siddhartha Duggirala)

On this note, I would like to express sincere thanks to each and everyone in the
whole team for letting me be a part of this book and helping me out. My unfeigned
thanks to Dr. Pethuru Raj and Anupama Raman for their guidance and support
throughout the execution of this book.

I would like to thank each and every one from IIT Indore for being a part of my
life. Especially Dr. Abhishek Srivatsava, Dr. Aruna Tiwari, and Dr. Siddharth Malu
for believing in me and encouraging me to pursue whatever my heart bleeds for.
I would like also to thank Sarfraz Qureshi my senior in IIT Indore and Dr. Kaushik
Pavani my mentor who introduced me to the world of data.

I'd take this opportunity to thank my parents, brother, and cousins for helping me
out, keeping me motivated, and showering their love. Without these great people,
their support, and motivation, none of this would've been achievable. I am really
grateful to all my friends for helping me and supporting me till the completion of
the book. So, thanks everyone!

Contents

Chapter 1
The Brewing Trends and Transformations in the IT Landscape

1.1 Introduction

As widely reported, there are several delectable transitions and some disruptions in the IT landscape. Definitely, the consequences are vast and varied: the incorporation of nimbler and next-generation features and functionalities into existing and emerging IT solutions, the grand opening for scores of fresh possibilities and opportunities for not only businesses but also individuals, the fabulous eruption of altogether new IT products and solutions for the humanity, etc. There are a number of disruptive and transformative technologies emanating and evolving as being vouched by leading market analyst and research firms. For an instance, Gartner regularly reports the top ten technology trends every year. The technologies have the inherent verve to bring forth numerous subtle and succinct transformations for business organizations as well as common people. In this chapter, to set up an appropriate context for the book, the most prevalent and pioneering trends in the IT landscape are to be detailed for inquisitive minds.

Someone wrote like this. The first wave of IT belongs to the aura of hardware engineering. A variety of electronic modules (purpose specific and generic) had been meticulously designed and aggregated in order to fulfill the various computing, networking, and storage requirements. The miniaturization technologies have been playing a very indispensable role in shaping up the hardware industry in bringing forth scores of micro- and nano-level components. We are on the track towards the era of ubiquitously deployed, disappearing, and disposable computers. The second wave of IT heralded a shift from hardware to software. The software engineering started to improvise decisively from there, and today software is pervasive and persuasive. Software brings in the much-needed adaptivity, modifiability, extensibility, and sustainability. Every tangible thing is being empowered to be smart through the embedding and imbedding of software. The third and current wave of IT began a couple years ago and is based on the utilization of data (big and fast) to derive benefits from the advantages gained in hardware and software. The capture and investigations

© Springer International Publishing Switzerland 2015
P. Raj et al., *High-Performance Big-Data Analytics*, Computer Communications and Networks, DOI 10.1007/978-3-319-20744-5_1

of data lead to actionable and timely insights that can be sagaciously used for realizing smarter applications and appliances.

Thus, data analytics is the most endearing and enduring subject of study and research in order to come out with viable and venerable methods for the envisaged smarter planet. Especially considering the faster growth of disparate and distributed data sources, there is a special liking for data virtualization, processing, mining, analysis, and visualization technologies that invariably fulfill the goals of knowledge discovery and dissemination. Data-driven insights enable taking right decisions for people as well as systems in time with all clarity and confidence. You can find the most promising trends sweeping the IT landscape in order to bring in the enhanced care, choice, convenience, and comfort for people at large.

1.2   The Emerging IT Trends

IT Consumerization The much discoursed and deliberated Gartner report details the diversity of mobile devices (smartphones, tablets, wearables, etc.). Increasingly, the IT is coming closer to humans. People at any point of time, any place, any device, any network, and any media could access and use any remotely held IT resources, business applications, and data for their personal as well as professional purposes. The massive production of slim and sleek input/output devices empowers end users to directly connect and benefit immensely out of all the telling improvisations of the IT discipline. The IT consumer trend has been evolving for some time now and peaking these days. That is, IT is steadily becoming an inescapable part of consumers directly and indirectly. And the need for robust and resilient mobile device management software solutions with the powerful emergence of "bring your own device (BYOD)" is being felt and is being insisted across. Another aspect is the emergence of next-generation mobile applications and services across a variety of business verticals. There is a myriad of mobile applications, maps, and service development/delivery platforms, programming and markup languages, architectures and frameworks, tools, containers, and operating systems in the fast-moving mobile space. Precisely speaking, IT is moving from enterprise centricity to be consumer oriented.

IT Commoditization Commoditization is another cool trend sweeping the IT industry. With the huge acceptance and adoption of cloud computing and big data analytics, the value of commodity IT is decisively on the rise. Typically, the embedded intelligence is being consciously abstracted out of hardware boxes and appliances in order to make hardware modules voluminously manufactured and easily and quickly used. The infrastructure affordability is another important need in getting realized with this meticulous segregation, and the perennial problem of vendor lock-in is steadily eased out. Any product can be replaced and substituted by another similar device from other manufacturers. With the consolidation, centralization, and commercialization of IT infrastructures heat up, the demands of commoditized hardware go up furiously. All kinds of IT infrastructures (server machines, storage appliances, network solutions such as routers, switches, load balancers, firewall gateways, etc.) are being commoditized with the renewed focus on IT industrialization. The commoditization through virtualization and containerization is pervasive and persuasive. Therefore, the next-generation IT environment is specifically software defined to bring in programmable and policy-based hardware systems in plenty.

The Ensuing Era of Appliances The topic of hardware engineering is seeing a lot of hitherto unheard improvisations. Undoubtedly, appliances are the recent hit in the IT market. All the leading vendors are investing their treasure, time, and talent in unearthing next-generation smartly integrated systems (compute, storage, network, virtualization, and management modules) in the form of instant-on appliances. IT appliances are fully customized and configured in the factory itself so that they could just be turned on to get their verve at customer location in minutes and hours rather than days. In order to incorporate as much automation as possible, there are strategic appliance-centric initiatives on producing pre-integrated and pretested and tuned converged IT stacks. For example, FlexPod and VCE are leading in the race in the converged IT solution category. Similarly, there are expertly integrated systems such as IBM PureFlex System, PureApplication System, and PureData System. Further on, Oracle engineered systems, such as Oracle Exadata Database Machine and Exalogic Elastic Cloud, are gaining in the competitive market.

Infrastructure Optimization and Elasticity The entire IT stack has been going for the makeover periodically. Especially on the infrastructure front due to the closed, inflexible, and monolithic nature of conventional infrastructure, there are concerted efforts being undertaken by many in order to untangle them into modular, open, extensible, converged, and programmable infrastructures. Another worrying factor is the underutilization of expensive IT infrastructures (servers, storages, and networking solutions). With IT becoming ubiquitous for automating most of the manual tasks in different verticals, the problem of IT sprawl is to go up, and they are mostly underutilized and sometimes even unutilized for a long time. Having understood these prickling issues pertaining to IT infrastructures, the concerned have plunged into unveiling versatile and venerable measures for enhanced utilization and for infrastructure optimization. Infrastructure rationalization and simplification are related activities. That is, next-generation IT infrastructures are being realized through consolidation, centralization, federation, convergence, virtualization, automation, and sharing. To bring in more flexibility, software-defined infrastructures are being prescribed these days.

With the faster spread of big data analytical platforms and applications, commodity hardware is being insisted to accomplish data and process-intensive big data analytics quickly and cheaply. That is, we need low-priced infrastructures with supercomputing capability and infinite storage. The answer is that all kinds of underutilized servers are collected and clustered together to form a dynamic and huge pool of server machines to efficiently tackle the increasing and intermittent needs of computation. Precisely speaking, clouds are the new-generation infrastructures that fully comply to these expectations elegantly and economically. The cloud technology, though not a new one, represents a cool and compact convergence of several proven technologies to create a spellbound impact on both business and IT in realizing the dream of virtual IT that in turn blurs the distinction between the cyber and the physical worlds. This is the reason for the exponential growth being attained by the cloud paradigm. That is, the tried and tested technique of "divide and conquer" in software engineering is steadily percolating to hardware engineering. Decomposition of physical machines into a collection of sizable and manageable virtual machines and composition of these virtual machines based on the computing requirement are the essence of cloud computing.

Finally, software-defined cloud centers will see the light soon with the faster maturity and stability of competent technologies towards that goal. There is still some critical inflexibility, incompatibility, and tighter dependency issues among various components in cloud-enabled data centers; thus, full-fledged optimization and automation are not yet possible within the current setup. To attain the originally envisaged goals, researchers are proposing to incorporate software wherever needed in order to bring in the desired separations so that a significantly higher utilization is possible. When the utilization goes up, the cost is bound to come down. In short, the target of infrastructure programmability can be met with the embedding of resilient software so that the infrastructure manageability, serviceability, and sustainability tasks become easier, economical, and quicker.

The Growing Device Ecosystem The device ecosystem is expanding incredibly fast; thereby, there is a growing array of fixed, portable, wireless, wearable, nomadic, implantable, and mobile devices (medical instruments, manufacturing and controlling machines, consumer electronics, media players, kitchen wares, household utensils, equipment, appliances, personal digital assistants, smartphones, tablets, etc.). Trendy and handy, slim and sleek personal gadgets and gizmos are really and readily appealing and eye-catching to people today. With the shine of miniaturization technologies such as MEMS, Nanotechnology, SoC, etc., the power and smartness of devices are on the climb. IBM has stunningly characterized the device world with three buzzwords (instrumented, interconnected, and intelligent). Connected devices are innately proving to be highly beneficial for their owners. Machine-to-machine (M2M) communication enables machines, instruments, equipment, and any other devices to be self-aware and situation and surroundings aware. The cloud-enabled devices are extremely versatile in their operations, outputs, outlooks, and offerings. For example, cloud-enabled microwave device downloads the appropriate recipe for a particular dish from the Web and accordingly does the required in an automated fashion. Similarly, multifaceted sensors and actuators are attached with any ordinary devices to make them extraordinary in their decisions and deeds.

The implications of the exorbitant rise in newer devices for different environments (smart homes, hospitals, hotels, etc.) are clearly visible. On the data generation front, the volume of machine-generated data is higher and heavier than man-generated data. This clearly vouches the point that there is a direct proportion between data growth and new devices. The explosion of connected devices is unprecedented, and these special entities are slated to be in billions in the years ahead. However, the number of digitized elements will be easily in trillions. That is, all kinds of casual items in our midst are bound to be smart enough through the methodical execution of tool-supported digitization processes. Another vital trend is that everything is service enabled with the surging popularity of the RESTful service paradigm. Every tangible element is being service enabled in order to share their unique capabilities and to leverage others' capabilities as well programmatically. Thus, connectivity and service enablement go a long way in facilitating the production of networked, resource-constraint, and embedded systems in greater volumes.

When common things are digitized, standalone objects are interlinked with one another via networks, and every concrete thing gets service enabled, there would be big interactions, transactions, and collaborations resulting in big data that in turn lead to big discovery. All these clearly portray one thing. That is, the data volume is big and transmitted to be analyzed at an excruciating speed to come out with actionable insights. Having a large number of smart and sentient objects and enabling them to be interconnected to be intelligent in their requests and responses are being pursued with vengeance these days. Further on, all kinds of physical devices getting emboldened with remotely hosted software applications and data are bound to go a long way in preparing the devices in our everyday environments to be active, assistive, and articulative. That is, a cornucopia of next-generation people-centric services can be produced to provide enhanced care, comfort, choice, and convenience to human beings.

People can track the progress of their fitness routines. Taking decisions becomes an easy and timely affair with the prevalence of connected solutions that benefit knowledge workers immensely. All the secondary and peripheral needs will be accomplished in an unobtrusive manner people to nonchalantly focus on their primary activities. However, there are some areas of digitization that need attention, one being energy efficient. Green solutions and practices are being insisted upon everywhere these days, and IT is one of the principal culprits in wasting a lot of energy due to the pervasiveness of IT servers and connected devices. Data centers consume a lot of electricity, so green IT is a hot subject for study and research across the globe. Another area of interest is remote monitoring, management, and enhancement of the empowered devices. With the number of devices in our everyday environments growing at an unprecedented scale, their real-time administration, configuration, activation, monitoring, management, and repair (if any problem arises) can be eased considerably with effective remote correction competency.

Extreme Connectivity The connectivity capability has risen dramatically and become deeper and extreme. The kinds of network topologies are consistently expanding and empowering their participants and constituents to be highly productive. There are unified, ambient, and autonomic communication technologies from research organizations and labs drawing the attention of executives and decision-makers. All kinds of systems, sensors, actuators, and other devices are empowered to form ad hoc networks for accomplishing specialized tasks in a simpler manner. There are a variety of network, and connectivity solutions in the form of load balancers, switches, routers, gateways, proxies, firewalls, etc. for providing higher performance, network solutions are being embedded in appliances (software as well as hardware) mode.

Device middleware or Device Service Bus (DSB) is the latest buzzword enabling a seamless and spontaneous connectivity and integration between disparate and distributed devices. That is, device-to-device (in other words, machine-to-machine (M2M)) communication is the talk of the town. The interconnectivity-facilitated interactions among diverse categories of devices precisely portend a litany of supple, smart, and sophisticated applications for people. Software-defined networking (SDN) is the latest technological trend captivating professionals to have a renewed focus on this emerging yet compelling concept. With clouds being strengthened as the core, converged, and central IT infrastructure, device-to-cloud connections are fast materializing. This local as well as remote connectivity empowers ordinary articles to become extraordinary objects by distinctively communicative, collaborative, and cognitive.

The Trait of Service Enablement Every technology pushes for its adoption invariably. The Internet computing has forced for Web enablement, which is the essence behind the proliferation of Web-based applications. Now, with the pervasiveness of sleek, handy, and multifaceted mobiles, every enterprise and Web applications are being mobile enabled. That is, any kind of local and remote applications is being accessed through mobiles on the move, thus fulfilling real-time interactions and decision-making economically. With the overwhelming approval of the service idea, every application is service enabled. That is, we often read, hear, and feel service-oriented systems. The majority of next-generation enterprise-scale, mission-critical, process-centric, and multipurpose applications are being assembled out of multiple discrete and complex services.

Not only applications, physical devices at the ground level are being seriously service enabled in order to uninhibitedly join in the mainstream computing tasks and contribute for the intended success. That is, devices, individually and collectively, could become service providers or publishers, brokers and boosters, and consumers. The prevailing and pulsating idea is that any service-enabled device in a physical environment could interoperate with others in the vicinity as well as with remote devices and applications. Services could abstract and expose only specific capabilities of devices through service interfaces, while service implementations are hidden from user agents. Such kinds of smart separations enable any requesting device to see only the capabilities of target devices and then connect, access, and leverage those capabilities to achieve business or people services. The service enablement completely eliminates all dependencies and deficiencies so that devices could interact with one another flawlessly and flexibly.

1.3   The Realization and Blossoming of Digitalized Entities

Digitization has been an ongoing and overwhelming process, and it has quickly generated and garnered a lot of market and mind shares. Digitally enabling everything around us induces a dazzling array of cascading and captivating effects in the form of cognitive and comprehensive transformations for businesses as well as people. With the growing maturity and affordability of edge technologies, every common thing in our personal, social, and professional environment is becoming digitized. Devices are being tactically empowered to be computational, communicative, sensitive, and responsive. Ordinary articles are becoming smart artifacts in order to significantly enhance the convenience, choice, and comfort levels of humans in their everyday lives and works.

Therefore, it is no exaggeration to state that lately, there have been a number of tactical as well as strategic advancements in the edge-technology space. Infinitesimal and invisible tags, sensors, actuators, controllers, stickers, chips, codes, motes, specks, smart dust, and the like are being produced in plenty. Every single tangible item in our midst is being systematically digitized by internally as well as externally attaching these miniscule products onto them. This is for empowering them to be smart in their actions and reactions. Similarly, the distribution aspect too gains more ground. Due to its significant advantages in crafting and sustaining a variety of business applications ensuring the hard-to-realize quality of service (QoS) attributes, there are a bevy of distribution-centric software architectures, frameworks, patterns, practices, and platforms for Web, enterprise, embedded, analytical, and cloud applications and services.

Ultimately all kinds of perceptible objects in our everyday environments will be empowered to be self-aware and surroundings and situation aware, remotely identifiable, readable, recognizable, addressable, and controllable. Such a profound empowerment will bring forth transformations for the total human society, especially in establishing and sustaining smarter environments, such as smarter homes, buildings, hospitals, classrooms, offices, and cities. Suppose, for instance, a disaster occurs. If everything in the disaster area is digitized, then it becomes possible to rapidly determine what exactly has happened, the intensity of the disaster, and the hidden risks inside the affected environment. Any information extracted provides a way to plan and proceed insightfully, reveals the extent of the destruction, and conveys the correct situation of the people therein. The knowledge gained would enable the rescue and emergency team leaders to cognitively contemplate appropriate decisions and plunge into actions straightaway to rescue as much as possible, thereby minimizing damage and losses.

In short, digitization will enhance our decision-making capability in our personal as well as professional lives. Digitization also means that the ways we learn and teach are to change profoundly, energy usage will become knowledge driven so that green goals can be met more smoothly and quickly, and the security and safety of people and properties will go up considerably. As digitization becomes pervasive, our living, relaxing, working, and other vital places will be filled up with a variety of electronics including environment monitoring sensors, actuators, monitors, controllers, processors, projectors, displays, cameras, computers, communicators, appliances, gateways, high-definition IP TVs, and the like. In addition, items such as furniture and packages will become empowered by attaching specially made electronics onto them. Whenever we walk into such kinds of empowered environments, the devices we carry and even our e-clothes will enter into collaboration mode and form wireless ad hoc networks with the objects in that environment. For example, if someone wants to print a document from their smartphone or tablet and they enter into a room where a printer is situated, the smartphone will automatically begin a conversation with the printer, check its competencies, and send the documents to be printed. Smartphone would then alert the owner.

Digitization will also provide enhanced care, comfort, choice, and convenience. Next-generation healthcare services will demand deeply connected solutions. For example, Ambient Assisted Living (AAL) is a new prospective application domain where lonely, aged, diseased, bedridden, and debilitated people living at home will receive remote diagnosis, care, and management as medical doctors, nurses, and other caregivers remotely monitor patients' health parameters.

In summary, there are macro- and nano-scale, disposable, and diminutive sensors, actuators, chips and cards, tags, speckles, labels, stickers, smart dust, and dots being manufactured in large quantities and deployed randomly in our everyday environments in order to gain the environment intelligence. Further on, they are seamlessly attached on a growing array of commonly found, fixed, wireless, and portable artifacts and articles in our midst (personal, social, and professional locations) for enabling them to be computational, communicative, sensitive, adaptive, and responsive. That is, every kind of physical, mechanical, electrical, and electronic items is being empowered to join in the mainstream computing. The overall idea is to empower ordinary objects to become extraordinary in their actions and reactions. These technologically enabled objects gather any noteworthy state changes (events) and transmit them to the centralized control applications to initiate appropriate counter measures. Such kinds of smart objects and sentient materials are to capture various happenings in our environments in real time and pass them to the correct systems to proactively and preemptively initiate the right and relevant actions.

1.4   The Internet of Things (IoT)/Internet of Everything (IoE)

Originally, the Internet was the network of networked computers. Then, with the heightened ubiquity and utility of wireless and wired devices, the scope, size, and structure of the Internet have changed to what it is now, making the Internet of Device (IoD) concept a mainstream reality. With the service paradigm being positioned as the most optimal, rational, and practical way of building enterprise-class applications, a gamut of services (business and IT) are being built by many, deployed in World Wide Web and application servers, and delivered to everyone via an increasing array of input/output devices over networks. The increased accessibility and auditability of services have propelled interested software architects, engineers, and application developers to realize modular, scalable, and secure software applications by choosing and composing appropriate services from those service repositories quickly. Thus, the Internet of Service (IoS) idea is fast growing. Another interesting phenomenon getting the attention of press these days is the Internet of Energy. That is, our personal as well as professional devices get their energy through their interconnectivity. Figure 1.1 clearly illustrates how different things are linked

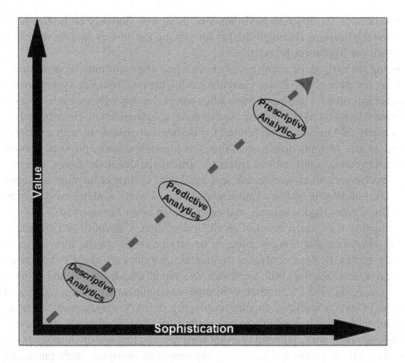

Fig. 1.1 The evolution of the data analytic world

with one another in order to conceive, concretize, and deliver futuristic services for the mankind (Distributed Data Mining and Big Data, a Vision paper by Intel, 2012).

As digitization gains more accolades and success, all sorts of everyday objects are being connected with one another as well as with scores of remote applications in cloud environments. That is, everything is becoming a data supplier for the next-generation applications, thereby becoming an indispensable ingredient individually as well as collectively in consciously conceptualizing and concretizing smarter applications. There are several promising implementation technologies, standards, platforms, and tools enabling the realization of the IoT vision. The probable outputs of the IoT field are a cornucopia of smarter environments such as smarter offices, homes, hospitals, retail, energy, government, cities, etc. Cyber-physical systems (CPS), ambient intelligence (AmI), and ubiquitous computing (UC) are some of the related concepts encompassing the ideals of IoT. The other related terms are the industrial Internet of things, the Internet of important things, etc.

In the upcoming era, unobtrusive computers, communicators, and sensors will be facilitating decision-making in a smart way. Computers in different sizes, look, capabilities, and interfaces will be fitted, glued, implanted, and inserted everywhere to be coordinative, calculative, and coherent. The interpretation and involvement of humans in operationalizing these smart and sentient objects are almost nil. With autonomic IT infrastructures, more intensive automation is bound to happen. The devices will also be handling all kinds of everyday needs, with humanized robots extensively used in order to fulfill our daily physical chores. With the emergence of specific devices for different environments, there will similarly be hordes of services and applications coming available for making the devices smarter that will in turn make our lives more productive.

During the early days, many people were using one mainframe system for their everyday compute needs. Today everyone has his/her own compute system to assist in his/her information needs and knowledge works. Increasingly multiple devices in and around us assist us in fulfilling our compute, communication, content, and cognition needs. Not only that, the future IT is destined to provide us with a variety of context-aware, insights-driven, real-time, and people-centric physical services. IBM in its visionary and seminal article has articulated that in the future, every system is instrumented, interconnected, and intelligent in their obligations and operations. The budding technology landscape is tended towards making every common thing smart, every device smarter, and every human being the smartest.

On another note, the concept of service orientation is all set to be conspicuous. That is, every tangible thing is going to be service centric in the form of service provider, broker, booster, consumer, auditor, etc. Services are going to be ambient, articulative, and adaptive. With micro-services are all encompassing and with containers emerging as the best-in-class runtime environment for micro-services, the activities of service crafting, shipping, deploying, delivery, management, orchestration, and enhancement are going to be greatly simplified. Further on, every system is to be ingrained with right and relevant smartness so that our environments (personal as well as professional), social engagements, learning, item purchasing, decision-making, scientific experiments, projects execution, and commercial activities are bound to exhibit hitherto unheard smartness during their accomplishments and delivery. The easily embeddable smartness through a surfeit of pioneering technologies is to result in smarter homes, hotels, hospitals, governments, retail, energy, healthcare, etc.

Lastly, as energy efficiency is being insisted everywhere as one of the prime requirements for the sustainability target, the worldwide luminaries, visionaries, and stalwarts are focusing on unearthing green, lean, and clean technologies and applying them in a methodical manner to make our digital assistants and artifacts power aware. In short, everything is self-aware and situation and surroundings aware in order to be cognizant and cognitive in all things for which they are artistically ordained. Thus, the service-orientated nature, the ingraining of smartness, and the guarantee of sustainability are the part and parcel of everything in our increasingly digital living.

1.5   The Tremendous Adoption of Social Media Sites

Social sites are not only prominent for not only reading but also for putting our comments, compliments, and complaints, for expressing our transient likes and dislikes, and sharing our views, photos, announcements, etc. There are blogging sites for posting musings and tweets for everyone and well-laid professional sites for exposing our education qualifications, industry experiences and technical expertise, etc. All these energize our thoughts, and sharing them instantaneously to the whole world via mass platforms and thereby the amount, variety, and velocity of personal and social information in public forums are decisively mind-boggling. With the faster maturity and stability of Web 2.0 (social Web) platforms, the phenomenon of social networking is gaining immense popularity across the globe. Digital communities for sharing knowledge are being realized, people data with their social leanings and product information are being published, search engines are very easy to work with, etc. In short, the future Internet is the world largest, ubiquitous, and service-centric repository of publicly findable, accessible, composable, and usable data, information, software applications, etc. The Internet is all set to comprise not only compute systems but also all kinds of devices and digitized entities, and hence, the Internet complexity is to increase exponentially.

Businesses emphasize having connected applications. Increasingly, it is being mandated to have highly integrated, multifaceted, multi-platform, multi-net, multi-device, and multimedia applications. With the arrival of splendid and sparkling array of social Websites, enterprise, Web, cloud, embedded, analytical, transactions, operational, and mobile applications are mandated to have a linkage with these sites to realize highly robust and resilient social applications. There are connectors, engines, and adaptors in plenty to enable a seamless and spontaneous synchronization with faraway social networking sites. With this integration, the topics of social media analytics (SMA) are booming in order to find appropriate ways and means for brand optimization, to realize outside-in thinking, to refine product marketing strategies, to have 360° view of customers, and to find the pulse of the people on various social aspects. Thus, for people empowerment, social computing is bound to play a very remarkable role in association with the praiseworthy advancements in the IT landscape.

1.6   The Ensuring Era of Predictive, Prescriptive, and Personalized Analytics

These days, machines and men generate data at an unprecedented pace. For example, in an average day, AT&T transfers about 30 petabytes of data through its network, every car produces 1.3 gigabytes (GB) of sensor data per hour, and, with 60 million cars manufactured per year, it is estimated that 103 exabytes of data are getting created just from cars alone. The widely used Twitter system processes around 340 million tweets a day, most of which are from mobile users. The Facebook generates about 10 terabytes (TB) every day. By 2016, the annual Internet traffic is expected to reach 1.3 zettabytes, and the 80 % of that data will be in unstructured formats. The traditional IT infrastructures, data bases and warehouses, data mining techniques, and analytical platforms are bound to face definite challenges and constrictions in efficiently storing and processing the massive volume of highly variable data to make informed and real-time business decisions to help their businesses to stay ahead of the competition.

As we all know, the big data paradigm is opening up a fresh set of opportunities and possibilities for businesses and individuals. As data explosion is actually occurring according to the forecasts of leading market research and analyst reports, the key challenge in front of enterprise and cloud IT teams is how to efficiently and rapidly capture, process, analyze, and extract tactical operation as well as strategic insights in time to act upon swiftly with all the confidence and clarity. The Fig. 1.1 vividly illustrates the increasing sophistication and value through next-generation analytical competencies.

There are two distinct trends prevailing in the data world: big data (volume and variety) and fast data (velocity and volume). There is an overwhelming realization among people that it is not the intuition but the data-inspired insights are to play a very significant role in arriving at correct and strategically sound decisions in the hypercompetitive and knowledge-filled world. Thus, data virtualization, analytics, and visualization disciplines are attracting a lot of attention these days in order to streamline the heavily complicated process of transitioning data to information and to knowledge. That is, all the generated, garnered, and crunched data ought to be taken to the logical conclusion in the form of pragmatic and dependable knowledge, which in turn has to be disseminated to people as well as actuating systems in order to ponder about the next course of actions in time. Not only knowledge discovery but also knowledge dissemination is very important in order to realize the vision of smart computing. Considering the ideals associated with the ensuing knowledge era, the data analytic domain has been very active and in accelerated mode in the industry as well as in the academic side.

There are industry-strength and open platforms and infrastructures coming up fast in order to enable seamless and spontaneous data integration, mining, and analytics. In the recent past, for real-world and real-time insights, the new concept of in-memory computing is being recommended and used extensively. In terms of nimbly responding to market sentiments, delighting customers, and reducing risks as well as costs, the capability of real-time analytics readily affords any organization the laser-like focus and the flexibility that corporate executives once only dreamed of.

The prominent contribution of in-memory computing is to do fast/real-time data analytics with ease. This hugely popular computing paradigm has brought in a series of paradigm shifts in data ingestion, storage, management, and analytics towards facilitating instant generation and delivery of actionable insights for enabling executives and even actuators, robots, etc. to take right decisions in time. There are noteworthy advances in the memory technology resulting in drastic decline in memory costs. Further on, there is a considerable increase in storage capacities, whereas faster access and higher durability are being readily facilitated in modern memory modules. Another point is that recent processors are predominantly blessed with multiple cores.

(continued)

Data can be captured and loaded from different and distributed sources into the system memory directly. This technique eliminates the data latency significantly and helps in taking faster business decisions. The performance gets improved as storage and operations are performed in the memory. In the traditional case of databases, data is stored in tables through relationships and interconnection among the tables. For data warehouses, multidimensional cubes are created to answer complex queries. In the case of in-memory analytics, the creation of multidimensional cubes is being avoided. The immediate benefits include the faster query and calculation which almost nullifies the need of building aggregate and pre-calculated cubes. There are different approaches for successful in-memory computing. The prominent ones among them are associative model, in-memory OLAP, Excel in-memory add-in, in-memory accelerator, and in-memory visual analytics. In addition, there are many software platforms and solutions such as SAP HANA, and there are products such as VoltDB and Oracle Exalytics giving tough competition to HANA in the in-memory compute space. The exceptional velocity and subsecond latency of an in-memory database are becoming important for worldwide companies to gain powerful and personalized analytic capabilities.

As per a document published by Intel, the key advantages of embracing the in-memory processing include the ability to offload processing from expensive database appliances; the ability to integrate data from different sources and eliminate or reduce the time spent on performance-tuning tasks such as query analysis, cube building, and aggregate table design; the easy deployment for self-service analytics, providing intuitive and unconstrained data exploration; and the instant visualization capabilities for complex data sets.

The new mechanism insists on putting all incoming data in memory instead of storing it in local or remote databases so that the major barrier of data latency gets eliminated. There are a variety of application domains and industry verticals yearning for in-memory big data analytics. Timeliness is an important factor for information to be beneficially and confidently leveraged. As we know, the hardware appliances are in general high performing, thus guaranteeing higher throughput in all they do. Here too, considering the need for real-time extraction of trustworthy insights, several product vendors have taken the route of software as well as hardware appliances for substantially accelerating the speed with which the next-generation big data analytics get accomplished. For a rapid generation of insights out of a large amount of multi-structured data, the new entrants such as in-database analytics are highly insisted.

In the business intelligence (BI) industry, apart from realizing real-time insights, analytical processes and platforms are being tuned to bring forth insights that invariably predict something to happen for businesses. Therefore, executives and other serious stakeholders proactively and preemptively could formulate well-defined schemes and action plans, course corrections, fresh policies and optimizations for business efficiency, new product offerings and premium services, and viable and value-added solutions based on the inputs. Prescriptive analytics, on the other hand, is to assist business executives by prescribing and formulating competent and comprehensive schemes and solutions to safely reach the targets predicted by the predictive analytics.

IBM has introduced a new computing paradigm "stream computing" in order to capture streaming and event data on the fly and to come out with usable and reusable patterns, hidden associations, tips, alerts and notifications, impending opportunities as well as threats, etc. in time for executives and decision-makers to contemplate appropriate countermeasures (James Kobielus (2013).

As a key enabler for this new generation of analytic processing methods, IBM InfoSphere Streams provides a state-of-the-art computing platform that can help organizations transform burgeoning data into actionable information and business insights. InfoSphere Streams is a critical component of the IBM big data platform and delivers a highly scalable, agile software infrastructure to perform in-motion analytics on a wide variety of relational and non-relational data types at unprecedented volumes and speeds and from thousands of real-time sources. With InfoSphere Streams, organizations can capture and act on key business data just in time, all the time.

Thus, highly competent processes, products, patterns, practices, and platforms take care of the vastly varying data volume, variety, velocity, veracity, variability, and viscosity to bring in enhanced business value, productivity, optimization, and transformation. The well-known multi-structured data types are:

- Business transactions, interactions, operations, and analytical data
- System and application infrastructures (compute, storage, network, application, Web and database servers, etc.) and log files
- Social and people data
- Customer, product, sales, and other business data
- Multimedia data
- Machine and sensor data
- Scientific experimentation and observation data (genetics, particle physics, climate modeling, drug discovery, etc.)

Thus, data comes in different size, structure, scope, and speed to polish the rough edges and accelerate the journey towards the envisaged smarter world. The following steps are the most prominent ones in formulating a winning enterprise-wide data strategy:

- *Aggregate* all kinds of distributed, different, and decentralized data.
- *Analyze* the formatted and formalized data.
- *Articulate* the extracted actionable intelligence.
- *Act* based on the insights delivered and raise the bar for futuristic analytics (real-time, predictive, prescriptive, and personalized analytics).
- *Accentuate* business performance and productivity.

There are several kinds of domain-specific and agnostic analytical disciplines emerging and evolving with the corporates gaining the capability of big data capture, storage, and processing.

Context Analytics With all the machines, robots, actuators, and sensors in our places that are getting connected, we easily conceive connected applications and environments. One distinct capability being derived out of these instrumented, interconnected, and intelligent devices is the context awareness, which is rapidly becoming the currency of the twenty-first century. Typically, machines' data are fast, and hence for gaining actionable context information, the fast/real-time data analytics is the way forward. As discussed above, there are in-memory, streaming, and other real-time analytical platforms to make context analytics pervasive. As connected machines are in the range of billions, the machine data points per second in association with spatial and temporal data will enable the grand arrival of autonomous things. Another brewing trend is that all kinds of physical items are being empowered through a direct association with cyber applications and data (cyber physical systems (CPS)). The era of autonomous machines providing cognitive and context-aware services to people is all set to dawn upon us. Self-services will be common and cheap. Dane Coyer, the CEO of SpaceCurve, has come out with the following use cases of context awareness.

- *The Connected Cow* – The Dutch company Sparked has developed sophisticated sensors that cattle farmers could easily implant in a cow's ear. The data from the cows, transmitted wirelessly to the farmer, could be used to determine the precise location and health of individual cows and even entire herds. Farmers also could learn about fluctuations in diet, how cows respond to environmental factor and general herd behavior. Looking forward, companies such as Vital Herd are to introduce powerful yet minuscule sensors that will be ingested by the cows to provide detailed information about practically every biological parameter imaginable. The days are not too far away for connected cows in helping themselves in diagnosing health issues and enabling automatic collaboration with veterinarian services, which may deliver medication through autonomous drones.
- *The Connected Car* – Automobiles currently in production contain an increasing array of disappearing yet dexterous sensors to collect everything from wiper

blade speed to frequency of braking to patterns of acceleration. Predominantly, sensors and actuators are being used in automobiles for safety and security. The external connectivity is facilitated through in-vehicle infotainment system, which in synchronization with car-attached sensors enables to detect when an accident happened, the exact location, etc. Further on, car can automatically dial to emergency/ambulance. There are other use cases being visualized for connected cars. Knowing how many cars are currently braking on a specific stretch of road is an immediate indication of road conditions. Such information could inform those currently approaching that area. This data also could be a very accurate representation of the weather at that specific location. The next wave of auto-based sensors will center on collision/accident avoidance. This wave will require the auto/driver combination not only to contextualize data being collected on board but also to integrate information from vehicles nearby as well as the surrounding environment. This all leads, of course, to the driverless vehicle.

- *Connected Air* – An autonomous drone flies to a predetermined location in a valley. The drone opens a small hatch and drops small, pill-sized sensors along a road. The sensors activate, setting up a communication network that is able to detect and identify an oncoming convoy. The network also can determine the speed and direction of the convoy, communicating that information back to a base station.

In summary, the delectable advancements in miniaturization technologies have paved the way for bringing forth diminutive, disposable, and deft sensors and actuators in plenty. There are sensors in the size of a grain of rice, and new-generation sensors are available in sand size. There are smart dust, motes, specks, tags, stickers, codes, etc. When these edge technologies are implanted and embedded with any tangible things in our everyday environments, the result is the mesmerizing world of smart and sentient materials. The random deployment of highly low-cost, power, range, and size sensors in any remote and rough environments by drones or aerial vehicles enables to capture everything in that environment in digital form in time goes a long way in pondering about hitherto unheard and unforeseen things and providing them with ease. The vision, sensing, perception, and decision-making will become ubiquitous and accurate. The principal use cases include physical security and asset management, measuring air quality, anticipating any risks in dangerous and hard-to-reach places, etc. There is one common thread in all these discussions. The amount of data streaming in from swarms of smart objects will be immense.

The data explosion is a litmus test and lingering challenge for enterprise and cloud IT teams. Thus, the IT organizations are mandated to have elastic yet economic and efficient IT infrastructures and end-to-end synchronized platforms in order to make sense out of big as well as fast data. IT infrastructures for data analytics need to be high performing. In the subsequent chapters, we are to discuss various high-performance mechanisms and solutions being rolled out by product vendors. Researchers are unearthing a variety of techniques and tools for ensuring high performance while doing analytics on both big and fast data. We have given a host of best practices, key guidelines, hardened evaluation metrics, easily applicable know-hows, and pilots and proofs of concepts to have high-performance IT environments especially for next-generation data analytics.

1.7 Apache Hadoop for Big Data and Analytics

In simple terms, the data growth has been phenomenal due to a series of innovations happening together. An astronomic amount of data is getting collected and stored in large-scale data storage appliances and networks. A few sample tips and tidbits on the worldwide data growth prospects. Very precisely, EMC and IDC have been tracking the size of the "Digital Universe (DU)." In the year 2012, both EMC and IDC estimated that the DU would double every two years to reach 44 zettabytes (ZB) by the year 2020. The year 2013 actually generated 4.4ZB DU, which is broken down into 2.9ZB generated by consumers and 1.5ZB generated by enterprises. EMC and IDC forecast that the IoT will grow to 32 billion connected devices by 2020, which will contribute 10 % of the DU. Cisco's large-scale data tracking project focuses on data center and cloud-based IP traffic estimating the 2013 amount at 3.1ZB/year (1.5ZB in "traditional" data centers, 1.6ZB in cloud data centers). By 2018, this is predicted to rise to 8.6ZB with the majority of growth happening in cloud data centers. Precisely speaking, the deeper connectivity and service enablement of all kinds of tangible things in our everyday locations open up the path-breaking possibility of data-driven insights and insight-driven decisions.

With the Web-scale interactions being facilitated by Yahoo, Google, Facebook, and other companies, the amount of data being collected routinely would have easily overwhelmed the capabilities of traditional IT architectures of these companies. The need for fresh, elastic, and dynamic architectures has been felt, and hence, the emergence of Hadoop is being felicitated and celebrated widely.

Apache Hadoop is an open-source distributed software platform for efficiently storing and processing data. Hadoop software runs on a cluster of industry-standard and commodity servers configured with direct-attached storage (DAS). On the storage front, Hadoop could store petabytes of data reliably on tens of thousands of servers and enables horizontal scalability of inexpensive server nodes dynamically and cost-effectively in order to guarantee the elasticity mandated for big and fast data analytics.

MapReduce is the core and central module to simplify the scalability aspect of Apache Hadoop. MapReduce helps programmers a lot in subdividing data (static as well as streaming) into smaller and manageable parts that are processed independently. The parallel and high-performance computing complexities are being substantially lessened through the leverage of the hugely popular MapReduce framework. It takes care of intra-cluster communication, task monitoring and scheduling, load balancing, fault and failure handling, etc. MapReduce has been modernized in the latest versions of Hadoop, and YARN is the new incarnation blessed with

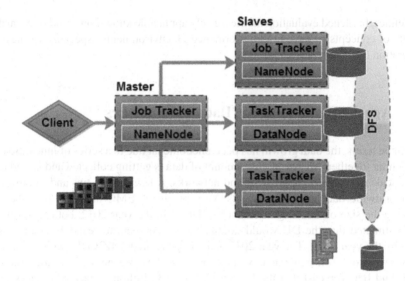

Fig. 1.2 The HDFS reference architecture

additional modules to bring in more automation such as cluster management and to avoid any kind of fallibility.

The other major module of the Apache Hadoop platform is the Hadoop distributed file system (HDFS), which is designed from the ground up for ensuring scalability and fault tolerance. HDFS stores large files by dividing them into blocks (usually 64 or 128 MB) and replicating the blocks on three or more servers for ensuring high data availability. HDFS (as illustrated in the Fig. 1.2) provides well-written APIs for MapReduce applications to read and write data in parallel. DataNodes can be incorporated at run time to maintain the performance mandate. A separate node is allocated for managing data placement and monitoring server availability. As illustrated above through a pictorial representation (the source is from a white paper published by Fujitsu), HDFS clusters easily and reliably holds on to petabytes of data on thousands of nodes. In addition to MapReduce and HDFS, Apache Hadoop includes many other vital components as explained in the box below.

Ambari A Web-based tool for provisioning, managing, and monitoring Apache Hadoop clusters which includes support for Hadoop HDFS, Hadoop MapReduce, Hive, HCatalog, HBase, ZooKeeper, Oozie, Pig, and Sqoop. Ambari also provides a dashboard for viewing cluster health such as heatmaps and ability to view MapReduce, Pig, and Hive applications visually along with features to diagnose their performance characteristics in a user-friendly manner.

(continued)

Avro It serves for serializing structured data. Structured data is converted into bit strings and efficiently deposited in HDFS in a compact format. The serialized data contains information of the original data schema. By means of the NoSQL databases such as HBase and Cassandra, large tables can be stored and accessed efficiently.

Cassandra A scalable multi-master database with no single points of failure.

Chukwa A data collection system for managing large distributed systems. Chukwa monitors large Hadoop environments. Logging data is collected, processed, and visualized.

HBase A scalable and distributed database that supports structured data storage for large tables.

Mahout A Scalable machine learning and data mining library.

Pig A high-level data-flow language and execution framework for parallel computation. It includes a language, Pig Latin, for expressing these data flows. Pig Latin includes operators for many of the traditional data operations (join, sort, filter, etc.) as well as the ability for users to develop their own functions for reading, processing, and writing data. Pig runs on Hadoop and makes use of both HDFS and MapReduce.

Apache Flume It is a distributed system for collecting, aggregating, and moving large amounts of data from multiple sources into HDFS. With the data sources that are multiplying and diversifying, the role and responsibility of Flume software grow up. Flume is suited in particular for importing data streams, such as Web logs or other log data into HDFS.

Apache Sqoop It is a tool for transferring data between Hadoop and the traditional SQL databases. You can use Sqoop to import data from a MySQL or Oracle database into HDFS, run MapReduce on the data, and then export the data back into an RDBMS.

Apache Hive It is a simpler programming language for writing MapReduce applications. HiveQL is a dialect of SQL and supports a subset of the SQL syntax. Hive is being actively enhanced to enable low-latency queries on Apache HBase and HDFS.

ODBC/JDBC Connectors ODBC/JDBC Connectors for HBase and Hive are the components included in Hadoop distributions. They provide connectivity with SQL applications by translating standard SQL queries into HiveQL commands that can be executed upon the data in HDFS or HBase.

(continued)

Spark Spark is a framework for writing fast, distributed programs. Spark solves similar problems as Hadoop MapReduce does but with a fast in-memory approach and a clean functional style API. With its ability to integrate with Hadoop and inbuilt tools for interactive query analysis (Shark), large-scale graph processing and analysis (Bagel), and real-time analysis (Spark Streaming), it can be interactively used to quickly process and query big data sets.

To make programming faster, Spark provides clean, concise APIs in Scala, Java, and Python. You can also use Spark interactively from the Scala and Python shells to rapidly query big data sets. Spark is also the engine behind Shark, a fully Apache Hive-compatible data warehousing system that can run 100× faster than Hive.

JAQL It is a functional, declarative programming language designed especially for working with large volumes of structured, semi-structured, and unstructured data. The primary use of JAQL is to handle data stored as JSON documents, but JAQL can work on various types of data. For example, it can support XML, comma-separated values (CSV) data, and flat files. An "SQL within JAQL" capability lets programmers work with structured SQL data while employing a JSON data model that's less restrictive than its SQL counterparts. Specifically, JAQL allows you to select, join, group, and filter data that is stored in HDFS, much like a blend of Pig and Hive. JAQL's query language was inspired by many programming and query languages, including Lisp, SQL, XQuery, and Pig.

Tez A generalized data-flow programming framework, built on Hadoop YARN, which provides a powerful and flexible engine to execute an arbitrary DAG of tasks to process data for both batch and interactive use cases. Tez is being adopted by Hive, Pig, and other frameworks in the Hadoop ecosystem, and also by other commercial software (e.g., ETL tools), to replace Hadoop MapReduce as the underlying execution engine.

ZooKeeper A high-performance coordination service for distributed applications.

1.8   Big Data into Big Insights and Actions

We have talked about the data explosion and the hard realization that if data is crunched deftly, then the free flow of actionable insights empowering decision-makers to take precise and perfect decisions well ahead of time is being helped with the availability of competent analytical platforms and optimized infrastructures. In this section, let us discuss why organizations are hell bent on adopting the technology advancements being achieved in the analytical space to be ahead. With big and fast data analytics becoming common and casual, the IT systems are more reliable and resilient. With IT resuscitation and versatility, the business efficiency and adaptivity are set to rise significantly.

Customer Centricity IT has been doing a good job of bringing in highly visible and venerable business automation, acceleration, and augmentation. However, in the recent past, technologies are becoming more people centric. Business houses and behemoths across the globe, having captured the essence of IT well in their journey previously, are renewing their focus and re-strategizing to have greater impacts on the elusive goal of customer delight through a variety of captivating premium offerings with all the quality of service (QoS) attributes implicitly embedded. Traversing extra miles for maintaining customer relationships intact, precisely capturing their preferences, and bringing forth fresh products and services to retain their loyalty and to attract newer customers are some of the prickling challenges before enterprises to retain their businesses ahead of immediate competitors. Personalized services, multichannel interactions, transparency, timeliness, resilience, and accountability are some of the differentiating features for corporates across the globe to be ensured for their subscribers, employees, partners, and end users. People data is the most sought after for understanding and fulfilling customers' wishes comprehensively.

There are social sites and digital communities to enable different sets of people to express their views and feedbacks on various social concerns, complaints, product features, thoughts, musings, knowledge share, etc. The recent technologies have the wherewithal to enable various customer analytic needs. The first and foremost aspect of big data analytics is the social data and its offshoots such as 360° of customers, social media and networking analytics, sentiment analytics, etc. With businesses and customers that are synchronizing more closely, the varying expectations of customers are resolutely getting fulfilled.

Operational Excellence The second aspect of big data analytics is the machine data. Machines produce a huge amount of data to be systematically captured and subjected to a series of deeper and decisive investigations to squeeze out tactical as well as strategic insights to enable every kind of machines to be contributing to their fullest capacity and capability.

Business agility, adaptivity, and affordability through the promising IT innovations are gaining momentum. IT systems are pruned further and prepared to be extra lean and agile, extensible, and adaptive in their structural as well as behavioral aspects. There is a continued emphasis in closing down the gaps between business and IT. Operational data are being captured meticulously in order to extract all kinds of optimization tips to keep IT systems alive. Any kind of slowdown and breakdown is being proactively nipped in the bud in order to continuously fulfill customers' needs.

Thus, highly optimized and organized IT in synchronization with customer orientation does a lot for any kind of enterprising initiative to achieve its originally envisaged success. The new-generation analytical methods come handy in visualizing opportunities and completing them with ease.

Fig. 1.3 The big picture

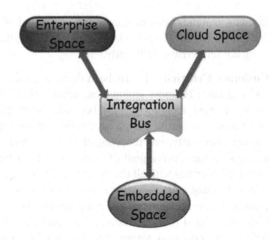

Data center executives face big data-induced several major problems and challenges. The current compute, storage, and network infrastructures are bound to face capacity and capability problems with the more generic and specific usage of big and fast data for knowledge discovery. Capacity planning is a key issue. Scalability and availability of IT resources are very important in the big data world. Therefore, the cloud idea captured the imagination of people widely in order to have highly efficient, consolidated, centralized and federated, converged, mixed (virtualized and bare metal) servers; automated, shared, and orchestrated IT centers; and server farms. And in the recent past, software-defined data centers are seeing the reality with the availability of software-defined compute, storage, networking, and security solutions.

A white paper titled "Big Data Meets Big Data Analytics" by SAS indicates that there are three key technologies that can help you get a handle on big data and even more importantly extract meaningful business value from it:

- *Information Management for Big Data* – Capturing, storing, and managing data as a strategic asset for business empowerment
- *High-Performance Analytics for Big Data* – Leveraging data using high-performance IT for extracting real-time and real-world insights to solve a variety of professional, social, as well as personal problems
- *Flexible Deployment Options for Big Data* – Choosing better options (on premise (private cloud), off premise (public cloud), or even hybrid cloud) for big data and analytics

The Big Picture With the cloud space growing fast as the optimized, automated, policy-based, software-defined, and shared environment comprising highly sophisticated and synchronized platforms and infrastructure for application development, deployment, integration, management, and delivery, the integration requirement too has grown deeper and broader as pictorially illustrated in the Fig. 1.3. Thus, there will be extreme integration among all kinds of entities and elements in the physical world and software services in the cyber world in order to have a growing array of versatile and vivacious applications for the total humanity.

All kinds of physical entities at the ground level will have purpose-specific inter-actions with services and data hosted on the enterprise as well as cloud servers and storage appliances to enable scores of real-time and real-world applications for the society. This extended and enhanced integration would lead to data deluges that have to be accurately and appropriately subjected to a variety of checks to promptly derive actionable insights that in turn enable institutions, innovators, and individuals to be smarter and speedier in their obligations and offerings.

1.9 Conclusions

It has been a mesmerizing journey for IT, which has been the greatest enabler of worldwide businesses. However, there is a paradigm shift now. That is, IT is all set to empower and enable individuals substantially in their everyday works and walks. Technologies are coming closer to people, easily accessible, consumable, and usable. Technologies participate and contribute in every aspect of human lives in this connected world. Our everyday environments (roads, offices, manufacturing plants, retail stores, airports, eating joints and junctions, etc.) are being stuffed with disappearing yet smart sensors and actuators. All these clearly lead to the explosion of data that needs to be carefully collected and analyzed to bring forth tactical as well as strategically sound intelligence to set the path straight and smooth for the knowledge-driven, service-oriented, and people-centric digital era.

1.10 Exercises

1. Discuss the IT trends which have necessitated the evolution of big data analytic paradigms.
2. Write short note on Internet of things (IoT).
3. Discuss the concept of context analytics
4. Describe the HDFS reference architecture for high-performance big data analytics.
5. Discuss the various components of Apache Hadoop for high-performance big data analytics.

Chapter 2
The High-Performance Technologies for Big and Fast Data Analytics

2.1 Introduction

The slogan of "more with less" has been intense these days due to several reasons. The IT budget is being pruned ceaselessly due to the uncertain economic scene across the globe. Decision-making is very tardy, and every kind of project expenditure is being planned and audited meticulously. There are different kinds of responses for this clarion call. Business executives incessantly mandate their IT department to explore and execute both tactically and strategically sound methods such as systematic IT rationalization, simplification, and automation, standardization, commoditization, and decommissioning of superfluous elements in order to considerably cut costs (capital as well as operational). There is another inspiring approach. Systems are internally empowered to be high performing by leveraging a number of proven tactics and tips. That is, high-performance computing is one such collective endeavor to deliver this goal of "more with less" even for data and process-intensive workloads. Compute machines, storage appliances, and network solutions are hence readied accordingly to be high performing and scalable. That is, systems need to deliver their full potential in the midst of expected and unexpected constraints. Towards its direct facilitation, appropriate approaches and algorithms are being unearthed by concerned researchers and IT stalwarts in order to enable systems to work all the time to their ultimate capability. Exascale computing is another buzzword bulldozing and bombarding the IT world in the recent past. HPC is definitely a purposeful compute paradigm, which is consistently and continuously throwing solutions for effectively and economically tackling the new-generation I/O and process-intensive workloads.

© Springer International Publishing Switzerland 2015 25
P. Raj et al., *High-Performance Big-Data Analytics*, Computer Communications and Networks, DOI 10.1007/978-3-319-20744-5_2

As per Wikipedia, there are many differences between high-throughput computing (HTC) and high-performance computing (HPC). HPC tasks are characterized as needing large amounts of computing power for short periods of time, whereas HTC tasks also require large amounts of computing, but for much longer times (months and years, rather than hours and days). HPC environments are often measured in terms of floating-point operations per second (FLOPs).

The HTC community, however, is not concerned about operations per second, but rather operations per month or per year. Therefore, the HTC field is more interested in how many jobs can be completed over a long period of time instead of how fast an individual job can complete. As an alternative definition, the European Grid Infrastructure defines HTC as "a computing paradigm that focuses on the efficient execution of a large number of loosely-coupled tasks," while HPC systems tend to focus on tightly coupled parallel jobs, and as such they must execute within a particular site with low-latency interconnects. Conversely, HTC systems are independent, sequential jobs that can be individually scheduled on many different computing resources across multiple administrative boundaries. HTC systems achieve this using various grid computing technologies and techniques. HPC systems enable users to run a single instance of parallel software over many processors, whereas HTC is a serial system more suited to running multiple independent instances of software on multiple processors at the same time. Speeding up of task execution and data processing through the leverage of parallelization has been the most sought-after high-performance approach.

There are many HPC domains such as climate modeling, financial services, scientific computing, big data analytics (BDA), electronic design automation (EDA), computer-aided engineering (CAE), oil and gas explorations, drug discovery, DNA sequencing and homology searching, Monte Carlo simulations, computational fluid dynamics (CFD), and structural analysis.

If decision makers could access and analyze enterprise data a hundred times faster, they would be able to make smarter decisions in time to improve business productivity and profitability. Consultants, architects, and developers have a big job here in appropriately choosing and architecting IT infrastructures and platforms and coding to condense hour-long analytical queries into just seconds to gain deeper and decisive insights into critical business issues and to comprehensively support real-time strategies and tactics.

In this chapter, we would like to give a stimulating foundation on the strategic convergence of HPC and BDA, and in the ensuing chapters, you will find detailed content on the tactic as well as the strategic impacts of this cool synchronization on the forthcoming era of knowledge.

2.2   The Emergence of Big Data Analytics (BDA) Discipline

Lately, there are several data and process-intensive workloads emerging and evolving fast. This natural phenomenon puts professionals and professors to ponder about the means of efficiently running them to extract the expected results in time. The HPC paradigm is being mandated in order to tackle the challenges being posed by this special category of applications. With the heightened complexity, the leverage of special infrastructures and platforms in association with adaptive processes is being insisted for cost-effective BDA.

High-performance systems are being mandated here in order to efficiently crunch a large amount of data emanating from different and distributed sources. Therefore, HPC acquires special significance with the maturity and stability of big data computing. For the forthcoming era of big data-inspired insights, HPC is bound to play a very prominent and productive role in fulfilling the hard requirements of capturing, indexing, storing, processing, analyzing, and mining big data in an efficient manner.

The Intricacies of the "Big Data Paradigm"

- The data volume gets bigger (in the range of tera-, peta-, and exabytes).
- The data generation, capture, and crunching frequency have gone up significantly (the velocity varies from batch processing to real time).
- The data structure too has got diversified (poly-structured data).

That is, data structure, size, scope, and speed are on the rise. Big data and large-scale analytics are increasingly important for optimizing business operations, enhancing outputs and rolling out newer offerings, improving customer relations, and uncovering incredible opportunities. BDA therefore has greater benefits for businesses to explore fresh avenues for additional revenues. In addition, BDA has long-lasting implications on IT infrastructures and platforms as enlisted below.

- The data virtualization, transformation, storage, visualization, and management
- Preprocessing and analyzing big data for actionable insights
- Building insight-driven applications

The Key Drivers for Big Data There are a number of new technologies and tools constantly coming up in order to fulfill the varying expectations of businesses as well as people. The prominent ones among them are:

- Digitization through edge technologies
- Distribution and federation
- Consumerization (mobiles and wearables)
- Centralization, commoditization, and industrialization (cloud computing)
- Ambient, autonomic, and unified communication and ad hoc networking
- Service paradigm (service enablement (RESTful APIs) of everything
- Social computing and ubiquitous sensing, vision, and perception
- Knowledge engineering
- The Internet of Things (IoT)

In short, enabling the common things to be smart and empowering, all kinds of physical, mechanical, and electrical systems and electronics to be smarter through instrumentation and interconnectivity are the key differentiators for the ensuing smarter world. The resulting sentient objects (trillions of digital objects) and smarter devices (billions of connected devices) in sync up with the core and central IT infrastructure (Cloud) are to produce a wider variety and a large amount of data that in turn has the wherewithal to formulate and facilitate the implementation and delivery of situation-aware and sophisticated services for humanity ultimately. The promising and potential scenarios are as follows: Sensors and actuators are to be found everywhere, and machine-to-machine (M2M) communication is to pour out voluminous data which is to be carefully captured and cognitively subjected to a number of decisive investigations to emit out useful knowledge, the raging concepts of the Internet of Things (IoT), cyber physical systems (CPS), smart environments, etc. Similarly, the cloud enablement of every tangible thing in our midst is turning out to be a real game changer for every individual to be the smartest in his daily deeds, decision-making capabilities, and deals. Thus, with data being categorized as the strategic asset for any organization and individual across the globe, the purpose-specific HPC resources are being given prime importance to turn data into information and to generate pragmatic knowledge smoothly.

2.3   The Strategic Implications of Big Data

1. The Unequivocal Result: The Data-Driven World

   - Business transactions, interactions, operations, master, and analytical data
   - Log files of system and application infrastructures (compute, storage, network, application, Web and database servers, etc.)
   - Social and people data and weblogs
   - Customer, product, sales, and other business-critical data

- Sensor and actuator data
- Scientific experimentation and observation data (genetics, particle physics, financial and climate modeling, drug discovery, etc.)

2. *Newer Kinds of Analytical Approaches*

   There are several fresh analytical methods emerging based on big data as enlisted below. Big data analytics are the new tipping point for generating and using real-time and actionable insights to act upon with all confidence and clarity. For example, there will be substantial renaissance on predictive and prescriptive analytics for any enterprise to correctly and cogently visualize the future and accordingly to set everything in place to reap all the visible and invisible benefits (business and technical).

Generic (horizontal)	Specific (vertical)
Real-time analytics	Social media analytics
Predictive analytics	Operational analytics
Prescriptive analytics	Machine analytics
High-performance analytics	Retail and security analytics
Diagnostic analytics	Sentiment analytics
Declarative analytics	Financial analytics

3. *Next-Generation Insight-Driven Applications*

   With a number of proven methods and tools for precisely transitioning data into information and into workable knowledge on the horizon, the aspect of knowledge engineering is fast picking up. Next, timely and technically captured insights of big data by meticulous leveraging of standards-compliant analytical platforms are to be disseminated to software applications and services to empower them to behave distinctively. The whole idea is to build, host, and deliver people-centric services through any handheld, portable, implantable, mobile, and wearable devices. Big data is going to be the principal cause if leveraged appropriately for the proclaimed smarter world.

The Process Steps: Big Data → Big Infrastructure → Big Insights The big data challenges are common for nearly all businesses, irrespective of the industry. Ingest all the data, analyze it as fast as possible, make good sense of it, and ultimately drive smart decisions to positively affect the business all as fast as possible. There are different methodologies being disseminated for timely extraction of all kinds of usable and useful knowledge from data heap. The most common activities involved in bringing forth actionable insights out of big data are:

- Aggregate and ingest all kinds of distributed, different, and decentralized data.
- Analyze the cleansed data.
- Articulate the extracted actionable intelligence.

- Act based on the insights delivered and raise the bar for futuristic analytics (real-time, predictive, prescriptive, and personal analytics) and to accentuate business performance and productivity.

2.4   The Big Data Analytics (BDA) Challenges

Definitely, there will be humungous IT challenges because of the enormity, variability, viscosity, and veracity of big data. Therefore, big data mandates high-quality IT infrastructures, platforms, DBs, middleware solutions, file systems, tools, etc.

The Infrastructural Challenges

- Compute, storage, and networking elements for data capture, transmission, ingestion, cleansing, storage, preprocessing, management, and knowledge dissemination
- Clusters, grids, clouds, mainframes, appliances, parallel and supercomputers, etc.
- Expertly integrated and specifically engineered systems for powering up big data requirements efficiently

- *The Platform Challenges*: We need end-to-end, easy-to-use, and fully integrated platforms for making sense out of big data. Today, there are pieces for data virtualization, ingestion, analytics, and visualization. However, complete and comprehensive platforms are the need of the hour in order to accelerate the process of extracting knowledge from big data.

  - Analytical, distributed, scalable, and parallel databases
  - Enterprise data warehouses (EDWs)
  - In-memory systems and grids (SAP HANA, VoltDB, etc.)
  - In-database systems (SAS, IBM Netezza, etc.)
  - High-performance Hadoop implementations (Cloudera, MapR, Hortonworks, etc.)

- *The File Systems and Database Challenges*: Having realized the shortcomings of traditional databases for big data, product vendors have come out with a few analytical, scalable, and parallel SQL databases to take care of the heightened complexity of big data. In addition to that, there are NoSQL and NewSQL DBs that are more compatible and capable for handling big data. There are new types of parallel and distributed file system solutions such as Lustre from NetApp with many newly added capabilities for the big data world.

Figure 2.1 clearly illustrates the challenges associated with big data analytics.

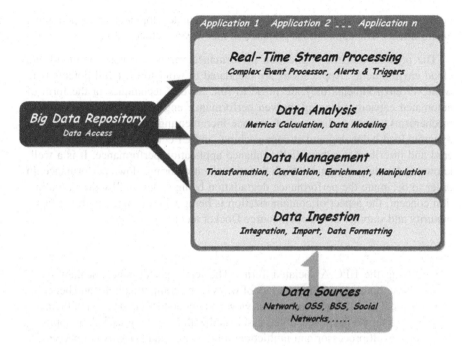

Fig. 2.1 The challenging big data world

2.5   The High-Performance Computing (HPC) Paradigms

The challenges of knowledge engineering are growing steadily due to several game-changing developments in the data front. Large data sets are being produced in different speeds and structures; there is a heightened complexity of data relationships, there is a sharp rise in routine and repetitive data, the aspects of data virtualization and visualization requirements are becoming crucial, etc. HPC is being prescribed as the best way forward as HPC facilitates businesses to see exponential performance gains, an increase in productivity and profitability, and the ability to streamline their analytic processes.

Clearing the Mystery of HPC The performance of software applications varies widely due to several reasons. The underlying infrastructure is one among them, and hence application designers and developers are always forced to come out with a code that is critically optimized for the execution container and the deployment environment. Now with clouds emerging as the core, central, and converged environment for applications, software engineers are tasked with bringing in the necessary modifications on the legacy software to be seamlessly migrated, configured, and delivered via clouds. This process is touted as the cloud enablement. Now applications are being built directly in cloud environments and deployed there too in order to eliminate the standard frictions between development and operational environments. The applications prepared in this way are cloud native.

The point is that the application performance varies between non-cloud and cloud environments. Applications are mandated to work to their full potentials in whatever environments they are made to run. Several techniques in the form of automated capacity planning, proven performance engineering and enhancement mechanisms, auto-scaling, performance-incrementing architectural patterns, dynamic load balancing and storage caching, and CPU bursting are being considered and inscribed to substantially enhance application performance. It is a well-known and widely recognized truth that virtualization brings down performance. In order to decimate the performance degradation being sponsored by the virtualization concept, the aspect of containerization is being recommended with the faster maturity and stability of the open-source Docker technology.

Clarifying the HPC-Associated Terms The terms performance, scalability, and throughput are used in a variety of ways in the computing field, and hence it is critical to have an unambiguous view and understanding on each of them. When we say performance, it gets associated with IT systems as well as applications. Multiprocessor and multicore architectures and systems are becoming common.

An application performance can be calculated based on a few characteristics. The user load and processing power are the deciding factors. That is, how many users an application can handle per second or the number of business transactions being performed by it per second. A system performance is being decided based on the number of floating-point operations per second it could achieve. A high-performance system is one that functions above a teraflop or 10^{12} floating-point operations per second.

The performance of an application depends on the application architecture, the application infrastructure, and the system infrastructure. As we all know, every infrastructure component has a theoretical performance limit. But due to several internal and external reasons, the performance practically achieved is much below the theoretically quoted one. A network with the data transfer speed of 1 Gbps does not provide the fullest speed at any point of time due to multiple dependencies and deficiencies surrounding it. The same story lies for other hardware modules too. Ultimately, the performance of any application that runs on them suffers ignominiously. The Joyent white paper [1] says that limited bandwidth, disk space, memory, CPU cycles, and network connections can collectively lead to poor performance. Sometimes poor performance of an application is the result of its architecture that does not properly distribute its processes across available system resources. The prickling challenge is how to empower the system modules technologically to achieve its stated theoretical performance so that applications can be high performing.

(continued)

Throughput is the performance number achieved by systems and applications. The effective rate at which data is transferred from point A to point B is the throughput value. That is, throughput is a measurement of the raw speed. While speed of moving or processing data can certainly improve system performance, the system is only as fast as its slowest element. A system that deploys ten gigabit Ethernet yet its server storage can access data at only one gigabit effectively has a one gigabit system.

Scalability is closely synchronized with performance. That is, even with the number of users going up suddenly and significantly, the same performance metric has to be maintained. That is, with the unplanned appreciation in user load, the processing performance has to be adequately enhanced to maintain the earlier response time to all the users. The only way to restore higher effective throughput and performance is through the addition of compatible resources. Auto-scaling at the system level as well as at the application level is being made mandatory in cloud environments. Leading cloud service providers (CSPs) ensure auto-scaling, whereas cloud management platforms such as OpenStack ensure auto-scaling of resources. For big data analytics, the project of Savanna/Sahara is to ensure automated scaling out as well as scaling down.

There are several popular computing types emerging exclusively for realizing the goals of high-performance computing. There are primarily centralized and distributed computing approaches to bring in high-performance computation. Without an iota of doubt, parallel computing is the most widely used for ensuring high performance and throughput. There are symmetric multiprocessing (SMP) and massively multiprocessing (MPP) solutions in plenty. As the number of domains yearning for high performance is consistently on the rise, the focus is more intense on HPC technologies these days. Especially for the forthcoming world of knowledge, the domain of data analytics for extraction of knowledge is bound to play a very stellar role in shaping up the data-driven world. With data becoming big data, the need for HPC significantly goes up. In the ensuing sections, we would like to throw more light on different HPC models that are being perceived as more pragmatic for the big data analytics. The Hadoop standard has been widely embraced for its ability to economically store and analyze large data sets. By exploiting the parallel computing techniques ingrained in the "MapReduce," the data-processing framework of Hadoop, it is possible to reduce long-computation times to minutes. This works well for mining large volumes of historical data stored on disk, but it is not suitable for gaining real-time insights from live and operational data. Thus, there are concerted efforts to formulate realistic high-performance methods towards real-time and high-performance big data analytics.

2.6   The High-Performance Approaches Through Parallelism

The following are the prominent approaches for parallelizing work using additional hardware:

- Shared memory
- Shared disk
- Shared nothing

Shared Memory Symmetric multiprocessor (SMP) machines are the widely used ones for shared memory. All the CPUs share a single and shared memory and a collection of disks. The complexity arises here in distributed locking. There is no need for any commit protocols as both the lock manager and buffer pools are in the memory system. All the processors therefore could access the memory in a controlled manner. The scalability is the problem as all I/O and memory requests have to be carried out over the same bus that all the processors share. The bandwidth of this overcrowded bus gets quickly clogged. In addition, the shared-memory multiprocessors require complex and customized hardware to keep their L2 data caches consistent. Therefore, shared-memory systems find it difficult to scale on the basis of varying demands.

Shared Disk In this architecture, there are several independent processor nodes and each one of them has its own dedicated memory. However, these nodes all access a single collection of disks typically in the form of storage area network (SAN) system or a network-attached storage (NAS) system. Shared-disk architecture too has the severe scalability problem as the above one. The network connecting each of the CPUs to the shared-disk system can become the I/O bottleneck. Secondly, as the memory is not shared, there is no central place for the lock table or buffer pool to reside. To set locks, the lock-manager module has to be centralized in one processor or to involve a complex distributed locking protocol. This protocol must use messages to implement the same sort of cache-consistency protocol implemented by shared-memory multiprocessors in hardware. Either of these approaches to locking is likely to become a bottleneck as the system is getting scaled. To make shared-disk technology work better, vendors implement a "shared-cache" design which works much like shared disk.

Such a mechanism works fairly well on online transaction processing (OLTP), but for data warehousing/online analytical processing (OLAP), this setup is not up to the mark. Warehouse queries are answered through the sequential scans of the fact table of the data warehouse. Unless the full fact table is in the aggregate memory of the cluster, the disk needs to be used. Therefore, a shared cache limits scalability. Further on, the same scalability problems in the shared-memory model also get repeated in the shared-disk architecture. The bus between the disks and the processors can become a bottleneck, and the problem of resource contention for certain disk blocks arises particularly when the number of CPUs goes up.

Shared Nothing In this arrangement, each processor has its own set of disks. There is no sharing of any of the critical compute resources. For the big data world, data is being horizontally partitioned across several nodes such that each node has a subset of the rows from each table in the database. Each node is then responsible for processing only the rows on its own disks. Such architectures are especially well suited to the star schema queries present in standard data warehouse workloads as only a very limited amount of communication bandwidth is required to join one or more (typically small) dimension tables with the (typically much larger) fact table.

Every node maintains its own lock table and buffer pool thereby totally eliminating the need for the complicated locking and software or hardware consistency mechanisms. Because shared-nothing architecture does not have the bus or resource contention issues, it facilitates the realization of dynamic scale-out of hundreds or even thousands of machines. Shared-nothing clusters also can be constructed using commodity hardware. All the Hadoop-based big data systems are predominantly leveraging this proven and potential architecture to ward off all kinds of constrictions. There are state-of-the-art software solutions to ensure scale-out and scale-in of compute resources based on changing demands.

With the surging popularity of the shared-nothing architecture, increasingly compute and data clusters and grids are being formed out of commodity servers in order to achieve high performance in a cost-effective fashion. For big data analytics, even clouds in order to be commercially viable use commodity servers extensively. There are other hardware-imposed performance acceleration ways and means. Appliances are the other high-performance and turnkey alternatives, but the total cost of ownership (TCO) is on the higher side. Appliances offer scale-up to ensure the higher performance. For readers' benefits, we have incorporated a lot of details on the brewing appliance trends and the business transformations being brought forward in other chapters. Hence shared-nothing database systems crafted out of commodity hardware modules seem to be a better bet for most of the scenarios in the big data world. Scientists and researchers are in unison in exploring and expounding venerable hardware and software solutions to bring the smoothened and steadied high performance/throughput through the compact parallelization.

2.7   Cluster Computing

Clusters are more visible these days as they are ensuring scalability, availability, and sustainability in addition to the original goal of higher performance. Besides providing the cost-effectiveness, the simplicity of bringing up clusters is the main noteworthy point. Technologies for cluster formation, monitoring, measurement, management, and maintenance are already matured and stabilized. The massive acceptance of x86-based clusters is clearly facilitating the uptake of HPC in big way. The unprecedented success of clusters is due to the simplified architecture, which originates from traditional commoditized servers linked together by powerful interconnects such as Gigabit Ethernet and InfiniBand.

Clusters typically follow the MPP model. The main drawback is that every cluster node has its own memory space, which needs to be accessed by other nodes via the system interconnect. The unmistakable result is the added complexity in software development, namely, slicing up an application's data in such a way as to distribute it across the cluster and then coordinating computation via internode message passing. Such an architectural approach also necessitates maintaining an operating system (OS) and associated software stack on each node of the cluster. Clusters are often complicated to manage at both the system and the application levels.

On the other side, SMP platforms implement a shared-memory model, where the entire address space is uniformly accessible to all the processors in the system. This is implemented by aggregating multiple processors and associated memory into a single node using NUMA-aware communication fabric. This means there is no need to carve up application data and to coordinate distributed computation. Such an arrangement offers a much more natural programming model for the development community and can implicitly take advantage of existing software packages. Such systems also need only a single OS instance and software environment, thus simplifying system upgrades and patches. Unfortunately, the SMP model has lost out to the cluster model due to several reasons. The custom NUMA fabric requires additional hardware components, and the cost is running high for the SMP model. Gartner defines a big data cluster as a set of loosely coupled compute, storage, and network systems, with a few specialized nodes suitable for administration, combined to run a big data framework. The advantages of big data clusters include:

- Lower acquisition costs and clusters can reuse existing hardware.
- Ease of scaling the cluster and ability to mix high-end hardware for master nodes and commodity hardware for worker nodes.
- Ability to easily modify hardware configuration to suit the quirks of workloads.

The negative factors are the Hadoop stack component availability, and the version releases vary widely among distributions. Further on, depending on the vendor chosen, the support capabilities can change sharply.

The Virtual SMP Alternative (www.scalemp.com) Clusters are currently very popular, and due to the abovementioned reasons, SMPs could not do well in the market as expected. However, there is a renewed interest in consolidating their advantages together to enable businesses substantially. The distinct capabilities of SMPs are being embedded in clusters, whereas the reverse is also being attended seriously. If clusters are made to function like SMPs, then business IT can easily realize the advantages of relatively cheap and scalable hardware with the highly decreased management complexity. On the other hand, if SMPs can also run MPI applications built for distributed memory architectures without the management overhead of a traditional cluster, there will be strong pick up for SMPs. Having realized the need for having the distinct advantages of clusters in SMPs, ScaleMP has come out with a converged product, that is, the value proposition offered by

Fig. 2.2 The leverage of a
single virtual machine
(VM)

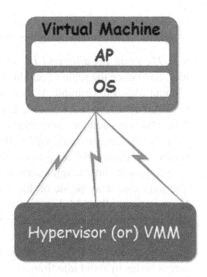

ScaleMP, a company whose vSMP Foundation (Versatile SMP) product turns a conventional x86 cluster into a shared-memory platform. It does so in software, employing a virtual machine monitor (VMM) that aggregates multiple x86 nodes, I/O, and the system interconnect into a single (virtual) system (Fig. 2.2). The cluster's indigenous interconnect is used in lieu of an SMP's custom network fabric to maintain memory coherency across nodes. The current-generation vSMP Foundation product is able to aggregate as many as 128 nodes and up to 32,768 CPUs and 256 TB of memory into one system.

vSMP Foundation creates a virtual shared-memory system from a distributed infrastructure providing the best of both worlds for big data and analytics problems. It allows scaling just by adding "one more node" but still keeps the OPEX advantage of a shared-memory system. It provides benefits for small Hadoop deployments where the OPEX costs are high and can handle big data cases where data cannot be easily distributed by providing a shared-memory processing environment.

The Elevation of Hadoop Clusters Hadoop is an open-source framework for running data-intensive applications in compute clusters made out of scores of heterogeneous commodity servers. There are several business and technical use cases for Hadoop clusters. There are advanced mechanisms being incorporated in Hadoop sensors for scalability, availability, security, fault tolerance, etc. Automated scale-out and scale-in are being achieved through extra and externally imposed techniques. For large-scale data crunching, Hadoop clusters are turning out to be indispensable due to its simple architecture. There are better days ahead for Hadoop clusters. Hadoop is designed from the ground up to efficiently distribute large amounts of processing across a set of machines from a few to over 2000 servers. A small-scale Hadoop cluster can easily crunch terabytes or even petabytes of data. The steps for efficient data analytics through Hadoop clusters [2] are given below.

Step 1: The Data Loading and Distribution—the input data is stored in multiple files, and hence the scale of parallelism in a Hadoop job is related to the number of input files. For example, if there are 10 input files, then the computation can be distributed across ten nodes. Therefore, the ability to rapidly process large data sets across compute servers is related to the number of files and the speed of the network infrastructure used to distribute the data to the compute nodes. The Hadoop scheduler assigns jobs to the nodes to process the files. As a job is completed, the scheduler assigns another job to the node with the corresponding data. The job's data may reside on local storage or on another node in the network. Nodes remain idle until they receive the data to process. Therefore, planning the data set distribution and a high-speed data center network both contribute to better performance of the Hadoop processing cluster. By design, the Hadoop distributed file system (HDFS) typically holds three or more copies of the same data set across nodes to avoid idle time.

Steps 2 and 3: Map/Reduce—the first data-processing step applies a mapping function to the data loaded during step 1. The intermediate output of the mapping process is partitioned using some key, and all data with the same key is next moved to the same "reducer" node. The final processing step applies a reduce function to the intermediate data; and the output of the reduce function is stored back on disk. Between the map and reduce operations, the data is shuffled between the nodes. All outputs of the map function with the same key are moved to the same reducer node. In between these two key steps, there could be many other tasks such as shuffling, filtering, tunnelling, funnelling, etc.

Step 4: Consolidation—after the data has been mapped and reduced, it must be merged for output and reporting.

Hadoop clusters can scale from hundreds of nodes to over ten thousand nodes to analyze some of the largest data sets in the world. Hadoop clusters are the most affordable and adept mechanism for high-performance big data storage, processing, and analysis. It is hence obvious that the Hadoop framework in sync up with well-designed compute clusters is to tackle scores of data-intensive applications through efficient parallelizing of data across. Clusters are bound to be pervasive as enterprise IT is under immense pressure to reduce cost and take business services and solutions to the market in double quick time.

2.8   Grid Computing

For high-performance workloads across industry verticals, the current IT systems are found to be ineffective. Another interesting mandate is to reuse existing IT resources to the fullest while preparing additional resources for running high-end applications. There are several domains such as financial services, manufacturing, life sciences, technical computing, etc. demanding fresh ways and means for HPC. Grid computing is being positioned as one of the exceptionally powerful HPC paradigms. Grids follow the ideals of distributed computing. The real beauty is not the distributed deployment of servers but the centralized monitoring, measurement, and management of them. Computational grids allow you to seamlessly establish a fruitful linkage among the processors, storage, and/or memory of distributed computers to enhance their utilization to a new high to solve large-scale problems more quickly. The benefits of grids include cost savings, improved business agility by decreasing time to deliver results, and purpose-specific collaboration and enhanced sharing of resources. Grid computing is an extensible compute environment for ensuring scalability, high availability, and faster processing in a cost-effective manner. "Divide and conquer" has been a success mantra, and here too, grids exploit it to come out with flying colors in assuaging and accomplishing the needs of HPC. All kinds of parallelizable workloads and data volumes could benefit out of this computing paradigm.

There are business factors and forces that are paving the way for the systematic realization of grid computing capabilities widely. Today everyone is being assisted by many differently enabled devices collaborating with one another in understanding our needs and delivering them in time unobtrusively. Devices enable us to be connected with the outside world. As machines are empowered to communicate with one another in the vicinity as well as with remote systems, the amount of data getting generated through various interactions among machines and men is incredibly tremendous. The hugeness of data is making existing IT systems stressful. That is, the window of opportunity for capturing and turning the data into information and into knowledge gets shrunken sharply. Increasingly, industry applications are being subjected to process large volumes of data and to perform repetitive computations that exceed the existing server capabilities. In this sickening scenario, grid computing came as a boon in order to overcome the brewing data-imposed challenges. The conspicuous benefits include:

- *Scalability*—long-running applications can be decomposed as manageable execution units, and similarly large data sets can be precisely segmented into data subsets. Both of these can be executed together at the same time to speed up the execution process. As there is sufficient number of commodity servers joining in the processing process, the application segregation and data division are bound to do well. Further on, the unique capability of runtime addition of newer servers is to ensure the fluent scalability.
- *User Growth*—several users can access a virtualized pool of resources in order to obtain the best possible response time by maximizing utilization of the computing resources.
- *Cost Savings*—leveraging unutilized and underutilized compute machines in the network is the prime move for IT cost reduction. Resource sharing is another noteworthy factor in a grid environment.

- *Business Agility*—grid computing sharply enhances the IT agility, which in turn leads to business agility. That is, IT is being empowered to listen to business changes and challenges quickly.
- *Heightened Automation*—with the implementation and incorporation of powerful algorithms in grid environments, the automation of managing grid applications and platforms is elevated to a new level.

For big data analytics, the grid concepts are very contributive and constructive. Grids provide exemplary workload management, job scheduling and prioritization, and the subdivision of analytics job for higher productivity. As indicated above, system availability, scalability, and sustainability are fully entrenched through software in grids. Elimination of single point of failure, embedded fault tolerance, etc. is the principal key drivers for grid-based big data analysis. Grid computing can parse and partition large-scale analytics jobs into smaller tasks that can be run, in parallel, on smaller and cost-effective servers than on high-end and expensive symmetric multiprocessor (SMP) systems.

In-Memory Data Grid (IMDG) [3] Although the Hadoop's parallel architecture can accelerate big data analytics, when it comes to fast-changing data, the Hadoop's batch processing and disk overheads are overly prohibitive. In this section, we are to explain how real-time and high-performance analytics can be realized by combining an IMDG with an integrated and stand-alone MapReduce execution engine. This new convergence delivers faster results for live data and also accelerates the analysis of large and static data sets. IMDG provides low-access latency, scalable capacity and throughput, and integrated high availability. IMDGs automatically store and load balance the data across an elastic cluster of servers. IMDGs also redundantly store data on multiple servers to ensure high availability just in case a server or network link fails. An IMDG's cluster can easily scale up its capacity by adding servers to handle additional workloads dynamically.

IMDGs need supple storage mechanisms to handle widely differing demands on the data that they store. IMDGs could host complex objects with rich semantics to support features such as property-oriented query, dependencies, timeouts, pessimistic locking, and synchronized access from remote IMDGs. Typically MapReduce applications are being used for crunching large populations of simple objects. There are other applications envisaging the storage and analytics of huge numbers of very small objects such as sensor data or tweets. To handle these divergent storage requirements and to use memory and network resources efficiently, IMDGs need multiple storage APIs, such as the Named Cache and Named Map APIs. Through these APIs, applications can create, read, update, and delete objects to manage live data. This comes as a handle for application developers to store and analyze both heavyweight objects with rich metadata and lightweight objects with highly optimized storage with the same ease.

Operational systems generally process live data, and if IMDGs are integrated with operational systems, then the access of in-memory data gets significantly accelerated for special-purpose analysis, providing real-time insights to optimize IT operations and helping to identify any exceptional and risky conditions in time. Integrating a MapReduce engine into an IMDG minimizes the analysis and response times remarkably because it avoids data movement during processing. Advanced IMDGs demonstrate parallel computing capabilities to overcome many of the MapReduce-introduced limitations and also enable the semantics of MapReduce to be emulated and optimized. The result is the same with the advantage of faster delivery. If a MapReduce application is programmed to analyze both live data and historical data, then the same code can be utilized in the IMDG-based real-time environment as well as in the Hadoop batch environment.

IMDGs for Real-Time Analytics There are a few activities to be considered and done towards real-time analytics. The first step is to eliminate batch-scheduling overhead introduced by Hadoop's standard batch scheduler. Instead, IMDGs can pre-stage a Java-based execution environment on all grid servers and reuse it for multiple analyses. This execution environment consists of a set of Java Virtual Machines (JVMs), one on every server within the cluster alongside each grid service process. These JVMs form IMDG's MapReduce engine. Also the IMDG can automatically deploy all necessary executable programs and libraries for the execution of MapReduce across the JVMs, greatly reducing start-up time down to milliseconds.

The next step [3] in reducing the MapReduce analysis time is to eliminate data motion as much as possible. Because an IMDG hosts fast-changing data in memory, MapReduce applications can get data directly from the grid and put results back to the grid. This accelerates data analysis by avoiding delays in accessing and retrieving data from secondary storage. As the execution engine is integrated with the IMDG, key/value pairs hosted within the IMDG can be efficiently read into the execution engine to minimize access time. A special record reader (grid record reader) can be used to automatically pipeline the transfer of key/value pairs from the IMDG's in-memory storage into the mappers. Its input format automatically creates appropriate splits of the specified input key/value collection to avoid any network overhead when retrieving key/value pairs from all grid servers. Likewise, a grid record writer enables pipelined results from Hadoop's reducers back to the IMDG storage. Thus, IMDGs are turning out to be an excellent tool for accomplishing data analytics to extract actionable intelligence in time.

In-memory data grids are popular because they address two related challenges:

- Access to big data for real-time use
- Application performance and scale

In-memory data grids present a smart solution posed by these two challenges:

- Ensuring that the right data is available in memory with simple access. In-memory data grids promote extremely fast, scalable read-write performance.
- Automatically persisting unused data to a file system or maintaining redundant in-memory nodes to ensure high reliability and fault tolerance.
- Elastically spinning up and down distributed nodes.

- Automatically distributing information across the entire cluster so the grid can grow as your scale and performance needs change.

GridGain is a JVM-based application middleware that enables companies to easily build highly scalable real-time compute and data-intensive distributed applications that work on any managed infrastructure from a small local cluster to large hybrid clouds.

To achieve this capability, GridGain provides a middleware solution that integrates two fundamental technologies into one cohesive product:

- Computational grid
- In-memory data grid

These two technologies are for any real-time distributed application as they provide the means for co-located parallelization of processing and data access, and they are the cornerstone capability for enabling scalability under extreme high loads.

Compute Grid Computational grid technology provides means for distribution of the processing logic. That is, it enables the parallelization of computations on more than one computer. More specifically, computational grids or MapReduce type of processing defines the method of splitting original computational task into multiple subtasks, executing these subtasks in parallel on any managed infrastructure and aggregating (reducing) results back to one final result. GridGain provides the most comprehensive computational grid and MapReduce capabilities.

In-Memory Data Grid This provides capability to parallelize the data storage by storing partitioned data in memory closer to application. IMDGs allow treating grids and clouds as a single virtualized memory bank that smartly partitions data among the participating computers and providing various caching and accessing strategies. The Goal of IMDGs is to provide extremely high availability of data by keeping it in memory and in highly distributed (i.e., parallelized) fashion.

On summary, it is clear that using an IMDG with an integrated MapReduce engine opens the door to real-time analytics on live and operational data. The IMDG's integrated MapReduce engine also eliminates the need to install, configure, and manage a full Hadoop distribution. Developers can write and run standard MapReduce applications in Java and these applications can be executed as a stand-alone by the execution engine. In a nutshell, in-memory data grids in association with Hadoop engines are capable of producing results in time efficiently so that informed decisions can be taken to embark on the execution journey with all confidence and clarity. The productivity of IT infrastructures goes up considerably with the smart leverage of grids. There are specific use cases emerging and evolving across industry verticals, and they are bound to benefit immensely by utilizing the subtle and sublime concepts of grid computing.

2.9   Cloud Computing

We have discussed about the roles of clusters and grids in fulfilling the high-performance requirements of big data analytics. In this section, we are to explain how the raging cloud paradigm is to contribute for the exclusive high-performance needs of BDA. As we all know, the cloud idea is very popular due to its immense potential in seamlessly bringing up infrastructure optimization. Typically, the utilization rate of IT infrastructures stands at 15 %, and hence there have been a string of endeavors at different levels and layers to sharply enhance the utilization rates of capital-intensive and expensive-to-operate IT resources. The cloud paradigm is a growing collection of pragmatic techniques and tips such as consolidation, centralization, virtualization, automation, sharing, etc. of various IT resources (compute machines, storage appliances, and network solutions) towards well-organized and optimized IT environments. There are competent solutions even for clustering virtualized machines towards high-performance and high-throughput systems for specific uses.

A variety of enhancements are being worked out to make IT environments cloud-ready. As prevalent in software engineering, the API-backed hardware programmability is being brought in these days in order to automate the activation of hardware elements over any network. That means the remote discoverability, accessibility, maneuverability, manageability, and maintainability of hardware elements are being facilitated towards the elevation of their usability and utilization level. Another noteworthy point here is that the concentrated intelligence in hardware components is being segregated and presented as a software layer so that the long-standing goals of IT commoditization and industrialization are fulfilled. The introduction of software layer is to extremely simplify the operations of hardware modules, which means that the configurability, policy-based replaceability, substitutability, etc. of hardware modules through software are to see the light soon. This is the reason these days we often hear and read about the buzzwords such as software-defined infrastructures, networking, and storage. In short, a number of game-changing advancements are being rolled out to make IT programmable, converged, and adaptive.

Businesses need automated ways to expand and contract their IT capability as per the changing needs. Production-ready appliances and cloud-based software delivery provide flexible answers to this ongoing challenge. However, extending these approaches to address the extreme demands of mission-critical enterprise-scale applications requires innovation on many levels. Cloud enables ubiquitous and on-demand access to a dynamic and shared pool of highly configurable computing resources such as servers, storages, networking, applications, and services. These resources can be rapidly deployed and redeployed with minimal human intervention to meet changing resource requirements. That is, the IT agility, adaptability, affordability, and autonomy being realized through the leverage of the cloud concepts have a positive impact on business efficiency.

Scalability in Cloud Environments When cloud as a technology began trans-forming the IT industry, the buzz was all about IT infrastructure. Spinning up virtual machines (VMs) on demand was like a social utility (gas, electricity, and water). The cloud landscape thereafter continued to evolve, and today it is all about data and applications as the goal of infrastructure on demand is seeing the light fast. Now the ability of cloud service providers to orient their infrastructures to incoming work-loads is the new rat race. As this paradigm continues to expand in different dimen-sions and directions, today's business buyers are learning that "time to value" is more important than the commodity servers in cloud.

For the enigmatic cloud idea, there have arisen a number of use, business, and technical cases that are being overwhelmingly illustrated and articulated through a string of white papers, data sheets, case studies, research publications, magazine articles, and keynote talks in various international conferences and confluences. But the scalability attribute definitely stands tall among all of them. When adding more resources on the cloud to restore or improve application performance, administra-tors can scale either horizontally (out) or vertically (up). Vertical scaling (up) entails adding more resources to the same computing pool (e.g., adding more RAM, disk, or virtual CPU to handle an increased application load). On the other hand, horizon-tal scaling (out) requires the addition of more machines or devices to the computing platform to handle the increased demand.

Big Data Analytics in Clouds With data becoming big data, insights are bound to become big, and hence any futuristic applications are going to be definitely big insight driven. It is hence easy to understand that, in any enterprise, technically captured and tremendously stocked data volumes are ultimately to impact it tacti-cally and strategically. That is, no industry sector and business domain are to be left out of this data-inspired disruption and transformation. As this trend picks up, increasingly we read about and experience big data applications in the areas of capi-tal market, risk management, energy, retail, brand and marketing optimization, social media analysis, and customer sentiment analysis. Considering the hugeness of processing and data storage, businesses are yearning for parallel processing capa-bilities for analysis and scalable infrastructures capable of adapting quickly to an increment or decrement in computing or storage needs. Therefore, many big data applications are being readied to be cloud enabled and deployed in cloud environ-ments so as to innately avail all the originally envisaged cloud characteristics such as agility, adaptability, and affordability.

High-Performance Cloud Environments There is a common perception that vir-tualized environments are not suitable for high-performance applications. However, cloud infrastructures are increasingly a mix of both virtualized and bare-metal serv-ers. Therefore, for meeting the unique requirements of HPC applications, bare-metal systems are being utilized. Even VMware has conducted a series of tests in order to identify the fitment of big data analytics in virtualized environments, and the results are very encouraging as per the report published in the VMware website. The real beauty of cloud environments is the auto-scaling. Besides scaling up and down, scaling out and in is the key differentiator of clouds. Automatically, adding new resources and taking away the resources allocated as per the changing needs put cloud on top for cost-effective HPC. Any parallelizable workloads are tackled efficiently in clouds.

There are parallel file systems; scale-out storages; SQL, NoSQL, and NewSQL databases; etc. to position cloud infrastructures as the next-generation and afford-able HPC solution. For example, multiple computer-aided engineering (CAE) loads can process faster in an environment that is able to scale to meet demand, which makes cloud efficient, flexible, and collaborative. By applying the proven cloud principles to established HPC and analytics infrastructures, silos simply vanish, and shared resources can be leveraged to maximize the operational efficiency of existing clusters. The meticulous transition to the promising cloud paradigm can help in many ways. Due to extreme and deeper automation in cloud environments, there is an optimized usage of resources for achieving more powerful and purposeful computations.

Cloud Platforms for HPC Not only software-defined infrastructures but also hosting of pioneering HPC platforms in cloud environments enables clouds to be positioned as viable and venerable HPC environments. In the recent past, there have come a number of parallelizing platforms for real-time computing. The prominent platforms among them are IBM Netezza, SAP HANA, and SAS High-Performance Analytics. An instance of IBM Netezza was deployed in a public cloud environment (IBM SoftLayer) and tested to gain an insight into how it functions in a cloud envi-ronment. The data-processing speed was found to be excellent, and it has been deduced that a seamless synchronization of HPC platforms with cloud infrastruc-tures ensures the required high-performance goals.

Similarly, SAP and Intel came together to verify how their products go together in a cloud environment. Their engineering teams have deployed SAP HANA in a new Petabyte Cloud Lab that provides 8000 threads, 4000 cores, and 100 TB of RAM in a server farm consisting of 100 four-socket Intel Xeon processor E7 family-based servers. The cluster currently hosts a single instance of SAP HANA, and engineers continue to see near-linear scalability operating across a petabyte of data.

SAS is using Amazon Web Services (AWS) to help organizations improve busi-ness functions by creating flexible, scalable, and analytics-driven cloud applica-tions. This marks a critical step forward in helping organizations execute their big data and Hadoop initiatives by applying advanced analytic capabilities in the cloud with products. This not only reduces the costs considerably but also enables custom-ers to be benefited immensely and immediately because the cloud migration can make critical decisions to be taken quickly by being able to analyze data from any-where at any time in an efficient fashion. It is an irrefutable truth that the prime factors driving businesses towards the cloud paradigm include faster access to new functionality, reducing capital IT costs and improving the use of existing resources.

Without an iota of doubt, cloud is the happening place for all kinds of technical advancements as far as IT optimization, rationalization, simplification, standardization, and automation tasks are concerned. With the convergence of several technologies, clouds are being positioned as the next-generation affordable supercomputer for comprehensively solving the storage, processing, and analytical challenges thrown up by big data. The availability of massively parallel, hybrid, and application-specific computing resources being accessed through a loosely coupled, distributed, and cloud-based infrastructure brings forth a bevy of fresh opportunities for a range of complex applications dealing with large data sets.

2.10   Heterogeneous Computing

Heterogeneity is becoming a common affair in IT these days due to the multiplicity of competitive technologies and tools. Therefore, it makes sense to have a new model of heterogeneous computing to run heterogeneity-filled heavy workloads. Recently, heterogeneous computing has been gaining traction in a number of domains. Heterogeneous computing, a viable mechanism to realize the goals of accelerated computing, refers to systems that use a variety of different computational units such as general processors and special-purpose processors (digital signal processors (DSPs), graphics processing units (GPUs), and application-specific circuits often implemented on Field-Programmable Gate Arrays (FPGAs)). The GPU is a many-core machine with multiple SIMD multiprocessors (SM) that can run thousands of concurrent threads. Application-specific integrated circuit (ASIC) is another application-specific circuit. For example, a chip designed to run in a digital voice recorder or a high-efficiency bitcoin miner is an ASIC. Accelerators are the paramount solution approaches these days to substantially speed up specific parameters under some circumstances. Some applications have specific algorithms which can be offloaded from general-purpose CPUs to specific hardware which can accelerate those parts of the application. Mainly, GPUs are the leading force in sustaining the ideals of heterogeneous computing.

Why GPU Clusters?   This is the era of multicore computing as the performance of single-core CPUs has stagnated. Therefore, with the greater awareness, the adoption of GPUs has skyrocketed these days. Due to a series of advancements in micro- and nanoscale electronics, the value and power of GPUs have increased dramatically with a broad variety of applications demonstrating order-of-magnitude gains in both performance and price performance. GPUs particularly excel at the throughput-oriented workloads that are characterizing data and compute-intensive applications.

However, programmers and scientists focus most of their efforts on single-GPU development. The leverage of GPU clusters to tackle problems of true scale is very minimal as programming of multiple GPU clusters is not an easy one due to lack of powerful tools and APIs. As with MapReduce, parallel processing of data is handled well by GPUs. But existing GPU MapReduce targets solo GPUs and only in-core algorithms. Implementing MapReduce on a cluster of GPUs definitely poses a few challenges. Firstly, the multi-GPU communication is difficult as GPUs cannot source or sink network I/O, and hence supporting dynamic and efficient communication across many GPUs is hard. Secondly, GPUs do not have inherent out-of-core support and virtual memory. Thirdly, a naive GPU MapReduce implementation abstracts away the computational resources of the GPU and possible optimizations. Finally, the MapReduce model does not explicitly handle the system architecture inherent with GPUs. Armed with the knowledge of these critical restrictions, the authors [4] have come out with a well-defined library "GPU MapReduce (GPMR)" that specifically overcomes them.

Heterogeneous Computing for Big Data Analytics In this section, we are to discuss how this newly introduced computing paves the way for high-performance BDA. Many researchers across the globe have done considerable work to improve the performance of MapReduce by efficiently utilizing CPU cores, GPU cores, and multiple GPUs. However, these novel MapReduce frameworks do not aim to efficiently utilize heterogeneous processors, such as a set of CPUs and GPUs.

Moim: A Multi-GPU MapReduce Framework [5] As we all know, MapReduce is a renowned parallel-programming model that considerably decreases the developmental complexity of next-generation big data applications. The extra simplicity originates from the fact that developers need to write only two different functions (map and reduce). The map function specifies how to convert input <key, value> pairs into intermediate <key, value> pairs, and the reduce function receives the intermediate pairs from the map function as the input and reduces them into final <Skey, value> pairs. The MapReduce runtime innately takes care of data partition, scheduling, and fault tolerance in a transparent manner. However, MapReduce has several limitations. Although it is carefully designed to leverage internode parallelism in a cluster of commodity servers, it is not designed to exploit the intra-node parallelism provided by heterogeneous parallel processors such as multicore CPUs and GPUs. There are other concerns too. In MapReduce, the intermediate pairs of a job are shuffled to one or more reducers via the hashing mechanism based on the keys. Unfortunately, this approach may result in serious load imbalance among the reducers of a job as the distribution of keys is highly skewed. As the speed of a parallel job consisting of smaller tasks is determined by the slowest task in the chain, a larger degree of load imbalance may translate into a longer delay.

To tackle these challenges, the authors [5] have designed a new MapReduce framework, called Moim, which, while overcoming the abovementioned drawbacks, provides a number of new features as follows in order to increase the data-processing efficiency of MapReduce:

- Moim efficiently utilizes the parallelism provided by both multicore CPUs and GPUs.
- It overlaps CPU and GPU computations as much as possible to decrease the end-to-end delay.
- It supports efficient load balancing among the reducers as well as the mappers of a MapReduce job.

- The overall system is designed to process not only fixed but also variable-size data.

Heterogeneous Computing in Cloud We have discussed about the impending role of clouds as the futuristic and flexible HPC environment. Now as chipsets and other accelerated solutions that fully comply with the specifications of heterogeneous computing are hitting the market, the days of full-fledged heterogeneous computing is not far off. Another path-breaking development is that the combination of heterogeneous computing and cloud computing is emerging as a powerful new paradigm to meet the requirements for HPC and higher data-processing throughput. Cloud-based heterogeneous computing represents a significant step in fulfilling the advancing HPC needs. "The Intel Xeon Phi coprocessor represents a breakthrough in heterogeneous computing by delivering exceptional throughput and energy efficiency without the high costs, inflexibility, and programming challenges that have plagued many previous approaches to heterogeneous computing."

Cloud-Based Heterogeneous Computing via Nimbix Cloud Nimbix launched the world's first Accelerated Compute Cloud infrastructure (a non-virtualized cloud that featured the latest co-processors for advanced processing), and the focus had always been on time to value. Thereafter, they had introduced JARVICE (Just Applications Running Vigorously in a Cloud Environment), and this is the central platform technology developed in order to run applications faster at the lowest total cost. One of the benefits of running a big data application in the Nimbix Cloud is that it automatically leverages powerful supercomputing-class GPUs underneath. This can comfortably speed up rendering by tens or even hundreds of times depending on the model vs. even very powerful desktops and laptops. The NVIDIA Tesla GPUs support computation, not just visualization, and are much more powerful than most graphics processors available on PCs. Thus, there are providers working on delivering high-performance heterogeneous computing from cloud environments.

Several companies are attracted towards heterogeneous computing. The OpenPOWER Foundation consortium was initiated by IBM and sustained by many other organizations to make the Power architecture pervasive and persuasive. This is for bringing in the extreme optimization in next-generation compute systems to comfortably achieve the success on compute-intensive workloads and for lessening the workloads of application developers. It was announced that the future versions of IBM Power Systems will feature NVIDIA NVLink technology, eliminating the need to transfer data between the CPU and GPUs over the PCI Express interface. This will enable NVIDIA GPUs to access IBM POWER CPU memory at its full bandwidth, improving performance for numerous enterprise applications. Power Systems are at the forefront of delivering solutions to gain faster insights from analyzing both structured information and unstructured big data—such as video, images and content from sensors—and data from social networks and mobile devices. To draw insights and make better decisions, businesses need solutions that consist of proprietary and open system software to solve their specific pain points.

To drive those solutions, secure and flexible Power Systems servers are designed to keep data moving by running multiple concurrent queries that take advantage of industry-leading memory and I/O bandwidths. All of this leads to highly supported utilization rates.

2.11 Mainframes for High-Performance Computing

The essential architecture of a mainframe system, with its ready-made network of specialized devices, centrally managed and organized, delivers the performance and scalability required for BDA workloads. The reliability of the mainframe at a level that distributed systems still cannot match, a result of decades of development and refinement, makes it the ideal platform for mission-critical workloads. The mainframe system virtualizes its physical resources as part of its native operation. Physically, the mainframe is not a single computer but a network of computing components including a central processor with main memory, with channels that manage networks of storage and peripheral devices. The operating system uses symbolic names to enable users to dynamically deploy and redeploy virtual machines, disk volumes, and other resources, making the shared use of common physical resources among many projects a straightforward proposition. Multiple such systems may be blended together.

Mainframe computers still rule the IT division of many organizations across the world. The mainframe is the undisputed king of transactional data, and anywhere from 60 to 80 % of all the world's transactional data is said to reside on the mainframe. Relational data only represents a fraction of all the data held on the mainframe. Other prominent data assets are stored in record-oriented file management systems such as VSAM that predates the advent of RDBMS. XML data is another kind of data getting produced, captured, and stored in large quantities. And in the recent past, a huge and largely untapped source of data comes in the form of unstructured or semi-structured data from multiple internal as well as external sources. This non-mainframe data is growing at exponential rates. Consider social media data. Twitter alone generates 12 terabytes of tweets every day. It is not desirable or practical to move such volumes of non-mainframe data into the mainframe for analysis. But there are tactic and strategic use cases for multi-structured data. For example, it would be very useful to comb through social media for information that can augment the traditional analytics that you already do against your relational mainframe data.

IBM's InfoSphere BigInsights, the commercial-grade implementation of the Hadoop standard, running on a Power or IBM System x server is certainly well suited to ingest and process this sort of poly-structured data. Connectors available with DB2 for z/OS enable a DB2 process to initiate a BigInsights analytics job against the remote Hadoop cluster and then ingest the result set back into a relational database or traditional data warehouse to augment the mainframe data. Mainframe data never leaves the mainframe and is simply augmented and enhanced by data ingested from other sources.

Veristorm [6] has delivered a commercial distribution of Hadoop for the mainframe. The Hadoop distribution coupled with state-of-the-art data connector technology makes z/OS data available for processing using the Hadoop paradigm without that data ever having to leave the mainframe. Because the entire solution runs in Linux on System z, it can be deployed to low-cost and dedicated mainframe Linux processors. Further on, by taking advantage of the mainframe's ability to activate additional capacity on demand as needed, vStorm Enterprise can be used to build out highly scalable private clouds for BDA. vStorm Enterprise includes zDoop, a fully supported implementation of the open-source Apache Hadoop. zDoop delivers Hive for developers who prefer to draw on their SQL background and Pig for a more procedural approach to building applications.

In the mainframe environment, users can integrate data held in Hadoop with various NoSQL, DB2, and IMS databases in a common environment and analyze that data using analytic mainframe software such as IBM Cognos and SPSS, ILOG, and IBM InfoSphere Warehouse. Mainframe users can take advantage of such factory-integrated capabilities [7].

- The IBM DB2 Analytics Accelerator for z/OS, which is based on IBM Netezza technology, substantially accelerates queries by transparently offloading certain queries to the massively parallel architecture of the Accelerator appliance. The DB2 for z/OS code recognizes the Accelerator is installed and automatically routes queries that would benefit from this architecture to the appliance. No application changes are required.
- IBM PureData System for Hadoop is a purpose-built, standards-based system that architecturally integrates IBM InfoSphere BigInsights Hadoop-based software, server, and storage into a single system.
- IBM zEnterprise Analytics System (ISAS) 9700/9710 is a mainframe-based, high-performance, integrated software and hardware platform with broad business analytic capabilities to support data warehousing, query, reporting, multidimensional analysis, and data and text mining.
- The ability to integrate real-time analytics transactional scoring in DB2 for z/OS allows for efficient scoring of predictive models within the milliseconds of a transaction by integrating the IBM SPSS Modeler Scoring within IBM DB2 for z/OS.

On summary, IBM Big Data Analytics on zEnterprise provides a truly modern and cost-competitive analytics infrastructure with an extensive and integrated set of offerings that are primed for delivering on today's business-critical analytics and big data initiatives across all of your data sources.

2.12 Supercomputing for Big Data Analytics

Cray is bringing in an integrated open-source Hadoop big data analytics software to its supercomputing platforms. Cray cluster supercomputers for Hadoop will pair Cray CS300 systems with the Intel distribution for Apache Hadoop software. The Hadoop system will include a Linux operating system, workload management software, the Cray Advanced Cluster Engine (ACE) management software, and the Intel distribution. Thus, the BDA has successfully penetrated into supercomputing domain too. Other corporates are not lagging behind in synchronizing big data with their powerful infrastructures. Fujitsu brings out the high-performance processors in the Fujitsu M10 enterprise server family to help organizations meet their everyday challenges. What once was reserved for data-intensive scientific computing is now made available for meeting the distinct challenges of mission-critical business computing especially for BDA. From high-throughput connectivity to data sources to high-speed data movement and to high-performance processing units, Fujitsu Japan has been in the forefront serving data-driven insights towards realizing and deploying mission-critical intelligent systems.

IBM wants to unlock big data secrets for businesses with a new free Watson Analytics tool. This offering leverages IBM's Watson technology and allows businesses to upload data to IBM's Watson Analytics cloud service and then query and explore results to spot trends and patterns and conduct predictive analysis. Watson Analytics parses data, cleans it up, preps it for analysis, identifies important trends, and makes it easily searchable via natural language queries. The tool could help companies better understand customer behavior or connect the dots between sales, weather, time of day, and customer demographic data.

Thus, big data analytics has become an important trend drawing the attentions of many. Product innovators and vendors focusing on supercomputing, cognitive, and parallel computing models are consciously redrawing their strategy in tweaking their solutions and services in order to bring forth quantifiable value for the challenging proposition of BDA.

2.13 Appliances for Big Data Analytics

Undoubtedly, appliances represent the next-generation IT delivery. They are purpose built and are pre-integrated devices that club together the right size of the hardware modules and the relevant software libraries to run specific workloads quickly, easily, and effectively. This is turning out to be a cheaper and viable option for small and medium enterprises. Certain applications produce better results in the appliance mode, and appliances rapidly and religiously deliver better returns on the investment made, whereas the total cost of ownership (TCO) remains on the lower side. Due to the smart bundling, making appliances up and running is furiously fast due to the automated configuration facility, and the functioning is smooth. This is a kind of accelerated computing, and human intervention, instruction, and involvement are very minimal. The powerful emergence of appliances is a significant part of the series of innovations in the IT field in order to streamline and sharpen the IT delivery. IT productivity is bound to go up significantly with the incorporation of appliances in the enterprise IT environments and cloud centers.

Bundling has been a cool concept in IT, and in the recent past, the containerization aspect, which is a kind of bundling of all the relevant stuff together to automate and accelerate IT, has received a solid boost with the simplified engine introduced by the Docker initiative. Appliances are hence bound to score well in this competitive environment and acquire greater space in the world market in the days ahead. Appliances are much more varied and vast in the sense that there are multiple varieties emerging as per the changing requirements. Appliances can be virtual appliances too. That is, virtual or software appliances can easily get installed in specified hardware. This segregation enhances the appliance flexibility, and different hardware vendors can easily move into the world of appliances. The result is the pervasive and persuasive nature of appliances. In the ensuing sections, we are to discuss about the enhanced role of appliances for different purposes as listed below:

- Data warehouse appliances for large-scale data analytics
- In-memory data analytics
- In-database data analytics
- Hadoop-based data analytics

2.13.1   Data Warehouse Appliances for Large-Scale Data Analytics

The growing number of data sources and the resulting rises in data volumes simply strain and stress traditional IT platforms and infrastructures. The legacy methods for data management and analytics are turning out to be inadequate for tackling the fresh challenges posed by big data. The data storage, management, processing, and mining are the real pains for conventional IT environments. The existing systems, if leveraged to crunch big data, require huge outlays of technical resources in a losing battle to keep pace with the demands for timely and actionable insights. Many product vendors have come out with appliances to accelerate the process of data analytics in an easy manner.

IBM PureData System for Analytics Revolution Analytics® and IBM have teamed together to enable organizations to incorporate R as a vital part of their big data analytics strategy. With multiple deployment options, organizations can simply and cost-effectively optimize key steps in the analytic process (data distillation, model development, and deployment), maximize performance at scale, and gain efficiencies.

PureData System for Analytics, powered by Netezza technology, architecturally integrates database, server, and storage into a single, purpose-built, easy-to-manage system that minimizes data movement, thereby accelerating the processing of analytical data, analytics modeling, and data scoring. It delivers exceptional performance on large-scale data (multiple petabytes), while leveraging the latest innovations in analytics. Revolution R Enterprise "plugs-in" to IBM Netezza Analytics, a built-in analytical infrastructure. With IBM Netezza Analytics, all analytic activity is consolidated into a single appliance. PureData System for Analytics delivers integrated components to provide exceptional performance, with no indexing or tuning required. As an appliance, the hardware, software (including IBM Netezza Analytics), and storage are completely and exceptionally integrated, leading to shorter deployment cycles and faster time to value for business analytics.

EMC Greenplum Appliance We know that business intelligence (BI) and analytical workloads are fundamentally different from online transaction processing (OLTP) workloads, and therefore we require a profoundly different architecture for enabling online analytical processing (OLAP). Generally, OLTP workloads require quick access and updates to a small set of records, and this work is typically performed in a localized area on disk with one or a small number of parallel units. Shared-everything architectures, wherein processors share a single large disk and memory, are well suited for OLTP workloads. However, shared-everything and shared-disk architectures are quickly overwhelmed by the full-table scans, multiple complex table joins, sorting, and aggregation operations against vast volumes of data that represent the lion's share of BI and analytical workloads.

EMC Greenplum is being presented as the next generation of data warehousing and large-scale analytic processing. EMC offers a new and disruptive economic model for large-scale analytics that allows customers to build warehouses that harness low-cost commodity servers, storage, and networking to economically scale to petabytes of data. Greenplum makes it easy to expand and leverage the parallelism of hundreds or thousands of cores across an ever-growing pool of machines. The Greenplum's massively parallel and shared-nothing architecture fully utilizes every single core with linear scalability and unmatched processing performance. Supporting SQL and MapReduce parallel processing, the Greenplum database offers industry-leading performance at a low cost for companies managing terabytes to petabytes of data.

Hitachi Unified Compute Platform (UCP) The ability to store data in memory is crucial to move business from traditional business intelligence to business advantages through big data. SAP High-Performance Analytic Application (HANA) is a prominent platform for in-memory and real-time analytics. It lets you analyze business operations in real time based on large volumes of structured data. The platform can be deployed as an appliance or delivered as a service via the cloud. The convergence of Hitachi UCP and SAP HANA has resulted in a high-performance big data appliance that helps you accelerate adoption and achieve faster time to the value.

Oracle SuperCluster is an integrated server, storage, networking, and software system that provides maximum end-to-end database and application performance and minimal initial and ongoing support and maintenance effort and complexity at the lowest total cost of ownership. Oracle SuperCluster incorporates high-speed on-chip encryption engines for data security, low-latency QDR InfiniBand or 10 GbE networking for connection to application infrastructure; integrated compute server, network, and storage virtualization through Oracle Solaris Zones; and the mission-critical, Oracle Solaris operating system. Oracle SuperCluster provides unique data-base, data warehouse, and OLTP performance and storage efficiency enhancements and unique middleware and application performance enhancements, is engineered and pre-integrated for easy deployment, and minimizes overhead backed by the most aggressive support SLAs in the industry. The large 4 terabyte memory foot-print of SuperCluster T5-8 allows many applications to run entirely in memory. SuperCluster M6-32 allows even greater memory scaling with up to 32 terabytes in a single configuration. Running Oracle in-memory applications on Oracle SuperCluster provides significant application performance benefits.

SAS High-Performance Analytics (HPA) SAS HPA is a momentous step forward in the area of high-speed and analytic processing in a scalable clustered environment. Teradata's innovative Unified Data Architecture (UDA) represents a signifi-cant improvement for meeting up all kinds of recent challenges thrown by big data. The UDA provides 3 distinct, purpose-built data management platforms, each inte-grated with the others, intended with specialized needs:

- *Enterprise Data Warehouse*—Teradata database is the market-leading platform for delivering strategic and operational analytics throughout your organization, so users from across the company can access a single source of consistent, cen-tralized, and integrated data.
- *Teradata Discovery Platform*—Aster SQL-MapReduce delivers data discovery through iterative analytics against both structured and complex multi-structured data, to the broad majority of your business users. Prepackaged analytics allow businesses to quickly start their data-driven discovery model that can provide analytic lift to the SAS Analytics Platform.
- *Data Capture and Staging Platform*—Teradata uses Hortonworks Hadoop, an open-source Hadoop solution to support highly flexible data capture and staging. Teradata has integrated Hortonworks with robust tools for system management, data access, and one-stop support for all Teradata products. Hadoop provides low-cost storage and preprocessing of large volumes of data, both structured and file based.

SAS HPA software platform in sync up with Teradata UDA infrastructure pro-vides business users, analysts, and data scientists with the required capabilities and competencies to fulfill their analytic needs. SAS in-memory architecture has been a significant step forward in the area of high-speed and analytic processing for big data. One of the major themes of new SAS offerings over the last couple of years has been high-performance analytics largely using in-memory clustered technology to provide very fast analytic services for very large data sets. SAS visual analytics has also made significant strides towards the affordable analytic processing using largely a very similar in-memory architecture.

The key to SAS HPA and SAS visual analytics (VA) is the clustered processing (massively parallel processing (MPP)), and this proven and promising model enables SAS deployments to scale cluster size to support larger data, higher user concurrency, and greater parallel processing. However, the most significant benefit for SAS users is the blazing speed. Both environments with high-speed memory-centric techniques are to achieve extremely fast analytic processing. For example, for a Teradata customer, the SAS HPA reduced the analytic processing time from 16 h to 83 s for an analytical requirement, which is a dramatic improvement in speed. The biggest impact for that customer was that it now enabled their users to "experiment more," try more advanced model development techniques, and utilize the mantra of "failing faster." That is, if it only takes a couple of minutes to fail, then people would go for more trials and errors towards producing better models.

For SAS VA users, it is the same story. That is, one billion row analytical data sets can be pulled up and visualized in a couple of seconds. Users can apply different analytic techniques, slice and filter their data, and update different visualization techniques, all with near instantaneous response time. The SAS in-memory architecture comes in two data management flavors. The first one utilizes an MPP database management platform for storage of all of the data, and the second one utilizes a Hadoop file system cluster for persistence. Both work fast and can scale, especially when working with advanced clustered MPP style database models. However, for many complex organizations undertaking large-scale big data projects, neither is a "one-size-fits-all" solution.

The most economical model utilizes Hadoop running HPA directly against data scattered across the nodes of a distributed file system. With this model, relatively low-cost servers can be used to support the Hadoop workers, connected together by high-speed networking, with processing managed via the MapReduce. This distributed process gives the same benefits of many of the MPP model databases, but with fewer bells and whistles, at a lower cost. The Teradata appliance for SAS HPA extends the analytic capabilities of the Teradata environment, enabling SAS in-memory architecture directly onto the Teradata environment. With the HPA Appliance, Teradata extends any UDA data platform with new HPA capabilities.

The Aster Big Analytics Appliance The Aster Big Analytics Appliance is a powerful and ready-to-run platform that is pre-configured and optimized specifically for big data storage and analysis. As a purpose-built, integrated hardware and software solution for analytics at big data scale, this appliance runs the Aster SQL-MapReduce and SQL-H technology on a time-tested and fully supported Teradata hardware platform. Depending on workload needs, it can be configured exclusively with Aster nodes, Hadoop nodes, or a mixture of both Aster and Hadoop nodes. Additionally, integrated backup nodes for Aster nodes are available for data protection. By minimizing the number of moving parts required for deployment, the appliance offers easy and integrated management of an enterprise-ready information discovery solution with the benefits of optimized performance, continuous availability, and linear scalability. The appliance comes with Aster Database, which features more than 80 prepackaged SQL-MapReduce functions to enable faster insights. The SQL-MapReduce framework allows developers to write powerful and highly expressive SQL-MapReduce functions in various programming languages such as Java, C#, Python, C++, and R and push them into the discovery platform for advanced in-database analytics. Business analysts can then invoke SQL-MapReduce functions using standard SQL through Aster Database, and the discovery platform allows applications to be fully embedded within the database engine to enable ultrafast, deep analysis of massive data sets.

2.13.2   In-Memory Big Data Analytics

The need is for a highly productive environment which enables the data analyst to carry out analysis swiftly and implement the knowledge that has been discovered quickly so that it is delivered to the individual or software application that can use it just in time or sooner. Even so, there are three different latencies that an organization will experience with the new BI.

- *The Time to Discovery*—the time it takes for a data scientist to explore a collection of data and discover useful knowledge in it
- *The Time to Deployment*—the time it takes to implement the discovered knowledge within the business processes that it can enrich
- *Knowledge Delivery Time*—the time it takes for the BI application to deliver its knowledge in real time

Organizations are constantly seeking out for better ways to make informed decisions based on the trustworthy insights extracted by deeper analytics on the huge volumes of data. However, the worrying point is that the amount of data we have to analyze is expanding exponentially. Social and sentiment data (Facebook), weblogs, people profiles (LinkedIn), opinionated tweets (Twitter), actuator and sensor data, business transactional data, lab data, biological information, etc. are pumping out a tremendous amount of data to be systematically captured and subjected to a variety of drills. At the same time, the pressure to make better, fact-based decisions faster has never been greater than now.

Salient MPP (http://www.salient.com/) is a super scalable, in-memory, and multidimensional analytical data platform that defeats traditional limitations of speed, granularity, simplicity, and flexibility in use. When combined with Salient's discovery visualization user interface, it provides an overall analytical solution preferred by executives, analysts, and basic users to perform simple through complex analytics much faster than previously possible.

The GridGain In-Memory Data Fabric is a proven software solution, which delivers unprecedented speed and unlimited scale to accelerate the process of extracting timely insights. It enables high-performance transactions, real-time

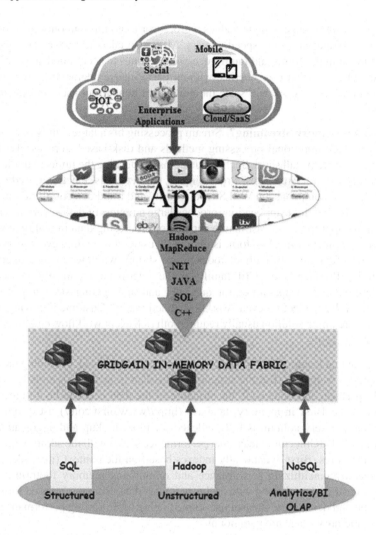

Fig. 2.3 The GridGain in-memory data fabric

streaming, and faster analytics. The GridGain In-Memory Data Fabric provides a unified API that spans all key types of applications (Java, .NET, C++) and connects them with multiple data stores containing structured, semi-structured, and unstructured data (SQL, NoSQL, Hadoop). Figure 2.3 depicts the GridGain In-Memory Data Fabric.

Keeping data in random access memory (RAM) allows a system to process data hundreds of times faster than by electromechanical input/output (processor to disk) operations. Through advanced data compression techniques, MPP can handle very large volumes and, at the same time, take advantage of the speed of in-memory processing. This speed advantage is enhanced by Salient's proprietary n-dimensional

GRID indexing scheme, which enables a processor to go through only that portion of data most relevant to the specific query. MPP also takes full advantage of both multi-threading platforms and multiprocessor machines to accommodate very large numbers of concurrent user queries, without performance degradation. Increasing the number of processors will scale the number of concurrent users in near-linear fashion.

What Is In-Memory Streaming? Stream processing fits a large family of applications for which traditional processing methods and disk-based storages like databases or file systems fall short. Such applications are pushing the limits of traditional data-processing infrastructures. Processing of market feeds, electronic trading by many financial companies on Wall Street, security and fraud detection, and military data analysis—all these applications produce large amounts of data at very fast rates and require appropriate infrastructure capable of processing data in real time without any bottlenecks. Apache Storm is mainly focused on providing event workflow and routing functionality without focusing on sliding windows or data querying capabilities. Products in the CEP family, on the other hand, are mostly focused on providing extensive capabilities for querying and aggregating streaming events, while generally neglecting event workflow functionality. Customers looking for a real-time streaming solution usually require both rich event workflow combined and CEP data querying.

It is true that keeping data in memory removes the bottleneck of reading data for large queries from disk. But the structure of the data in memory is equally important. To perform and scale well, the structure of the data needs to be designed for analytics. The Birst in-memory database (http://www.birst.com/) uses columnar data storage. Every column is fully indexed for rapid lookup and aggregation. A highly parallel architecture means that performance scales with the addition of more processing cores. Birst dynamically indexes based on the context (join, filter, and sort), thereby maximizing performance and minimizing memory footprint. Birst uses hash maps when dealing with arbitrary, sparse data. Bitmaps are used for more structured and dense data. Rowset lists come to play when sorting performance and efficient memory usage are paramount.

2.13.3 In-Database Processing of Big Data

This is the ability to perform analytical computations in the database management system where the data resides rather than in an application server or desktop program. It accelerates enterprise analytics' performance, data manageability, and scalability. In-database processing is ideal for big data analytics, where the sheer volume of the data involved makes it impractical to repetitively copy it over the network.

By leveraging in-database processing, analytics users are leveraging the power of the database platform, designed specifically for highly efficient data access methods, even with enormous data sets consisting of millions or billions of rows. SAS enables in-database processing for a set of core statistical and analytical functions and model scoring capabilities within Teradata, leveraging the MPP architecture for scalability and performance of analytic computations. These capabilities allow analytic computations to be run in parallel across potentially hundreds or thousands of processors. Parallel execution greatly accelerates the processing time for analytics calculations, providing very significant performance gains for faster results.

This is for predominantly simplifying and accelerating the analytics field, and an embedded, purpose-built, and advanced analytics platform delivered with every IBM Netezza appliance is to empower worldwide enterprises' analytic needs to meet and exceed their business demands. This analytical solution fuses data warehousing and in-database analytics together into a scalable, high-performance, and massively parallel platform to crunch through petascale data volumes furiously fast. This platform is specifically designed to quickly and effectively provide better and faster answers to the most sophisticated business questions. This allows the integration of its robust set of built-in analytic capabilities with leading analytic tools from divergent vendors such as Revolution Analytics, SAS, IBM SPSS, Fuzzy Logix, and Zementis.

2.13.4 Hadoop-Based Big Data Appliances

Hadoop is an open-source software framework for big data crunching and is composed of several modules. The key modules are MapReduce, the large-scale dataprocessing framework, and Hadoop distributed file system (HDFS), the data storage framework. HDFS supports the Hadoop distributed architecture that puts compute engines into the same physical nodes that store the data. This new arrangement and approach brings computation to the data nodes rather than the other way around. As data sizes are typically huge, it is prudent to move the processing logic over data. The data heaps are therefore segregated into a number of smaller and manageable data sets to be processed in parallel by each of the Hadoop data nodes. The results are then smartly aggregated into the answer for the original problem.

It is anticipated that the Hadoop framework will be positioned as the universal preprocessing engine for the ensuing big data era. The coarse-grained searching, indexing, and cleansing tasks are being allocated to Hadoop module, whereas the fine-grained analytics are being accomplished via the fully matured and stabilized data management solutions. Ultimately apart from the preprocessing, Hadoop comes handy in eliminating all kinds of redundant, repetitive, and routine data to arrive at data that are really rewarding at the end. The second major task is to transform all multi-structured data into structured data so that traditional data warehouses and bases can work on the refurbished data to emit pragmatic information to users. There are both open-source (Cloudera, Hortonworks, Apache Hadoop, Map R, etc.) and commerce-grade (IBM BigInsights, etc.) implementations and

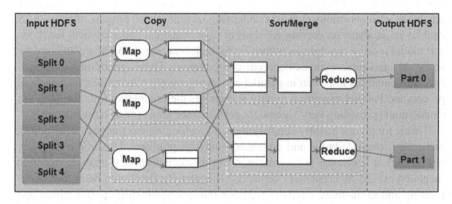

Fig. 2.4 The macro-level Hadoop architecture

distributions of the Hadoop standard. Datameer is the end-to-end platform for data ingestion, processing, analysis, and visualization. Figure 2.4 clearly tells how data are being split, mapped, merged, and reduced by MapReduce framework, while HDFS is the data storage mechanism.

Why Hadoop Scores Well? The plummeting cost of physical storage has created a bevy of tantalizing opportunities to do more with the continuous rise of data volumes like extracting and delivering insights. However, there is still the issue of processor cost. A 1 TB, massively parallel processing (MPP) appliance could run $100,000 to $200,000. The total cost for an implementation could go up to a few millions of dollars. In contrast, a terabyte of processing capacity on a cluster of commodity servers can be had for $2000 to $5000. This is the compelling factor for IT consultants to incline towards the Hadoop framework. This enormous gain in computational costs being achieved by Hadoop clusters is due to the proven distributed architecture of commodity clusters for low-cost data processing and knowledge dissemination. Appliances follow the contrast method and impose a hefty amount on IT budgets. Hadoop operates in a shared-nothing mode. All Hadoop data is stored locally on each node rather than on a networked storage. Processing is distributed across an array of commodity servers with independent CPUs and memory. The system is intelligent in the sense that the MapReduce scheduler optimizes for the processing to happen on the same node storing the associated data or located on the same leaf Ethernet switch.

Hadoop is natively fault tolerant. Hardware failure is expected and is mitigated by data replication and speculative processing. If capacity is available, Hadoop will start multiple copies of the same task for the same block of data. Results are accepted from the task that finishes first, while the other task is canceled and the results discarded. Speculative processing enables Hadoop to work around slow nodes and eliminates the need to restart a process if a failure occurs during a long-running calculation. Hadoop's fault tolerance is based on the fact that the Hadoop cluster can be configured to store data on multiple worker nodes. A key benefit of Hadoop is the ability to upload unstructured files without having to "schematize" them first. You can dump any type of data into Hadoop and allow the consuming programs to determine and apply structure when necessary.

As written above, Hadoop is being positioned as a vehicle to load formalized and formatted data into a traditional data warehouse for performing activities such as data mining, OLAP, and reporting or for loading data into a BI system for advanced analytics. Organizations can also dump large amounts of data into a Hadoop cluster, use a compatible visual analytics tool to quickly make sense out of the data, aggregate it, and export the data into analytic solution. In addition, the distributed processing capability of Hadoop can be used to facilitate the extract-transform-load (ETL) processes for getting the data from disparate and distributed sources into the warehouse.

Gartner defines a big data appliance as an integrated system that delivers a combination of server, storage, and network devices in a pre-integrated stack, together with a big data distributed processing framework such as Hadoop. The well-known advantages include:

- Standard configuration with maintenance and support provided by the vendor
- Converged hardware and software that can potentially lower setup time
- Unified monitoring and management tools that can simplify administration

The negative points include:

- Expensive acquisition and incremental expansion costs.
- Rigid configuration with minimal ability to tune the infrastructure.
- When operating at scale, vendor lock-in poses a significant barrier for safe exit.

Oracle Big Data Appliance   Oracle Big Data Appliance is a high-performance and secure platform for running Hadoop and NoSQL workloads. With Oracle Big Data SQL, it extends Oracle's industry-leading implementation of SQL to Hadoop and NoSQL systems. By combining the newest technologies from the Hadoop ecosystem and powerful Oracle SQL capabilities together on a single pre-configured platform, Oracle Big Data Appliance is uniquely able to support rapid development of big data applications and tight integration with existing relational data. It is pre-configured for secure environments leveraging Apache Sentry, Kerberos, both network encryption and encryption at rest, as well as Oracle Audit Vault and Database Firewall.

Oracle Big Data SQL is a new architecture for SQL on Hadoop, seamlessly integrating data in Hadoop and NoSQL with data in Oracle Database. Oracle Big Data SQL radically simplifies integrating and operating in the big data domain through two powerful features: newly expanded External Tables and Smart Scan functionality on Hadoop. Oracle Big Data Appliance integrates tightly with Oracle Exadata and Oracle Database using Big Data SQL and Oracle Big Data Connectors, seamlessly enabling analysis of all data in the enterprise.

Dell In-Memory Appliance for Cloudera Enterprise   Hadoop platforms are being increasingly embedded into powerful hardware to derive powerful appliances. It is absolutely clear that across all industries and markets, data is the new currency and competitive differentiator. But in the recent past, data has become big data. And to realize the promised competencies out of big data, organizations need competent solutions in place to facilitate faster and easier data ingestion, storage, analysis, and building of insights from big data. That's the idea behind the Dell In-Memory Appliance for Cloudera Enterprise. Building on a deep engineering partnership among Dell, Intel, and Cloudera, this next-generation analytic solution solves the big data challenge with a purpose-built turnkey and an in-memory advanced analytics data platform.

To enable fast analytics and stream processing, the Dell In-Memory Appliance for Cloudera Enterprise is bundled with Cloudera Enterprise, which includes Apache Spark. Cloudera Enterprise allows your business to implement powerful end-to-end analytic workflows, comprising batch data processing, interactive query, navigated search, deep data mining, and stream processing, all from a single common platform. With a single common platform, there is no need to maintain separate systems with separate data, metadata, security, and management that drive up the complexity and cost.

High-Performance Big Data Networking The unprecedented speed with which the prime IoT technologies are being adapted powerfully sets the stage for the explosion of poly-structured data. Scores of breakthrough edge technologies and their meticulous usage have collectively facilitated the realization of a growing array of digitized entities. The pioneering connectivity technologies and tools are enabling every smart and sentient object in our personal and professional environments to seamlessly find and connect with one another in the neighborhood and with the remotely held cyber applications and data. All types of purposeful interactions among IT-enabled physical, mechanical, electrical, and electronic systems result in data getting produced in plenty and accumulated in massive storage systems.

Hadoop deployments can have very large infrastructure requirements, and therefore hardware and software choices made at design time have a significant impact on performance and return on investment (ROI) of Hadoop clusters. Specifically, Hadoop cluster performance and ROI are highly dependent on network architecture and technology choices. While Gigabit Ethernet is the most commonly deployed network, it provides less than ideal bandwidth for many Hadoop workloads and for the whole of range of I/O-bound operations comprising a Hadoop job.

Typical Hadoop scale-out cluster servers utilize TCP/IP networking over one or more Gigabit Ethernet network interface cards (NICs) connected to a Gigabit Ethernet (GbE) network. The latest generation of commodity servers offers multi-socket and multicore CPU technology, which outstrips the network capacity offered by GbE networks. Similarly, with noteworthy advances in processor technology, this mismatch between server and network performance is predicted to grow further. Solid-state disks (SSDs) are evolving to offer equivalent capacity per dollar of hard disk drives (HDDs), and they are also being rapidly adopted for caching and for use with medium-sized data sets. The advances in storage I/O performance offered by SSDs exceed the performance offered by GbE networking. All these clearly make network I/O increasingly the most common impediment to improved Hadoop cluster performance.

There is a concern expressed in different quarters on the viability of transferring huge quantities of data from on-premise systems to cloud-based big data analytics. The transmission of tens of terabytes of data over the open and shared public Internet, which is the prominent communication infrastructure for cloud-based data processing and service delivery, evokes some inconvenient questions.

IBM Aspera Solution   Built on top of the patented FASP transport technology, IBM Aspera's suite of On Demand Transfer products solves both technical problems of the WAN and the cloud I/O bottleneck, delivering unrivaled performance for the transfer of large files or large collections of files, in and out of the cloud. Aspera's FASP transport protocol eliminates the WAN bottleneck associated with conventional file transfer technologies such as FTP and HTTP. With FASP, transfers of any size into and out of the cloud achieve perfect throughput efficiency, independent of the network delays, and are robust to extreme packet loss.

Aspera has developed a high-speed software bridge, Direct-to- Cloud, which transfers data at line speed, from source directly into cloud storage. Using parallel HTTP streams between the Aspera on-demand transfer server running on a cloud virtual machine and the cloud storage, the intra-cloud data movement no longer constrains the overall transfer rate. The files are written directly to cloud storage, without a stop-off on the cloud compute server.

In summary, as big data gets even bigger, the demand to increase processing power, storage capacity, storage performance, and network bandwidth grows even greater. To meet this demand, more racks and data nodes may be added to Hadoop clusters. But this solution is neither economical nor efficient. It requires more space, increases the power consumption, and adds to the management and maintenance overheads while ignoring the fact that slow 1 GbE interconnects continue to handicap Hadoop's node to node and overall input/output speed and cluster performance. 10 Gigabit Ethernet has the potential of bringing the Hadoop cluster networking into balance with the recent improvements in performance brought by server CPUs and advances in storage technology. However, to achieve optimum balance, the network I/O gains delivered by 10GbE must come with optimal efficiency so that the impact of high-speed network I/O on the server CPU is minimized.

2.13.5   High-Performance Big Data Storage Appliances

With the amount of data getting stored doubling every two years and the energy required to store that data exceeding 40 % of data center (DC) power consumption, nearly every organization has a critical need for massively scalable and intelligent storage solutions that are highly efficient, easy to manage, and cost-effective. As organizations of all sizes face the daunting task of the big data era, many struggle with maintaining their productivity and competitiveness as the overpowering waves of big data simply bog them down or negatively impact their performance. The unprecedented growth rate of data, particularly the unstructured data, has brought them a series of challenges. As per the IDC report, by the end of 2012, the total amount of digital information captured and stocked in the world reached 2.7 zettabytes (ZB). It also clearly reports that 90 % of it is unstructured data like multimedia files (still and dynamic images, sound files, machine data, experimentation results, etc.). Searching for useful information in those data mountains poses a real challenge to enterprise IT teams of business organizations across the globe with the existing IT infrastructures. But along with this unprecedented explosion of data comes an incredible opportunity for monetizing better products and services. Data-driven insights ultimately lead to fresh possibilities and opportunities. Companies are armed to seek out hitherto unexplored avenues for fresh revenues.

One critical requirement in BDA is a file system that can provide the requisite performance and maintain that performance while it scales. HDFS is a highly scalable and distributed file system that provides a single, global namespace for the entire Hadoop cluster. HDFS comprises of DataNodes supporting the direct-attached storage (DAS), which store data in large 64 MB or 128 MB chunks to take advantage of the sequential I/O capabilities of disks and to minimize the latencies resulting from random seeks. The HDFS NameNode is at the center of HDFS. It manages the file system by maintaining a file metadata image that includes file name, location, and replication state. The NameNode has the ability to detect failed DataNodes and replicate the data blocks on those nodes to surviving DataNodes.

HDFS has some limitations in scale and performance as it scales due to its single namespace server. File system is the standard mechanism for storing, organizing, retrieving, and updating the data. File system solutions have placed an additional burden on most commercial organizations, requiring technical resources and time as well as financial commitments. And, to complicate matters further, the myriad of file system choices has only created more confusion for organizations seeking a big data solution. Network-attached storage (NAS) appliances have been a popular choice for workgroup and departmental settings where simplicity and utilization of existing Ethernet networks were critical requirements. However, the various NAS solutions do not scale adequately to meet the needs of managing big data and delivering high-throughput to data-intensive applications. Thus, there is a clarion call for fresh solutions to take on big data with confidence and clarity. Some file system solutions do not allow the parallelization of multiple paths of data flow to and from the application and the processing cores. The end result with this approach is a large file repository that cannot be utilized effectively by multiple computer-intensive applications.

Considering these constrictions, parallel file systems (PFS) like Lustre have become popular these days especially for the stringent requirements imposed by big data. As a more versatile solution, PFS represents the hope for the big data era. A PFS enables a node or file server to service multiple clients simultaneously. Using a technique called file striping, PFS significantly increases IO performance by enabling reading and writing from multiple clients concurrently and thus increases available I/O bandwidth. In many environments, a PFS implementation results in applications experiencing a five- to tenfold increase in the performance. However, a major hurdle to wider commercial adoption of PFS is the lack of technical expertise required to install, configure, and manage a PFS environment.

Having realized this huge and untapped opportunity, the company Terascala has come out with an innovative storage appliance that addresses the big and fast data challenges. It is the first company to introduce a scalable high-performance storage appliance that stands up quickly; is easy to manage; augments existing systems available through Dell, EMC, and NetApp; and enables achieving a level of investment protection previously unavailable with parallel file systems.

ActiveStor ActiveStor is a next-generation storage appliance that delivers the high-performance benefits of flash technology with the cost-effectiveness of enterprise SATA disk drives. It scales linearly with capacity without the manageability and reliability compromises that often occur at scale. The principal benefits include:

• High parallel performance
• Enterprise-grade reliability and resiliency
• Easy management

For many big data applications, the limiting factor in performance is often the transportation of large amount of data from hard disks to where it can be processed (DRAM). In the paper [8], the authors have explained and analyzed an architectural pattern for a scalable distributed flash store which aims to overcome this limitation in two ways. First, the architecture provides a high-performance, high-capacity, and scalable random access storage. It achieves high throughput by sharing large numbers of flash chips across a low-latency and chip-to-chip backplane network managed by the flash controllers. The additional latency for remote data access via this network is negligible as compared to flash access time. Second, it permits some computation near the data via an FPGA-based programmable flash controller. The controller is located in the data path between the storage and the host and provides hardware acceleration for applications without any additional latency. The authors had constructed a small-scale prototype whose network bandwidth scales directly with the number of nodes and where average latency for user software to access flash store is less than 70 microsecond, including 3.5 microsecond of network overhead.

It is clear that state-of-the-art file systems and storage solutions are becoming indispensable for the world of big data. High-performance storage appliances are hitting the market these days to facilitate big data analytics efficiently and effectively.

2.14 Conclusions

As the cloud era is hardening, where the world creates 2.5 exabytes of data every day, traditional approaches and techniques for data ingestion, processing, and analysis are found to be limited because some lack parallelism and most lack fault tolerance capabilities. Path-breaking technologies in the form of converged and resilient infrastructures, versatile platforms, and adaptive applications are being prescribed as the correct way of working with massive data volumes.

Insight-driven strategizing, planning, and execution are very vital for world businesses to survive in the knowledge-driven and market-centric environment. Decision-making has to be proactive and preemptive in this competitive environment in order to keep up the edge earned by businesses. Innovation has to be fully ingrained in all the things businesses do in their long and arduous journey.

Data-driven insights are the most validated and venerable artifacts to bring forth next-generation customer-centric offerings. These days, worldwide corporations are getting stuffed and saturated with a large amount of decision-enabling and value-adding data, dealing with more complicated business issues and experiencing increased globalization challenges. Thus, it is essential to transform data assets into innovation and maximize the productivity of resources to drive sustainable growth.

In this chapter, we have explained the importance of high-performance IT infrastructures and platforms besides end-to-end big data frameworks in order to substantially speed up data crunching to derive actionable insights in time to empower people to be the smartest in their personal as well as professional lives. Today, it is simple and straightforward that to out-compute is to out-compete.

2.15   Exercises

1. Write a short note on converged infrastructure for big data analytics.
2. Explain IMDG.
3. Write short notes on the following:

   - Hadoop as a service
   - Data warehouse as a service

4. Explain the different data models of NoSQL databases.
5. Explain the Apache Tajo Reference Architecture.
6. Describe event processing architecture and its variants.

References

1. Performance and Scale in Cloud Computing, a white paper by Joyent, 2011. https://www.joyent.com/content/09-developers/01-resources/07-performance-and-scale-in-cloudcomputing/performance-scale-cloud-computing.pdf
2. Hadoop Cluster Applications, a white paper by Arista, 2013. https://www.arista.com/assets/data/pdf/AristaHadoopApplication_tn.pdf
3. Brinker DL, Bain WL (2013) Accelerating hadoop MapReduce using an in-memory data grid, a white paper from ScaleOut Software, Inc
4. Stuart JA, Owens JD (2012) Multi-GPU MapReduce on GPU clusters
5. Mengjun Xie, Kyoung-Don Kang, Can Basaran (2013) Moim: a multi-GPU MapReduce framework
6. The Elephant on the Mainframe, a white paper by IBM and Veristorm, 2014. http://www.veristorm.com/sites/g/files/g960391/f/collateral/ZSW03260-USEN-01.pdf
7. Olofson, CW, Dan Vesset (2013) The mainframe as a key platform for big data and analytics, a white paper by IDC
8. Sang-Woo Jun, Ming Liu, Kermin Elliott Fleming, Arvind (2014) Scalable multi-access flash store for big data analytics, FPGA'14, February 26–28, 2014, Monterey, CA, USA
9. Chandhini C, Megana LP (2013) Grid computing-a next level challenge with big data. Int J Sci Eng Res 4(3)
10. Colin White (2014) Why dig data in the cloud?, a white paper by BI Research

Chapter 3
Big and Fast Data Analytics Yearning for High-Performance Computing

3.1 Introduction

The data growth has been phenomenal in the past few years due to several things happening together. There are pioneering technologies and tools for extreme and deeper connectivity among various hardware and software entities; the service enablement of devices, applications, and IT infrastructures for seamless and spontaneous integration and orchestration is being facilitated through potential standards; data virtualization and information visualization platforms are flourishing; analytic processes and products are hardened for timely knowledge discovery and dissemination; the need for intelligent systems are being felt across; etc. The end result is that there are billions of digitized objects and connected devices; millions of operational systems, software services in enterprise, web, and cloud environments, and state-of-the-art infrastructures; etc. Further on, the surge in the number of everyday and everywhere services and applications (e.g., smartphones are the inspiration for millions of mobile services being hosted in faraway mobile clouds today, similarly, the emergence of smart home devices is bound to conceptualize next-generation home services, etc.), the increasing popularity of social sites and knowledge communities, the explosion of value-adding scientific experiments and technical computing, the powerful emergence of highly programmable and software-defined IT infrastructures (server machines, storage appliances, and networking solutions), etc. are immensely contributing for the exponential growth of usable data. There are trendy and handy, implantable, macro- and nanoscale, and disposable and disappearing sensors, actuators, codes, chips, controllers and cards, tags, labels, stickers, speckles, smart dust, and dots being manufactured in large quantities and randomly deployed in different environments for gathering environmental data, any perceptible state changes, and specific events and for transitioning any ordinary entities in our midst into extraordinary articles.

© Springer International Publishing Switzerland 2015
P. Raj et al., *High-Performance Big-Data Analytics*, Computer Communications and Networks, DOI 10.1007/978-3-319-20744-5_3

In our daily lives, there are distinct and decisive data generation, capture, buffering, and transmission elements in abundance. There is no doubt that the size of man as well as machine-made data is massively growing. This transformational turn and trend is bringing in several challenges while laying a stimulating and sustainable foundation for fresh opportunities for individuals, innovators, and institutions across the globe.

The Flourishing Device Landscape The device ecosystem is expanding fast; therefore, there is a growing array of fixed, portable, wireless, wearable, nomadic, implantable, and mobile devices, instruments, machines, consumer electronics, kitchen wares, household utensils, equipment, etc. Elegant, slim, and sleek personal gadgets and gizmos are really appealing to people today and are turning out to be the most intimate input/output modules in our everyday works and walks. Self, situation, and surrounding awareness are being projected as the next-generation mandatory feature for any commonly and casually found and cheap things in our environments to be useful for people. That is, every tangible artifact is being empowered to be aware, active, and articulate so that they can individually as well as collectively join in the mainstream computing. As the contemporary computing is tending to be cognitive, intelligent systems are the most sought-after ones for fulfilling the goals behind smarter computing.

There is a strategic, seamless, and spontaneous convergence between the virtual and the physical worlds. All these clearly insist the point that the IT needs for data creation/generation, transfer, storage, and leverage have been growing ceaselessly. This positive and progressive trend is indicating and conveying a lot of key things to be seriously contemplated by worldwide business and IT executives, evangelists, exponents, and experts. New techniques, tips, and tools need to be unearthed in order to simplify and streamline the knowledge discovery process out of growing data heaps. The scope is bound to enlarge, and there will be a number of fresh possibilities and opportunities for business houses out of data mountains. Solution architects, researchers, and scholars need to be cognizant of the niceties, ingenuities, and nitty-gritty of the impending tasks of transitioning data to information and then to knowledge. That is, the increasing data volume, variety, and velocity have to be smartly harnessed and handled through a host of viable and valuable mechanisms in order to extract and sustain the business value and the edge earned. Knowledge extraction, engineering, and exposition will become a common affair.

In this chapter, we try to bring up a strategically sound synchronization between big data and high-performing computing technologies. We start this chapter with a brief on big data analytics. Further on, we have given the details of fresh data sources emanating for the widespread leverage of fresh analytical methods on big data. This chapter is mainly crafted in order to give the business-centric as well as the technical view of high-performance big data analytics. The readers can find the major application domains of high-performance big data analytics and the compelling reasons for wholeheartedly embracing this new paradigm.

3.2   A Relook on the Big Data Analytics (BDA) Paradigm

Big data analytics is now moving beyond the realm of intellectual curiosity and propensity to make tangible and trendsetting impacts on business operations, offerings, and outlooks. It is no longer a hype or buzzword and is all set to become a core and central requirement for every sort of business enterprise to be relevant and rightful to their stakeholders and end users. Being an emerging and evolving technology, it needs a careful and cognitive analysis before its adoption and adaption. Its maturity, stability, and strategic fitment need to be investigated thoroughly so that all kinds of visible as well as hidden risks (feasibility, financial implications, technology maturity and stability, resource availability, etc.) can be fully identified and articulated well in the beginning stage itself. Any kind of discrepancies and deficiencies can be understood and nipped in the budding stage itself or mitigated to a major extent before embarking on the long and arduous big data journey. Big data analytics is a generic and horizontally applicable idea to be feverishly leveraged across all kinds of business domains and hence is poised to become a trendsetter for worldwide businesses to march ahead with all clarity and confidence. Real-time analytics is the hot requirement today and everyone is working on fulfilling this critical need. The emerging use cases include the use of real-time data such as the sensor data to detect any abnormalities in plant and machinery and batch processing of sensor data collected over a period to conduct root cause and failure analysis of plant and machinery.

Describing the Big Data World   We have discussed about the fundamental and fulsome changes happening in the IT and business domains. Service enablement of applications, platforms, infrastructures, and even everyday devices besides the varying yet versatile connectivity methods has laid down strong foundations for man- as well as machine-generated data. The tremendous rise in data collection along with all the complications has instinctively captivated both business and IT leaders to act accordingly to take care of this huge impending and data-driven opportunity for any growing corporates. This is the beginning of the much-discussed and much-discoursed big data computing discipline. This paradigm is getting formalized with the deeper and decisive collaboration among product vendors, service organizations, independent software vendors, system integrators, innovators, and research organizations. Having understood the strategic significance, all the different and distributed stakeholders have come together in complete unison in creating and sustaining simplifying and streamlining techniques, platforms and infrastructures, integrated processes, best practices, design patterns, and key metrics to make this new discipline pervasive and persuasive. Today the acceptance and activation levels of big data computing are consistently on the climb. However, it is bound to raise a number of critical challenges, but at the same time, it is to be highly impactful and insightful for business organizations to confidently traverse in the right route if it is taken seriously. The continuous unearthing of integrated processes, platforms, patterns, practices, and products is a good indication for the bright days of the big data phenomenon.

The implications of big data are vast and varied. The principal activity is to do a variety of tools-based and mathematically sound analyses of big data for instantaneously gaining big insights. It is a well-known fact that any organization having the innate ability to swiftly and succinctly leverage the accumulating data assets is bound to be successful in what they are operating, providing, and aspiring. That is, besides instinctive decisions, informed decisions go a long way in shaping up and confidently steering organizations. Thus, just gathering data is no more useful, but IT-enabled extraction of actionable insights in timeout of those data assets serves well for the betterment of businesses. Analytics is the formal discipline in IT for methodically doing data collection, filtering, cleaning, translation, storage, representation, processing, mining, and analysis with the aim of extracting useful and usable intelligence. Big data analytics are the newly coined word for accomplishing analytical operations on big data. With this renewed focus, big data analytics is getting more market and mind shares across the world. With a string of new capabilities and competencies being accrued out of this recent and riveting innovation, worldwide corporates are jumping into the big data analytics bandwagon. This chapter is all for demystifying the hidden niceties and ingenuities of the raging big data analytics.

Big Data Characteristics Big data is the general term used to represent massive amounts of data that are not stored in the relational form in traditional enterprise-scale databases. New-generation database systems are being unearthed in order to store, retrieve, aggregate, filter, mine, and analyze big data efficiently. The following are the general characteristics of big data:

- Data storage is defined in the order of petabytes, exabytes, etc. in volume to the current storage limits (gigabytes and terabytes).
- There can be multiple structures (structured, semi-structured, and less structured) for big data.
- Multiple types of data sources (sensors, machines, mobiles, social sites, etc.) and resources for big data.
- The speed of data collection, ingestion, processing, and mining straddles to both extremes. That is, the speed varies between real-time and batch-oriented processing.

High-Performance Analytics High-performance analytics enables organizations to quickly and confidently take strategically sound decisions, seize new incoming opportunities, make better choices, and create new value from big data. It is all about creating big insights in time. There are resilient platforms and other solutions forthcoming to simplify and streamline this complicated process. As the data volume is tremendously huge, it usually takes days or even weeks to extract hidden information, pattern, and other details if traditional methods are leveraged here. However, with the maturity and stability of high-performance analytic processes and products, the analytics task has shrunken to just minutes or seconds enabling faster knowledge discovery and dissemination. That is, discovering precise answers for complex problems to achieve better organizational performance and value is the one-point agenda for the overwhelming success of big data analytics.

Today's organizations are looking for ways and means to gain right and relevant insights from big and fast data quickly. Analytics go a long way in extracting previously unseen patterns, sentiments, associations, insights, opportunities, and relationships from data mountains and delivering that information to the right people, at the right time and at the right place. It is all about big data turning to be big insights for organizations to plan ahead and execute what is planned with all perfection and efficiency. There are several distributed processing mechanisms such as in-memory, in-database, and grid computing emerging to do decisive analytics on big data.

- *In-memory analytics* divide analytic processes into easily manageable pieces with computations distributed in parallel across a dedicated set of blades. One can use sophisticated analytics to tackle complex problems quickly and solve dedicated, industry-specific business challenges faster than ever before. Considering the speed with which data gets generated, in-memory database is a refreshing approach in the industry these days in order to allow companies the requisite freedom to access and analyze the data to make sense out of it quickly. The delectable point here is that the data access, processing, and mining are exponentially faster compared to the same tasks when traditionally accomplished via disk-based databases. This means that either decisions can be made quicker as data can be analyzed faster or more precisely informed as more data can be analyzed in the same amount of time. The timeliness and accuracy of insights being extrapolated and emitted through a variety of analytical mechanisms is bound to climb up sharply

- *In-database processing* uses a massively parallel processing (MPP) database architecture for faster execution of key data management and analytic development and deployment tasks. Relevant tasks are moved closer to the data, and computations are run inside the database to avoid time-consuming data movement and conversion. This reduces or even eliminates the need to replicate or move large amounts of data between a data warehouse and the analytical environment or data marts.

- *Grid computing* lets you create a managed, shared environment for processing large volumes of data and analytic programs quickly using dynamic, resource-based load balancing. You can split individual jobs and run each piece in parallel across multiple symmetric multiprocessing (SMP) machines using shared physical storage. This enables IT to build and manage a low-cost, flexible infrastructure that can scale to meet rapidly changing computing requirements. Central administration helps you monitor and manage multiple users and applications under a given set of constraints. IT can meet service-level demands by easily reassigning computing resources to manage peak workloads and changing business needs. Multiple servers in a grid environment enable jobs to run on the best available resource. If a server fails, you can transition its jobs seamlessly to other servers—providing a highly available business analytics environment. Multiprocessing capabilities let you divide individual jobs into subtasks that are run in parallel with the best available hardware resource in a grid environment. Faster processing of data integration, reporting, and analytical jobs speeds decision-making across the enterprise.

There are several other solutions being proposed for applying IT-enabled high-performance analytics on big data. We have discussed most of the pragmatic computing types and solutions in the very first chapter of this book.

3.3   The Implications of Big and Fast Data

It is being visualized that there can be multiple opportunities and possibilities with the rise of big and fast data domains. Businesses, IT teams, and researchers have a bigger role to play here in order to immeasurably benefit out of this evolutionary as well as revolutionary development. A flexible and futuristic strategy has to be in place for businesses to reap the differentiating advantages, whereas IT managers and consultants smartly sync up with the business direction to be the prime enabler for establishing and sustaining insights-driven enterprises. Researchers and even end users are supposed to bring forth new kinds of applications to make sense out of the ubiquitous data explosion from a growing set of diverse and distributed data sources. The key impacts include:

- The data management (end-to-end data life cycle) infrastructures
- Data analytics platforms
- Building next-generation insights-driven applications

Big Data Infrastructures From the data capture to the subjection of cleaned-up data for the quicker and easier extraction of usable insights mandates a variety of consolidated IT infrastructures and seamlessly synchronized platforms. Hence, leveraging big data for the grand realization of smarter systems across industry verticals is going to be a challenging affair. There are storage appliances, network connectivity solutions, bare metal servers, virtual machines (VMs), and, in the recent past, Docker containers for Hadoop-inspired big data analytics. Thus, compute machines in association with storages and networks are the epitome of the domains of data science and analytics for the foreseeable future. Precisely speaking, the life cycle management of big data is definitely a time-consuming and tough task for enterprise and cloud IT teams in the days to unfold. Elastic and efficient infrastructures are the most rightful requirement for the big data world.

Big Data Platforms Apart from the converged and dynamic infrastructures, platforms play a very vital role in shaping up the data world. On the platform front, the most plausible scenario is to have integrated platforms for data ingestion, analytics, knowledge discovery, and visualization. There are connectors, drivers, and adaptors for retrieving data from different data sources such as files, databases, devices, sensors, operational systems, social sites, etc. Hadoop platforms dominantly are enabling coarse-grained data searching and retrieval. The Hadoop is for transitioning multi-structured data into structured data for the business intelligence (BI) platforms to work on the formatted and formalized data beneficially. Hadoop is for the removal of all kinds of redundant and repetitive data so that the total data size would come down sharply and hence the traditional relational database systems and business intelligence (BI) solutions can accommodate the data for fine-grained queries and retrievals. MapReduce is the prominent data processing framework. Any programming and script languages can be used for programming MapReduce applications. Hadoop distributed file system (HDFS) is the key data storage framework. Even traditional database management systems are being refurbished accordingly to take up the brewing challenges of data analytics in an efficient and effective manner. There are parallel, analytical, clustered, and distributed database managements emerging to cater to BDA. There are other popular data management systems such as NoSQL databases, NewSQL databases, etc. adding value and verve for big data analytics. There are middleware solutions in the form of data hubs, message buses and fabrics, brokers, etc. in order to smoothen up rough edges.

There is an integrated approach too. Datameer (http://www.datameer.com/) is one such platform for simplifying and streamlining big data analytics tasks. That is, it provides end-to-end synchronized solution for performing analytics with just a click. There are appliances for exclusively accomplishing big data analytics. Hadoop is the prime method for big data analytics especially for batch processing. However, there are open source frameworks such as Storm and Spark for real-time processing of big data. Similarly, there are several specific analytical methods such as operational analytics. IBM has a couple of products, namely, SmartCloud analytics for predictive insights (SCAPI) and SmartCloud analytics—log analytics (SCALA). Splunk has a comprehensive platform for machine analytics. As there are a growing market and mind shares for analytics, there are several start-ups as well as established product vendors investing heavily in crafting well-oiled analytical platforms.

Big Data Applications The BDA is fast becoming a key discipline for study and research across academic institutions and research labs of IT organizations, and there are renewed endeavors by IT product vendors to bring forth standardized and smart solutions to enable big data analytics. Thus, with the maturity and stability of big data infrastructures and platforms, the route for producing knowledge applications and systems is getting cleared. All the peripheral and plumbing tasks associated with the building of insights-driven services and knowledge-filled solutions are abstracted and made as plug and play through a bevy of automation and standardization procedures. That is, infrastructures and platforms are made available on demand so that software engineers and program developers are more concerned with their core capabilities in conceptualizing and concretizing next-generation systems. Thus, connectivity, service enablement, and now cognition enablement through real-time and reliable insights are seeing the light to facilitate both IT and business applications to be intelligently active and articulate. In short, analytics lead to pragmatic knowledge that can be seamlessly fed to and appropriately used by systems and human beings· to be smart and sophisticated in exhibiting their innate capabilities. With software-defined infrastructures (SDI) and cloud-based platforms fast-stabilizing, the days of Analytics as a Service (AaaS) are not far away. Knowledge engineering, enhancement, and exposition will become ambient and affordable.

3.4 The Emerging Data Sources for Precise, Predictive, and Prescriptive Insights

Firstly, the key drivers for the data explosion are the adoption and adaption of technologies as listed below. Then there are illustrious advancements in miniaturization technologies resulting in scores of multifaceted sensors, actuators, robots, consumer electronics, connected machines, cars, etc.:

- Trillions of sentient and smart objects due to the sweeping digitization through edge technologies
- Smartphones and wearables in billions due to IT consumerization
- The unprecedented growth of the device and the service ecosystems
- The exponential growth of operational, transaction, real-time, and interactive systems
- Billions of connected devices and systems via deeper and extreme networking and communication
- Large-scale technical computing and scientific experiments
- The booming and blooming of social sites (Web 2.0) and knowledge communities
- IT centralization, commoditization, and industrialization (cloud computing)
- The adoption and adaption of technologies such as the Internet of Things (IoT), the cyber physical systems (CPS), the Ambient Intelligence (AmI), etc.

Precisely speaking, computing becomes distributed yet centrally managed; communication is all set to be ambient, autonomic, and unified; sensing becomes ubiquitous; sentient objects are everywhere; vision, perception, decision enabling, and actuation are pervasive; knowledge capture and leverage are mandated in system and service implementation; etc.—the prevailing and path-breaking trends in the IT field. Further on, the interconnectivity of every tangible thing; the networking (local as well as remote) of resource-constrained embedded devices; the standards-compliant service enablement for device/application integration and programmable infrastructures for remote discovery, accessibility, diagnostics, reparability, manageability, and sustainability; the fast-tracking of the commoditization of infrastructures; the end-to-end converged and dynamic big data platforms; etc. are being touted as the main cause for such a huge amount of data getting generated, garnered, and subjected to a different set of generic and purpose-specific investigations for systematically acquiring and leveraging the value hidden inside. Figure 3.1 clearly put big data in the middle of a number of game-changing people-centric technologies.

Figure 3.2 throws light on how various sorts of generic and specific networks (BAN, CAN, LAN, PAN, etc.) produce a lot of useful data.

Further on, all kinds of electronic transactions and interactions lead to a big amount of incredible data. With the integration scene heats up with anything to anything else connectivity and integration, the scope for big and trustworthy insights is on the climb as pictorially represented in Fig. 3.3.

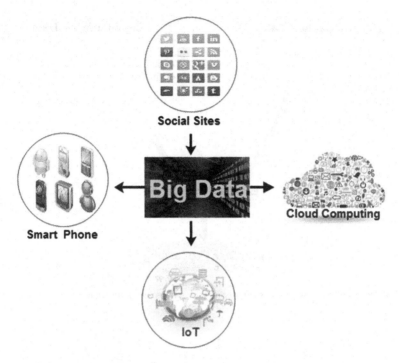

Fig. 3.1 A variety of technologies push for the big data world

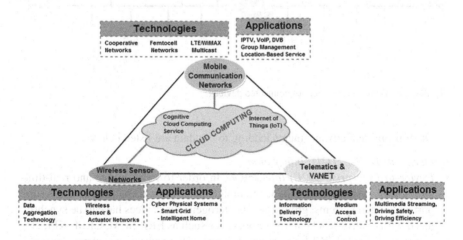

Fig. 3.2 The networking of every system, device, and empowered objects together producing big data

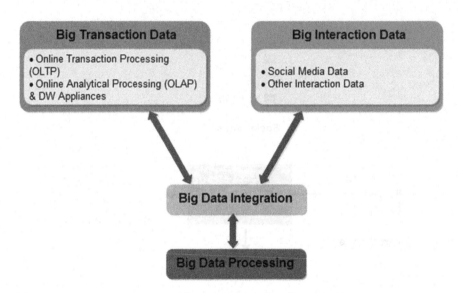

Fig. 3.3 The integration of big transactions and interactions lead to big data

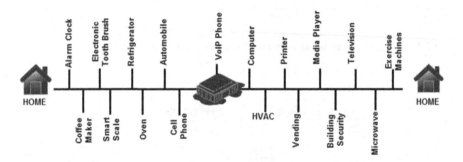

Fig. 3.4 The growing ecosystem of connected devices

Other prominent advancements leading to big data are listed below.

- *Device-to-Device (D2D) Integration*
- *Device-to-Enterprise (D2E) Integration*: In order to have remote and real-time monitoring, management, repair, and maintenance and for enabling decision support and expert systems, ground-level heterogeneous devices have to be synchronized with control-level enterprise packages such as ERP, SCM, CRM, KM, etc.
- *Device-to-Cloud (D2C) Integration*: As most of the enterprise systems are moving to clouds, device-to-cloud (D2C) connectivity is gaining importance.
- *Cloud-to-Cloud (C2C) Integration*: Disparate, distributed, and decentralized clouds are getting connected to provide better prospects.

Figure 3.4 clearly insists the emerging scenario of every kind of device gets integrated with one another in the vicinity.

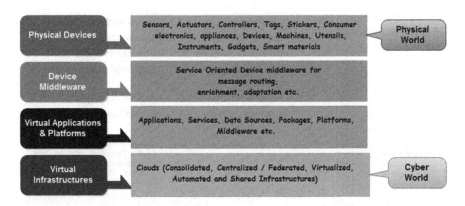

Fig. 3.5 The reference architecture for the Internet of Things (IoT)

Figure 3.5 lays out the reference architecture for the fast emerging domain of the Internet of Things (IoT) facilitating the seamless and spontaneous linkage of the physical world with the virtual world.

3.5   Why Big Data Analytics Is Strategically Sound?

The large-scale collection, indexing, and stocking of data from different and distributed sources have laid a stimulating foundation for the eruption of fresh and transformational analytical domains. There are both domain-specific and agnostic analytics flourishing these days with the maturity and stability of enabling technologies, tricks, and tools on the information management side. We have put forth some of the famous and widely applied analytics on different kinds of data in Table 3.1.

Figure 3.6 vividly illustrates the estimated business value to be obtained by different industry verticals when embracing the big data analytics capabilities and competencies in a calculated manner. The leading market analysis and research watchers have come out with encouraging business results and suddenly everything is data-driven. The transition from intuition-based decisions to data-driven insights is spot on and smooth to the exuberance of the IT world. For example, it is calculated the US government spends one trillion dollar every year on healthcare alone. Now it is forecast that the same government can simply save around 300 billion dollars if big data analytics (BDA) is comprehensively implemented for the people's healthcare across the nation. Similarly, there are validated reports for all the leading 11 industry segments, and hence the data analytics is picking up fast across the industry.

Figure 3.7 depicts and describes what to do with the accumulating data from a growing array of big and fast data.

The Leading Application Domains of Big Data Analytics Every business domain is being stuffed with an enormous amount of data. With the data processing and

Table 3.1 The specific as well as generic analytical disciplines

Real-time analytics	Social media analytics
Predictive analytics	Operational analytics
Prescriptive analytics	Machine analytics
High-performance analytics	Retail and security analytics
Diagnostic analytics	Sentiment analytics
Streaming analytics	Context-aware analytics

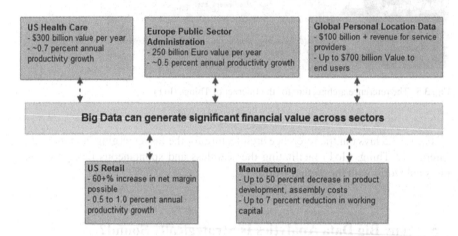

Fig. 3.6 The McKinsey findings on the business value of big data analytics

Fig. 3.7 What to do with data in motion, usage, and persistence

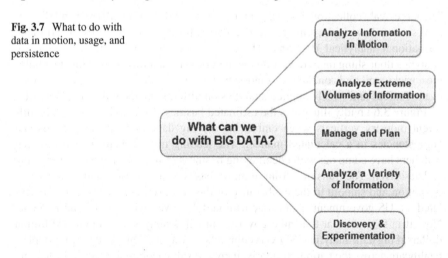

mining technologies maturing fast, knowledge discovery and dissemination needs are heavily simplified. Every domain is therefore knowledge packed and hence bound to be insightful and incredible to their stakeholders. For example, retail analytics brings in a number of tactical as well as strategic advantages for shoppers, suppliers, OEMs, store owners, retail IT team, and other stakeholders. Figure 3.8 shows the key significant beneficiaries of big data analytics.

Fig. 3.8 The dominant
analytics-inspired domains

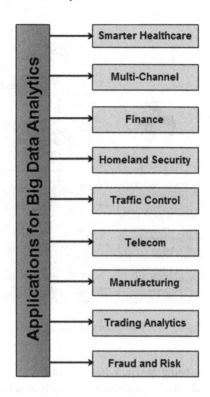

3.6   A Case Study for Traditional and New-Generation Data Analytics

Generally monthly once, our home electricity meter readings are captured and transmitted wirelessly to the centralized servers (say, a data warehouse (DW)). Extraction, transformation, and loading (ETL) tools are extensively used to format any incoming data to be compatible for the DW environment. Querying DW emits the expected results. From DW, several other analytical, customer-centric, report-generation, and other visualization systems receive for further actions. For example, electricity bills are generated and dispatched to every home in time, electricity consumption is being monitored and analyzed for pondering about energy conservation methods or for exploring the possibility of levying additional taxes for those who use electricity energy more, etc. Here the data capture frequency is monthly, and the data format is homogeneous because officials feed the data manually in the format compatible for the target environment. Thus, traditional analytics has been working perfectly. Figure 3.9 illustrates the traditional architecture.

Now there are automated and connected electricity meters from multiple producers leveraging different technologies. There are diverse data transmission technologies, the data capture frequencies are varying from minutes to hours and to months, and the data being emitted by energy meters are hugely disparate in their format. The key point here is the data getting generated is huge and hence big data platform

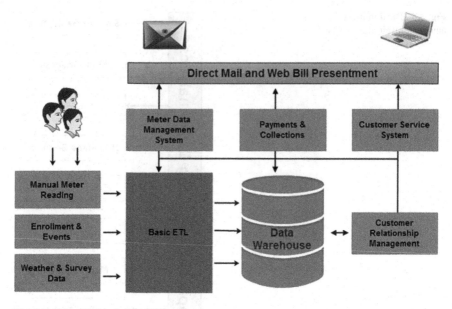

Fig. 3.9 The traditional smart energy architecture

is being insisted here in order to do the justice for consumers, departments (electricity generation, transmission, and distribution), government ministries, etc. Figure 3.10 depicts the new-generation application architecture embedding big data platform modules.

The new architecture is necessitated due to the tremendous increase in the data generation of hundreds of thousands of automated electricity meters, and the data collection frequency swings from real-time to batch method. The data variety too grows noticeably. The Hadoop platform acts as a soothing mechanism. That is, multi-structured data gets transitioned into structured data to be seamlessly used by enterprise data warehouse (EDW), and the unwanted and irrelevant data gets eliminated at the source stage in order to enable traditional data management platforms to handle only the value-adding data. Precisely speaking, Hadoop presents itself as a powerful preprocessing platform. For most of the situations, Hadoop is slated to complement with the conventional business intelligence (BI) technologies in order to substantially increase the comprehensiveness, completeness, and accuracy of data analytics.

The Big Data Analytics Technical Architecture For conveying different facets and the fact, there are a number of distinct architectural expositions. The highest one is the reference architecture, which is mandatory for any new concept to flourish. The big data paradigm is expected to be a huge hit for industries to zoom ahead in their operations, outputs, and outlooks. As explained above, data sources, acquisition, organization and storage, analysis for knowledge extraction, and finally the dissemination of actionable insights are the principal components in a big data architecture. As pictorially represented in Fig. 3.11, there are multiple technologies, tools, and tricks made available in order to streamline the tasks under each head.

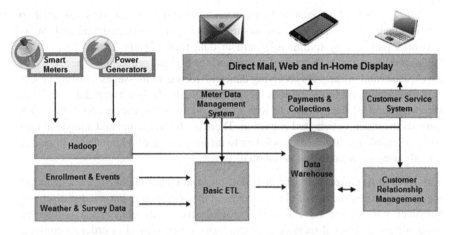

Fig. 3.10 The architecture for the big data era

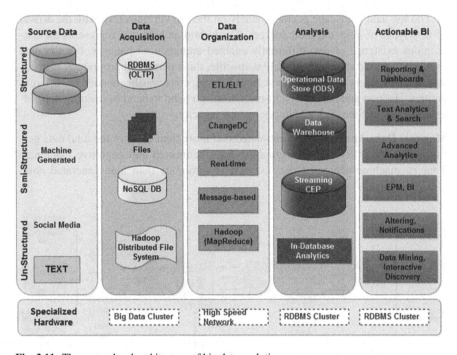

Fig. 3.11 The macro-level architecture of big data analytics

The highly optimized infrastructures in association with synchronized platforms are the main pillars for fluently attaining the envisioned success out of the big data domain. Besides data virtualization, ingestion, preprocessing and analysis platforms, there are middleware/broker/connector/driver/adaptor solutions and different sets of data management platforms such as the clustered and analytical SQL databases and

NoSQL and NewSQL databases. Then visualization tools are very essential for timely impart any acquired to correct users and systems. High-speed and unified networks play a very telling role here in data transmission across data centers. Hadoop is emerging as the powerful standard for big data crunching. There are message queues and brokers for receiving data and document messages, evening processors for decoupled events, engines for fast and streaming data, batch data, etc. Thus, for every kind of data, there are appropriate platforms to capture and crush them towards the much-anticipated cognition. There are transactional and analytical databases to enable the transition from data to information and to knowledge to be confidently used to sustain what is initiated.

The Hybrid Architecture The arrival of big data technologies does not dismantle the existing infrastructure or platform or even the approach of knowledge discovery. However, considering the threatening complexity of big data and data-intensive applications, additional technologies and tools are employed in order to considerably eliminate the impacts. Figure 3.12 clearly tells the additional modules to accomplish the big data analytics in a standardized and smart manner.

The big data landscape is continuously on the growth trajectory with the arrival of new types of data and their sources. The hybrid architecture represents the harmonious existence of two differently enabled architectural patterns. For the data capture, there are standards as well as specific, third-party, and proprietary connectors. In short, every aspect of data science is being consciously attended by different entities. Hadoop and data warehouse solutions go hand in hand in emitting dependable insights in time with all simplicity and sagacity.

Machine Data Analytics It is estimated that more than 75 % of the total data getting generated every day is originating from connected and cognitive machines. That is, machine-generated data is more voluminous than man-generated data.

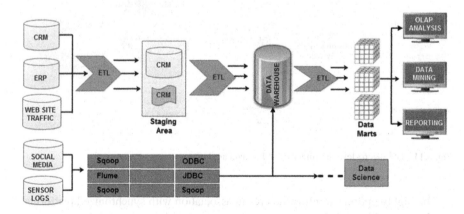

Fig. 3.12 The hybrid architecture of traditional as well as new-generation analytics

Therefore, machine analytics is one of the strategic analytical domains making waves in the IT corridors. There are data centers accommodating a large number of enterprise-class operational and analytical systems; data management systems; packaged, home-grown, and turnkey systems; and integration engines. These traditional data centers are tending towards powerful private cloud environments with the adoption of cloud technologies. On the other side, the prescribed paths such as industrialization, consumerization, commoditization, centralization, consolidation, optimization, etc. for IT to be critically right and relevant for the future are being fulfilled through hundreds of massive cloud centers for public consumption. Then for building smarter environments (smarter homes, hospitals, hotels, manufacturing, retail, energy, etc.), sentient objects, connected devices, adaptive applications, programmable infrastructures, integrated platforms, etc. are paramount. Smart sensors and actuators are being trumpeted as the eye and ear of future IT. As repeated above, resource-constrained embedded devices are instrumented and interconnected vigorously. Every kind of systems and services is bound to generate and dispatch a lot of useful data about their functions, issues, risks, alerts, etc. Figure 3.13 explains how all kinds of data files are captured and subjected to a series of deep investigations to squeeze out actionable insights.

Operational analytics come handy in visualizing the performance, security, and other pain points of IT systems and other electronics.

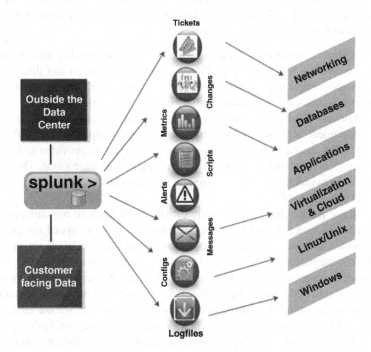

Fig. 3.13 The reference architecture for machine data analytics

3.7   Why Cloud-Based Big Data Analytics?

Public Clouds for Big Data Analytics Most traditional data warehousing and business intelligence (BI) projects to date have involved collecting, cleansing, and analyzing data extracted from on-premise business-critical systems. However, this age-old practice is about to change forever. However, for the foreseeable future, it is unlikely that many organizations will move their mission-critical systems or data (customer, confidential, and corporate) to public cloud environments for analysis. Businesses steadily are adopting the cloud idea for business operational and transactional purposes. Packaged and cloud-native applications are primarily found fit for clouds, and they are exceedingly well in their new residences. The biggest potential for cloud computing is the affordable and adept processing of data that already exists in cloud centers. All sorts of functional websites, applications, and services are bound to be cloud based sooner rather than later. The positioning of clouds as the converged, heavily optimized and automated, dedicated and shared, virtualized, and software-defined environment for IT infrastructures (servers, storage, and networking), business infrastructure, and management software solutions and applications is getting strengthened fast. Therefore, every kind of physical assets, articles, and artifacts is seamlessly integrated with cloud-based services in order to be smart in their behavioral aspects. That is, ground-level sensors and actuators are increasingly tied up with cloud-based software to be distinct in their operations and outputs. All these developments clearly foretell that the future data analytics is to flourish fluently in clouds.

The number of transnational organizations is growing steadily and the direct implication on IT is to have diverse and distributed applications and data sources getting hosted in multiple environments including hardened private, public, and even hybrid clouds. Customer, confidential, and corporate information are majorly stocked in private clouds considering the security needs. Having taken the customer-facing requirement, all kinds of enterprise-scale business applications (ERP, SCM, CRM, KM, CM, etc.) are being taken to public clouds and are provided as software as a service (SaaS) by various cloud service providers across the globe. The hybrid nature evolves in order to provide a seamless and spontaneous connectivity among public and private clouds.

These days' public clouds are natively providing all kinds of big data analytics tools, platforms, and tools on their infrastructures in order to speed up the most promising data analytics at a blazing speed at an affordable cost. WAN optimization technologies are maturing fast to substantially reduce the network latency while transmitting huge amount of data from one system to another among geographically distributed clouds. Federated, open, connected, and interoperable cloud schemes are fast capturing the attention of the concerned, and hence we can see the concept of the inter-cloud getting realized soon through open and industry-strength standards and deeper automations. With the continued adoption and articulation of new capabilities and competencies such as software-defined compute, storage, and networking, the days of cloud-based data analytics are to grow immensely. In short, clouds are being positioned as the core, central, and cognitive environment for all kinds of complex tasks.

Hybrid Clouds for Specific Cases It is anticipated that in the years to unfold, the value of hybrid clouds is to climb up sharply as for most of the emerging scenarios, a mixed and multi-site IT environment is more appropriate. For the analytics space, a viable and venerable hybrid cloud use case is to filter out sensitive information from data sets shortly after capture and then leverage the public cloud to perform any complex analytics on them. For example, if analyzing terabytes worth of medical data to identify reliable healthcare patterns to predict any susceptibility towards a particular disease, the identity details of patients are not too relevant. In this case, just a filter can scrape names, addresses, and social security numbers before pushing the anonymized set to secure cloud data storage.

All kinds of software systems are steadily being modernized and moved to cloud environments especially public clouds to be subscribed and used as a service over the public web. The other noteworthy factor is that a variety of social sites for capturing and captivating different segments of people across the world are emerging and joining in the mainstream computing. We therefore hear, read, and even use social media, networking, and computing aspects. A statistics says that the widely used Facebook pours out at least 8 terabytes of data every day. Similarly, other social sites produce a large-scale of amount of personal, social, professional data apart from musings, blogs, opinions, feedbacks, reviews, multimedia files, comments, compliments, complaints, advertisements, and other articulations. These poly-structured data play a bigger role in shaping up the data analytics domain.

The other valuable trends include the movement of enterprise-class operational, transactional, commercial, and analytics systems to public clouds. We all know that www.salesforce.com is the founding public cloud providing CRM as a service. Thus, most of the enterprise data originates in public clouds. With public clouds projected to grow fast, the cloud data is being presented as another viable and venerable opportunity towards cloud-based data analytics.

There are concerns expressed in different quarters about the suitability of clouds for high-performance analytics. However, this fear is being overcome through a host of fresh approaches. One is by hosting high-performance platforms such as in-memory and in-database systems on cloud infrastructures. Thus, synchronized processing, mining, and analytics of big and fast data in public clouds for knowledge extraction are gaining immense momentum. Filtering, deduplication, compression, and other prominent WAN optimization techniques come handy in efficiently transmitting big data to public clouds for specific analytical requirements.

Enterprise Analytics Most corporates today have accumulated plenty of data in scores of enterprise-grade storages. Creating intelligence and gleaning big insights and value from this data heaps are the need of this hour for enterprises to chalk out strategy and some worthwhile tactics towards business transformation and optimization. Thus far, scorecards and metrics, gut feelings, intuitions, and experience have been the everyday guides for making business-critical decisions. It has been proved beyond any iota of doubt that business analytics has a direct bearing on business performance. However, with the availability of powerful analytical technologies and tools, data-driven insights in time are being seen as the next-generation business analytics for organizations solve complex business problems, improve performance, and drive sustainable growth through innovation. Demands on enterprise IT to deliver an elastic environment are to increase as more data, users, and applications are being utilized to solve complex business problems. Typically enterprise analytics departments drive the need for:

- Workload management and prioritization
- Governance of the entire IT environment
- Optimized performance across all business processes

In short, high-performance computing (HPC) delivers faster business analytics that can have a pioneering effect on an organization's performance and value. HPC enables organizations to drive proactive, evidence-based business decisions and agile strategies to anticipate and manage change in a volatile market.

The Prominent Use Cases   As indicated above, cloud-based analytics for data getting originated and made available in clouds makes sense for business houses. On the other side, considering the security and network latency issues, on-premise analytics is also happening. Both the approaches have some pros and cons, and it is prudent to make use of public cloud services if the business requirements such as productivity, less TCO, high returns, affordability, sustainability, extensibility, etc. are met.

Social Media Analytics (SMA)   As indicated above, the size of social data is growing rapidly. The increasing volume of social data leads to multiple value additions if appropriately subjected to a variety of specific probes. Social media and network analytics provide a 360° view of customers for various customer-centric organizations to accelerate decision enablement. The sentiment of customers can be easily captured through customer sentiment analysis. Other renowned use cases include brand enhancement options, product innovation, and sales multiplication opportunities for business organizations. There are other data sources such as click-streams, telemetric devices, cars on the road, and sensors combining with social data (Facebook, twitter, etc.). In this use case, data from each source is uploaded in small batches or streamed directly to the cloud-based analytical services for extracting actionable insights in time.

Digital Commerce Analytics   Increasingly physical stores become e-stores. These days' online stores and businesses are in plenty catering to different populations distinctly. There are digital commerce software and other related solutions for quickly facilitating the setup and running of e-commerce, business, auction/market, and gaming sites. For these companies, monitoring business operations, analyzing customer and user behavior, and tracking marketing programs are top priorities. The user base has grown exponentially, and today every second, millions of people go to electronic commerce sites to procure products. Hundreds of servers, storage, and network connectivity solutions are being involved in order to enhance customer experience while doing electronic transactions. The operational and transactional systems generate enormous amount of data every second, and they need to be carefully captured for analyzing them meticulously towards proactive addressing of any concerns, risks, opportunities, alerts, patterns, and any other fruitful information. A cloud-based system is ideally suited for collecting and analyzing all of these data to help business managers effectively track and beneficially analyze overall business operations and performance.

Operational Analytics Operational analytics is the emerging discipline in the growing analytics space as the number, size, scope, and variety of operational systems in every model of business under the sun are on the increase due to more users, complicated business applications, and sophisticated IT platforms. In order to preserve the performance level and to prevent any kind of slowdowns and breakdowns, the well-established operational analytics of IT infrastructures and platforms is very paramount.

Data Warehouse Augmentation Cloud-based Hadoop platform is a cost-effective data ingestion, storage, processing, and archiving one for big data. Hadoop is being prescribed as the most efficient and contemporary mechanism for preprocessing a massive amount of data pouring in. Once filtered, cleansed, and retrofitted by Hadoop, formatted and formalized data travel to data warehouse for fine-grained and posterior analytics. Thus, there is a clear-cut synchronization between Hadoop and traditional business intelligence (BI) platforms in order to cater different data management and analytics scenarios. That is, a hybrid environment for smart analytics is steadily emerging and evolving.

There can be many more use cases for cloud-based analytics with clouds being empowered with newer capabilities. Fresh analytical features and facilities are being unearthed to leverage the unique potentials of cloud environments in order to make analytics precise, pervasive, and productive.

3.8 The Big Data Analytics: The Prominent Process Steps

Data is the raw material for actionable insights, and with more data, the outpouring insights are going to be precise and perfect. Data analytics is therefore being accepted as the game-changing engagement for any organization and institution in their long and arduous journey. As illustrated widely, there are many advantages arising out of technology-inspired data analytics. Businesses can get a comprehensive and complete view of their customers in a capsule form; business strategy and tactics can be accordingly modified as per emerging trends; the aspects such as infrastructure optimization, technology choice, architecture assimilation, etc. can be simplified; the currently running business processes can be succulently improved to reap and realize better business performance; etc.

All the tasks starting from data collection to knowledge discovery and dissemination are really getting complex due to several developments occurring together. There are several data sources emerging insisting for automated data capture, cleansing, polishing, formatting, filtering, etc. Preprocessing activities need to be systematically performed, and with increasing data complexity, it is not an easy task anymore. Highly competent platforms and toolsets in association with adaptors, connectors, and drivers need to be in place in order to accelerate the preprocessing functionalities. Hadoop is being categorized as the most promising one here and is being proposed as the new-generation ETL/ELT platform for the impending big data era.

Data Acquisition Data is captured and uploaded to a cloud-based data services. For example, Datameer, an end-to-end big data platform, ignores the limitations of ETL and static schemas to empower business users to integrate data from any source into Hadoop. Datameer has pre-built data connector wizards for all common structured and unstructured data sources; therefore, data integration is immensely simplified. Datameer loads all data in raw format directly into Hadoop. The process is optimized and supported with robust sampling, parsing, scheduling, and data retention tools that make it simple and efficient for any user to get the data they need quickly. Some use cases, such as analyzing constantly changing user data, lend themselves to streaming the data into Hadoop as analytics are run. This ensures that user data is always up to date. Datameer provides data links to any data source for just that purpose. Integrate all of your data fast and easy.

Treasure Data service (another big data platform service provider) uses a parallel bulk data import tool or real-time data collection agents that run on the customer's local systems. The bulk data import tool is typically used to import data from relational databases, flat files (Microsoft Excel, comma delimited, etc.), and application systems (ERP, CRM, etc.). Data collection agents are designed to capture data in real time from Web and application logs, sensors, mobile systems, and so forth. Since near-real-time data is critical for the majority of customers, most data comes into the Treasure Data system using data collection agents. Data collection agents filter, transform, and/or aggregate data before it is transmitted to the cloud service. All data is transmitted in a binary format known as MessagePack. The agent technology has been designed to be lightweight, extensible, and reliable. It also employs parallelization, buffering, and compression mechanisms to maximize performance, minimize network traffic, and ensure no data loss or duplication during transmission. Buffer sizes can be tuned based on timing and data size.

Data Storage There are SQL, NoSQL, and NewSQL databases for big data storage. There are discussions and debases on choosing SQL and NoSQL databases. Based on the current needs and emerging situations, architects choose an appropriate database management system. Here the Treasure Data service stores data in Plazma, which is an elastically scalable, secure, cloud-based, columnar database developed by Treasure Data. Plazma is optimized for time-series data. Real-time streaming data is loaded first into a row-based store, and older data is held in a compressed columnar store. Queries are automatically executed across both data sets so the analytics can include the freshest data. This is ideal for dynamic data sources or use cases that rely on analyzing the most recent available data. Data is converted into JSON before being loaded into Plazma for schema-flexible access.

Data Analysis This is the key phase or stage for big data analytics. Hadoop platforms are the most sought-after ones for effectively accomplishing big data analytics. There are multiple Hadoop implementations and distributions. There is a stream of open source as well as commercial-grade Hadoop software solutions in the marketplace.

Datameer is an end-to-end big data solution enabling business users to discover insights in any data via wizard-based data integration, iterative point-and-click analytics, and drag-and-drop visualizations, regardless of the data size, structure, source, and speed. Instead of having its own Hadoop-compliant analytical platform, Datameer has tied up with established product vendors (Cloudera, Hortonworks, IBM, etc.) for providing seamless and synchronized data analytics. That is, any data analytics platform can be integrated with Datameer. Datameer is a fully extensible solution that can integrate with existing data warehouse (DW) and business intelligence (BI) solutions. Datameer users can also gain instant insights via the Datameer App Market, which offers dozens of pre-built analytic applications across a variety of use cases and data types. Datameer provides the most complete solution to analyze structured and unstructured data. It is not limited by a pre-built schema and the point-and-click functions take the data analytics to greater heights. Even the most complex nested joins of a large number of datasets can be performed using an interactive dialog. User queries are being received and processed by a query engine, and then data crunching and interpretation module are also utilized for extracting and producing appropriate answers in time for enabling users to plunge into precise and perfect decision-making.

Knowledge Visualization Knowledge discovery has to be disseminated to authorized and authenticated systems and people in order to empower them to sagaciously ponder about the best course of actions. Visualization has been an intense subject of study and research to bring in as much automation as required, and these days, visualization is being facilitated through a host of fresh mechanisms such as hi-fi dashboards, reports, charts, maps, graphs, tables, infographics, and other visualizations. Further on, not only fixed compute machines but also a variety of portables, mobiles, wearables, gadgets and gizmos, etc. are emerging to be leveraged for next-generation visualizations.

There are simultaneous enhancements to make analytics smarter. High-end algorithms and methods are being experimented and espoused. The already matured data mining field is going through a number of disruptions and transformations especially to be right and relevant for the big data era. Clustering, classification, and other data mining methods are being deftly strengthened to capitalize the ensuing opportunities.

3.9   Real-Time Analytics

Big data has been a prominent and progressive aspect in the industry for some time now due to the unprecedented data explosion, and the realization is that data is turning out to be a strategic asset for any enterprise to march ahead. Real-time data is a relatively new phenomenon sweeping the IT field lately. Systems in running state typically generate a lot of real-time data to be speedily and systematically captured and crushed intelligently by advanced infrastructures and platforms for emitting any impactful insights. Sensors and machines in millions pour out large quantities of data in higher velocities. The world-famous Twitter is another interesting trend gripping millions of people across the globe at any point of time generating billions of tweets that need to be processed on the fly in order to predict many things in our real-world lives.

Thus, fast data or continuous data is an emerging trend capturing and captivating the imaginations of people. That is, the data being generated, garnered, and transmitted is being done at greater speeds these days. Data is being streamed from different places and sources, and hence the discipline of stream processing is growing by leaps and bounds in order to bring forth a set of technologies, tools, and tricks to effectively make sense out of streaming data. Thus, the challenge is how to receive real time and do the appropriate analytics to extract useful information and knowledge in time to act on the extracted with all the confidence.

Messaging has been a kind of standardized wrapping mechanism on data and documents for a long time now for integrating different and distributed systems locally as well as remotely via networks and for gaining each one's special capabilities interchangeably. There are a number of open and standards-compliant message brokers, queues, and middleware services in order to work on messages. Not only data messages but also event messages are very popular. Business events occur in millions in certain fast-moving industry verticals. There are simple as well as complex event engines from different product innovators for precisely capturing and processing hundreds of thousands of business events and even for aggregating simple events into complex events to simplify the data and process-intensive activity of knowledge extraction and engineering.

In summary, as pictorially represented in Fig. 3.14, often, masses of structured and semi-structured historical data are stored in Hadoop (volume + variety). On the other side, stream processing is used for fast data requirements (velocity + variety). Both complement each other very well.

In short, modern technologies such as social, mobile, cloud, and the Internet of Things (IoT) are directly or indirectly the prominent causes for big data. The datasets associated with these evolve rapidly, are often self-describing, and can comprise complex types such as JSON and Parquet.

Hadoop is typically a batch-processing solution for the brewing big data era. That is, data is collected and stored in commoditized servers and disk storages to be subjected to a slew of different processing techniques to extract insights at scheduled

Fig. 3.14 The pictorial representation of big data characteristics

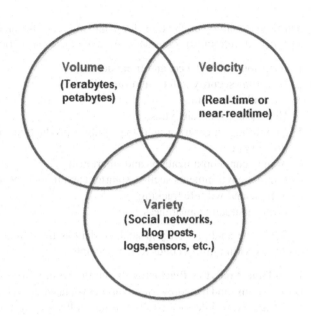

times. Batch processing often takes a few minutes to generate an output from data, and with the recent phenomenon of huge data explosion, the processing can go up for a few hours. However, there are fresh business requirements insisting for capturing and crunching data on the fly in order to produce timely results. Thus, the data speed turns out to be an important ingredient in the ensuing big data era. As discussed above, real-time or fast, event, continuous, and streaming data demand for real-time analytical capabilities. Operational data is a sort of real-time data for bringing forth operational intelligence. Not only IT infrastructures and platforms but also bespoke, home-grown, and packaged business applications generate a lot of operational data in the form of log, configuration, and policy files to be analyzed then and there to eliminate any kind of loss associated with system breakdown or maintenance.

For a real-world example, count the number of vehicles at different traffic lights within a city limit and feed the details into a Hadoop platform or a Spark system to analyze the data on different perspectives and parameters. The prominent outputs could be "traffic hotspots" and other related insights to be leveraged fully. On using the extracted insights, a variety of remarkable improvements can be brought forth for effectively and efficiently regularizing traffic flow, a better plan can be worked out, the execution quality is bound to shore up further, the traffic prediction and action prescription will be much more concrete and cognitive, etc.

On the business side, there are several scenarios gradually getting noticed and voiced for fast data. Thus, for establishing and sustaining newer real-time applications and services across the industry verticals, the faster maturity and stability of real-time technologies and tools for achieving real-time analytics is being viewed as a positive development. Following are few of use cases for real-time analytics:

1. Intrusion, surveillance, and fraud detection
2. Real-time security, safety, and surveillance
3. Algorithmic trading
4. Healthcare, sport analytics, etc.
5. Monitoring, measuring, and managing a production, operational, and transactional systems
6. Supply chain optimizations and smart grid
7. Smarter environments such as smarter cars, homes, hospitals, hotels, etc.
8. Vehicle and wildlife tracking
9. Context/situation awareness

Real-time analytics let you analyze data as they come in and make important decisions within milliseconds to few seconds.

Real-Time Analytics Platforms Batch processing first collects data for a certain period of time and then only tries to process data when all the data has been received. Basically, we sit idle for first 30 min just collecting data and try to do it as fast as possible when 30 min has passed. However, real-time processing is quite different. Traditional Hadoop platforms would find it difficult to cope up with the overwhelming requirements of real-time analytics. When the number of events goes up sharply, the size of the data is bound to grow exponentially. Querying and receiving responses within a few seconds is not an easy task. We need modern technologies and out-of-the-box approaches for breaking up and processing the incoming data. Data are not stored and processed. Instead while data is on the move, analytics need to happen. For that to see the light, leveraging multiple machines in parallel smartly to emit pragmatic, predictive, and even prescriptive information out of the data sets in a few seconds seems to be the viable and venerable solution. Figure 3.15 pictorially presents the difference between batch and real-time processing.

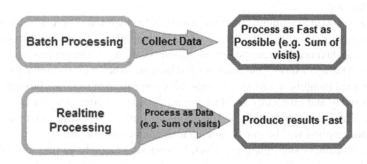

Fig. 3.15 Batch vs. real-time data processing

Apache Drill is an open source, low-latency SQL query engine for Hadoop and NoSQL. Apache Drill is built from the ground up to provide low-latency queries natively on such rapidly evolving multi-structured datasets at scale. Apache Drill provides direct queries on self-describing and semi-structured data in files (such as JSON and Parquet) and HBase tables without needing to define and maintain schemas in a centralized store such as Hive metastore. This means that users can explore live data on their own as it arrives vs. spending weeks or months on data preparation, modeling, ETL, and subsequent schema management.

Drill provides a JSON-like internal data model to represent and process data. The flexibility of this data model allows Drill to query, without flattening, both simple and complex/nested data types as well as constantly changing application-driven schemas commonly seen with Hadoop/NoSQL applications. Drill also provides intuitive extensions to SQL to work with complex/nested data types.

In-Memory Analytics The status quo of data processing is to use Hadoop MapReduce and processing data from disks. This kind of processing is bound to induce the latency issue on most of the occasions. That is, the CPU stays idle until data arrives from the disk. Herein the new paradigm of in-memory computing comes to the rescue.

We all would have heard SAP HANA, which is very famous for the in-memory computing approach. VoltDB and MemSQL are the other renowned in-memory databases gaining sufficient traction in the market. While the cost of memory modules is coming down considerably, memory-based temporal storage, processing, and analytics gain the wider acceptance. The MemSQL [Fig. 3.16] database conveniently and cognitively converges both transactions and analytics for fast data processing and real-time reporting. As per the information published in the website, the key differentiators include:

- Accelerate applications and power real-time operational analytics.
- Flexible scale-out on commodity hardware to maximize performance and ROI.
- Analyze real-time and historical data together.
- Combine relational and JSON data.

MemSQL's in-memory store is vehemently pronounced as an ideal way for mixed transactional and analytical workloads serving the most demanding applications and real-time analytics. With its fully integrated column store, MemSQL expands beyond an in-memory workload as illustrated in the architectural diagram (Fig. 3.16).

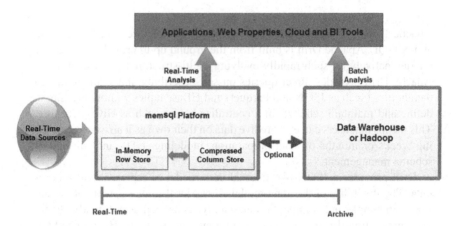

Fig. 3.16 The MemSQL DB's reference architecture

VoltDB, the latest NewSQL database, successfully handles fast data generated from the cloud, mobile, and social applications and smart devices. The availability and abundance of fast and continuously streaming data presents an enormous opportunity to extract actionable intelligence in time, gain reliable insights, and make sense out of them. The insights in turn are fed or disseminated in time into every kind of everyday systems, services, and applications to enable them individually as well as collectively to be smart in their behavior. That is, smart systems network with one another as well as with remotely held applications in cloud environments to visualize and elegantly realize smart grids, homes, hospitals, hotels, cities, etc. Software applications increasingly mandated to exhibit adaptive behavior need appropriate insights-driven augmentation, acceleration, and automation in time.

SAP HANA converges database and application platform capabilities in memory to transform transactions, analytics, and predictive and spatial processing so businesses can operate in real time. By eliminating the divide between transactions and analytics, SAP HANA allows you to answer any business question anywhere in real time. SAP HANA drives performance, expedites processes, and truly revolutionizes business.

In-Database Analytics In-database analytics is a technology that allows data processing to be performed within the database by embedding the appropriate analytic logic into the database itself. This arrangement eliminates the time and the efforts required to transform data and move it back and forth between a database and a separate analytics application. Typically an in-database analytics system consists of an enterprise data warehouse (EDW) built on an analytic database platform. This combination of platforms provides parallel processing, partitioning, scalability, and optimization capabilities to simplify and streamline the analytical needs. Further on, in-database analytics allows analytical data marts to be seamlessly consolidated in the data warehouse. In such a setup, data retrieval and analysis are faster and corporate/customer/confidential information is fully secured because it does not need to leave the data warehouse at all. This unique approach is highly beneficial in enabling companies and corporates make data-driven decisions and insights-inspired predictions about any future business risks and opportunities, identify trends, and spot anomalies to make informed decisions more efficiently and affordably.

Companies use in-database analytics for applications requiring intensive processing. For example, fraud detection, credit scoring, risk management, trend and pattern recognition, and balanced scorecard analysis are being touted as the most promising applications for in-database analytics, which also superbly facilitates ad hoc analysis.

PureData System for Analytics This is an advanced data warehouse appliance powered by Netezza technology to bring in a series of game-changing transformations for the big data world. In addition to the features and benefits of the data warehouse appliance itself, this new appliance comes with additional software to exploit big data opportunities and leading business intelligence capabilities. Included with the data warehouse appliance are software licenses to get started with IBM Cognos for business intelligence (BI), IBM InfoSphere DataStage for data integration, IBM InfoSphere BigInsights to augment data warehouse with Hadoop data services, and IBM InfoSphere Streams for real-time streaming analytics.

3.10   Stream Analytics

Analytic platforms that generate insights from data in real time are attracting enterprises to adopt and adapt them accordingly. There are streaming analytics platforms by open source community as well as commercial-grade vendors with a variety of features and facilities. With a sudden spike in event, operational, and streaming data, the discipline of real-time, fast, and continuous data analytics is red hot at this point of time. In the last decade, we heard a lot about event processing. There are simple as well as complex event processing engines to squeeze out insights on streams of events. Simple events generally do not contribute much, and hence discrete, atomic, and basic events are clubbed together to craft complex events that are destined to realize usable intelligence. It is expected that these two ideas (events and streams) are converging to have a greater impact across industry verticals. With Hadoop emerging as the de facto standard for big data, there are a few noteworthy enhancements such as Storm and Spark on Hadoop to accelerate the process of streaming analytics. That is, if Hadoop platforms are very popular for knowledge discovery from big data, then the real excitement of real-time analytics platforms is all about capturing, compressing, and processing streaming data towards accelerating "time to insights."

The real-time processing is turning out to be indispensable because of the new phenomenon called as "perishable insights." That is, if enterprises are not setting up competent technologies in place, then there is every possibility for them to miss out tactical as well as strategic insights. Firms need to detect and act upon the extracted at a moment's notice. Streaming analytics is the one being portrayed and prescribed for harnessing and turning out any perishable insights emanating from sentient objects, smart sensors, connected devices, hardware as well as software infrastructures, application transactions and interactions, etc. into applicable insights for firms to surge ahead against their competitors.

Developers are fast familiarizing themselves with a handful of streaming operators for real-time analytics. The prominent ones include filters, aggregators, correlators, and locators, time-window operators, temporal operators, enrichment operators, and various custom and third-party operators. Software developers need to understand and compose these operators intelligently to realize actionable insights in timeout of streaming data. Sensor data are typically not value-adding unless they are getting composed with data from other sensors, actuators, operational, transactional and analytical systems, etc. to derive pragmatic and potential actions, alerts, triggers, associations, patterns, etc. Streaming has been there for a long time now and has been leveraged extensively in financial service industry. For example, stock trading is one of the renowned use cases out of streaming data. The idea is to create a graph of processing nodes (to maintain state), and data are processed when they are flowing through the graph. The primary use cases for streaming analytics include the following:

- Business process management and automation (process monitoring, BAM, reporting exceptions, operational intelligence)
- Finance (algorithmic trading, fraud detection, risk management)
- Network and application monitoring (intrusion detection, SLA monitoring)
- Sensor network applications (RFID reading, scheduling and control of fabrication lines, air traffic)

3.11 Sensor Analytics

There are clear indications that sensors and actuators are turning out to be the eye and ear of future IT. The quality and quantity of sensor applications are growing steadily across many industry verticals with the ready availability of smart sensors that could form ad hoc networks wirelessly in order to cooperatively finish tough and rough tasks in risky and hazardous environments. The focus on smarter environments got a strong fillip with the arrival of powerful sensors and networked and resource-constrained embedded devices. Environmental monitoring, asset management, the realization of digitized artifacts out of commonly found and cheap objects in our everyday environs, etc. are some of the distinctive derivatives out of all the noteworthy advancements in the sensor field.

For building adaptive business and IT applications, sensor values are steadily subjected to a variety of fusion with the emergence of highly advanced data fusion algorithms. Sensor data fusion has therefore become a deeper and decisive subject these days as there is a greater awakening that instead of using a single sensor in a particular place for a particular cause, differently enabled sensors could be deployed in plenty and used for extracting different data points. Such an accumulation of sensor data leads to derive more accurate results. For an instance, some years back, there was a fire alarm in the UK prime minister house, and hence all the emergency and fire extinction vehicles are quick enough to reach the spot in time in ready form to face any eventuality. Fortunately, there was no fire. The reason told was that there were only fire sensors. The solution proposed was that if there were different sensors for different parameters such as fire, temperature, pressure, gas, presence, etc. and powerful algorithms were utilized for calculating the probability for the eruption of fire, the whole rush of vehicles could have been easily avoided. Thus, sensors in unison are being proclaimed as the best course of actions for bringing forth scores of people-centric smart systems.

Further on, not only multiple sensor values but also sensor values in synchronization with a variety of web, social, mobile, embedded, enterprise, and cloud applications are destined to bring in sophisticated and smarter systems. That is, capturing and analyzing sensor values in association with IT and business data is to result in a steady stream of pioneering and people-centric applications. There are powerful platforms and toolsets for quickly making sense out of streaming and event data as we discussed in real-time and streaming analytics. Sensor analytics is to smartly integrate sensor data with other decision-enabling data emanating from other data sources to squeeze out actionable insights.

3.11.1 The Synchronization Between Big Data Analytics (BDA) and High-Performance Computing (HPC): The Value Additions

As enunciated many times, HPC is a grandiose enabler of the following new capabilities and competencies by cognitively fulfilling the infrastructural requirements of big data analytics. The HPC solutions could optimally use and manage IT infrastructure resources providing superior scalability and reliability and their contribution in transforming big data assets into real business value instantaneously is immense. There are other HPC solutions being recommended to simplify and streamline big and fast data analytics. In-database analytics is for significantly reducing the data movement and for deploying models quickly. As indicated in the beginning of this chapter, in-database solutions execute data management and analytic tasks inside the database. This promotes data consistency by reducing unnecessary data movement. In-database solutions by using massively parallel processing (MPP) database architecture provide enterprises to deploy predictive models and get results quickly. In-memory computing is another popular HPC method to solve complex problems. In the recent past, with the surging popularity of in-memory computing solutions, concurrent and multiuser data access is made possible in addition to extremely fast analytic operations. Cloud computing is being empowered to be high performing. Clouds increase the efficiency with distributed deployment and central monitoring. Grid and cloud computing paradigms epitomize the distributed computing and are the optimized and cost-effective version of supercomputing. Big data analytics is the most appropriate one for distributed computing.

Finally, data warehouse and Hadoop appliances are hitting the market with all force. There are several product vendors such as IBM, Oracle, Cisco, Teradata, EMC, etc. that produce a host of purpose-specific appliances as a high-performance IT solution. For small- and medium-scale enterprises, appliances are the most effective one.

3.12   Conclusions

So we have discussed a variety of big data-induced analytics in this chapter. Apart from the MapReduce-enabling batch processing of big data, real-time processing is also being given its share of importance as real-time analytics has a lot of use cases to offer. There are in-database as well as in-memory analytics platforms emerging and evolving fast to facilitate real-time analytics. SAP HANA is one popular in-memory database solution with higher market share for interactive and ad hoc analytics. Figure 3.17 clearly illustrates what solutions need to be leveraged for what requirements.

The Y-axis represents the amount of data (in size or as number of events), while the X-axis is time taken to produce the results. It outlines when each technology is

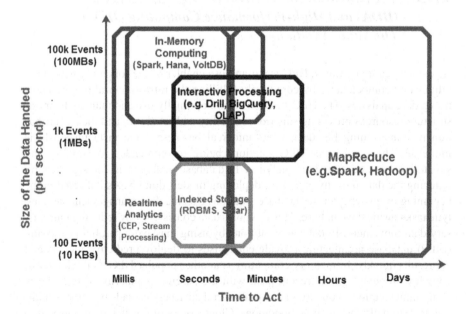

Fig. 3.17 The evolving needs of big and fast data analytics

useful. The HPC route is being specified as the best fit for tackling the distinct needs of big data analytics.

3.13   Exercises

1. Describe the macro-level architecture of big data analytics.
2. Discuss the reference architecture of Internet of Things.
3. Discuss the reference architecture of machine data analytics.
4. Write short notes on:

    • Sensor analytics
    • Stream analytics

5. Discuss the hybrid architecture of traditional as well as new-generation analytics

Chapter 4
Network Infrastructure for High-Performance Big Data Analytics

4.1 Introduction

Organizations at all levels are increasing their focus on big data, and it is one of the most spoken about technology nowadays. Present-day organizations are realizing more value from huge data sets like audio, video, and other social media sources. But handling these types of data is not an easy task, and it requires reconstruction of all aspects pertaining to IT hardware like network infrastructure, storage devices, servers, middleware components, and even the applications. In order to meet the ever-increasing demands of big data, the IT infrastructure is undergoing drastic changes. Some of the notable trends are replacement of hard drives with solid-state devices and design of new file systems which have the capability to process huge amounts of data in parallel and decoupling of functions from the underlying hardware components by using software-enabled techniques. However, there still exists a huge gap in the infrastructure readiness to store and process big data as depicted in the graph which is given below:

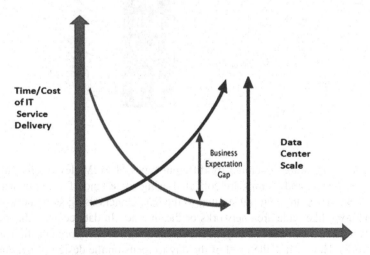

© Springer International Publishing Switzerland 2015
P. Raj et al., *High-Performance Big-Data Analytics*, Computer Communications and Networks, DOI 10.1007/978-3-319-20744-5_4

One of the key requirements of IT infrastructure to bridge this gap is the scale-up and scale-out of the existing infrastructure. Let us understand more about the meanings of these terms in the context of IT infrastructure:

- Scale-up: Infrastructure is scaled up by using components which offer enhanced performance and higher capacity. For example, in case of servers, it could mean having servers with more CPUs, cores, and memory. In case of storage devices, it could mean using devices which offer better performance and storage capacity like solid-state drives. In case of networks, it could mean replacing the 10 Gbps Ethernet pipes with 20 Gbps or 40 Gbps pipes for better data transmission rates.
- Scale-out: Infrastructure is scaled out by adding more components which can perform more processing in parallel which in turn speeds up the pace of processing. In case of servers, it could mean adding more servers. In case of storage devices, it could mean adding more storage devices. However, in case of networks, scaling out cannot happen instantaneously as network has many interwoven components and scaling the network could mean increasing each of these components which in turn may need a lot of reconfiguration. However, networks play a pivotal role in the processing of big data as depicted in the diagram which is given below:

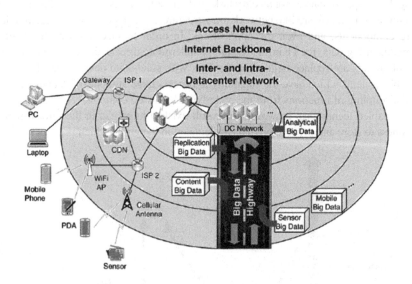

The data which are generated by different types of M2M devices like mobile phones, sensor, and laptops are collected using some kind of wired or wireless networks. They are then transmitted to the data centers using some networking technology like wide area networks or the Internet. In data centers, this data is analyzed and the result of analyzes is delivered back to users/organizations using networks. Hence, it is the need of the day to focus on the design of networking technologies and components which are ready to handle big data efficiently.

Before getting into more details about the design of networking components which are big data ready, it is necessary to understand the limitations of the present networks in terms of their capability to handle big data. Let us examine this aspect in detail in the next section.

4.2   Network Infrastructure Limitations of Present-Day Networks

In this section, we will analyze some of the limitations of the present-day networks in terms of their capabilities to handle big data:

1. *Static nature of networks*: The present-day network infrastructure has a bunch of protocols which are used to interconnect systems over long distances reliably and with good performance and security. However, most of these protocols are designed for specific requirements, and hence they tend to isolate the network into silos which in turn increases the complexity of handling them and altering them when there is a need. For example, in order to add any specific networking device, it is required to alter multiple network components like access control lists, switches, routers, firewalls, and in some cases portals also. Due to the complexity of altering each of these components, networks of today are more or less static in nature as IT personnel defer not to create service disruption in an attempt to alter these huge numbers of network components. But is this the present-day requirement? In the present-day infrastructure, server virtualization is a common trend in an attempt to optimize the use of server resources. With server virtualization, each server in a data center may have the necessity to communicate with hundreds and thousands of servers which may be colocated or in geographically dispersed data centers. This is in contrast to the existing architectures which typically support interactions between one server to multiple clients and one server to a limited number of other servers. But with virtualization becoming very prominent, each server has to communicate with hundreds of servers which may be running several other applications on their virtual machines. To add onto this complexity, virtual machines have several techniques like live VM migration to increase fault tolerance and disaster recovery. All these aspects which are related to virtual machines pose tough challenges for many design aspects of conventional networks like addressing schemes, namespaces, and routing.

   In addition to virtualization, another aspect which poses a tough challenge for the existing network infrastructure is the concept of converged network or the use of the same IP network for handling different types of IP data like voice, data, and video streams. Though most of the networks have the capability to adjust the quality of service parameters for each type of data differently, most of the provisioning tasks to handle each of this type of data need to be done manually. Owing to the static nature of the network design, the networks lack the capability to change their parameters like QoS, bandwidth, etc. as per the changing demands of applications and users.

2. *Rigid network policies*: It is a very cumbersome task to implement new network policies in the existing network infrastructure because of its rigid and siloed nature. In order to change a specific network policy, it may be necessary to change hundreds of different network devices which are a part of the network. In an attempt to alter each of the network component as per a new policy, the network administrators may induce several attacking surfaces for hackers and other malicious elements.

3. *Inability to scale*: Today's infrastructures are designed with massively parallel algorithms to speed up the pace at which data is processed. These parallel algorithms involve a huge number of data exchanges between the various servers which are involved in processing/computation. This kind of scenario demands hyper-scale high-performance networks with limited or no manual intervention. The rigid and static nature of present-day networks leaves no options to cater to this type of requirements of organizations.

    Another prominent trend which is evolving nowadays is the concept of multi-tenancy due to the proliferation of cloud-based model of service delivery. This model requires servicing different groups of users with different applications which may have different performance needs. These aspects are very difficult to implement in the traditional network infrastructure.

4. *Vendor dependence*: Present-day organizations demand a lot of new features in the network infrastructure which will help them to scale as per the changing needs of the business environment. But in many situations, it may not be possible to implement those features as they may not be supported by the network infrastructure equipment vendors. This makes things very difficult for present-day organizations and necessitates decoupling of components from the underlying hardware as this will go a long way in eliminating vendor dependence.

Activity Time ☺

Now that you have learnt the limitations of the traditional network infrastructure, what could be the techniques that can be used to overcome these limitations and make the network infrastructure big data ready?

Hint: Use each challenge discussed above and convert them into a possibility. Summarize your observations in the space which is given below:

1. ....
2. ....
3. ....

Some Interesting Facts About YouTube Videos [1]
- More than 1 billion unique users visit YouTube each month.
- Over 6 billion hours of video are watched each month on YouTube—that's almost an hour for every person on Earth.

(continued)

- 100 h of video are uploaded to YouTube every minute.
- 80 % of YouTube traffic comes from outside the United States.
- YouTube is localized in 61 countries and across 61 languages.
- According to Nielsen, YouTube reaches more US adults aged 18–34 than any cable network.
- Mobile makes up almost 40 % of YouTube's global watch time.

An Interesting Use Case of Big Data Analytics
A mobile device manufacturer can monitor several parameters of your mobile usage like average screen brightness, Wi-Fi connectivity, signal strength, and more using the manufacturer's monitor component which can be installed in your mobile device at the time of purchase. This device data can be collected daily and sent to a high-performance cluster which is maintained by the device manufacturer. This cluster can then analyze the usage data and provide useful recommendations to the user in the form of push notifications. Some examples of notifications could be to turn on auto screen brightness, start using wireless network when the signal strength gets low, etc.

4.3 Approaches for the Design of Network Infrastructures for High-Performance Big Data Analytics

The following are the approaches which we are going to use to describe the network infrastructure which is required for high-performance big data analytics.

Network virtualization	Software Defined Networking
Two tier leaf spine architecture	Network Functions virtualization

Network Virtualization Network virtualization decouples the network functions from the underlying hardware that delivers them. This is done by creating virtual instances which can be plugged onto any off-the-shelf platforms and used immediately.

Software-Defined Networking (SDN) *SDN* offers a centralized point for the orchestration and control of the underlying network traffic. This is done with the help of specialized components called SDN controllers which function as the brain of the network.

Two-Tier Leaf Spine Architecture This is a fat tree architecture with two types of switches: one to connect the servers and the other one to connect the switches. This provides more scalability when compared to traditional three-tier architecture.

Network Functions Virtualization (NFV) It refers to the virtualization of network services. This refers to set of techniques which accelerates the provisioning of network services without much of dependencies on the underlying hardware components. This is something which is still evolving.

Each of these techniques will be discussed in detail in this chapter.

4.3.1   Network Virtualization

Network virtualization refers to the creation of multiple logical network partitions over a single network infrastructure. This segments the network into multiple logical networks. A network which is logically segmented using the network virtualization technique is called a virtualized network or a virtual network. A virtual network appears as a physical network to the nodes connected to it. Two nodes connected to a virtual network can communicate among themselves without routing of frames, even if they are in different physical networks. Network traffic must be routed when two nodes in different virtual networks are communicating, even if they are connected to the same physical network. Network management traffic including "network broadcast" within a virtual network does not propagate to any other nodes that belong to a different virtual network. This enables functional grouping of nodes with a common set of requirements in a virtual network, regardless of the geographic location of the nodes. The logical network partitions are created using many networking techniques like virtual local area network (VLAN), VXLAN, virtual storage area network (VSAN), and so on which will be described later in this chapter. The diagram given below gives a high-level overview about the concept of network virtualization.

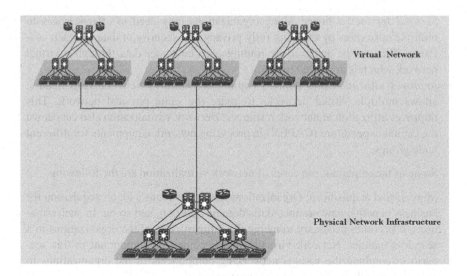

Network virtualization is performed by the hypervisor and physical switch operating system (OS). These software allow an administrator to create virtual networks on physical and virtual machine networks.

A physical switch runs an operating system which performs network traffic switching. The operating system must have network virtualization functionality to create virtual networks on the switch. Hypervisor has built-in networking and network virtualization functionalities. These functionalities can be leveraged to create a virtual switch and configure virtual networks on it. These functionalities are also provided by third-party software, which may be installed onto the hypervisor. Then, the third-party software module replaces the native networking functionality of the hypervisor.

The following are the key benefits of network virtualization:

- *Secure guest and partner access*: Many organizations allow customers and other business partners to access some of their resources using the Internet. A virtualized network helps to provide separate access to these parties. This in turn will help to protect the confidential information and other confidential assets of the organizations.
- *Role-based access control implementation*: Information access policies define who can access what data and resources. Using network virtualization techniques, it is possible to create separate user groups or business divisions. This in turn helps to ensure that individuals of only specific user group/ business division will have access to certain sensitive information pertaining to them.
- *Device isolation*: Certain devices/device components may need to be isolated from others for security or performance reasons. For example, banks can isolate ATMs on a dedicated virtual network to protect transactions and customer privacy.

- *Secured services delivery*: Many organizations may need to offer services to multiple customers by ensuring fully privacy and security of data for each customer. This can be achieved by routing each customer data through a virtual network which is dedicated to them.
- *Improves utilization and reduces capital expenditure*: Network virtualization allows multiple virtual networks to share the same physical network. This improves utilization of network resources. Network virtualization also cuts down the capital expenditure (CAPEX) in procuring network equipments for different node groups.

Some of the important use cases of network virtualization are the following:

- Mergers and acquisitions: Organizations nowadays focus a lot on acquisition for business benefits, new product skills/domain addition, and so on. In such situations, it becomes necessary to merge the infrastructure of the organizations in a seamless manner. Network virtualization becomes very important in this scenario to combine the various networking components of the organizations to ensure a smooth and synchronized functioning.
- Globalization of enterprises: Present-day organizations have branches distributed across the world. But they tend to work more or less using the concept of borderless enterprises. Network virtualization proves very handy to handle such situations by creating multiple virtualized domains according the business divisions, guest and partner access, IT maintenance and administration, geographic regions, and so on. One important aspect which needs to be mentioned in this regard is that the creation of virtualized domains does not act as a barrier for sharing of resources, tools, and staff members from time to time as per the changing business requirements. Network virtualization also helps to optimize the use of networks and provides improved performance.
- Retail sector: Retail is a fast-growing sector across the world with new retail giants with worldwide presence emerging every now and then in the market. Most of the retail groups have the tendency to outsource many maintenance aspects to a third-party agency/partner. In such situation, virtualized networks help to isolate the traffic of each third-party agency/partner from the retail store traffic. This ensures optimal usage of network resources and also provides improved performance.
- Regulatory compliance: Healthcare organizations in the United States are required to ensure the privacy of patient data as per the Health Insurance Portability and Accountability Act (HIPAA). Network virtualization is very helpful in these situations as it helps to create separate networks for different categories of people as per their access control permissions.
- Government sector: There are many departments in a government sector. Many times it becomes necessary to ensure that these departments use separate networks for security and privacy reasons. IT departments of governments can segment department services, applications, databases, and directories by using network virtualization techniques. This in turn facilitates resource consolidation and cost benefits.

Now that we have seen enough use cases of network virtualization, in the next section, we will discuss some of the key components of a virtual network.

Components of a Virtual Network   Virtual machines run on top of a complete system on which some kind of virtualization software has been implemented. But these virtual machines (VM) need a virtual network which has all the characteristics and components of a physical network. They also need to be connected to a virtual switch in the server. A virtual switch is a logical layer 2 (OSI model) switch that resides inside a physical server within the hypervisor. Virtual switches are created and configured using hypervisor. The high-level diagram of a virtual switch is given below:

Virtual Switch

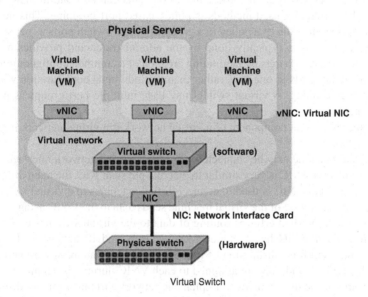

Virtual Switch

Virtual switches provide traffic management by routing packets to the virtual machines which are hosted within a hypervisor. Routing of packets requires a media access control (MAC) address to specify the destination VM to which a packet needs to be routed. These MAC addresses of the virtual machines are stored and maintained in a MAC address table. Apart from MAC addresses, this table also maintains the details of the virtual switch ports to which packets need to be forwarded.

Virtual switches also facilitate communication among VMs within a physical server and direct VM traffic to physical network. Switching of VM traffic to physi-cal network allows VMs to communicate with their clients or VMs hosted on another physical server. A virtual switch may be connected to multiple physical network interface cards (NIC). This helps in traffic management by distributing outbound traffic to multiple physical NICs. It also provides fault tolerance capabilities by allowing virtual switches to route traffic to an alternate NIC in case of failure of a specific NIC. For handling different types of traffic, different types of virtual ports are configured on a virtual switch. The different types of virtual switch ports are given below:

- Uplink ports: They connect a virtual switch to the physical NICs present in the server on which the virtual switch is present. Virtual switches can transfer data to a physical network only when it has multiple or at least one NIC attached to its uplink port.
- VM ports: They connect VNICs to a virtual switch.
- Hypervisor kernel port: They connect hypervisor kernel to a virtual switch.

Port grouping is a mechanism used to group the ports according to specific criteria like security, type of traffic, and so on. This can be done in many ways. One of the commonly used methods is policy-based port grouping. This involves creation and application of a policy to a group of virtual switch ports as per specific requirements. This is typically done by the administrator and provides a lot of flexibility and time savings by facilitating creation of a common configuration for a group of switch ports at one time rather than the individual configuration which is very time consuming. A virtual switch may have multiple port groups as per the requirement.

Another important component of a virtual network is a virtual network interface card (VNIC).

A virtual machine may be connected to multiple virtual network interface cards. The working of a VNIC is very similar to that of a physical NIC, the main difference being the fact that VNIC is used to connect virtual machines to a virtual switch.

The guest operating of the virtual machine sends data to the VNIC using a device driver software. VNIC performs routing of data to the virtual switches in the form of frames. Each VNIC has a unique MAC address and IP address and follows Ethernet protocol for transmission of frames. These MAC addresses are generated by the hypervisor, and they are assigned to each VNIC during virtual machine creation. Some of the mechanisms to implement network virtualization are discussed in the next section.

4.3.1.1   Techniques to Implement Network Virtualization

Virtual LAN (VLAN)

A VLAN is a logical network created on a LAN or across multiple LANs consisting of virtual and/or physical switches. VLAN technology can divide a large LAN into smaller virtual LANs or combine separate LANs into one or more virtual LANs. A VLAN enables communication among a group of nodes based on functional requirements of an organization, independent of nodes location in the network. All nodes in a VLAN may be connected to a single LAN or distributed across multiple LANs.

A virtual LAN is implemented by grouping switch ports in such a way that all the workstations connected to those specific switch ports receive the data that is sent to those switch ports. This creates a logical grouping or partition among the workstations in a LAN based on specific business requirements like projects, domain, business unit, and so on. This in short ensures that the entire network is segmented into multiple virtual networks. As this grouping mechanism mainly uses switch ports as a basis for grouping, these types of VLANs are also called port-based VLANs. A high-level implementation of port-based VLAN technique is shown in the diagram given below. In the diagram given below, VLANs are created based on various departments in an organization.

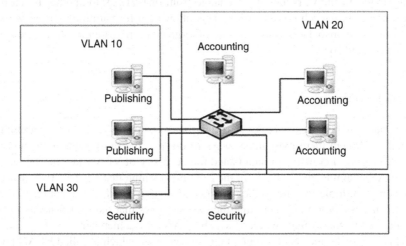

In port-based VLANs, switch ports are just assigned a VLAN ID. Workstations which are connected to a particular switch port will automatically receive the membership of that specific VLAN. One simple scenario pertaining to the example given above is summarized in the table given below:

Port number	VLAN ID
1	10
2	10
3	20
4	30

The benefits of VLAN are as follows:

- Broadcast traffic within a specific VLAN is restricted from propagating to another VLAN. For example, a node receives all broadcast frames within its associated VLAN but not from other VLANs. This imposes a restriction on the traffic which enters a specific VLAN. This restriction on VLAN traffic frees bandwidth for user traffic, which thereby improves performance.
- VLANs facilitate easy, flexible, and less expensive way to manage networks. VLANs are created using software. Therefore, they can be configured easily and

quickly compared to building separate physical LANs for various communication groups. If it is required to regroup nodes, an administrator simply changes VLAN configurations without moving nodes and doing re-cabling.

- VLANs also provide enhanced security by isolating sensitive data of one VLAN from any other VLANs. It is also possible to impose restrictions at the OSI layer 3 routing device to prevent inter-VLAN routing.
- Since a physical LAN switch can be shared by multiple VLANs, the utilization of the switch increases. It reduces capital expenditure (CAPEX) in procuring network equipments for different node groups.
- Facilitates the easy formation of virtual workgroups as VLANs provide the flexibility to the workstations to change from one VLAN to another by easily changing the switch configuration. This allows the formation of virtual workgroups and also facilitates sharing of organization resources like printers, servers, and so on.

VLAN Tagging

Many times it becomes necessary to distribute a single VLAN across multiple switches. Though there exist many ways to do this, the most popular method is VLAN tagging. Let us try to understand the necessity of VLAN tagging by using the VLAN example given above. In the example, assume that VLAN 20 is distributed across multiple switches. When a switch receives a broadcast packet for VLAN 20, it is necessary to make sure that the switch knows that the packet needs to be broadcasted to some other switch of which VLAN 20 is a member.

This is done by means of a frame tagging technique which is called VLAN tagging. The only limitation of this technique is the fact that it requires a change to the fundamental format of an Ethernet header. VLAN tagging involves insertion of 4 additional bytes to the header of an Ethernet packet. The Ethernet header structure after addition of 4 bytes is given below:

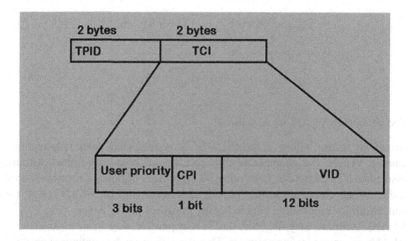

The main fields of the header are TPID and TCI.

TPID: This is the tag protocol identifier. The main purpose of TPID is to represent the fact that there is tag header which is present and contains the following fields:

User priority: This is a 3 bit field and conveys the priority information which need to be included in the frame. There are eight priority levels which are allowed: zero denotes the lowest priority level and seven denotes the highest priority level.

CFI: This is a 1 bit field which is always set to zero for Ethernet switches. This field is mainly used to indicate priority between Ethernet and token ring networks. If this field has a value of 1, then it indicates the fact that the frame should not be bridged to a port which is untagged.

VID: This field corresponds to the virtual LAN identifier, and this field plays a key role for the distribution of VLAN across multiple switches.

Now let us try to understand how this tagging mechanism helps to solve the problem which we described in the previous section. To understand it better, let us consider a broadcast packet which arrives at a specific switch port. This packet is associated with VLAN 20, i.e., its VLAN ID is 20. Let us assume that port 10 of this switch is connected to port 15 of another switch which also is a part of VLAN 20. Now what needs to be done to configure VLAN tagging is to ensure that ports 10 and 15 should be configured as tagged member ports of VLAN 20. This is typically done by the network administrator. Once this is done, it makes switch 1 aware of the fact that once it receives a broadcast, it needs to send it out through port 10 as a broadcast packet with VLAN ID = 20 in the tag. It makes switch 2 aware of the fact that it should receive the tagged packet and associate it with VLAN 20. Switch 2 will also send out the packet to all the member ports of VLAN 20. This makes it very easy for switch 2 to understand what needs to be done with the packets belonging to VLAN 20. So in short, this concept can be summarized as follows:

- If a port is tagged to be a member of a particular VLAN, then all packets which are sent to that port by the VLAN should have a VLAN tag inserted into it.
- If a port receives a tagged packet with a specific VLAN ID, then the packet needs to be associated with that VLAN.

Virtual LAN has its limitations and the main limitation is its scalability. Scalability becomes a bigger concern if the network under consideration is used in cloud infrastructure. These scalability concerns can be addressed using another technique called Virtual Extensible Local Area Network (VXLAN). This technique is used extensively in data centers where massive scalability is a key requirement. More details are explained in the next section.

4.3.1.2 Virtual Extensible Local Area Network

Many times it becomes necessary to move or migrate virtual machines from one server to another for purposes like load balancing, disaster recovery, and traffic management. Many techniques to ensure the live migration of VMs are available.

But the key consideration in this regard is to make sure that VMs must remain in their native subnet so that they remain accessible during migration. This becomes a serious concern especially when the number of subnets, virtual machines, and servers are huge in the count. This is where VXLAN comes into the picture. VXLAN helps to overcome the limitations posed by IP subnetting by using layer 2 tunneling feature. It helps the data center administrators to implement a good layer 3 architecture and also ensure that VMs can be moved across the servers without any limitations. VXLAN uses techniques to combine multiple layer 3 sub-networks to a layer 3 infrastructure. This allows the virtual machines on multiple networks to communicate as though they are a part of the same subnet. The high working level of a VXLAN is shown in the diagram given below.

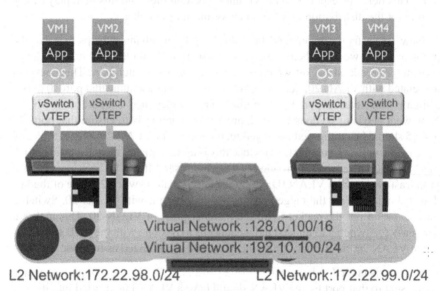

VXLAN traffic is managed transparently by most of the networking devices. For VXLAN, IP-encapsulated traffic is routed like normal IP traffic. The encapsulation or decapsulation is done by the VXLAN gateways which are also called Virtual Tunnel End Points (VTEP). These VTEPs play a major role in VXLAN. VTEPs can be implemented in one of the following ways:

- Virtual bridges in the hypervisor
- VXLAN aware virtual machine applications
- VXLAN-enabled switch hardware

Each VXLAN network segment has a 24 bit identifier which is unique. This identifier is also called VXLAN Network Identifier or VNI. The 24 bit address space allows massively scalable virtual networks. However, in most of the cases, the number of useable virtual network addresses is limited by multicast and by the limitations of the network hardware. Virtual machines in a logical layer 2 domain use the same subnet and are mapped using a common VNI. This common mapping allows the virtual machines to communicate with one another. It should be noted that the IP addressing rules which are followed in the physical layer 2 are applicable to virtual networks as well.

VXLANs maintain the uniqueness of the virtual machines by combining the virtual machine's MAC address and the VNI. This sometimes leads to the duplication of MAC addresses within a data center. The only restriction in this scenario is that duplication of MAC addresses cannot happen within the same VNI. Virtual machines which belong to a particular subnet do not require any special configuration to support VXLAN traffic. This is mainly due to the presence of VTEP which is typically a part of hypervisor itself. The configuration on the VTEPs should include layer 2 or IP subnet to VNI network mapping and VNI to IP multicast group mapping. The first mapping allows building of forwarding tables to facilitate VNI/MAC traffic flow. The second mapping helps VTEPs to perform broadcast or multicast functions across the network.

Next, we will try to understand virtual networking in storage area networks. This is referred to as virtual storage area network and is described below.

Virtual Storage Area Network (VSAN)

Virtual SAN is a logical grouping of servers or storage devices, created on a storage area network, in order to facilitate communication among a group of nodes with a common set of requirements regardless of their physical location. VSAN conceptually functions in the same way as that of a VLAN.

Each VSAN acts as an independent fabric and are being managed independently. Each VSAN has its own set of fabric services, configuration, and set of unique Fiber Channel addresses. Configurations on a specific VSAN do not affect any other VSAN. Similar to VLAN tagging, VSAN has its tagging mechanism. The purpose of VSAN tagging is similar to VLAN tagging in LAN.

4.3.1.3 Traffic Management in a Virtual Network

Network traffic must be managed in order to optimize performance and availability of networked resources. Many techniques exist to monitor and control the network traffic in a physical network. Some of them could be applied to manage the virtual network traffic. Load balancing is a key objective of managing network traffic. It is a technique to distribute workload across multiple physical or virtual machines and parallel network links to prevent overutilization or underutilization of these resources and optimize performance. It is provided by dedicated software or hardware.

It is possible for the network administrators to apply a policy for distribution of network traffic across VMs and network links. Network traffic management techniques can also be used to set a policy to ensure failover of network traffic across network links. In the event of a network failure, the traffic from the failed link will failover to another available link, based on predefined policy. Network administrators have the flexibility to change a policy as per the requirement.

When multiple VM traffics share bandwidth, network traffic management techniques ensure guaranteed service levels of traffic generated by each VM. Traffic management techniques allow an administrator to set priority for allocating bandwidth for different types of network traffic such as VM, VM migration, IP storage, and management. In this section, we will understand some techniques which are used for traffic management.

4.3.1.4   Link Aggregation

Link aggregation is a technique used to aggregate multiple network connections into a single connection in order to provide an increased throughput which in turn provides significant performance improvement. Some variants of the link aggregation techniques which may be applied to virtual networks are:

- VLAN trunking: VLAN trunking is a technique which allows traffic from multiple VLANs to traverse through a single link or network connection. This technology allows for a single connection between any two networked devices such as routers, switches, VMs, and storage systems with multiple VLAN traffic traversing the same path. The single connection through which multiple VLAN traffic can traverse is called a trunk link. VLAN trunking enables a single port on a networked device to be used for sending or receiving multiple VLAN traffic over a trunk link. The port capable of transferring traffic pertaining to multiple VLANs is called a trunk port. To enable trunking, it is necessary to ensure that the sending and receiving networked devices should have at least one port configured as trunk port. A trunk port on a networked device is included to all the VLANs defined on the networked device and transfers traffic for all those VLANs. The mechanism used to achieve VLAN trunking is called VLAN tagging which was described earlier.
- NIC teaming: NIC teaming is a technique that logically groups (to create a NIC team) physical NICs connected to a virtual switch to form a team. This is done to balance the network traffic and to ensure failover in the event of a NIC failure or a network link outage. NICs within a team can be configured as active and standby. Active NICs are used to send frames, whereas standby NICs remain idle. Load balancing allows distribution of all outbound network traffic across active physical NICs, giving higher throughput than a single NIC could provide. A standby NIC will not be used for forwarding traffic until a failure occurs on one of the active NICs. In the event of NIC or link failure, traffic from the failed link will failover to another physical NIC. The load balancing and failover across NIC team members are governed by policies which are configured on the virtual switch.

4.3.1.5   Traffic Shaping

Traffic shaping controls network bandwidth to prevent impact on business-critical application traffic by restricting the noncritical traffic flow. It also helps to guarantee the required quality of service. Traffic shaping can be enabled and configured on the virtual switch level. Traffic shaping uses three parameters to throttle and shape network traffic flow: average bandwidth, peak bandwidth, and burst size.

Average bandwidth is configured to set the allowed data transfer rate (bits per second) across a virtual switch over time. Since this is an averaged value over time, the workload at a virtual switch port can go beyond average bandwidth for a small time interval. The value provided for the peak bandwidth determines the maximum data transfer rate (bits per second) allowed across a virtual switch without queuing or dropping frames. The value of peak bandwidth is always higher than the average bandwidth.

When the traffic rate at a virtual switch exceeds the average bandwidth, it is called burst. Burst is an intermittent event and typically exists in a small time interval. The burst size defines the maximum amount of data (bytes) allowed to transfer in a burst, provided it does not exceed the peak bandwidth. The burst size is a calculation of bandwidth multiplied by the time interval during which the burst exists. Therefore, the higher the available bandwidth, the less time the burst can stay for a particular burst size. If a burst exceeds the configured burst size, the remaining frames will be queued for later transmission. If the queue is full, the frames will be dropped.

4.3.2 Software-Defined Networking (SDN)

Software-defined networking is a paradigm in which network control is decoupled from the underlying network devices and is embedded into a software-based component called SDN controller. This separation of control enables the network services to be abstracted from the underlying components and helps network to be treated like a logical entity. The high-level architecture of SDN is depicted in the diagram which is given below:

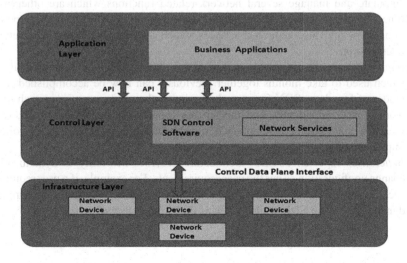

All the business applications which run in the network are a part of the application layer. All the components of the network are a part of the infrastructure layer. The SDN software component resides in the control layer and interacts both with the applications and with the infrastructure components.

The core of the SDN is the software component which is called the SDN controller. The entire network can be controlled by means of the SDN controller, and the SDN controller appears to all other components of the network as a logical switch. SDN controller can be used to monitor and control the operations of the entire network. This greatly eliminates the hassles of configuring hundreds of network devices. The network administrators can now change network settings dynamically using SDN programs. SDN controller interacts with the business applications using SDN APIs. SDN controller interacts with infrastructure components of the network using control some protocols like OpenFlow. OpenFlow is one of the most prominent protocols used in SDN, though there are many other protocols as well for SDN. SDN helps intelligent orchestration and provisioning of the network quickly using software programs which are written in the control layer. The development of open APIs is in progress for SDN architecture, and this will give a great deal of vendor independence for the SDN architecture. As of now, all the vendor devices which use a common SDN protocol for communication can be controlled centrally from an SDN controller.

4.3.2.1   Benefits of SDN

- *Centralized control of multi-vendor network equipments*: All network equipments which use a common SDN protocol for communication can be controlled centrally using an SDN controller irrespective of the vendors who have manufactured the equipments.
- *Reduced complexity through automation*: SDN framework provides features to automate and manage several network-related functions which are otherwise time consuming when done manually. This automation will bring down operational cost and also reduce the errors which are introduced due to manual intervention.
- *Improved network reliability and security*: Network policy implementation which used to take months together previously can now be accomplished in a matter of few days. SDN framework eliminates the need to configure each network device individually, and this in turn reduces the possibility of security breaches and other noncompliance aspects which may arise during policy implementation.
- *Better user experience*: SDN architecture provides flexibility to dynamically change configuration as per the user requirements. For example, if a user requires specific level of QoS for audio data streams, it can be configured to happen dynamically using SDN controller. This offers better user experience.

Some of the prominent use cases for SDN are:

- Campus
- Data center
- Cloud
- Carriers and service providers

OpenFlow

OpenFlow is the one of the first standard communications interfaces which was defined for an SDN architecture [2]. It allows direct access and configuration of network devices such as switches and routers (these components can be both physical and virtual (hypervisor based)). It is the absence of such open interfaces that have led to the monolithic, closed, and mainframe-like nature of traditional networks. OpenFlow is so popular in the field of SDN that many a times, SDN and OpenFlow are used interchangeably.

Activity Time

Divide the class into groups of two, each comprising of equal number of members. For each group assign the task of finding out a protocol other than OpenFlow which is used in SDN architecture/framework.

4.3.2.2   Two-Tier Leaf/Spine Architecture

The traditional network fabric architecture has three tiers as shown in the diagram which is given below:

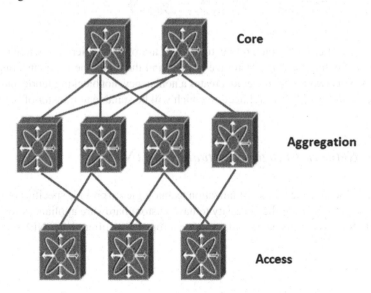

The functions of the three tiers of switches are as follows:

Tier 1 (access switches): The access switches are used to connect servers and other storage devices which are part of the network.

Tier 2 (aggregation switches): The access switches are connected using Ethernet media to aggregation switches. The aggregation switches aggregate and forward traffic from the access switches to the core switches.

Tier 3 (core switches): The core switches or routers forward traffic flows from servers and storage devices to the intranet and Internet.

The main limitation of this architecture is that they use layer 2 forwarding techniques as opposed to layer 3 forwarding techniques. In addition to this, it is common to have oversubscription of bandwidth in the access layer and less bandwidth in the aggregation layer. This in turn will lead to latency. All these factors limit the scalability of the architecture as per the present needs. In order to overcome the limitations imposed by this architecture, the two-tier leaf/spine network fabric architecture has been designed. The high-level architecture of two-tier leaf/spine network fabric is depicted in the diagram which is given below:

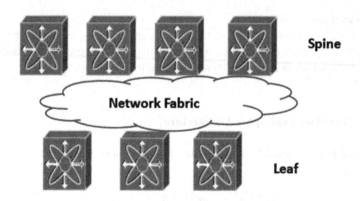

In the two-tier leaf/spine architecture, there are only two tiers of switches: one tier for connecting the servers/storage devices and the other one for connecting the switches. This two-tier architecture creates a nonlatency, nonblocking fabric and thus provides a highly scalable architecture which will be suitable to transfer of big data.

4.3.3 Network Functions Virtualization (NFV)

NFV is a concept which uses virtualization technologies to provide specific network-related services without the necessity to have custom hardware appliances for each network function. This is the main value proposition offered by NFVs. Some examples of NFVs are virtual firewalls, load balancers, WAN accelerators, and intrusion detection services. NFV can be visualized as a combination of virtualization and SDN, and the relationship is depicted in the diagram which is given below:

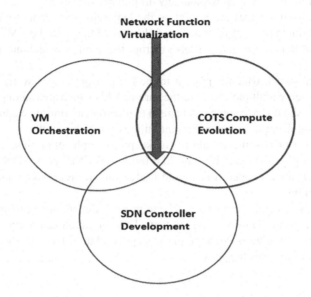

It is not necessary to use SDN to implement NFV; present-day virtualization techniques are robust enough to build NFVs. However, the orchestration and management capabilities of SDN greatly enhance the capabilities of NFV, and hence the use of SDN is being advocated during the development of NFVs. Virtualization of network services doesn't necessarily mean separate hypervisor partitioned VMs that contain each service instance; instead, it could also mean [3]:

- Services which are implemented in a machine which has multiple/compartmentalized OS(s)
- Services which are implemented within a single hypervisor
- Services which are implemented as distributed or clustered as composites
- Services which are implemented on bare metal machines
- Services which are implemented in Linux virtual containers

These techniques may use some kind of storage device like NAS to share their state.

NFV is still an evolving area; however, the following are some of the concerns which should be kept in mind during design of NFVs [3]:

- The use of hypervisor and delivering virtualized services using the same underlying physical hardware can lead to a conflict for physical resources. This may cause a performance drop in the delivery of services which are related to that specific component. NFV orchestration system should monitor such performance degradation very carefully. The NFV orchestration system should also keep track of the hypervisor and the physical resources so that any contention for resources can be carefully sorted out without any drop in performance.

- The virtualized services are hosted on the hypervisor component which could become a single point of failure. This failure will impact all the VMs which are running on that server and will also disrupt the services which are offered by those VMs.
- The virtual switch which is present in the hypervisor can get overloaded in an attempt to serve multiple vNICs of the various VMs which are running on it. The hypervisor should have some mechanism to identify and prioritize control traffic in so that application and management failures can be avoided.
- The hypervisor has the capability to keep the applications unaware of the changes in physical machine state like failure of a NIC port. SDN controller and orchestration cooperation should bridge this awareness gap and perform timely actions.
- In some cases, virtual machines can be migrated from one server to another as a part of a high-availability (HA) strategy. This migration can impact a service delivery in several ways. So appropriate steps need to be taken to ensure that no disruption of services happens.

4.4   Wide Area Network (WAN) Optimization for Transfer of Big Data

In the present world of big data, it is important to ensure fast and reliable movement of big data over global distances. This factor is turning out to be a decisive one for the success of business in every industry vertical. The Transmission Control Protocol (TCP) has been the key protocol which is used for data transfer across wide area networks. But TCP has many performance bottlenecks, more so for networks which have high round-trip time (RTT) and packet loss, and these bottlenecks become more pronounced and evident for high-bandwidth networks. The graph given below clearly depicts this scenario [4].

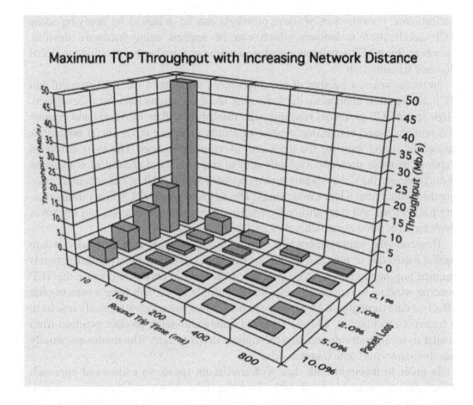

These performance bottlenecks are caused due to TCP's additive-increase/multiplicative-decrease (AIMD) congestion avoidance algorithm. This AIMD algorithm works in the following manner:

1. Probes the available bandwidth of the network
2. Increases the packet transmission rate according to available bandwidth
3. Increases the packet transmission rate until packet loss is detected
4. After detecting packet loss, packet transmission rate is exponentially reduced which in turn causes a drastic dip in performance of the network.

To add on to this, some parameters like losses due to physical network media also create a dip in packet transmission rate in TCP networks. However, the loss-based congestion control in TCP AIMD is the major factor which reduces the throughput in a TCP network. In TCP AIMD, loss of very packet leads to the retransmission of the packet and also stops the data delivery to the destination until retransmission of the lost packet happens. This causes a major bottleneck for reliable transmission of large bulk data like big data which does not require in-order (byte-stream) delivery of data. This TCP limitation severely impacts the performance of traditional file transfer protocols which are built on TCP like FTP, HTTP, CIFS, and NFS. These performance bottlenecks become more evident when it comes to long-distance transmission over wide area networks. Some level of performance optimization of these protocols can be achieved by applying some TCP acceleration techniques which can be applied using hardware devices. However, these TCP acceleration techniques are not found to be effective for global distance transmission.

In recent years, a number of new high-speed versions of the TCP protocol and TCP acceleration appliances implementing these variations have been developed. High-speed TCP protocols recognize the fundamental flaw of AIMD and revamp this window-based congestion control algorithm to reduce the artificial bottleneck caused by it and improve the long-term average throughput. The most advanced versions of these protocols typically aim to improve the detection of congestion through measuring richer signals such as network queuing delay, rather than increasing throughput until a loss event occurs. This helps to prevent TCP flows from creating packet loss, and thus artificially entering congestion avoidance, and improves the long-term throughput in nearly loss-free networks.

However, the improvement diminishes rapidly in wide area networks, where packet losses due to physical media error or buffer overflow by cross-traffic bursts become non-negligible. A single packet loss in these networks will cause the TCP sending window to reduce severely, while multiple losses will have a catastrophic effect on data throughput. More than one packet loss per window typically results in a transmission timeout, and the resulting bandwidth-delay-product pipeline from sender to receiver drains and data throughput drops to zero. The sender essentially has to re-slow-start data transmission.

In order to transport bulk data with maximum speed, an end-to-end approach which uses the available bandwidth along the entire data transfer path is required. Aspera FASP [4] is an efficient and innovative bulk data transport technology which provides a viable alternative for transferring files over public and private IP-based wide area networks. Aspera FASP is implemented at the application layer, and it acts as an endpoint application protocol. Hence, it does not require any changes to the standard networking infrastructure. FASP has the capability to deliver 100 % bandwidth efficient transport of bulk data over any IP network. Data transfer using FASP is independent of network delay and packet loss which in turn provides the high-performance next-generation approach for the transfer of big data.

Aspera FASP overcomes the disadvantages of TCP, and it provides reliable transport of data for applications that require bulk data transfer (which does not involve byte-stream delivery). Another key feature of FASP is that it completely separates out reliability and rate control aspects from data transmission. This is done by using standard UDP in the transport layer which helps in achieving decoupled congestion and reliability control in the application layer by using a theoretically optimal approach that retransmits precisely the real packet loss on the channel. On account of the decoupling of the rate control and reliability, new packets need not slow down for the retransferring of lost packets as in TCP-based byte streaming applications. Data that is lost in transmission is retransmitted at a rate that precisely matches the available bandwidth inside the end-to-end path, or a configured target rate, with zero duplicate retransmissions for zero receiving cost.

The amount of bandwidth which is available inside a specific path is found out using a delay-based rate control mechanism. FASP basically uses queuing delay as a means to measure the congestion of the network and maintains only a small queue in the network. The data transfer rate is adjusted according to the size of the queue (e.g., if the queue size becomes very small, it indicates that there is more unused bandwidth and hence more data is transferred and vice versa). FASP periodically sends probing packets into the network in order to assess the queuing delay that exists in the data transfer path. If FASP detects an increase in queuing delay, it reduces the data transfer proportional to the difference between the target queuing and the current queuing, therefore avoiding overdriving the network and vice versa when it detects a decrease in queuing delay.

FASP's adaptive rate control mechanism has many advantages. They are:

- It uses network queuing delay as primary congestion control parameters and packet loss ratio as secondary congestion control parameter. Using these parameters, FASP is able to precisely estimate the level of network congestion without slowing down data transmission due to packet loss.
- FASP uses embedded quick response mechanism to automatically slow down data transfer rate when there are many simultaneous data transfers. It also has mechanisms to speed up data transfer automatically, and this ensures efficient delivery times for data.
- Advanced feedback mechanism allows FASP session rate to quickly converge to a state of equilibrium. Steady data transmission rate provides QoS experience for the users without investing anything extra for QoS hardware or software.
- Steady use of network bandwidth always tends to keep network utilization and efficiency at 100 %.

File transfer bottlenecks can appear in various types and forms. Many times, there will be decreased speed when transferring a set of files of small sizes when compared to transferring a single file of the same size. With the help of a novel file streamlining technique, FASP provides high efficiency for transfers of a large number of small files as well. As a result, FASP has the capability to eliminate the fundamental bottlenecks of TCP- or UDP-based file transfer technologies such as FTP and UDT. FASP also speeds up data transfers over public and private IP networks. FASP removes the artificial bottlenecks caused by imperfect congestion control algorithms, packet losses (by physical media, cross-traffic burst, or coarse protocols themselves), and the coupling between reliability and congestion control. In addition, FASP innovation is eliminating emerging bottlenecks from disk IO, file system, CPU scheduling, etc. and achieves full line speed on even the longest, fastest wide area networks.

4.5   Conclusions

In the first part of this chapter, we discussed the various requirements of the present-day networks in order to transmit big data. We also analyzed the various concerns of the present-day networks which are making them unsuitable for the transfer of big data.

In the second part of this chapter, we discussed the various approaches which should be adopted by the organizations to make their network ready for big data. The various approaches which were discussed are network virtualization, software-defined networks, two-tier leaf and spine architecture, and network functions virtualization. The various methods to implement network virtualization and the key components of a virtual network were also discussed. The traffic management techniques used in virtual networks were also discussed in detail. The various aspects of SDN and the architecture of SDN were discussed in this chapter. The chapter finally concludes with the description of NFV and the concerns to be kept in mind while designing service delivery using NFV.

4.6 Exercises

1. Explain the shortcomings of present-day networks.
2. Write a short note on network virtualization techniques.
3. Explain the concept of VLAN tagging in detail.
4. Explain SDN architecture.
5. Write a short note on NFV.
6. Explain the design concerns to be kept in mind during the design of NFV.
7. Explain the concept of WAN optimization using FASP.

References

1. https://www.youtube.com/yt/press/en-GB/statistics.html
2. A white paper on Software Defined Networking -The New Norm for networks by Open Networking Foundation
3. A book on Authoritative review of network programming technologies by Thomas. D. Nadeau & Ken Gray and published by Oreilly publishers
4. http://bridgesgi.com/wp-content/uploads/2014/04/Bridge-Solutions-Group-Aspera-fasp_a_critical_technology_comparison.pdf

Chapter 5
Storage Infrastructures for High-Performance Big Data Analytics

5.1 Introduction

To get started with, we will examine the shortfalls which are present in the traditional HPC storage systems which make them unfit for the requirements of the present-day high-performance computing architecture and applications. Some of the key shortfalls are:

- *Integration of Technology Stacks from Multiple Vendors*: Present-day storage systems use different components of technology stacks from diverse vendors as they lacked the capability to design and deliver end-to-end HPC solutions. This drastically increases the system complexity and makes many aspects like testing and quality control extremely cumbersome. The multi-vendor HPC storage systems also occupy more floor space and have high-power requirements for their functioning. These storage systems also create I/O bottlenecks which will act as a hindrance for their adoption by HPC applications. This multi-vendor HPC storage systems will create concerns for the customer when it comes to various aspects like maintenance in the long run.
- *Limited Automation in Configuration and Tuning Processes*: Multi-vendor HPC systems often involve a piece meal installation process which is typically very lengthy and cumbersome because of the involvement of diverse components from multiple vendors. This time-consuming installation and configuration process might impact the project deadlines making the systems highly unsuitable for the dynamically changing requirements of present-day systems. A lack of an integrated setup also inhibits a user's capability to interact effectively with all the components of a multi-vendor system. Many tuning cycles might be required to tune the performance of the systems as per the requirements of the HPC applications. All these aspects reduce the efficiency and reliability aspect of conventional HPC systems.
- *Lack of Focus on Management Software*: Management software is a very critical component of HPC storage systems as they play a pivotal role in the smooth operation of the entire system. But ironically, the conventional HPC storage

© Springer International Publishing Switzerland 2015
P. Raj et al., *High-Performance Big-Data Analytics*, Computer Communications and Networks, DOI 10.1007/978-3-319-20744-5_5

systems gave limited or no importance to the design and development of management software for storage systems. As a result, HPC storage system users really have a tough time when they try to capture and record various parameters of the storage system like performance. A lack of sophisticated diagnostic tools also makes various aspects like log analysis and troubleshooting extremely difficult. All these limitations force organizations to spend more time and effort in managing and maintaining these HPC storage systems.

The scenario becomes all the more difficult when the organizations scale up. Configuration management, maintenance, and integration tasks become extremely difficult, and the cost required to address these challenges will grow exponentially as well. All these have made it the need of the day for organizations to adopt specialized storage infrastructure which is suitable to meet the demands of the high-performance computing applications. However, some conventional storage infrastructures have also found their way into the present HPC storage era with some modifications to their architecture and design. In this chapter, we will examine all aspects pertaining to storage infrastructure and also examine their suitability to meet the demands of present-day high-performance applications.

5.2   Getting Started with Storage Area Network

During the early stages of its evolution, storage area network (SAN) was typically designed as a client-server system with the server connected to a group of storage devices by means of some interconnection media which was called bus. In some situations, the client systems were communicating directly to the storage devices. These types of storage architectures in which the client-server systems communicated directly with the storage devices (without any communication network) were referred to as direct-attached storage (DAS). The high-level architectural overview of a DAS system is summarized in the diagram which is given below:

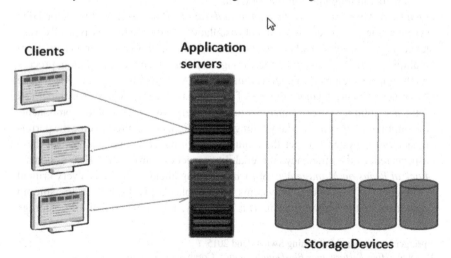

There are three main tiers in the architecture given above; they are:

> **Tier 1 : Client Systems which access the applications**
>
> - They are connected to the application servers typically using some kind of switch or connector

> **Tier 2 : Application servers where applications are hosted**
>
> - The application servers have (Input /Output) I/O controllers to control input/output operations to the attached storage devices. The I/O controllers are designed to work according to the specific interfaces which are used for connecting to the storage devices. If the attached storage devices support different types of interfaces, there will be an I/O controller for each type of interface.

> **Tier 3 : Storage Devices**
>
> - They are used for storing data which is generated by the application which runs in the application server.

Popular I/O Interfaces Supported by Storage Devices in DAS Architecture

Small Computer System Interface (SCSI)

It is one of the most popular electronic interfaces which were developed by American National Standards Institute (ANSI). Parallel SCSI (also called as SCSI) is one of the most popular forms of storage interface. SCSI connectors/ interfaces are mainly used to connect disk drives and tape drives directly to the servers or client devices. SCSI connectors can be also used to establish connection to other peripheral devices like printers and scanners. The source (client-server devices) communicates with the attached storage devices using the SCSI command set. The most recent version of SCSI which is called SCSI Ultra320 provides data transfer speeds of 320 MB/s. There is also another variant of SCSI which performs serial transmission and is called *Serial Attached SCSI (SAS)*. It offers enhanced performance and scalability features when compared to its parallel counterpart. SAS at present supports data transfer rates of up to 6 Gb/s.

Integrated Device Electronics/Advanced Technology Attachment (IDE/ATA)

The term IDE/ATA actually represents a dual-naming conventions. The IDE component in IDE/ATA denotes the specification of the controllers which are connected to the computer's motherboard for communicating with the attached devices. The ATA component specifies the interface which is used for connecting storage devices, such as CD-ROMs, disk drives, and tape drives, to the motherboard. The most recent version of IDE/ATA is called Ultra DMA (UDMA), and it supports data transfer rates of up to 133 MB/s. There is also

(continued)

a serial version of the IDE/ATA specification which is called serial ATA (SATA). SATA offers enhanced data transfer speeds when compared to its parallel variant, and it can offer data transfer speeds of up to 6 Gb/s.

Activity Time !!!!!

Open your computer and make a list of all the other I/O interfaces which are used for communication with storage devices in a DAS architecture. Make a comparative study and identify the best I/O interface option. Consider parameters like data transfer speeds, different types of peripheral devices supported, maximum number of devices supported, and so on.

Tape Drives vs. Disk Drives: Which Is a Better Option?
Disk drives are a more popular choice as storage media when compared to tape drives because of the following limitations of the tape drives:

- Data is stored linearly on the tape. Search and retrieval operations of data are performed using sequential operations which will take several seconds to complete. This imposes limitations on the usage of tapes by real-time and other performance-intensive--> application.
- In a multiuser environment, it is not possible for multiple applications to simultaneously access data stored on tape.
- In a tape drive, the read/write head touches the surface of the tape which leads to quick wear and tear of the tape surface
- The space requirements and the overhead for managing tape media are significant when compared to disk drives.

However, even with all these limitations, tape is still a preferred low-cost option to store backup data and other types of data which are not accessed frequently. Disk drives allow random access operations on data which is stored in them, and they also support access by multiple users/applications simultaneously. Disk drives also have more storage capacity when compared to tape drives.

Tier three comprises of the storage devices. The connections to these storage devices are controlled by means of an I/O controller which is attached to the application server.

5.2.1 Shortcomings of DAS

1. Static Configuration: If the configuration of the bus needs to be changed dynamically to add new storage devices in order to resolve I/O bottlenecks, that option
   is not supported by DAS architecture.
2. Expensive: Maintenance of DAS systems is quite expensive. DAS architecture
   does not allow sharing of storage devices among servers according to the variation in workloads of the servers. This in turn implies that each server needs to
   have its own spare storage capacity to be used in times of peak load. This would
   increase the cost drastically.
3. Limited Scalability/Supported Data Transmission Distance: The scalability of
   the DAS architecture is limited by a number of ports which are available in each
   storage device and also the data transmission distance supported by the bus and
   cables which are used to connect servers to the storage devices.

RAID (Redundant Array of Independent Disks) for Disk Drives
RAID is a mechanism which is used to combine a set of disk drives and use
them as a single storage device. The underlying objective of RAID is to
improve the performance and the fault tolerance of the disk drives. These
objectives are achieved using two techniques:

- Striping: The task of splitting the data to be written across multiple disk
  drives in order to improve the performance of disk drives by balancing the
  load across them equally
- Mirroring: The task of storing copies of data in multiple disks in order to
  ensure that even if one disk fails, the data in the other disk will serve as a
  backup copy

5.3 Getting Started with Storage Area Networks (SANs)

There are several shortcomings in DAS architecture, and this has led to the emergence
of a separate category of networks to connect servers to the storage devices. This
category of networks is referred to as storage area networks. The high-level generic
architecture of a SAN is depicted in the diagram which is given below (Fig. 5.1).

   In this architecture, as discussed above, the application servers access the storage
devices through a dedicated network. This dedicated network for accessing storage
devices is called storage area networks. Having a dedicated network for handling
storage device traffic facilitates centralized storage and management. It also adds a
lot of scalability to the architecture. The two main transmission protocols which are
used by a majority of the SANs are Fibre Channel Protocol (FCP) or Transmission
Control Protocol/Internet Protocol (TCP/IP). SANs are classified into FC SAN and

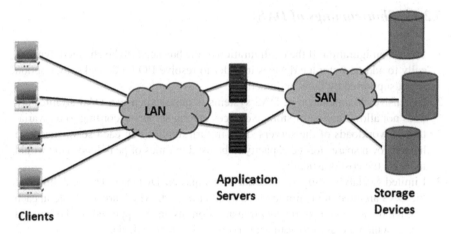

Fig. 5.1 Architecture of storage area networks

IP SAN based on the protocol used by them. There are mainly three ways in which data is accessed from the storage devices; they are block-level access, file-level access, and object-level access. Among these, object-based access mechanisms are prominently used by high-performance big data applications.

5.3.1   Block-Level Access

Block-level access mechanism is the typical data access mechanisms used in a SAN. In block-level access mechanism, data access is done in terms of blocks or chunks. The blocks are of fixed size, and it is typically 512 bytes in most of the scenarios. Block-level access of data is done by specifying linear block addresses which correspond to the location where the data is stored in the disk.

5.3.2   File-Level Access

In file-level access mechanism, data access is done in terms of files which are retrieved by specifying their name and path. This method is most commonly used for accessing files from file servers. File servers provide a shared storage infrastructure which can be accessed using an IP network. These file servers are referred to as network-attached storage (NAS). More details of NAS will be covered in the latter half of this chapter.

5.3.3   Object-Level Access

In object-level access mechanisms, data is accessed in terms of variable-sized chunks called objects. Each object is a container which holds data and its associated attributes. Object-based access mechanism is the preferred option for accessing unstructured data because of the following reasons:

- Immense scalability
- A flat address space instead of a hierarchical one which offers good performance
- Capability to store rich metadata associated with each object

One of the main features offered by object-based storage is the capability to provide rich metadata for each object which is stored in it. This metadata facilitates efficient data manipulation and management especially of unstructured data. The following figure shows a sample of the amount of metadata which can be attached to an object in an object-based storage system:

Picture properties   More

Type: JPEG Image
Dimensions: 3264 x 2448 pixels
Size: 3.42 MB
Modified: 11/3/2012 6:30:38 PM
Location: C:\Documents and Setting
Description:

Camera properties   More

Camera Model: iPhone 4S
Date Taken: 10/28/2012 8:43:13 AM

Data in object-based storage devices are manipulated using commands which include an object in its entirety. For example, some examples of commands used in object-based storage devices are create, delete, put, and so on. Each object is uniquely identified with the help of an identifier which is called object ID. Object ID is generated with the help of a 128 bit random number generator, and this helps to ensure that object ID is unique. Other details about the object like location, size, etc., are stored in the form of metadata.

Data that is stored in object-based storage devices can be accessed using Web service APIs such as Representational State Transfer (REST) and Simple Object Access Protocol (SOAP). Some types of object-based storage devices also offer support for protocols like Hypertext Transfer Protocol (HTTP), XML, etc. Object-based--> storage devices incur very less overhead to perform concurrent read/writes, file locks, and permissions. This provides significant performance improvement and massive scaling capabilities to object-based storage devices. In addition to that, the amount of rich metadata associated with each object offers support to perform analytical operations very efficiently, and hence, object-based storage devices are ideal candidates for storing data which is generated/used by high-performance big data applications. In the next section of this chapter, we will examine the storage infrastructure requirements for storing big data.

5.4   Storage Infrastructure Requirements for Storing Big Data

Big data comprises of huge volumes of constantly changing data which come in from a variety of sources and will be a mix of structured and unstructured data. The key objective of using big data is to derive actionable insights by performing analytical operations. Because of the peculiar nature of big data, the storage infrastructure which is used for storing big data should have some unique features which will make them suitable for handling big data. The unique features are:

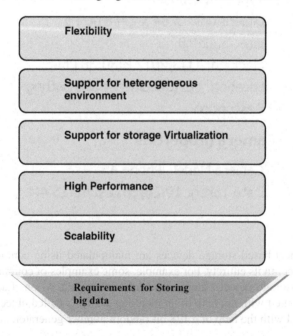

Flexibility: They should have the capability to store diverse types and formats of data. This is mainly to accommodate 3 Vs of big data, namely, volume, velocity, and variety.

Support for Heterogeneous Environment: They should have application servers which have the capability to access files from LAN or SAN. This will help them to access data from a variety of sources without any additional configuration changes.

Support for Storage Virtualization: Storagevirtualization is a technique which helps to manage storage resources efficiently. It provides the capability to aggregate heterogeneous types of storage devices and manage them as a single unit. This will be very helpful to allocate storage resources according to the constantly changing storage requirements of big data applications.

High Performance: One of the key requirements of big data applications is that many of them require real-time or near real-time responses for their operation. In order to support this requirement, the storage infrastructures should have high-speed data processing capabilities.

Scalability: They should be able to scale quickly as per the requirements of big data applications.

In the next section, we will analyze the various types of storage area networking technologies, and we will also map their suitability for big data applications.

5.4.1 Chapter Organization

The organization of the chapter is as follows. The first part provides a general explanation of the various storage area networking technologies. Their suitability for storing big data is also analyzed. In the second part of the chapter, we examine the most preferred storage options for big data.

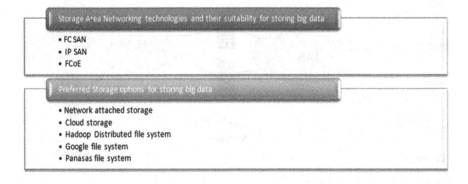

5.5   Fiber Channel Storage Area Network (FC SAN)

FC SAN is one of the most preferred storage area networking technologies which uses Fiber Channel Protocol (FCP) for high-speed data transmission. Storage area networking in simple terms refers to FC SAN. The high-level architecture of an FC SAN is depicted in the diagram which is given below:

Note: Please note that several variants of this architecture are possible (Fig. 5.2). The main components of an FC SAN are:

- Clients
- Storage devices/storage arrays which support FC protocol
- Fabric which facilitates transmission
- Switches/routers
- Host bus adapter which connects the application servers or host systems to storage devices

FC SAN uses block-level access mechanisms to access data from the storage devices. They offer excellent performance by providing very high data transmission speeds. Most recent versions of FC SAN offer data transfer speeds of up to 16 Gb/s. FC SAN architecture is highly scalable. The key concern with FC SAN is the fact that the cost to set up infrastructure is very high as FC SAN requires its custom set of cables, connectors, and switches.

The high infrastructure cost involved in setting up the FC network and its inability to support file-level access are the two major factors which have blocked their adoption by big data applications. Nowadays, the cost of 10Gb Ethernet and other IP-based technologies is far less when compared to FC technology.

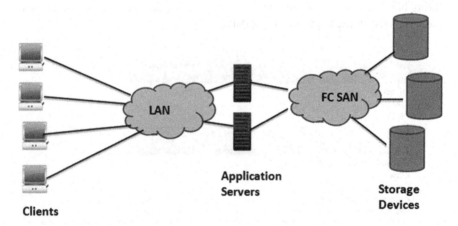

Fig. 5.2 Architecture of FC SAN

5.6   Internet Protocol Storage Area Network (IP SAN)

An IP SAN network is also referred to as iSCSI (SCSI over IP). In this network, storage devices are accessed over a TCP/IP-based network using SCSI commands. Ethernet is the physical media which is used for data transmission. Ethernet is a cost-effective option which makes IP SAN more popular when compared to FC SAN. Data in an IP SAN is also accessed by using block-level access mechanisms. The high-level overview architecture of IP SAN is depicted in the diagram given below (Fig. 5.3).

iSCSI is definitely a preferred technology choice for big data storage because of the following reasons:

• It uses 1/10 Gigabit Ethernet transport, which significantly reduces the network complexity.
• Less cost when compared to FC SAN.
• Offers more flexibility as it provides option to leverage the existing IP infrastructure.
• Offers excellent performance as there are several iSCSI-supported storage arrays which are capable of providing millions of iSCSI IOPS to handle the huge performance requirements of big data applications.

But the main disadvantages of choosing iSCSI for big data are its inability to support file-level access.

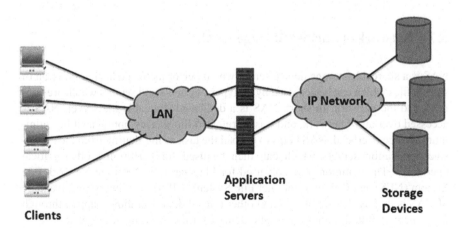

Fig. 5.3 Architecture of IP SAN

5.6.1   Fiber Channel Over Ethernet (FCoE)

The FCoE technology allows encapsulation and transmission of Fiber Channel frames over the conventional Ethernet network without using the Ethernet default forwarding scheme. This feature of FCoE allows transmission of SAN traffic and Ethernet traffic using a common 10 Gigabit network infrastructure. This allows organizations to perform consolidation of their LAN and SAN over the same network infrastructure. FCoE also allows organizations to cut down their infrastructure cost by reducing the number of cables, network interface cards (NICs), and switches. The main component of FCoE infrastructure is the FCoE switch which does the separation of LAN and SAN traffic.

FCoE is not a preferred technology for big data applications because of the following reasons:

- For FCoE to work properly, it is essential to ensure that storage traffic is fully separated from the LAN traffic. This is not a possibility in the case of big datastorage applications because of the unpredicted and huge amounts of data that needs to be stored and retrieved frequently.
- There should be some strong error detection and recovery mechanism in order to ensure that no storage packets are dropped during transmission. This is mainly due to the fact that Fiber Channel Protocol is slow in recovering from packet errors. This is also another consideration which has practical implementation difficulties.

5.7   Network-Attached Storage (NAS)

NAS is a shareable storage device/server which performs the dedicated function of storing files which can be accessed by all types of clients and servers which are connected to the network. In short, NAS is a dedicated shareable file server. NAS is accessed over an IP network, and it is a preferred file sharing option as it has minimum storage overhead. NAS helps to offload the task of file sharing from the expensive application servers which can then be used for performing other critical operations. The common protocols used for file sharing in NAS are Network File System (NFS) and Common Internet File System (CIFS). One major disadvantage of NAS is that as sharing of files and other related data operations happen through the same network, it often creates a bottleneck for the performance of NAS.

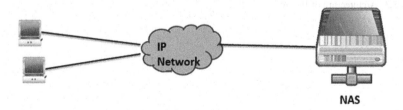

NAS

Nowadays, a variant of NAS called *scale-out NAS* is emerging as a popular storage option for big data application. Scale-out NAS provides an extremely scalable architecture in which the disk space can be expanded as per the requirement, by adding new disk drives from other storage disk arrays or other storage devices. This scalability feature of scale-out NAS makes it a preferred file storage option for big data applications. Scale-out NAS is also called clustered NAS. Another feature of scale-out NAS is that even if additional storage resources are added, they can all be managed as a single resource which offers a great deal of flexibility for the organizations.

To summarize, the following features of scale-out NAS make it a preferred big datastorage option for many organizations:

- Scalability: It is possible to add additional storage nondisruptively as per the requirements. This offers a lot of cost benefits for the organizations and also helps in storage consolidation.
- Improved Flexibility: It is compatible and can be accessed by clients and servers which are running on both UNIX and Windows platforms.
- High Performance: The use of 10Gb Ethernet media for data transfer offers high data transfer rates and improved performance.

Some of the prominent scale-out NAS storage providers in the market are EMC Isilon, IBM Scale-Out Network-Attached Storage (SONAS), and NetApp NAS.

5.8 Popular File Systems Used for High-Performance Big Data Analytics

In this section, we will discuss some of the popular file systems which are used by high-performancebig data analytical applications. Some of the prominent file systems are:

- Google File System (GFS)
- Hadoop Distributed File System (HDFS)
- Panasas file system

5.8.1 Google File System (GFS)

Some of the key characteristics of GFS which make it a preferred choice for high-performancebig data applications are the following:

- It has the capacity to store large number of files which are of huge size. The smallest file size which can be stored in GFS is assumed to be 1GB. This file system is optimized to store and process huge number of big files which is typically the characteristic of data which is generated and used by high-performancebig data analytical applications.

- GFS is made up of large number of commodity server components which are deployed in a clustered mode and are highly scalable. At present, some of the current deployments have over 1000 storage nodes, with over 300 TB of disk space. These deployments are very robust and highly scalable and are heavily accessed by hundreds of clients on a continuous basis. In addition to this, GFS has a fault-tolerant architecture.
- GFS has in-memory architecture which is best suited and used by majority of high-performance big data analytical applications.

The architecture of GFS is depicted in the diagram which is given below:

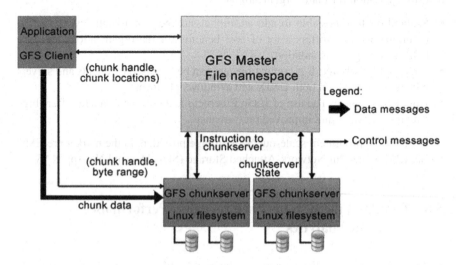

The key components of the architecture are the following:

- GFS master
- GFS chunkserver
- GFS clients which access the data from the file system

GFS architecture has a master-slave configuration with a single GFS master server and many chunkservers which in turn can be accessed by multiple clients as depicted in the diagram. Each chunkserver typically has Linux operating system with a user-level server process running on it. It is also possible to run chunkserver and GFS client run on the same server if the machine has the necessary configuration to support both the components.

Files are stored in GFS in the form of fixed-size chunks. Each chunk is identified using a unique 64 bit identifier which is also known as a chunk handle. This chunk handle is assigned to each chunk by the GFS master at the time of its creation.

The chunks are stored in local disks of the chunkservers in the form of Linux files. Each Linux file or chunk will have a chunk handle and byte range assigned to it. Each chunk at the time of storage is replicated and stored in multiple chunkservers which provides enhanced reliability to the data stored in the GFS. The default number of replicas which are created for each file is 3. However, there are also provisions to define different replication levels for different types of files as per the requirements.

GFS master stores the metadata information of file system. The metadata parameters which are stored by GFS master are the following:

- Namespace
- Access control information
- Mapping of files to chunks
- Current location of chunks

GFS master also performs the following chunk management aspects:

- Garbage collection of orphaned chunks
- Migration of chunks between chunkservers
- Chunk lease management

GFS is always deployed in a clustered configuration. Hence, it is necessary to periodically monitor the health of the various chunkservers. This task is done by GFS master by exchanging heartbeat messages with the chunkservers.

GFS clients from each application use the GFS file system API to communicate with the GFS master and chunkservers. GFS clients interact with GFS master only for metadata-related operations. All other types of file operations are performed by the GFS clients by interacting with chunkservers. Caching is not supported by the GFS clients and chunkservers. This is mainly to avoid the performance bottlenecks which are caused due to caching of huge files.

When a GFS client wants to access a file, the client will place a request to the master server. The master server will search and retrieve the file name associated with the location of that particular chunk. The chunk is later retrieved by the client system by going to the chunk location in the respective chunkserver. The security and access permissions are maintained by the master server. When a client places a request to a master server, the master server guides the client to the primary copy of the chunk, and it will also ensure that all other replicas of this chunk are not updated during this time period. After the modification of the primary chunk is complete, it is passed on to other replicas. The role of the master server can cause a bottleneck in this entire architecture, and the failure can also cause failure of the entire file system.

5.8.2 Hadoop Distributed File System (HDFS)

Apache™ Hadoop® is an open-source software platform which enables distributed processing of huge data sets across server clusters. It has massive scalability and can scale up from a single server to thousands of servers. Apache Hadoop has two main components; they are:

- Map Reduce—It is a framework that has the capability to understand and distribute work to various nodes that are a part of the Hadoop cluster.
- Hadoop Distributed File System (HDFS)—It is a file system that is spread across all the nodes that form a part of the Hadoop cluster and is used for data storage. It connects the file systems on many local nodes and converts them into one big file system.

5.8.2.1 Why Hadoop for High-Performance Big Data Analytics?

The following are the characteristics of HDFS which make it suitable for high-performancebig data analytics:

- *Massive Scalability*—New nodes can be added nondisruptively, i.e., new nodes can be added without changing the existing data format and without altering the existing data loading mechanisms and applications.
- *Cost Effectiveness*—Hadoop provides big data processing capabilities to commodity servers. This in turn drastically reduces the cost per terabyte of storage for organizations. In short, Hadoop is a cost-effective storage option for all types of organizations.
- *Flexibility*—Hadoop does not have any schema structure. This helps Hadoop to store and process all types of data whether it is structured or unstructured, from diverse types of data sources. This feature of Hadoop allows joining and aggregation of data from many sources which in turn facilitate deeper data analyses and better outcomes.
- *Fault Tolerance*—When a node in the cluster fails, the system redirects work to another location of the data and continues processing without any drop in performance.

5.8.2.2 Architecture of HDFS

HDFS has a massively scalable and fault-tolerant architecture. The main components of the architecture are NameNode and DataNode. These nodes work in a master-slave configuration. There is typically one NameNode per cluster, and it acts as the master and performs the following actions:

- Manages file system namespace
- Manages security and regulates access of files by the clients

Usually, there is a DataNode for every node present in the Hadoop cluster. These nodes keep track of the storage attached to the nodes. HDFS have a file system namespace, and data is stored and retrieved in terms of files. These files may be stored internally as a collection of blocks. These blocks may be split across several DataNodes. All file system namespace-related operations are handled by the NameNodes. They also keep track of the mapping of blocks to DataNodes. The DataNodes are responsible for performing read and write operations based on the client requests.

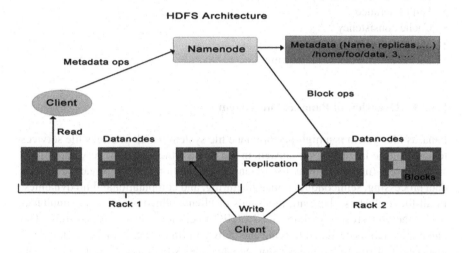

5.8.2.3   Architecture of HDFS

The main reason for the massive scalability of HDFS is the fact that the namespace and data are stored separately. Usually, metadata operations are very fast, whereas data access and transfer operations will take a long time to complete. If both data and metadata operations are done through the same server, it will create a bottleneck on the server. In the HDFS architecture, metadata operations are handled by the NameNode, and data transfer operations are distributed among the data servers utilizing the throughput of the whole cluster.

5.8.3   Panasas

Panasas is a high-performance storage system which is available as a file system that can be accessed using a POSIX interface. Hence, it is prominently referred to as Panasas file system, and in this chapter also, it will be referred to as Panasas file systems.

Panasas is a high-performance distributed file system which is used by big data analytical applications. Panasas has a clustered design which provides scalable performance to multiple clients which are accessing the file system simultaneously. The features of Panasas file system which make it suitable for high-performance big data analytics are the following:

- Per-file client-driven RAID
- Object-based storage
- Parallel RAID rebuild
- Fault tolerance
- Cache consistency
- Massive scalability
- Distributed metadata management

5.8.3.1 Overview of Panasas File System

Panasas file system is a high-performance file system which provides file services to some of the largest server clusters in the world which perform very data-intensive and real-time operations like scientific calculations, space research, seismic data processing, semiconductor manufacturing, and computational fluid dynamics. In all these clusters, there are thousands of clients which access data simultaneously, thereby creating a huge load of I/O operations on the file system. The Panasas system is designed to scale and deliver optimum performance in huge I/O load, and it also offers massive storage capacities which are in the range of petabytes or even more.

The Panasas file system is built using object storage technology and uses object-based storage devices for data storage. An object in Panasas file system contains both data and attributes packaged into a single container. It is very much similar to the concept of inode which is used in UNIX file system.

The key components of Panasas storage cluster are storage nodes and manager nodes. The default ratio of manager nodes to storage node is 1:10, though it is configurable as per requirements. The storage nodes have object stores which are accessed by the file system clients to perform I/O operations. These object stores are implemented on object-based storage devices. The manager nodes manage various aspects of the storage cluster. The functions of manager node are explained in detail later.

Each file is striped over two or more objects to provide redundancy and high-bandwidth access. The file system semantics are implemented by metadata managers that mediate access to objects from clients of the file system. The clients access the object storage using the iSCSI/OSD protocol for read and write operations. The I/O operations proceed directly and in parallel to the storage nodes, bypassing the metadata managers. The clients interact with the out-of-band metadata managers via RPC to obtain access capabilities and location information for the objects that store files.

Object attributes are used to store file-level attributes, and directories are implemented with objects that store name to object ID mappings. Thus, the file system metadata is kept in the object store itself, rather than being kept in a separate database or some other form of storage on the metadata nodes.

The main components of the Panasas file system are depicted in the diagram which is given below:

Activity

Open your desktop/laptop, and list down some live examples of Panasas file system implementation. Focus more on examples in scientific/research domain. Do a deep dive on the features of Panasas which are making it suitable for such implementations. Make a list in the space which is provided below:

1. ....
2. ....
3. ....

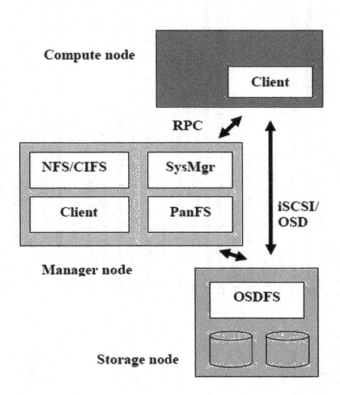

The role of different components of Panasas system is summarized in the table which is given below:

Panasas component	Description
Client	The Panasas client is available in the form of an installable kernel module. The client runs inside a Linux kernel. The client uses the standard VFS interface for its implementation. The host systems which have the Panasas client use a POSIX interface to connect to storage systems
Storage node	Each storage cluster node runs on a FreeBSD-based Linux platform. Each storage node has additional functions to perform the following services:
	Hardware monitoring
	Configuration management
	Overall control
	The storage node uses an object-based storage file system which is called object-based storage device file system (OSDFS). OSDFS is accessed as an iSCSI target, and it uses OSD command set for its operations. OSDFS mainly performs file management functions. Some of the additional functions performed by OSDFS:
	Ensures efficient disk arm utilization
	Media management
	Object-based storage device (OSD) interface management
SysMgr (cluster manager)	It maintains the global configuration and controls other services and nodes which are a part of the Panasas storage cluster. It has an application which provides both CLI and GUI. The key functions which are performed by the cluster manager are the following:
	Membership management of storage clusters
	Configuration management
	Fault detection
	Management of system operations like system restart, updates, etc.
Panasas metadata manager (PanFS)	It manages striping of data across object-based storage devices. PanFS runs on every cluster manager node as a user-level application. It performs the following distributed file system functions:
	Secure multiuser access
	Maintain consistency of file and object-level metadata
	Recovery from client, storage node, and metadata server crashes
NFS/CIFS services	They are used to provide Panasas file system access to clients which are unable to use the Linux file system installable client. CIFS is a user-level service which is based on Samba. NFS service makes use of tuned version of the standard FreeBSD and runs as a kernel-level process

Now It Is Activity Time Again

Match the items on column A correctly to the options which are listed under column B.

Column A	Column B
1. Cluster manager	(a) Manages striping of data
2. PanFS	(b) Maintains global configuration
3. Storage node	(c) Hardware monitoring

5.8.3.2   Storage Management in Panasas

Client systems which access Panasas have a single mount point through which they can access the entire system. Client systems can learn about the location of metadata service instances in cluster manager with the help of the /etc./fstab file. It is possible for a storage administrator to add new storage to the storage pool of Panasas nondisruptively. In addition to this, Panasas also has automatic storage discovery capabilities embedded in it.

In order to understand storage management in Panasas, it is necessary for you to understand two basic storage terms in the context of Panasas: BladeSet which is a physical storage pool and volume which is a logical quota tree. BladeSet refers to collection of StorageBlade modules which form part of the RAID fault domain. A BladeSet also marks the physical boundary for the volumes which are present in it. It is possible to expand the BladeSet any time either by StorageBlade modules or by combining multiple BladeSets together.

Volume refers to directory hierarchy and has a quota assigned to the particular BladeSet to which it belongs. Value of quota assigned to a volume can be changed any time. However, capacity is not allocated to a volume until it is used. This leads to competition between multiple volumes for space within their BladeSet which in turn will grow in size as per the demand. Volumes appear as directories in the file system namespace below the single mount point for the entire Panasas file system. It is not necessary to update mount points to Panasas file system when new volumes are added, deleted, or updated. Each volume is tracked and managed by a single metadata manager. The file system error recovery check is done independently on each volume, and errors on one volume do not disrupt the functioning of other volumes.

5.8.4   Luster File System

Luster high-performance parallel file system is the most prominent file system which is used by seven of the top 10 high-performance computing (HPC) systems on the international top 500 list. Luster is a Linux-based system, and it uses kernel-based server modules to deliver high-performance as per the requirements of HPC applications. Luster has an extremely flexible architecture which has the capability to support diverse types of clients and can run on almost any type of present-day hardware. Scalability is the key value-added feature offered by Luster and can be used to create a single namespace which can offer almost limitless capacity. Luster has widespread usage in diverse domains which use super-computers to fulfill their high-performance requirements. For example, one of the world's largest Luster installations is expected to begin at the German Climate Computing Centre in Hamburg, called DKRZ5, in 2015. This Luster installation requires the use of over 4B files.

Some of the key features of Luster are summarized in the table which is given below:

Luster features	Theoretical limits	Actual achieved production limits as of June 2014
Size of file system	512 PB	55 PB
Number of files	4 billion	Approximately 2 billion
Size of single file	2.5 PB	100 TB
Aggregate performance	7 TB/s	1.1 TB/s
No. of clients	>100,000	Approximately 50,000

5.8.4.1   Architecture of Luster File System

The different architectural components of Luster file systems and their features are summarized in the table which is given below:

Luster component	Functionality
Metadata Server (MDS)	Manages the metadata operations of the file system
Metadata Target (MDT)	Storage where the metadata information of all the files stored in the file system is maintained
Object Storage Target (OST)	This is the place where the actual data is stored. It is generally maintained as a RAID array
Object Storage Server (OSS)	These are the nodes which are responsible for managing I/O transfers of OSTs
LNET	This is the network layer which is responsible for abstracting the drives and other physical components from the file system
Luster client	Client which is used to access the file system
LNET router	A node used to do network fabric or address range translation between directly attached/remote clients and workstation resources

The architecture diagram of the Luster file system with all these components is summarized in the figure which is given below:

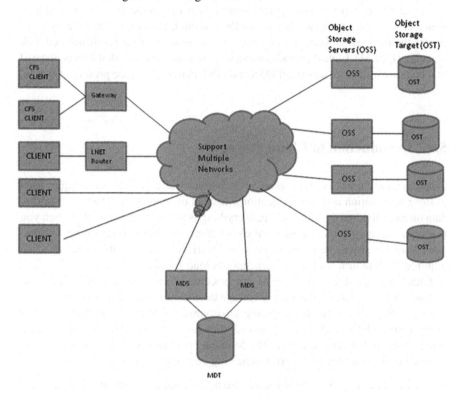

5.8.4.2 Working of Luster File System

Now let us look at the working of Luster file system. When a client system wants to issue a write operation to the file system, the file system first passes on the write request to the MDS component. MDS performs necessary user authentication checks and the intended location of the file. Based on the directory/file system settings, MDS responds back by providing a list of OSTs which can be used by the client to write the file. After the response from the MDS, the client interacts directly with the assigned OSTs and does not communicate with the MDS. This rule is applicable for all write operations irrespective of the file size. The mode of communication during write operation (if using InfiniBand) is done using remote direct memory access (RDMA) which offers excellent performance with minimum latency.

Luster file system is fully POSIX compliant. It has the capability to handle all transactions atomically. This means that requests for performing I/O operations are executed sequentially without any interruption in order to prevent conflicts. Data is not cached outside the client systems, and a file read or write acknowledgment is necessary to release the lock on the file system.

In order to achieve massive parallelism, Luster makes use of a distributed lock manager which has the capability to handle thousands of clients which are trying to access the file system. Each component runs an instance of Luster distributed lock manager (LDLM). LDLM provides a mechanism which ensures that data is updated in a consistent manner across all OSS and OST nodes which are present in the file system.

5.9   Introduction to Cloud Storage

Cloud computing has brought about a revolutionary change in the techniques used to store information and run applications. Instead of running programs and storing data on an individual desktop/laptop, everything is hosted in the "cloud." When you talk about accessing everything from cloud, there should be some storage mechanism also which will help you to store and retrieve data from the cloud as when required. This in turn leads to the concept of cloud storage.

Cloud storage does not refer to any specific storage device/technology, but instead refers to a large collection of storage devices and servers which are used for storing data within a cloud computing environment. Cloud storage users are not using a particular storage device; instead, they are using the cloud storage system using some kind of access service. The following parameters of cloud storage make it a preferred option for high-performance big data applications:

- Resource Pooling: Storage resources are maintained as a pool, and they are allocated instantaneously as per the demand.
- Capacity on Demand: From the storage pool, organizations can leverage storage resources as per the requirements of big data applications. There is no limit on the scalability as cloud infrastructure is highly elastic and scalable.
- Cost Effective: The ability to pay for the resources according to the usage provides significant economies of scale for organizations.

Note: The cloud storage architecture given below is not very specific to public or private cloud. It depicts the generic cloud storage architecture in any type of cloud. However, storage in private cloud is any day a preferred option because of the enhanced security it provides to the organization.

5.9.1   Architecture Model of a Cloud Storage System

The layered architecture of a cloud storage system is depicted in the diagram given below [2] (Fig. 5.4):

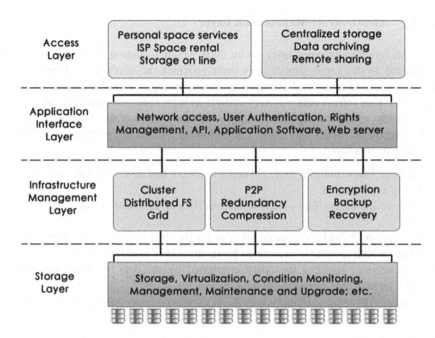

Fig. 5.4 Architecture of cloud-based storage

5.9.1.1 Storage Layer

Storage layer is the bottom most layer in the architecture of cloud storage which is given above. It contains different types of storage devices. Some example of storage devices in this layer could be:

- Fiber Channel storage devices
- IP storage devices such as NAS and iSCSI
- DAS storage devices such as SCSI
- Object-based storage devices

These storage devices may be present in geographically dispersed regions and connected to each other by means of some networking technology like Internet or wide area network (WAN). This layer has a unified storage management system which is capable of managing all these heterogeneous types of devices in a single storage pool and provisions them as per requirements in the form of a service like storage as a service or infrastructure as a service. The key underlying concept used in this layer is storage virtualization. This technology provides capabilities to manage heterogeneous storage devices with different performance levels as a single entity. Hence, the unified storage management activity which is performed in this layer can also be called as virtual storage management.

5.9.1.2   Infrastructure Management Layer

Infrastructure management layer is the layer which is present above the storage layer, and as the name implies, this layer provides the necessary infrastructure which is required for unified management of underlying storage devices in the storage layer. This infrastructure is very critical as it provides various vital functions like security, space management, backup, and storage consolidation using various techniques like clusters and grids. The following are the key services which are provided by this layer:

- Backup: Takes multiple copies in order to ensure that data stored in cloud is not lost in any situation.
- Disaster Recovery: Takes steps to recover data in the event of any kind of data loss
- Encryption: Provides enhanced security for the data by converting them into a format which cannot be interpreted by an attacker or malicious user
- Compression: Reduces the space consumed by the data by removing blank spaces which are present in the data
- Cluster: Aggregates multiple storage devices/servers to provide more storage capacity

5.9.1.3   Application Interface Layer

Application interface layer is used to provide various interfaces/APIs to support the cloud storage use cases which are provided/used by the organization. Some common examples of cloud storage use cases are data archive applications, backup applications, and so on. Different cloud storage service providers develop their own custom application interfaces as per the services offered by them.

5.9.1.4   Access Layer

Any authorized user who is registered to access the cloud services from the specific cloud service provider can login to the cloud storage system via a standard public application interface to use the required cloud storage service. Different cloud storage service providers use different types of access mechanisms. The access layer will have catalog which provides the pricing and other usage details and will also have the service level agreement details which are given by the specific service provider.

One of the important concepts which needs to be mentioned in this regard is the concept of cloud drive. Cloud drive acts as a gateway to access cloud storage which is provided by many vendors. The architecture of cloud drive is given in the figure below:

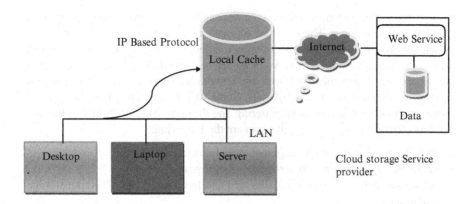

Cloud drive supports access to storage services offered by many leading cloud storage service providers including Microsoft Azure, Amazon S3 Amazon EC2, and EMC Atmos. Cloud drive masks the complexity of the underlying storage devices and allows the end user to access cloud storage like a local storage. Computers are connected to the LAN access data which is stored on cloud drive using some IP-based protocol. The cloud drive service communicates using Internet connection with the cloud storage service provider. Whenever data generated increases, cloud drive service starts moving data to the storage infrastructure of cloud storage service provider. If the data that is requested by the user is available in the local cache of the cloud drive, it will provide a significant performance improvement.

One of the most important requirements of any cloud storage system is that it should allow sharing of data between various heterogeneous commercial applications. In order to ensure smooth sharing of data among these applications, it is important to implement multilevel locking mechanisms for data. Another important aspect to be kept in mind is that cache consistency should be ensured in order to maintain consistent copies of the same data.

Apart from all these, the most important feature in the storage layer of cloud storage architecture is storage virtualization. Storage virtualization is the technology which is at the core of the cloud storage architecture. The concept of storage virtualization is explained in the next section.

5.9.2 Storage Virtualization

Storage virtualization is a mechanism to ensure that different heterogeneous types of storage devices are stored and managed as a single unit. This in turn will enable unified storage management, easier deployment, and integrated monitoring of entire storage infrastructure. Storage virtualization mainly involves splitting the available storage into virtual volumes. Virtual volumes can be created by combining different types of storage devices. These virtual volumes are then presented to the operating system as storage devices after abstracting the details of the storage devices which are present in that volume. Virtual volumes can be expanded, created, and deleted as per the storage requirements without any downtime. There are various techniques used in the creation of virtual volumes. Some of the most commonly used techniques in cloud storage are storage tiering and thin provisioning. Some of the key benefits offered by storage virtualization are the following:

- Provides unified storage management capabilities
- Facilitates aggregation of heterogeneous storage devices
- Allows storage resources to be allocated and freed as per the changing storage requirements
- Provides scalability to the storage infrastructure

5.9.2.1   Thin Provisioning

One of the major challenges faced by the present-day organizations is that most of the storage capacities allocated to various applications remain unused, and this turns out to be an expensive affair for the organizations. Majority of such situations arise due to over provisioning of storage needs. In some cases, this situation also arises due to upfront investment on storage capacity, though it may be changed later on. Let us consider a scenario to understand this situation better. It is estimated that the archival requirements of an ABC organization need approximately 50 TB of storage over a 2-year period with an average usage of 12.5 TB once in every 6 months. In most of the situations, the organization will purchase 50 TB of storage upfront and then plan to use it over the 2-year period. Imagine the cost invested by the organization upfront, though more than 50 % of the storage will be used only in the next year. Apart from the initial capital expenditure, the following are the other hidden costs involved in unused storage capacity management:

- Energy Wastage: The unused storage consumes power and generates heat which will add on to the power consumption requirements. This will also violate the "go green" policy which is adopted by most of the organizations.
- Floor Space: The unused storage devices will consume unnecessary floor space which could have been allocated otherwise to other useful infrastructure components.

It is also possible that the predicted storage needs of the archival application considered in the above example may drastically reduce due to various unanticipated factors. In such a situation, what happens to the amount invested in procuring the storage capacity? Situations like this are quite common across organizations. In order to tackle all such situations, virtual provisioning or thin provisioning comes as a lifesaver.

Virtual provisioning refers to the provisioning of storage as per the actual need. In this technique, logical storage is allocated to applications based on the anticipated requirements. Actual storage allocated is much lesser than the logical storage and is based on the current need of the applications. Whenever the storage need of the application increases, the storage is allocated to the applications from a common pool of storage. In this manner, thin provisioning provides efficient utilization of storage and reduces the waste due to unused physical storage. The concept of thin provisioning is depicted in the figure given below. In the example given below, application 1's anticipated storage requirement is 1 GB; however, it is allocated only 50 MB of storage as per the current requirements of the application. More storage will be given to the application as and when it needs it (the total available storage capacity is 5 GB) (Fig. 5.5).

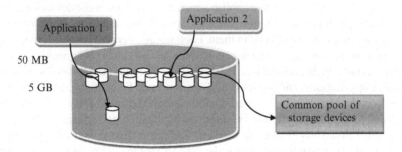

Fig. 5.5 Virtual provisioning

Activity for You

Based on the concept of virtual provisioning, how can the ABC organization described in the above example optimize their archival storage costs?

Interesting Fact About Virtual Provisioning
One example of virtual provisioning technique which is used in cloud storage is the concept of *ephemeral storage*. In ephemeral storage, storage allocated to a virtual machine instance exists only till the time of existence of the virtual machine instance. When the virtual machine instance is deleted, the storage gets destroyed along with it. In contrast to this concept, *persistent storage* is a form of storage which continues to exist even if the virtual machine instance with which it is associated currently is not being used or deleted. This allows persistent storage to be reused across virtual machine instances.

5.9.2.2   Storage Tiering

Let us consider the example of the ABC organization which was used to describe virtual provisioning concept. Imagine that the organization has purchased a mix of storage devices which offer varying performance, cost, etc. Applications like archival require only low-cost, low-performance storage devices. However, there will be other real-time applications which will require quick access to data which in turn is dependent on the number of input/output operations supported by the storage device. It would have been so helpful for the organization if there was a way to allocate storage as per the performance requirements of the various applications. In short, organizations require techniques that enable them to store the right data in the right type of storage device so that they can be made available at the correct point in time to the various applications. Storage tiering is a technique which provides this capability. It is a mechanism to establish a hierarchy/tier of storage devices and then store data in them based on performance and availability requirements of the application which uses the data stored in them. Each storage tier will have different levels of protection, performance, data access frequency, cost, and other considerations.

For example, high-performance FC drives may be configured as tier 1 storage for real-time applications, and low-cost SATA drives may be configured as tier 2 storage to keep less frequently accessed data like archival data. Moving the active data (frequently used data) to flash or FC improves application performance, while moving inactive data (less frequently used) to SATA can free up storage capacity in high-performance drives and reduce the cost of storage. This movement of data happens based on predefined policies. The policy may be based on parameters such as file type, frequency of access, performance, etc., and can be configured by the storage administrators. An example of storage tiering is depicted in the diagram which is given below:

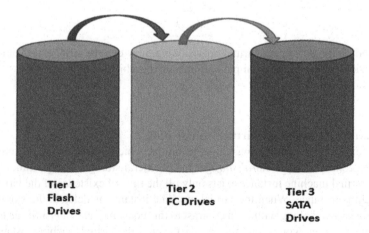

5.9.3   Storage Optimization Techniques Used in Cloud Storage

In this section, we will examine the various storage optimization techniques which are used in cloud storage. The two commonly used techniques are deduplication and compression:

- Deduplication: It is a technique to ensure that duplication of data is not present in the storage system or in other words ensure that no duplicate copies of data are stored in the system. This technique will drastically reduce the storage requirements. Deduplication works with the help of a hashing method. This hashing method is used to generate a unique hash value for each file based on the contents of the file. Each time a new file reaches the storage system, the deduplication software generates a hash value for the file and compares it with the existing set of hash values. If there is a matching hash value, it indicates that the same file is already stored in the system and will not be stored again. If there is a minimal change between the new version of the file and the file which is present in the system, the delta or difference is updated to the file stored in the system instead of storing the entire file. The process of deduplication is depicted in the diagram which is given below:

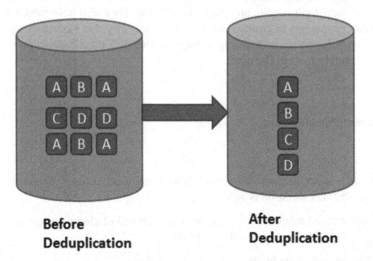

Before Deduplication

After Deduplication

Deduplication can be performed at two levels: file level and block level. File-level deduplication is done on the files, and it ensures that only a single copy of each file exists in the system. In block-level deduplication, the deduplication file is split into blocks, and the software ensures that only a single copy of the file is stored in each block. Identical files or blocks are detected by comparing the generated hash value with a preexisting list of hash values for files or blocks.

- Compression: Compression reduces the amount of data by removing the blank spaces which are present in the data. A major drawback of compression technique is that it consumes computing cycles. This in turn may cause performance concerns to users of storage services as transmission of data to the cloud is a continuous process.

5.9.4   Advantages of Cloud Storage

Storage technologies like storage area networks (SANs) and network-attached storage (NAS) provide benefits like high performance, high availability, and high accessibility using industry standard interfaces. However, these storage systems have many drawbacks:

- They are very costly.
- They have limited life.
- They require backup and recovery systems to ensure that data is fully protected.
- These technologies operate only under specific environmental conditions.
- They require storage personnel to manage them.
- They consume considerable amount of power for their functioning and cooling.

Cloud data storage providers provide cheap and unlimited data storage which can be used as per the requirements. Cloud storage can be accessed via the Internet or wide area network (WAN). Economies of scale enable providers to supply data storage cheaper than the equivalent electronic data storage devices/technologies [1]. Cloud storage is much cheaper when compared to other conventional storage systems, and they don't require any maintenance cost. They also have inbuilt backup and recovery systems to ensure data protection, and they don't consume any additional energy for power and cooling as they run on the cloud infrastructure which is hosted remotely most of the times.

Thought for the Brain

John Doe has a question in his mind, and he approaches his professor to get an answer. The question is as follows:

Is object-based storage the preferred storage choice of cloud storage service providers? If so, what are the reasons?

The answer given by the professor is as follows:

Yes it is the preferred choice of most of the cloud storage service providers because of the following reasons:

- They provide unlimited and highly scalable storage with multi-tenancy features.
- They have a scale-out architecture which can be accessed using Web interfaces like HTTP and REST.
- They have single flat namespace, location-independent addressing, and auto-configuring features.

5.10   Conclusions

In the first part of the chapter, various existing storage area networking technologies and their suitability for storing big data were discussed in detail. The advantages and disadvantages of each of the storage technology were analyzed. In the second half of the chapter, key focus was on storage technologies which were used for high-performance big data analytics. The concept of cloud storage and techniques which are deployed for cloud storage optimization was discussed in detail. The various popular file systems which were used for storing big data were also discussed in detail in this chapter.

5.11   Exercises

1. Describe the evolution of storage technologies.
2. Write short notes on the following topics:

    (a) Object-based storage
    (b) Limitations of DAS

3. Explain the two different types of storage area networking technologies.
4. Explain the features of NAS which make them suitable for big data storage.
5. Explain the layered architecture of cloud storage.
6. Explain deduplication technology and the benefits they offer to cloud storage.

References

1. Advantages of cloud data storage (2013) Retrieved from Borthakur D (2007) Architecture of HDFS. Retrieved from http://hadoop.apache.org/docs/r0.18.0/hdfs_design.pdf
2. Zhang Jian-Hua, Zhang Nan (2011) Cloud computing-based data storage and disaster recovery. In: International conference on future computer science and education, pp. 629–632. doi:http://doi.ieeecomputersociety.org/10.1109/ICFCSE.2011.157

Further Reading

Connel M (2013) Object storage systems: the underpinning of cloud and big-data initiatives. Retrieved from http://www.snia.org/sites/default/education/tutorials/2013/spring/stor/MarkOConnell_Object_Storage_As_Cloud_Foundation.pdf

Davenport TH, Siegel E (2013) Predictive analytics: the power to predict who will click, but, lie, or die [Hardcover]. Wiley, Hoboken. ISBN-13: 978–1118356852

IBM corporation (2014) What is hadoop? Retrieved from http://www-01.ibm.com/software/data/infosphere/hadoop/

Minelli M, Chambers M, Dhiraj A (2013) Big data, big analytics: emerging business intelligence and analytic trends for today's businesses [Hardcover]. Wiley (Wiley CIO), Hoboken

Chapter 6
Real-Time Analytics Using High-Performance Computing

6.1 Introduction

Real-time analytics is about using data and material when they are actually required. It is about aggressive analysis based on the data that is created in real time. It refers to analyzing data that can be accessed as and when they are fed into a system. A very practical example would be managing committee viewing orders done online as soon as a customer books an order. The benefit is that tracking becomes easy as real-time data can be accessed.

In this chapter, we will get into details about real-time analytics and how high-performance computing aids real-time analytics.

6.2 Technologies That Support Real-Time Analytics

There are a lot of technologies that support real-time analytics. Let's see a few of them in detail in the below section.

6.2.1 Processing in Memory (PIM)

Here, a processor is integrated into the memory chip. Processing-In-Memory ensures that partitioned data is scalable and also supports ultrafast data access. This ensures high support transactions and assures best consistency. It also supports various complex data models.

Below let's see a performance model created by XAP which ensures super performance and low latency using XAP in-memory data grid caching technology.

© Springer International Publishing Switzerland 2015
P. Raj et al., *High-Performance Big-Data Analytics*, Computer Communications and Networks, DOI 10.1007/978-3-319-20744-5_6

Before getting into the architecture details, let's see the benefits that can be achieved by managing and scaling data using XAP.

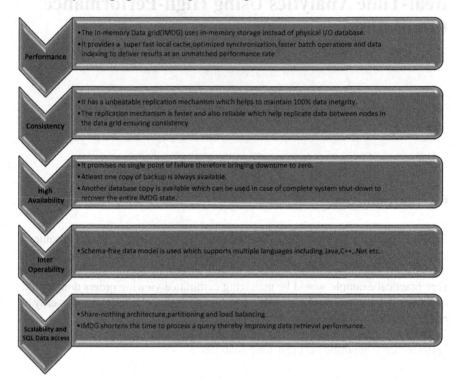

The IMDG has three deployment topologies:

All topologies mentioned below supports faster data processing and eliminates network overhead while accessing data. Regardless of the IMDG cluster deployment topology, a client can always run a near cache which allows to cache data locally within the process. This helps data to be reused without avoiding any remote access to the master data grid.

6.2.1.1   Fully Replicated

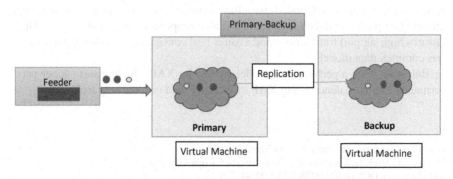

In this method, each member holds the complete data. Synchronous or asynchronous replication can be carried out.

6.2.1.2   Partitioned

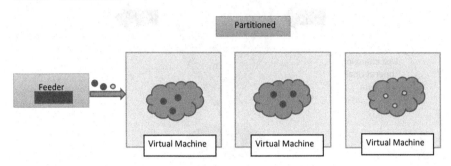

In this method, each node holds a different subset of data allowing different virtual machines to hold the entire data set. This is supported by multiple terabytes stored entirely in memory.

6.2.1.3   Partitioned + Backup

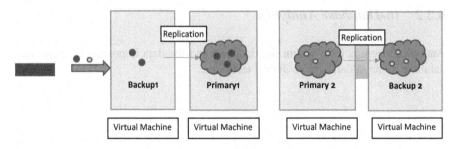

Here each node contains a different sub-portion of the data.

Real-Time Analytics Using Hadoop MapReduce

ScaleOut hServer V2

- The world's first Hadoop MapReduce engine integrated with a scalable, in-memory data grid.
- Full support for "live" fast-changing data.
- Faster and so can be used in e-commerce and management-related business applications.
- 20 times faster compared to other Apache models.
- Minimizes ease of use as installation is easy and does not take much time.
- Scale-out analytics server stores and analyzes "live" data.

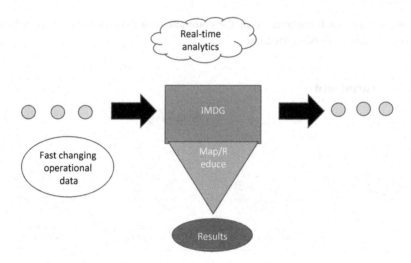

- In-memory data storage holds live data which are updated and accessed continuously.
- The analytical engine tracks important patterns and trends.
- The data-parallel approach delivers results in milliseconds to seconds.

6.2.2   In-Database Analytics

Analytical logic is built within the database and the data is processed inside the database in the in-database analytical technique.

In the traditional method, data is retrieved from the enterprise-level data warehouse and analytical operations are performed and the results are then sent to reporting tools like BusinessObjects and Excel applications.

Listed below are some limitations from the traditional method:

- Data retrieval from the data warehouse to the server takes more time as data increases exponentially.
- Cost of maintaining the server is high.
- The volume of data for running analytics depends on the volume of data that can be retrieved and stored in the server.
- Results obtained from analytics are not real time.
- Business users cannot run any analytics by changing any field or variable.

The in-database method solves all the above problems by eliminating the data extract as a separate process, and the server is a middle tier and it has an included redundant data storage which allows us to include analytics into the existing reporting tools so that the end users can run analytics when they require.

Did You Know?
Other technologies that support real-time analytics include:

- *Data warehouse applications*
- *In-memory analytics*
- *Massively parallel programming*

Activity Section

Activity No. 1:
Divide the class into three groups. Each group has to select one of the above technologies—data warehouse applications, in-memory analytics, and massively parallel processing—and create a presentation about the topic and present before the other groups. Working as a group is always fun!

6.3   MOA: Massive Online Analysis

MOA is used for data streaming and data clustering. It helps in running experiments and deploying algorithm by testing real-time data streams.

In today's real-time scenario, the rate at which data is generated is enormous. The data includes those coming from mobile apps, sensors, traffic management and network monitoring, log records, manufacturing products, call detail data, email, Facebook and Twitter post, etc. Here data that comes in arrives at high speed. MOA helps to deal with these kinds of new data types. Now let's see a typical data stream classification cycle.

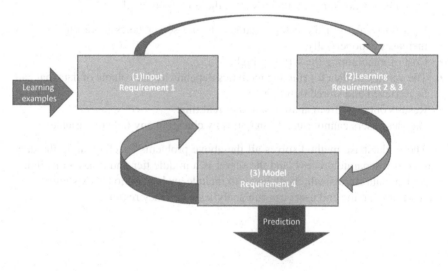

In the above figure:

Requirement 1 will process one query at a time and analyze the same only once.
Requirement 2 uses a reserved memory.
Requirement 3 works in a restricted time slot.
Requirement 4 is the prediction model to predict things at any time.

The above data streaming steps have few limitations.

MOA allows the evaluation of data stream learning algorithms in large stream and under unbound memory limits.

MOA allows the following features for stream clustering:

1. Data generators are available for the new data streams.
2. An extensive set of algorithms.
3. New evaluation techniques for stream clustering.
4. Analytical results can be visualized.

Activity Section

Activity No. 2:
Identify some of the data generators used for MOA and explain the same in details.

In the next session, we will discuss in detail about general parallel file system which is a widely used platform and we will also cover some use cases for the same.

6.4   General Parallel File System (GPFS)

For any system, file storage occupies a major share of the overall storage requirement. A huge increase of data in today's growing markets is forcing for innovative storage management approaches. Customers are not just looking for storage addition but are looking for a complete data management architecture solution that can address different forms of storage problems.

To address these file-based storage problems, the general parallel file system (GPFS) can be used which provides high performance, and the system is highly expandable for any future requirements. GPFS provides several options to deal with unstructured data. GPFS provides enterprise storage grids in the cloud environment which will be a mix of servers and storage.

GPFS has a TOKEN MANAGER which helps in coordinating with disks that are shared. The token manager controls the nodes and helps them to achieve direct access to data. A number of nodes can perform the role of a token manager for a sole file system preventing single points of failure.

In the next section, let us discuss about some of the use cases where GPFS is used and how it addresses customer problems related to file storage.

6.4.1   GPFS: Use Cases

GPFS has already been used in many global scientific applications starting from the online applications to manufacturing sectors.

Use Case for GPFS
1. Effectual load balancing for distributed systems
2. Data sharing for distributed area network
3. ILM
4. Disaster recovery (DR)
5. Hadoop MapReduce apps
6. Cloud application storage options
7. Smart data warehousing

The following section describes some common use cases of GPFS. Each of these use cases has a unique set of requirements related to scale, performance, data retention, access, availability, and capacity which can be effectively met using GPFS. In addition to the ones listed here, applications that need high-performance computing such as analytics, rendering, and sequencing also deploy and benefit from GPFS.

6.4.1.1   Effectual Load Balancing for Distributed Systems

GPFS was designed in such a way that by processes and nodes that are concurrently accessing a common data set, I/O workloads can be supported for read and write. Data is read and stored using the data striping technique where file data is distributed among several disk spaces. GPFS is used in real-time data applications that require massive storage and require real-time analytical capabilities.

In real-time media applications, the situation is that small storage units have to hold heavy loads during data processing. In order to handle such scenarios, different techniques such as file data striping (as we discussed previously), RAM caching, or file replication can be used. RAM caching can be cost effective only when running for large servers. Replication methods require additional space, and for cases where media has to be streamed, the load varies between different files and requires replication.

GPFS is an intelligent data balance system where data is shared parallel between nodes. It is very reliable and also expandable for any storage requirement which helps improve input-output processing.

Long-running jobs, for example, weather forecast/financial analysis, operate on a large number of separate blocks that run parallel. If one component fails, the job runtime is crashed and reduces application performance. By using GPFS, many existing problems are dealt with by storing and retrieving the application state back from a checkpoint in order to restart the failed node or replace it with a new one and restart the job from the last checkpoint. Also it is easy to add a new node to replace a failed node and restart the failed job from the last saved checkpoint. GPFS is designed not only for providing system scalability but is also highly available and reliable in large-scale storages with no single point of failure.

6.4.1.2   Data Sharing for Distributed Area Network

With the increase in data in all fields and sectors, the amount of data that is to be handled is extensively vast. Examples include data from different analytical platforms, healthcare, social networking sites and mobile applications, industries, and other market analysis. The huge amount of data looks for distributed storage methods for processing in these applications.

Example
In many real-time cases, data comes from multiple sites. For instance, let's consider the example of a healthcare industry where a health insurance company is required to provide a report for the state of New York, each state data being managed by different companies. So, different software organizations format the data collected from their internal systems required for the analysis. Each company provides data for one or more cities. Finally the data has to be collated to carry out the required analysis.

In the above example and manufacturing industry, previously the whole environment was divided into different partitions each having their own storage area, managed by different individual teams each having their own local policies. The technology used in each local partition was not able to expand itself for enterprise-level functions, and therefore the local team had to struggle in expanding their IT environments to meet the growing need.

One best example where GPFS has been used to share files across the globe is in DEISA, in Europe. DEISA is Distributed European Infrastructure for Supercomputing Applications. DEISA uses GPFS to distribute massive data across a WAN.

According to DEISA, their main storage objective was to:

1. Provide a globally effective file system that integrates heterogeneous architectures
2. Speed up system performance
3. Just like in a local file system, provide transparent access to data

6.4.1.3   Information Life Cycle Management

Information life cycle management is about managing information for a particular system and also storage systems. Information could be in any form including paper, images, videos, photographs, etc. ILM manages data protection, data backup, restoration of data, data archival, replication of data, and disaster recovery.

ILM is used by records and information management (RIM) to manage information which can be in any form as discussed above.

Efficiency of an information life cycle management (ILM) can be improved through GPFS through its automated storage management architecture.

The ILM tools that GPFS has can be used to automate the file management process. These tools can help determine where the user data can be stored physically irrespective of where it exists in the logical directory. GPFS helps use a common file system that is cost efficient. Data users can access their data without having to actually transfer the data. This saves cost and is also energy efficient as a lot of space and money can be saved in buying an additional disk space for storing all duplicate files. Data can be accessed in a parallel fashion which speeds up the time required to fetch a record.

Another advantage of GPFS is that the administrator can work with a zillion of files and also easily retrieve recently used files to create a backup strategy to store files.

ILM Tool Benefits

1. *Saves extra space and cost*
2. *Parallel accessing of files*

Now, let's talk about one of the use cases for ILM which is "improving database performance by data archiving."

Problem Statement

Today's main business problem is the amount of data that is generated which leads to very poor system performance. Though we do not use all this data every day, on the other hand unused data cannot be simply deleted as it is required for many analysis purposes and many other uses. Therefore, data has to be moved to another system from where it can be fetched when needed.

Problem Solution

ILM can help reduce the size of the database by archiving the data that is not used every day. ILM also ensures that the data that is archived is secure and can be fetched whenever required. The below diagram shows how the data archiving process works.

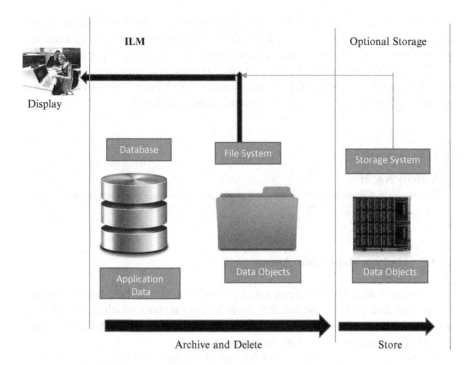

Benefits Realized
1. Reduction in database size with growth in data.
2. Backup and recovery takes less time.
3. Upgrade to new software is very fast and also easy.
4. Reduced cost.

6.4.1.4   Disaster Recovery (DR)

All companies and businesses dealing with real-time data need to make sure that
they have their policies set right to know what needs to be done during a failure, and
this is of utmost importance to them. GPFS has a number of features that help the
storage environments to withstand hardware failures. GPFS maintains a duplicate
file system at another location which at any point in time can be restored. The GPFS
cluster has three hardware sites which work together. Two hardware sites have

GPFS nodes that contain the replica of the file system. The third one has one single node which acts as a tiebreaker for the GPFS. When a network failure happens which disables the entire site operation, if the third site is still under operation, the system can be resumed using the duplicate file system that is maintained. If that also fails, the nodes lose access to GPFS. In such cases, GPFS has to be instructed manually to continue its operation with the resources that are available.

Activity Section

Activity No. 3:
Please look for more use cases of information life cycle management and explain the same in detail.

6.4.1.5 Hadoop MapReduce Apps

In the research area, GPFS is been used in many areas that include but not limited to real-time data analysis and InfoSphere. In all data analysis which is done in real time, data streaming happens first, and then data is analyzed when it becomes available. Here we concentrate on real-time streaming.

GPFS has an advanced feature which is called the shared-nothing cluster, and the architecture for the same is called as "GPFS-SNC." The additional feature here helps to have the system available at all times and also to provide better data replication.

In the architecture of GPFS-SNC, each node accesses a local storage network. The tasks get distributed between the individual systems that work independently. In a large financial organization, the risk is to analyze petabytes of data coming from different parts of the globe. Such critical applications require huge IT resource, and the cost involved is also very high. GPFS makes the analysis of these complex data efficient.

While using a Hadoop distributed file system, there are few limitations like files cannot be appended and no sections can be overwritten. GPFS helps system users to open, read, and append files and backup and archive files and allows data caching and data replication. The main feature of GPFS is its common file system which can be used by Hadoop MapReduce applications.

Hadoop	GPFS
1. Architecture based on master-slave technique	1. High-performance shared disk architecture
2. File locking not available	2. Distributed locking
3. Data striping—uniform-sized blocks	3. Data striping—multiple nodes
4. Write-once-read-many model	-1512305825.

Performance-wise, Hadoop and GPFS complement each other, whereas GPFS has outstanding data access patterns compared to Hadoop.

6.4.1.6   Cloud Application Storage Options

Cloud is the main reason for the tremendous increase in data in the world which offers infrastructure as a service. The amount of data in the world is said to rise almost 44 times as compared today on the next decade.

To meet the growing demand of data, many business organizations have started using cloud to meet their extreme demands. All these applications use the MapReduce technique where data is broken down into smaller parallel processes.

Some of the features of a cloud stack in a storage layer are:

1. *Scalability—can store up to petabytes of data*
2. *Reliability—can handle frequent failures occurring in large systems*
3. *Efficiency—can make the best use of network and disk resources*
4. *Lower cost—can maintain cloud computing at low cost*

Currently, cloud computing uses the normal Hadoop method or the Kosmos distributed file system to build the storage area. For cloud, using Lustre and GPFS is highly scalable and also less expensive. GPFS best suits cloud storage stack compared to Lustre.

Did You Know?
- *Lustre is a type of parallel distributed file system.*
- *They are mainly used for large-scale cluster computing.*
- *Lustre file systems have high-performance capabilities.*

  Source:http://en.wikipedia.org/wiki/Lustre_(file_system)

6.4.1.7 Smart Data Warehousing

Business analytics is more prominent in all business and organizations that want to use analytics in all their day-to-day work and to look for more innovation-based analytical techniques. The Smart Analytics System is designed to deliver faster analytical results on software that is already installed and configured to the server to add business value to their clients. The Smart Analytics System has a high-powered warehouse with exhaustive analytical options with an expandable environment.

For a data warehouse to run without any interruption or downtime, three important parameters are required—scalability, reliability, and availability. GPFS is an important feature of the Smart Analytics System which helps the system to be highly available even during a node failure. The system can be expanded so as to meet new business additions.

6.5 GPFS Client Case Studies

GPFS is used in many commercial applications where there is a great need for high-speed access to deal with huge volumes of data. Below, let's discuss few client use cases that use GPFS to support their organization's challenges.

6.5.1 Broadcasting Company: VRT

VRT is a broadcasting company which uses the traditional tape-based method which is considered to be an old method and also very slow. VRT used SAN switches to improve its audio and video content, but the system was not expandable. Along with these, other challenges that they faced include:

1. Dealing with the existing traditional architecture
2. Accessing and storing massive amounts of data
3. Dealing with compression-related issues

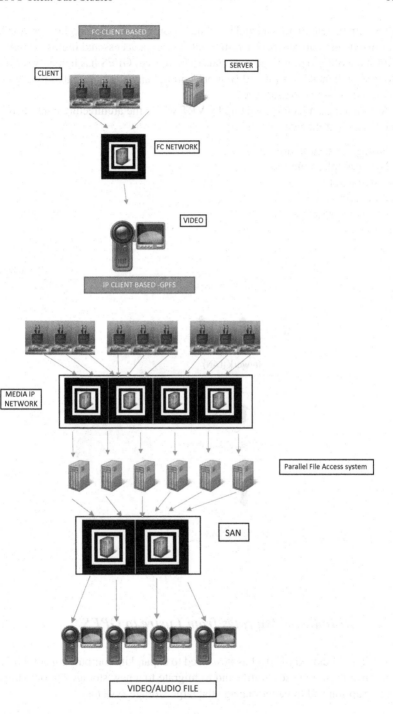

GPFS with its feature to read and write huge data content in a single operation helps minimize load. This allows for faster and easy data access and high scalability and enables the old programming materials to be reused. GPFS has helped VRT to capture new audiences at a rate 50 % more without any storage-related problems and parallel file system access issues.

A digital media factory is set up by VRT where the architecture consists of multiple layers that include:

1. Storage infrastructure
2. Network infrastructure
3. Data model
4. Production tools
5. Business process layer

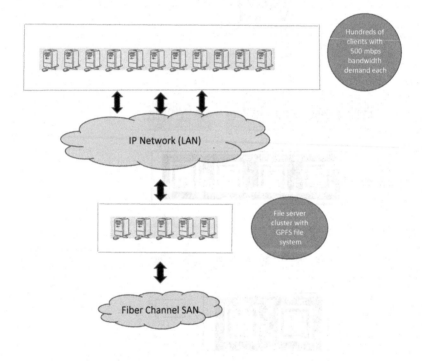

6.5.2   Oil Industry Migrates from Lustre to GPFS

An oil and gas industry had a business need to expand its compute capacity by 10 % to improve its storage scalability and to migrate to a new storage option which has no interruption and to better manage the large storage systems.

The current setup was based on the Lustre file system architecture method. The Lustre system had problems relating to scalability, reliability, storage, and archival issues.

GPFS can help optimize the existing storage requirements to the required performance rate. Based on GPFS file system features, an archiving method was set up. This helped them to archive data when required.

6.6 GPFS: Key Distinctions

GPFS has a shared disk access with global namespace which has an easily accessible cluster architecture. The capacity extension is unified across locations.

GPFS Key Distinctions
1. GPFS is primarily deployed and managed and also backed up.
2. Shared disk access with global namespace.
3. Easily accessible cluster architecture.
4. Unified capacity extension.
5. Accessible above 4000 nodes.
6. Parallel processing and extremely quicker performance.

More than 4000 nodes can be accessed in parallel using GPFS. GPFS has the advantage of quicker performance due to the parallel processing file system methodology that it uses.

6.6.1 GPFS-Powered Solutions

GPFS shares data across multiple nodes. GPFS provides the following benefits:

- *Highly available*: Advanced replication capabilities in the event of a failure.
- *Highly flexible*: Data can be easily shared across multiple locations.
- *Uninterrupted performance*: GPFS has a very good storage expansion feature.
- *Operational efficiency*: Lower cost of ownership due to simplified storage administration.

Activity Section

Activity No. 4:
List the above advantages in a pictorial format and explain the same.

6.7   Machine Data Analytics

Machine data analytics is one of the fastest developing areas in analytics. Machine data can be data generated from social Web applications, mobile devices, server, and network data.

Machine data analytics is about analyzing data like log data, alerts and message data, tickets, etc. generated from machine data and bringing out value from the data which can be used to create new insights.

Machine data is data generated by two kinds of interactions—machine to machine (M2M) and human to machine (H2M) which can be either structured or unstructured.

Now, spoken about what machine data analytics is, we will now talk about a company called Splunk which helps in analysis and visualization of the machine data that is generated very second.

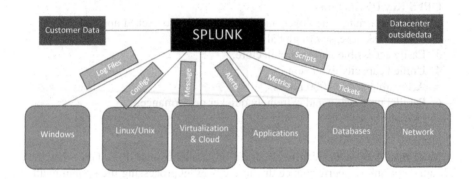

In the above figure, data from the customer-facing box denotes stream data, shopping cart data, and online transaction data. Data center outside data includes data from power center, manufacturing metrics data, GPS data, and other CDR and IPDR data.

Machine data is generated by various sources from different organizations. But these data were ignored as people were unaware of the value that can be retrieved from these data. Another problem is that most of the data generated is unstructured and it is not easy to handle such huge volumes of unstructured data. Legacy tools cannot handle unstructured data which is considered a big gap.

6.7.1 Splunk

Splunk started with using computer logs to solve security problems and other errors that come from machine data. The software is designed in such a way that it handles terabytes of data that is collected daily from different sources. The Splunk architecture enables users to run different queries with data that is collected at a higher speed.

Splunk can be deployed in a number of environments ranging from a single system to a distributed system where the data to be handled is huge. The Splunk architecture consists of forwarders, indexers, and search heads that allows for a secure and efficient collection and indexing of machine data for structured/unstructured data that comes from various sources.

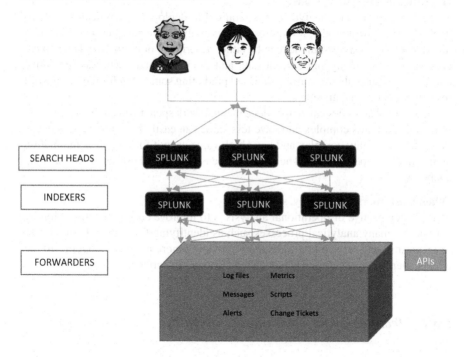

The above figure shows the Splunk deployment topology in a distributed environment by using the machine data fabric consisting of search heads, indexers, and forwarders.

6.8   Operational Analytics

Operational analytics is about improvising analytics with respect to business operations which involves data mining tools and techniques to get more value from data and to have a better business planning. The primary goal of operational analytics is to improve better decision-making in the operational systems.

A number of technologies and approach models can be used for operational analytics to obtain better decision-making results to take accurate decisions and make more effective business operations.

Many organizations have started implementing operational analytics in their business operations and are already seeing good results.

Operational Analytical Model
To perform operational analytics, it is required to deploy an analytical model. To deploy an analytical model, it requires various analytical techniques as well as historical data. An analytical model can be either descriptive or predictive. Descriptive analysis is about analyzing current data and drawing trends, whereas predictive analysis is about analyzing current data and predicting something for the future with respect to operational analytics.

Operational analytics can help reduce manual work spent to do analysis. Analysis of data that are less complex and have less value can easily be automated, whereas those that are highly complex and have high value cannot fully rely on automation as it requires expert advice. The area between the two is best suited for manual analytics.

When Customers Are Happy, so Are You
Another perspective of operational analysis is to improve customer satisfaction by automating many analytical processes such as identifying fraud in a claim process or increasing self-service in a website by providing more number of options to the clients, therefore providing a personalized customer experience.

6.8.1   Technology for Operational Analytics

For any analytics to work as expected and to deliver value, it requires few technologies that can run on an IT platform. Service-oriented architecture is required to integrate business with applications.

Shown below is the diagram showing the technologies required for operational analysis.

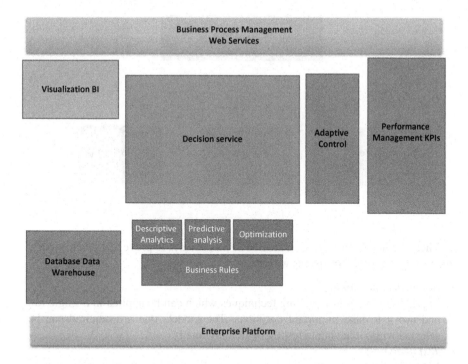

The most important technology required is a decision service. A decision service can be used to take the best decision by using good predictive models and techniques that support optimization. Also, since this is an approach where continuous improvement is required, technologies that can easily adapt to new changes are required.

The analytical models must be deployed on the operating systems. Some of the deployment models include batch database update, generation of code, database as an analytical platform, and domain-specific decision options.

6.8.2 Use Cases and Operational Analytics Products

6.8.2.1 IBM SPSS Modeler Features

The IBM SPSS Modeler is a predictive analytics platform which allows to bring out predictive decisions from data that is sent from systems and individuals. IBM SPSS provides a variety of techniques and algorithms that make decision-making more easy and effective. You can directly build your own predictive models and deploy them in your current business and take all important decisions with ease.

The attractive feature of IBM SPSS is that it combines predictive analysis with decision management. It helps users take the right decisions every time.

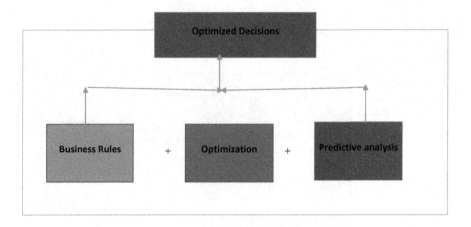

There are few other features that IBM SPSS provides to prove that it helps users/clients take important decisions with ease:

- *Automated modeling*:
  Provides a variety of modeling techniques which can be applied in a single run and use it to take important decisions. The models that are required can be selected without having to test them all individually.
- *Text analytics*:
  IBM SPSS allows unstructured data also to be used for effective data analysis which can be either text data or data coming from social websites, emails, feedbacks from customers, blog data, etc.
  It captures key data and shows trends which help to improve the most important factor of predictive models which is accuracy.
- *Entity analytics*:
  There are many entities that do not have much value when just looked upon as data. Entity analysis helps analyze data that might not have key benefits. Examples include fraud detection, site security, and customer relation management.
- *Social network analytics*:
  Social network analytics helps to analyze social entities and the impact it has with respect to individual's relationship.
- *Modeling algorithm*:
  There are a lot of modeling algorithms available in the IBM SPSS Modeler:

  1. Anomaly detector—this helps in detecting unusual records using the cluster-based algorithm.
  2. Apriori—to identify individual items in the database that occur frequently and the same can be extended to larger data sets.

3. Bayesian networks—takes care of conditional dependencies with graphical models and estimates the same.
4. C&RT, C5.0, CHAID, and Quest—helps in generating decision trees.
5. Decision list—helps in building interactive rules.
6. Logistic regression—to generate binary data
7. Neural network—it takes care of multilayer perceptrons.

Advantages of Using the SPSS Modeler

1. The most important advantage is that it helps analyze all data that exist anywhere.
2. The SPSS Modeler offers a variety of analytical algorithms to perform high-quality business analytics.
3. Very easy to build and deploy.
4. Very flexible—adapts to any environment you want it to analyze.

6.8.3 Other IBM Operational Analytics Products

There are many other products available in the market for operational analytics. Some of them include:

1. IBM SPSS Statistics —analyzes data by doing trend analysis and provides forecast

2. IBM SPSS Data Collection —gives an accurate view of society's opinion and their preferences and choices

3. IBM Cognos Business Intelligence —helps in improving business capabilities using analysis reports and scorecards

4. IBM Predictive Maintenance and Quality —improves operational performance and increases productivity

Activity Section

Activity No. 5:
There are many more products in the market today offered by many other companies. List one or two products with their specifications and benefits offered.

6.9   Conclusions

Real-time analytics help monitor data immediately and continuously and the changes that appear in real time. Mining big data is essential for future successes. Embracing new technologies and techniques helps provide a fast and reliable path to business success. Out of the thousands of analytical options that emerge today, choosing the right analytical tool is of utmost importance. Different tools have different advantages and disadvantages. The tools have to be chosen based on the current architecture requirements and how well it suits the current structure and what really can be achieved from the new tool.

6.10   Exercises

Objective Type:

1. Real-time analytics is the ability to use data and _____ when they are needed.

    a. Resource
    b. Data
    c. Time

2. HDFS is a _____ capability of big data.

    a. Storage and management
    b. Processing
    c. Database

3. Apache HBase is a _____ capability of big data.

    a. Storage and management
    b. Processing
    c. Database

4. IMDG stands for _____

    a. In-memory decision grid
    b. In-memory data grid
    c. In-memory division grid

5. MOA stands for _____

    a. Mass online application
    b. Mass-oriented application
    c. Massive online analysis

Detailed Type

1. Explain in detail the big data architecture capabilities.
2. Explain the types of IMDG in detail.
3. Explain in-database analytics in detail.
4. Write in detail about MOA.
5. What is GPFS—explain in detail two use cases.
6. What is machine data analytics and explain the importance of the same.
7. Explain IBM SPSS Modeler in detail.

Chapter 7
High-Performance Computing (HPC) Paradigms

7.1 Introduction

In the last few years, companies are seeing a growing demand in their business needs due to intense competition and many new innovative ways of accessing information in the growing market. This has resulted in a growing demand of computing power which in turn increases investment cost especially in the mainframe environments.

Also, at the same time, technology has evolved and more computing power is made available at a lower cost. Companies are looking for an opportunity to move their business from mainframe to open systems. Migrating a system from mainframe to open systems includes:

(a) Recoding all programs and recreating applications
(b) Redesigning systems
(c) Creating an altogether new software management procedures

The migrations also require the use of a new middleware to exchange data between the different platforms therefore adding additional costs and also requiring high-risk project developments. Another problem when doing batch processing is that in open systems, batch load is difficult to process and does not compare well with mainframe batch efficiency and duration.

At the end of the day, when IT managers analyze the results, the return on the investment has not provided the results that they had hoped for. This has actually slowed down or even stopped the undertaking of new migration projects. Therefore, the global question hopping around is if there is any solution to reduce mainframe costs without embracing the downsizing path.

© Springer International Publishing Switzerland 2015
P. Raj et al., *High-Performance Big-Data Analytics*, Computer Communications and Networks, DOI 10.1007/978-3-319-20744-5_7

7.2   Why Do We Still Need Mainframes???

A mainframe is called the engine of progress! When we take a closer look at the world's data, most of them still exist on mainframes. Many business-critical applications still run on mainframes. The mainframe systems are known for their long-life reliability, the ability to handle heavy workloads and the capability to handle Web applications as well. Mainframes are capable of executing thousands of processes within a second. Many systems in the areas of banking, finance, and research still run on mainframe servers, and it becomes very important to continue with them.

The only problem with mainframe systems are their backup and recovery processes that still exist on tapes. With the enormous increase in data from different fields, holding them on tape is not an efficient process, and also now all systems demand quicker recovery. The traditional methods of recovery are time-consuming as records are read in a sequential fashion and then have to be located and then be restored. Also, using tapes for huge volume systems becomes very costly too.

Therefore, it is important for companies in the research sector to come up with alternatives to the tape method which can process heavy workloads and also provide faster recovery process.

Let's now take a look at some of the solutions that are available now where mainframe systems use high-performance computing to serve their business better.

7.3   How Has HPC Evolved Over the Years in Mainframes?

1. The 1970s time-sharing mainframe
2. The 1980s distributed computing
3. The 1990s parallel computing
4. Centralization demand for HPC
5. Centralization with data security
6. Private cloud HPC

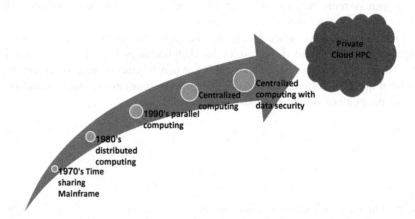

7.3.1   Cost – An Important Factor for HPC

When we invest in HPC, investors look for business value which may arise from either increased profits, through great engineering and innovation techniques, operational values, or IT values. Companies have started evaluating cost of HPC by focusing on not a single application but all available workloads leading to cloud computing.

7.3.2   Cloud Computing Centralized HPC

High-performance computing systems combined with huge storage applications connected by high-speed networks are required for today's high-performance computing. Using a centralized HPC allows us to balance workloads for large-running jobs and can help to manage data effectively by improving productivity. It also helps to enhance efficiency and secure data. It allows virtual desktop options along with mobile applications.

Now let's talk about the basic differences between local computing and cloud computing.

Local computing	Cloud computing
1. Processing done on a local desktop	1. Processing done on a centralized remote server
2. Files stored locally under a single control	2. Files stored centrally – time taken for file transfer is reduced
3. Limited capacity	3. No capacity limitation
4. Limited data management	4. Large files can be processed

7.3.3   Requirements to Centralized HPC

In order to centralize HPC and achieve operational efficiency, the following are required:

1. Maintain all data local to HPC using a data-centric view of all resources.
2. Use common tools for workload sharing.
3. Use graphical remote display for accessing data in the remote.

7.4   HPC Remote Simulation

Many companies are already working to create a remote workflow for centralized HPC or private cloud.

Let's have a look at a remote architecture for high-performance computing below.

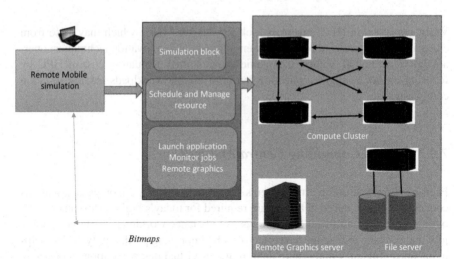

Now let's take a look at each of the components of the architecture.

1. Here, the portal has a remote user which has common integrated tools for the end users—to access data and for data management.
2. It also has a remote visualization tool. By sending bitmaps to the remote user from the remote graphics server, the results can be visualized. Desired processors can be run when required.
3. Easy to manage data—data can be accessed through the central server.

7.5 Mainframe Solution Using HPC

Let us now have a look about an important solution that helps reduce the mainframe costs.

7.5.1 Intelligent Mainframe Grid

Intelligent Mainframe Grid is a new solution based on grid computing technology which enables open distributed systems to run mainframe processes without software modification or data format changes.

Main Components in an IMG

Main Components in an IMG:

Grid Platform:

- Provides hardware and software virtualization services to assign resources to the mainframe processes when they need them

Communication and Storage Hardware:

- Allows sharing of high volume data between the mainframe and open systems

Mainframe Integration Architecture:

- Software architecture to synchronize the mainframe and open systems to obtain seamless execution of mainframe batch jobs on the open systems platform

The two main advantages of an IMG are the following:

1. From a mainframe perspective, the batch processes are executed as usual except that there are very few mainframe resources used which are close to 0 MIPS consumed.
2. It is not required to change any procedures, tools, or compilers (COBOL) during maintenance, training, and operation to allow batch jobs to be executed.

7.5.2   How Does an IMG Work?

A mainframe batch job (MBJ) is made of a collection of sequential steps, each one usually commands the execution of a program.

IMG provides the necessary tools, architecture, and execution platform to be able to execute a batch job outside the mainframe in three steps:

1. Translation of the original JCL instructions of the batch job into an equivalent version that can run on the IMSG Grid platform.
2. Access of the program source code and compilation of this code on the Grid platform to create a local executable version of the program on the Grid.
3. Allocate access and resources on the Grid platform for the execution of the job, give access to the input files, and allocate resources for the output files on the shared storage platform. The programs are executed locally.

In the above steps, 1 and 2 has to be executed only once during the batch job as long as no modifications are done to the JCL or the programs. Step 3 has to be repeated each time the batch job runs. This means that the batch jobs and their programs are catalogued on the mainframe the same way as they are on IMG. The translated JCL and the compiled programs are catalogued on the open systems ready to be executed whenever the need comes. When the programs have been recompiled and tested on the open systems, the mainframe is ready to run the batch jobs on the IMG platform.

All these steps discussed are completely automated, so that each time a new batch job is put in production on the mainframe, a set of JCL and programs are catalogued and compiled in the mainframe. The IMG-translated JCL is created along with the compilation of the corresponding programs for the IMG platform at the same time.

Mainframe operation decides then to use the mainframe or the IMG platform version at its will. Both can coexist simultaneously and can be used alternatively also.

7.5.3 IMG Architecture

Now, we will get into details about the IMG architecture. Each component affects the performance of the system. However, they are decoupled and can be substituted and adapted according to the evolution of technology to give the best possible overall results at any given time.

The architecture is designed in such a way that the execution platform is built on a grid of inexpensive nodes to provide the computing power necessary to compete with the mainframe execution efficiency, but without giving up its reputable reliability.

The main objectives of the IMG architecture as compared to the mainframe standards are the following:

- Faster execution
- Computing power on demand
- Scalability
- Improved reliability and fault tolerance
- Support of heterogeneous systems
- Parallel processing capabilities
- Less cost

The IMG Grid platform is based on open standards (Web services, SOA, and virtualization) to ensure compatibility, flexibility, and extensibility with the rest of the IT grids.

IMG components are tightly integrated so that they build a unique solution to solve the problem of mainframe batch job execution and decoupled so that they have their own purpose and independent operation. The IMG architecture is a full-fledged grid platform that can be used on its own to solve not only intensive batch computational problems but also online calculations of nearly any type, written in any language.

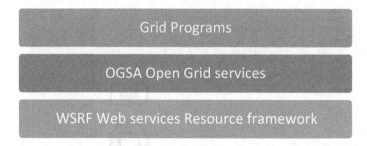

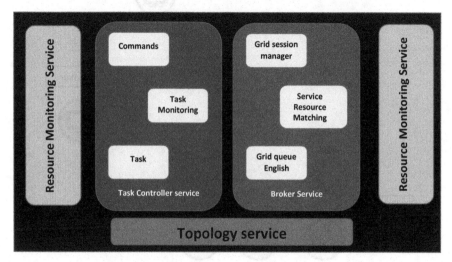

IMG architecture is built around four main components deployed as Web services within the IMG Grid Kernel, each one providing a unique functionality.

Now we will look into details of each component.

1. *Topology Service*:

   The main function of the topology service is to manage the node structure of the grid in such a way that any computer can have the freedom to play any role at any point in time. IMG is fault tolerant and there is no single point of failure by its design. The grid has three different roles.

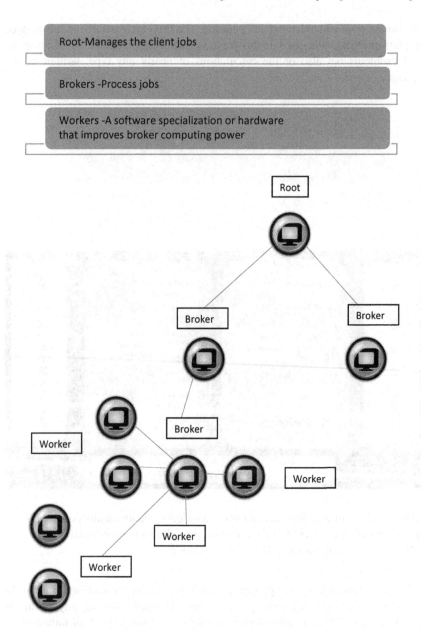

7.5.3.1　Root

The root manages all the client jobs.

7.5.3.2   Broker Service

The broker service maintains the resources in the grid in such a way that they match the best resource to allocate to a job.

7.5.3.3   Task Controller Service

The task controller takes care of executing processes in the grid. It has a storehouse of operations that a node is allowed to process. Each operation has commands that help each node to reuse functionality. The allowed operations can be combined with a new set of combination of existing commands to provide a new service altogether.

7.5.3.4   Monitoring Service

There are two types of monitoring services that are available:

- Grid Monitoring Service
- Resource Monitoring Service

Grid Monitoring Service:

This is to manage the grid internally.

Resource Monitoring Service:

This monitors all resources and provides status of running task, tasks that are pending, or task that are terminated in each of the node.

There is also a data-sharing platform available between the mainframe region and grid. This helps to process massive amounts of data to be processed without disturbing the mainframe. In case there is a disturbance caused to the mainframe, less resources are used than that would be required for the mainframe to execute.

Next, let us see the different architecture models that are available:

7.6   Architecture Models

7.6.1   Storage Server with Shared Drive

In this architecture, both the mainframe and the grid share a storage device which will allow direct access to data from both the environments without allowing any duplication.

7.6.2   Storage Server Without Shared Drive

Here also, the grid and mainframe shared a storage device where data can be copied from one environment to another in both directions, but each environment works on the data individually.

7.6.3   Communication Network Without Storage Server

In this architecture, the mainframe and the grid do not share a storage device, but they share a communication network that has all the messaging between both the environments. It also supports data interchange between the two environments.

The Intelligent Mainframe Grid supports all the three models but when we compare cost and performance, both reduces when we move from Architecture 7.6.1 to Architecture 7.6.3.

Activity Section

Activity No. 1:
Create the above architecture in model format in 2D or 3D.
Below are some of the points to be noted while creating the model.

1. The model you create should be a visualized view of the architecture diagram.
2. It can be in 2D or 3D format.
3. You can use Thermocole, plastic materials, and any material of your own.

7.6.3.1 Mainframe Integration Architecture

The mainframe integration architecture basically exists in the mainframe on some parts of the grid. This helps the mainframe to allow uninterrupted operation of the mainframe jobs by providing the required tools, commands, and necessary services. The execution remains under the control of the mainframe, and it integrates with any scheduler with which the mainframe is running. Here, there is no change in the plan or schedule that is required as the job return codes are sent by the mainframe integration architecture. It appears like the actual execution happened on the mainframe. The same happens in a case that when there is a program error, the error information is passed on to the programmer in such a way that the development of the program does not get affected by the platform on which the job is executed.

7.7 SMP (Symmetric Multiprocessing)

Now we are going to discuss about another interesting topic here which is the symmetric multiprocessing technique used in many mainframe systems that powers high-performance computing.

7.7.1 What Is SMP?

SMPs are symmetric multiprocessing systems that basically run on parallel architecture and has a global memory space.

7.7.2 SMP and Cluster Methods

In SMP, delivering high performance is very costly considering the amount of processors that are to be integrated in the shared memory environment. Due to this fact, many companies try to adopt the cluster method where a large number of servers are connected together and are then used as a single commodity. When we compare SMP and cluster method, clusters are difficult to manage and are also less efficient performance wise.

Activity Section

Activity No. 2:
Take a chart paper and write the differences between a cluster and SMP model with diagrams.
You can google the data for more information and you can write the same.
Once done, let each student present the same in the classroom.

7.7.3   Is SMP Really Important and Why?

SMPs are basically similar processors connected to a single storage and managed by a single operating system. SMP helps more workload to be executed at the same time because of parallel processing. The operating system in an SMP helps balance load across different processors.

Compared to the cluster method, SMP utilizes its load better. Another advantage of SMP is their less burden of management. SMPs have a single operating system and a single global storage space. Synchronizing the scheduling of jobs is much easier, and managing the storage space is also easy resulting in lesser cost compared to the cluster method.

Let's have a look at the below figure which shows the basic difference between SMP and a cluster method.

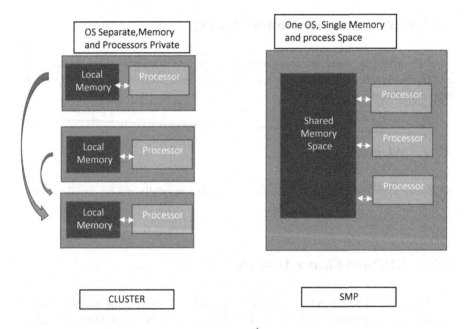

In the cluster model, we have a separate OS having a private memory and processor whereas SMP has one OS with a single memory and process space.

7.7.4   Thread Model

In an SMP model, parallel processing is based on special technique called the thread model. In this model, the main program is broken down into many subprograms which share the same memory as the main program does. Therefore, each thread can read and write the same memory space. The memory spaces can be protected and allow the threads to communicate in a variety of mechanism methods.

When we compare threads in a cluster environment, migrating threads across different nodes is very difficult. Therefore in clusters, message passing interfaces are used to share data across different servers. The main disadvantage of message passing interface is that it has to start its programs on multiple different servers.

When applications have to run on more than one server, message passing interfaces are preferred. MPIs or the message passing interface that we call can be used on an SMP model as well, but they are not suited for shared memory concept.

7.7.5 NumaConnect Technology

NumaConnect is a plug and play SMP solution where all the memory and processors are combined and controlled by a single OS. Ideally, in an SMP environment, due to limitations of shared memory, people go for something called the nonuniform memory access to get a global view of memory. Here, though the memory is accessible globally, it does not appear as local. The additional memory exists in another memory block where access times can differ based on the location. Another feature of global memory is its cache. Data can be present either in the main memory or cache memory. The data in the main memory will not be refreshed in the cache memory until both are not synchronized. NumaConnect provides a cache capability for all connected systems.

7.8 Virtualization for HPC

What is Virtualization? Virtualization is about allowing multiple applications to run on the same machine with added advantage of providing security and fault protection.

Some of the benefits that can be achieved by virtualization include the following:

1. Good server utilization
2. Improved business promptness to expand business due to future needs
3. Good security with a software-defined service
4. Can deal with power failure or equipment failure or any other disruptions

Activity Section

Activity No. 3:
Create a PowerPoint presentation about various innovation architecture that are done for mainframe systems using HPC.

Note: There are a lot of innovation activities happening in the area of mainframe computing especially in cloud environment.

Creating this PowerPoint presentation will help you realize the number of innovations happening in today's world and the competition between the different research organizations.

7.9 Innovation for Mainframes

Though there are a lot of rumors about mainframe getting vanished, they are the machines where 80 % of business-critical applications run today. A lot of innovations have been made which is a stunning comeback for mainframe machines. Mainframes are known for their agility and throughput that they provide.

Mainframes have proven to be very versatile. They support our traditional languages like COBOL and Assembler, and at the same time support all new platforms like XML, Java, and SOA. That's the power of mainframes. Mainframes are known for their backward compatibility which has made it a truly hybrid system of all times. Cloud platforms like infrastructure as a service turning out the way we work today. The concepts involved here have already been in the mainframe world for more than 40 years.

Mainframes are most often known to be very costly machines. But in today's growing world, mainframes are known to deliver results faster by providing security and reliability.

7.10 FICON Mainframe Interface

To improve performance of mainframe applications that require high-bandwidth data movements between the centers and to improve replication of data and quicker disaster recovery, a Brocade accelerator can be used.

FICON is an input/output interface that connects mainframe to other storage devices. The accelerator designed for FICON delivers excellent performance for high-bandwidth data.

Let's now see the architectural diagram of how the accelerator really works.

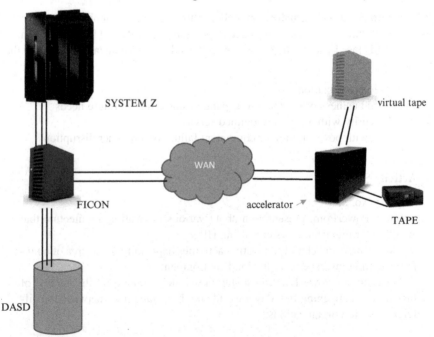

Here, the use of this accelerator speeds up performance, recovery, and backup by reducing operational costs. Emulation technique is used which helps to improve the performance of mainframe System Z applications by preventing them to degrade. The added advantage here is that of an enhanced data security while still providing faster recovery options. The use of accelerator reduces the cost needed for higher bandwidths.

Activity Section

Activity No. 4:
The next topic we are going to see is pretty interesting and one which you all can relate to your day-to-day activities.

What is it that we use every day and something that the world is living on? Yes it's MOBILE; the whole world has gone mobile now.

All day-to-day activities are done only with MOBILE.

What I want you all to do is take a paper and write down all things that you do using your mobile every day.

7.11 Mainframe Mobile

The world is going mobile today. The number of mobile users in the world has drastically increased. The populations prefer mobile to do all their personal transactions starting from paying your card bills, booking movie tickets online, and checking bank account balance online. With the increase in transactions via mobile, the number of mainframe processing through CICS has increased. Mainframe has the added advantage to handle huge volumes of data and process them in the fastest possible time.

Let's see the below figure to understand how extensively mainframes are used in a mobile transaction.

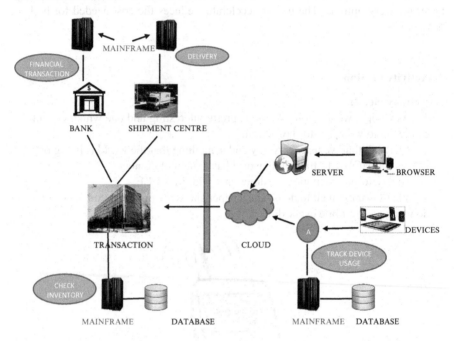

Taking a closer look at the mobile transaction, all the activities of the mobile transaction are driven from the mainframes starting from the cell phone accessing a mobile tower which is carried on with the inventory check, accessing bank account details for all financial transactions, or accessing the address details for any shipment-related transactions. In these days, there are a number of mobile applications like Amazon, cab apps, banking apps, etc. which have increased the number of the above processes. Therefore, there is a risk to keep the performance of mainframe systems constant as the data grows exponentially. With cloud computing gaining importance, mainframes systems are seeing more and more opportunities. More research on this area can really bring out enormous values out of the big iron mainframe systems.

7.12   Windows High-Performance Computing

Now let us talk about another innovation that is done for distributed systems through high-performance computing.

How does high-performance computing really work? A system where a node which acts as the header accepts the work request and distributes the work to smaller nodes. The smaller nodes perform the calculations and return the work to the header node through batch processing. This is how many mainframe computing usually work.

The only issue with high-performance computing is adding many additional nodes. If the nodes are fewer, work becomes slow and performance gets degraded. On the other hand, adding extra resources will add to infrastructure cost and power.

Below is the pictorial representation of the current high-performance computing architecture. There is a client workstation which sends the work requests. The header node receives the work requests and assigns them to smaller nodes. The smaller nodes return back the work after completion in a batch mode. The application network and private network are optional items which can be added based on the requirement.

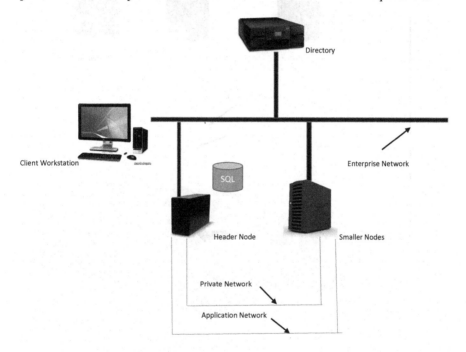

In order to avoid adding extra additional permanent nodes that add to infrastructure cost, Windows have come up with an option for high-performance computing. They have come up with two options.

1. You can add additional smaller nodes in the Windows Azure network using a broker node and pay for the same until you use it.
2. In the original network side, you can just install the header node and a broker node and all other smaller node in the Windows Azure network.

The above options can be used for critical financial applications which provide an alternate option of adding extra header nodes and reduce cost as you use them only when required and pay them for what you have actually utilized.

Below is the picture of how the Windows Azure nodes can be installed.

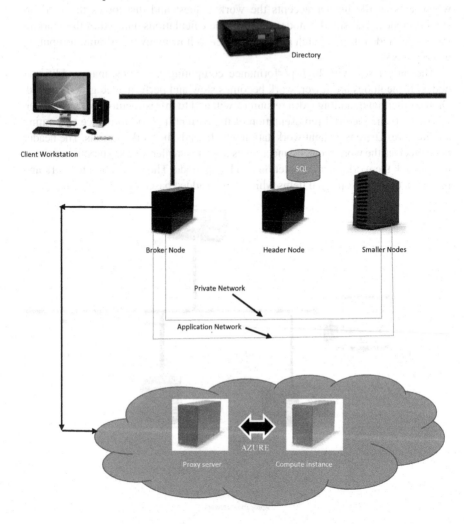

7.13 Conclusions

To summarize what we studied in this chapter:

- Importance of *mainframe systems* for today's growing data and how companies are investing trust of mainframe systems to run today's business-critical applications.

- Starting from healthcare, finance, banking, insurance, retail, and manufacturing companies still run on mainframes.
- For today's exponentially growing data, there is an increased need for *high-performance computing* and parallel computing.
- High-performance computing is looking for *betterstorage options* for growing data.
- HPC is looking for *performance improvement* of systems by reducing infrastructure, power, and other cost.
- *Better backup and quicker disaster recovery* options are of utmost importance with high-performance computing.
- There are a lot of *innovations* happening today in the field of mainframe using high-performance computing.
- The world has gone *mobile* with all important applications including shopping, banking, and healthcare available in mobile.
- *Mainframes and cloud computing* is considered as the best combination ever to deliver business value to clients.
- *Intelligent Mainframe Grid (IMG)* is considered as the best solution for grid-based computing systems.
- *Symmetric multiprocessing (SMP)* architecture works best for parallel processing dealing with huge data.

7.14 Exercises

Objective Type:

1. IMG refers to _____.

    (a) Intelligent Mainframe Grip
    (b) Intelligent Mainframe Grid
    (c) Intellect Mainframe Grid

2. HPC stands for _____.

    (a) High-performance cluster
    (b) High-performance computation
    (c) High-performance computing

3. SMP refers to _____.

    (a) Single-memory processing
    (b) Symmetric memory processing
    (c) Symmetric multiprocessing

4. _____ node accepts the work requests in a Window High performance computing.

   (a) Header
   (b) Smaller
   (c) Broker

5. _____ is a plug and play SMP model.

   (a) NumaConnect
   (b) IMG
   (c) Windows Azure

Answer the Following in More Than 100 Words:

1. What is IMG? Describe in detail.
2. Describe in detail about SMP architecture.
3. Describe the importance of mainframes and the evolution of HPC.
4. Talk about few innovation ideas that are implemented in mainframes.
5. Describe in detail with diagrams about Windows Azure high-performance computing.

Chapter 8
In-Database Processing and In-Memory Analytics

8.1 Introduction

We are increasingly digitizing our lives; this led to unparalleled growth in data. This data explosion is driven by exponential usage of mobiles and the Internet of things (IoT). With each waking day, more and more devices are connected to the Internet. Start-ups, venture capitalists, and stalwarts in computing world like CISCO, Google, and Microsoft are increasingly investing time and resources towards this growing phenomenon. The devices range from smartphones to thermostats to smart electric grids to driverless cars to solar panels to sports tracker monitors. We can safely prophesize that within the coming decade or two, everything electric will be connected to the Internet. According to the 2014 EMC/IDC Digital Universe report, data size is doubling every 2 years. In 2013 alone, in excess of 4.4 zettabytes of data was created; as per the report's prediction by 2020, that number will be 10–44 zettabytes, that is, 44 trillion gigabytes. Two-thirds of 2013 data was created by people, whereas in the coming decade, more data will be generated by things like embedded devices and sensors. In the report, IDC predicts that in 2020 the number of IoT devices will be around 300 billion. This data from these connected devices is powering a data economy, creating huge opportunities as well as challenges to future businesses. Furthermore, the exponential growth rate of this new data is crafting organizational change in the ways enterprises interact, manage, and make use of this data. As this data economy evolves, a vital distinction between the major ways of business interaction with data is evolving. Enterprises have already begun interaction big data which has huge volumes and varieties. Furthermore, as enterprises go on board with ever-more advanced analytics initiatives, they recognized the importance of interacting with fast data which corresponds to the velocity part of big data. The ability to process data instantaneously creates newer opportunities to recognize value via disruptive business models.

© Springer International Publishing Switzerland 2015
P. Raj et al., *High-Performance Big-Data Analytics*, Computer Communications and Networks, DOI 10.1007/978-3-319-20744-5_8

We must first learn differences between normal transactional workload and analytic workload. This distinction gives us an idea of whether normal databases can be used for analytics purposes or different kinds of data stores are required.

8.1.1   Analytics Workload vs. Transaction Workload

The characteristics of transactional processing workload include large number of short, discrete, atomic, and simple transactions. Updates to the data are frequent, and the data is generally up to date, detailed, and relational; response times are generally of order of few milliseconds. The major emphasis for online transaction processing (OLTP) systems is (a) maintaining data integrity in multiuser environments and (b) high throughput (transactions per second). These workloads correspond to day-to-day operations, batch processing, and analytical workloads

The Characteristics of Analytics Processing The characteristics of analytics processing [1, 7] include fewer users (business analysts, CEO's) submitting fewer yet long, complex, and resource-intensive requests. Response times are generally of order of tens to hundreds of seconds. Other major characteristics of analytic workloads are high data volumes, set-oriented bulk operations, temporary or intermediate staging of data, infrequent updates, and historical, multidimensional, and integrated data. This mainly comes into picture at the times of decision-making or making recommendations or in-risk analysis.

In 2008, a team of researchers led by Mike Stonebraker published a seminal paper in the ACM SIG-MOD entitled "OLTP through the Looking Glass, and What We Found There." The paper has shed light on the potential overheads that limit traditional RDBMS products and came to a conclusion that database performance can be increased multiple times if these limitations are overcome. Another major point mentioned is the change towards in-memory-based databases which we will see shortly.

The traditional RDBMS products' features which cause overhead in processing are as follows:

Locking: To maintain the consistency of a record, it is locked by a particular transaction trying to modify it. Due to this, no other transaction can access this record. But the extra processing required creates an overhead in case of analytical workloads where data consistency is not a big issue.

Buffer management: In conventional RDBMS, data is stored on fixed-size disk pages. At any point of time, a set of pages are cached in buffered pools. Locating records and field boundaries to be identified in the pages are overhead-intensive operations.

Latching: In multithreaded environment, updates to the shared data structures like indexes, lock tables, etc. must be done carefully. This creates potential overheads.

Index management: To increase the relative performance while searching for records, indexes are created. Maintaining these indexes requires significant CPU and I/O resources.

Write-ahead logging: To maintain the durability of data in the database, everything is written twice in traditional DBMS: once to the database and once to the log. Further, this log is forced onto the disk.

Originally designed to ensure that the ACID principles are achieved, these processes limit the databases from scaling linearly. That's the reason why modern NoSQL databases forgo any one of these principles to achieve linear or near linear scalability. Another limitation with the traditional databases is that the data is stored in row-oriented mechanism which is not efficient with analytical workloads.

To illustrate the points, let's take a database which specializes in transactional processing. If a company using this database platform needs to run analytics such as reporting or some other ad hoc analysis, then the company will maintain separate databases for transactions and analytics. Of course this would be the case even if the company employs analytical DBMS for analytics. SAP HANA is the platform supporting both transactional and analytical workloads, i.e., mixed workload.

The first step would be to extract the data from their transactional system. This data is first transformed to fit in the reporting database which usually forms enterprise warehouse or BW. Even then the reporting warehouse requires high amount of tuning configurations like aggregates and indexes but still has mediocre performance. This is the reason why modern-day analytical databases like Teradata database, Greenplum, and Vertica are created specifically designed for analytical workloads. Most also store data in columnar fashion, making it easy and flexible for the analytical data to be retrieved.

The demands of the businesses keep on increasing in the analytical sphere; this made the evolution of analytical products which we will briefly see. This evolution makes it easier for us to understand where the analytical world is going to and how we can achieve performance and provide businesses what they want—actionable insights.

8.1.2 Evolution of Analytic Workload

The idea of using data for making decisions is not new which came into existence in the last 10–15 years. This method dates back to precomputer era. With the advent of computers, it was made possible to collect large quantities of data and process it far more quickly; the field of business analytics came into existence. The first data systems were designed to capture transactions without any data loss. These systems are designed so as to achieve the ACID properties. Data query is done through SQL. Applications are developed on top of this database. Any analytical application simply generates static reports for further analysis by the analysts. The design goal of these systems is to capture transaction data accurately and store it efficiently for all of the mission critical systems. The analytical capabilities are limited to simple reporting. This was the time when answering the question what has happened is the major goal [3] (Fig. 8.1).

Then came the era of business intelligence where the emphasis is on understanding vital business phenomena and providing the managers with fact-based comprehension to make decisions. For the first time, data about customer interaction, sales, and production processes were recorded, analyzed, and aggregated.

Data sizes were small and almost static so data segregation was done into enterprise warehouses. However, loading of data and preparing data became a big hurdle where analytics spent most of the time. And the analysis was painstakingly slow which usually took weeks to months to perform. Most of the analysis is done on the historical data. The user was abstracted to some extent from the slow analysis by implementing something called online analytical processing system (OLAP). This analytical structure called cubes is generated with a multidimensional data structure, with each dimension being one query parameter. This allowed the users to do analysis, but unstructured processing and real-time analytics remained still a challenge. The data is also aggregated across dimensions to make it easier for querying. Thus, the major emphasis was on answering why something has happened.

Then the era of big data [4] came. Starting with Internet firms like Google and Amazon, new forms of data have been captured and analyzed. This big data changed the role of data and analytics at these firms. The big data has been distinguished from other small data as it was not completely generated by internal transactional system. Much of it came from external sources like weblogs, sensors, audio and

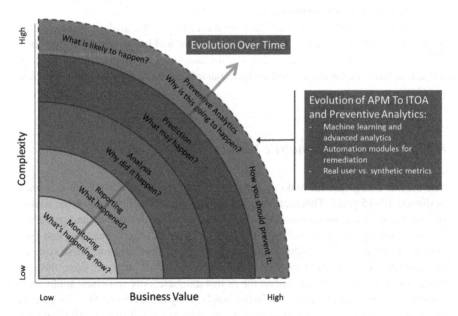

Fig. 8.1 Evolution of analytics

video recordings, etc. Extreme hype was built up, promoting unseen acceleration of new offerings.

The huge volumes of data can't be fitted and analyzed fast enough on a single server so systems like Hadoop, Spark, etc. have been created. With this, fast batch processing in parallel across interconnected distributed systems is mastered. To deal with newly created unstructured data, NoSQL databases like MongoDB, Redis, DynamoDB, Raik, Neo4j, etc. are created with some even supporting ACID properties with linear scalability. And cloud computing also made it possible for small firms to analyze and store data cheaply. New forms of analytics such as visual analytics, graph analytics, and text analytics are successfully deployed.

To make real-time analysis possible, mechanisms such as "in-memory" and "in-database" analytics were introduced. As such these were put in the front row due to the demands although these techniques existed for a while in different ways.

Using various machine learning and statistical techniques, the pioneer firms in big data developed customer facing applications such as recommendation engines, targeted ads, and even search algorithms.

Following the suite, many non-tech companies started integrating these newer forms of analytics. Some even started making applications integrated with analytics making it possible to make automatic decisions improving operational efficiency.

8.1.3 Traditional Analytic Platform

In a traditional analytical platform which is based on a relational data warehouse [2]. The data is first copied into the analytical server, and model development or cube creation is done on this server instead of the warehouse. These analytical servers usually store data in non-relationship data mart structures and are usually managed on distributed servers outside the data warehouse. The following problems creep in with these similar environments:

- Data extraction from relational data warehouse attracts high-performance penalty.
- Duplication of data from data warehouse and the data marts results in high infrastructure costs and non-efficient hardware utilization.
- Higher security due to multiple unmanageable replicas.
- Higher costs of skilled human resources for managing and developing programs to extract and perform computations.

Conventional BI [7] and analytical systems are completely based on data with fixed schema. These systems are designed of new types of un-/semi-structured data. As we have noted earlier, in-database analytics and in-memory analytics are introduced so as to deal with newer, complex analytical use cases with new and old kinds of data. The major bottleneck in traditional analytical systems is extracting, loading, and preparing the data for developing predictive or analytical model. Due to varied varieties of data, data is usually gathered from various data sources with different technologies. In times where the processing speeds are critical, inflexible or non-supporting agility is plainly unacceptable. Data assets are often gathered from across multiple sources that exist in a variety of repository technologies. In competitive times when speed of execution is critical, this lack of agility is just plainly unacceptable. This motivated the movement onto in-database processing which eliminates multiple of these limitations.

By now it is apparent that a single solution is not available to solve all the problems. "One size doesn't fit all." This has led companies to use technologies that are correct fit for a particular application. All these technologies are then integrated so as to achieve overall business goals. This has been termed as polyglot processing. Let's now study the in-database processing which aims at providing faster, agile analytical processing.

8.2   In-Database Analytics

In-database processing technique is not a new development introduced with big data analytics. In fact this is established with over 15 years of history. Addressing many challenges with the analytics in the market, Teradata introduced the concept of in-database processing. A lot of information is scattered across soloed data marts making it challenging for the analysts to gather the required data and manipulate and analyze it. While most of these jobs ran on servers or workstations, the iterative nature of these jobs made it necessary to extract a lot of samples to pull and transfer over systems causing hours of cycle time.

In database, analytical processing [5] is generally delivered as user-defined functions and a set of libraries of data and analytical functions so as to access data that lies in database, or even from pliable distrusted file system like Hadoop HDFS, direct usage of parallel processing capabilities, and interoperability with various operating systems and specialist analytical tools, be it for analysis or data management tasks.

Normal databases don't provide in-database processing feature which is touted as a primary feature in data warehouses and for analytical processing. A data warehouse is basically an analytical database which provides feasibility for reporting, storage, and providing data for advanced analytical tasks. These databases separate layers for different role holders, i.e., developers have access to raw data layer, some layer for the users to input the data.

In-database technology emphasizes on integrating/fusing analytical systems and data warehouses. As we have noted earlier, the conventional data warehouse system needs to export the information into analytical program to run complex computations on the data. In-database processing advocates pushing down the data processing to where the data is located instead of copying it to a central system and processing. Here the computations can be done using a single program, saving a lot of time that would've been waged in ETL tasks. Nowadays, many of the major vendors like Vertica, Teradata, Oracle, ExaSol, Accel, etc. are providing in-database functionality along with their offerings.

In-database [9] technology as we have noted came into existence to solve the limitations with the traditional analytical processing, where the data is loaded from enterprise data warehouses and fitted into analytical engines (SAS/SPSS, etc.) and the results are then fed into visualization tools like Tableau, MicroStrategy, etc. for user consumption or even visual analytics. First of all, as the data size grows, the extraction of data takes longer and more costs due to duplication and other factors as we have already jotted down. Although the extraction times (or data load times) can be reduced with incremental extraction of data, other problems still persist. Another major hurdle is the fact that scalability of analytics is limited by the amount of data that can be kept in the analytical engine at a particular point of time, which effectively means that the analytics or users of this system are working on smaller data sets, taking large amount of time and potentially outdated data. Most popular statistical language R is memory bound; that means that if the data to be analyzed doesn't fit in memory, this language doesn't work. With small enterprises, this problem might not be a major issue, but with large companies with huge amounts of data, this becomes an impeding problem. There is also a probability that the data consistency might be affected because of some human error or network partition while copying data. Data security and data governance are strict when the data resides in the corporate data warehouse, but as the data moves out of the warehouse to the analytical engines, the security and governance aspects might take a hit.

With a simple premise of pushing down the processing to the data, in-database technology has been able to address these issues and give a performance boost. This technology is heavily useful for user who wants to perform data mining tasks or processing on huge amounts of data, predictive analytics, and exploratory analytics. There are many use cases where in technology has been applied to provide not only advanced analytics but also analytics-based product offerings.

One of the major forms of processing that benefits in-database processing is predictive analytics. Predictive analytics in simple layman terms is to use the data stored to find a pattern or make an attempt to predict about what might happen in a particular context, for example, the books you may want to buy, what might happen with the stock market, etc. This is when an analytical program takes database information and attempts to predict a trend. This is not specific to in-database processing. Analytical computations—key performance indicator (KPI) calculations, data aggregations, model scoring, predictive analytics, temporal and geospatial analysis, and other functions—often touch large numbers of data records and multiple data fields. They may be carried out repeatedly. By using in-database analytics, these processing can be done faster.

In the new style of deployment, analytical engines are pre-integrated with the data warehouse repository. An added advantage due to this is that many of the data warehouses in the market today follow shared-nothing architecture with massive parallel processing capabilities. This MPP can be used to our advantage. Teradata database, for example, provides more than 1000 analytical functions through its partnerships with SAS, dedicated support to open-source R, and a lot more.

SAS In-Data Processing with Teradata Simplest way in which SAS can be integrated as an in-database functionality with Teradata is to translate the SAS operations to Teradata SQL. Let's take one standard SAS function PROC FREQ which according to SAS documentation "the FREQ procedure produces one- ® way to n-way frequency and cross-tabulation tables." Simply put this function calculates the table of frequencies. With SAS integration with Teradata, SAS compiler generates SQL for executing this function in the database itself rather than extracting data from the database in SAS engine. So there is no need for data duplication or data movement. The following figures illustrate the difference of execution without and with in-database processing, respectively. The SAS features which are too complex to be generated as SQL statements are implemented as compile C functions are user-defined constructs. The extensions make up the SAS libraries which are embedded into Teradata (Figs. 8.2 and 8.3).

An example of such complex function is scoring algorithms. These functions are transformed into optimized C code. These functions are wholly parallelized in the massively parallel processing (MPP) architecture inside the Teradata® RDBMS.

In-database processing is great for "big data" problems and for others problems that can greatly benefit from a centralized, managed analytics architecture. The following are some of the type of analytical problems which are best run in database:

- Data-intensive calculations, both simple and complex computations. In data-intensive calculations, a lot of data movement occurs which incurs huge costs on computing and network resources.
- Recurrent calculations which repetitively touch the same data. Movement of lesser amounts of data repetitively costs as much as moving big data less frequently.
- Cross-functional analytics. With a variety of data types supported by the DBMS, it becomes easy to join analytics across functional boundaries. For example, geo-spatial data with customer profile data and application access logs is one such form of cross-functional analytic application.

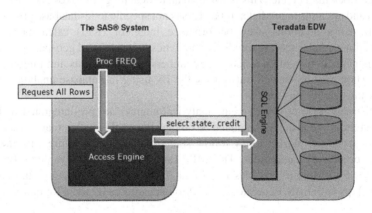

Fig. 8.2 SAS traditional processing in Teradata

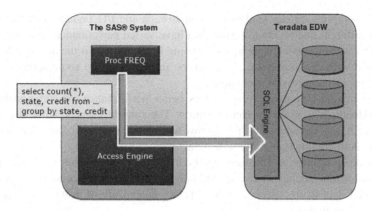

Fig. 8.3 In-database approach for Teradata and SAS

These in-database capabilities are vendor specific and also specific to a particular data warehouse or an appliance. Many a times vendors support multiple data infrastructure; while some capabilities are provided for these vendors, some others are gathered from specialty analytical vendors.

8.2.1 Architecture

Few architectural choices that make a good in-database analytical platforms are SQL support, high data loading throughput, and low latency along with the following functionalities:

- Integrated analytics such as machine learning, data mining, scoring of data, optimization techniques, and statistical techniques.
- Extensibility of functionalities through user-defined functions or MapReduce functions or even as stored procedures in MS SQL server or Oracle server.
- Scan friendliness and partitioning through which larger block sizes are used for efficient data reads from disks. I prove the processing speeds by eliminating portions which don't have the required input.
- Inherent parallelism is to be provided in a way of shared-nothing architecture, taking advantage of multiple cores in the processing units (CPU Processors or GPU), with some vendors like Greenplum, Netezza, and Teradata going further by using custom data transfer protocols as the network is considered to be a bottleneck in high-performance computing.
- Columnar data storage is advantageous in processing many analytical workloads, since most of the analytical processing requires only certain columns of records to process instead of the whole record as in the case of transactional processing.

- Data compression can lead to efficient storage and I/O savings. Keep in mind that different queries on different data have varied performance spectrum with different compression techniques. It would be even better if the data can be processed with decompressing. This can be implemented by some form of order preserving compression techniques.
- Even though columnar storage offers better performance for some analytical workloads, it is not a de facto solution. Their might even be some use cases where it is advantageous to store in row wise. HANA is the first such database to store both columnar and row wise data.
- Few other architectural features can be query pipelining, result set reuse, query optimization, batches writes, append only updates, lock less concurrency model, parallel data loads, specialized load nodes Aster Data nCluster from Teradata specializes in this.

8.2.1.1   Goals

The main goals of the in-database processing trace back to the evolution of these user demands:

- Lesser processing times: With inclusion of processing data in the database itself and utilizing the MPP and parallel capabilities of the database, the data processing takes comparatively lesser times.
- Effective resource utilization: Since the database infrastructure is put to work instead of just providing data, more work is done with the existing infrastructure, thereby increasing effective utilization.
- Less network load: Since the data is processed in the database itself, there is no need to move huge amounts of data throughout the network. Only solutions or the results are sent. This reduces the heavy burden on networks.
- Real-time analysis: In the traditional BI systems, the data is loaded into analytical engine. This data loaded can be old. But in case of in-database analytics, all the analytical processing is done on the latest data.

8.2.2   Benefits and Limitations

The major benefits of in-database analytics are reduction in data-access and data movement delays and execution time. The advantages gained by businesses while using in-database analytics are through faster shipment to market, improved accessibility and accuracy, decreased costs as an effect from increased resource utilization, higher reachability of the products, and reuse of existing hardware. The data retrieval and analysis is multifold times faster and more secure as the data never leaves the warehouse. The analysis can now work at scale and can easily utilize the parallel processing offered by the data warehouses.

The potential limitations can be that the processing capabilities provided are pretty specific to vendors. This might lead to vendor lock-in. The functionality provided by different vendors is implemented differently.

8.2.3   Representative Systems

8.2.3.1   Teradata Database

The Teradata database is a data warehouse system from Teradata [8]. Teradata database follows the shared-nothing architecture (i.e., each server node has its memory, processing, and network) with massively parallel processing capabilities (MPP). To increase the data storage, you just need to add more servers. Teradata now also supports unstructured and semi-structured data as well (Fig. 8.4).

There are three main components of Teradata architecture: *PE (Parsing Engine)*, *AMP (Access Module Processor)* and *BYNET*.

Parsing Engine (PE)
The primary job of this component is to control the user sessions and check authorizations, compiling and sending instructions to be executed on the AMPs. So whenever a user log in to Teradata, they first connect to PE. When a user submits a query, checks the syntax, and optimizes the code, he/she creates a plan and instructs AMPs

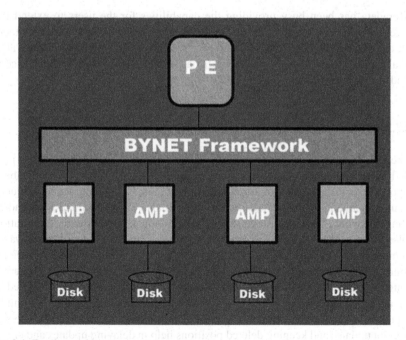

Fig. 8.4 Teradata architecture

to get the result for the query. The PE keeps track of everything about the table schema, number of records, and number of AMPs active. While making the plan, PE also checks the access right of the users.

Access Module Processor (AMP)
Access Module Processor (AMP) is the component which stores and retrieves the data. The AMPs receive the instructions from the PE, and the AMPs are designed to work in parallel. The data is divided among the AMPs, making it possible to divide the work among themselves. Each of the AMP is only responsible for its rows, and these cannot access each other's data rows.

Once the request has been processed, the results have to be sent back to the client. Since the rows are spread across multiple AMPs, they must be consolidated. This is done by the message passing layer, and each of the AMPs just sorts their own rows in parallel.

Message Passing Layer (BYNET)
When the components are distributed on different nodes, it becomes essential that each component should communicate with each other at high speeds. To enable this communications, Teradata uses the BYNET interconnect. It is a high-speed, dual redundant, multi-path communication channel. Another startling capability of the BYNET is that the bandwidth increases as the number of nodes in the system increases. This is done using virtual circuits. The dual redundancy helps in speed/ bandwidth and the availability. The messages routed are guaranteed to be delivered. When some failures occur, interconnect is reconfigured automatically.

Teradata has been busy providing the capabilities for the users to extend the native functions as extensions and leverage the parallelism in DBMS, and it partners with analytics companies like SAS and Fuzzy Logix to bring the in-database analytical capabilities to its platform. Teradata has started offering high-performance R for advanced analytical processing [10].

8.2.3.2 MonetDB

MonetDB [6] is an open-source column-oriented DBMS. This is designed to provide high performance on complex queries against large databases. This database supports vertical fragmentation for distribution of data, CPU tuning for faster query execution, and automatic and adaptive indexes. It also uses partial indexing and/or sorting of the data. This data database is ACID compliant. It uses Binary Association Tables to store data. Each BAT is a table consisting of an object identifier and value columns, representing a single column in the database. This DBMS is specially designed for bulk processing and data warehouse environments. The data is queried through SQL, JDBC, ODBC, and other clients, and the instructions are converted to BAT algebra. Each operator in BAT algebra corresponds to a MonetDB Assembly Language Instruction. The data is decomposed in a columnar fashion, and processes like delta updates and keeping deleted positions help in delaying updates and creating a cheap snapshot mechanism. Each memory is stored in memory mapped files.

Fig. 8.5 Fuzzy Logix
architectural view
in-database analytics

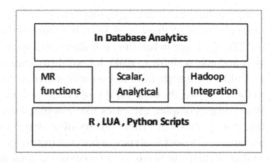

MonetDB provides in-database processing capabilities in two ways: through pre-defined and user-defined functions written in C. These UDFs don't run in sandboxes; instead they run in system space.

Other recent inclusion is to wrap R coding inside SQL functions. Wrapping R code in SQL lets the compiler know the I/O schema definitions. These SQL functions can be in either table forming statements (FROM clause), selection clause, or projection clause.

Exasol's Exapowerlytics is an enterprise analytical DBMS which provides interface through which user defined scripts can be developed and stored in database. These scripts can have scalar functions and MapReduce functions. These functions can directly be used in the SQl statements and are executed parallel in the cluster. This DBMS also stores data in compressed columnar fashion and is based on MPP architecture (Fig. 8.5).

8.2.3.3   Fuzzy Logic's DB Lytix

Fuzzy Logic's DB Lytix is a library of statistical and analytical functions which are used in predictive analytics and various other analyses. There is c/C++ function embedded in the data warehouse kernel. These functions run on the data warehouse providing the users with a whole suit of analytical functions to run in database. This library is available with almost all major vendors like Teradata, HP's Vertica, and Accel.

With this we turn our attention to other class of analytical problems like real-time analytics, stream processing, and complex event processing. Using in-database analytics is not the solution for every problem. This is where the in-memory analytics comes in. In the next section, we will study about the in-memory analytics.

8.3   In-Memory Analytics

We live in a world where data is coming at very high velocities, different types, and huge sizes. Fast data implies the velocity portion of 3 V's in big data. Handling this fast data is one of the biggest challenges of businesses. This availability of fast data brings us the enormous opportunity to gain insight and extract intelligence and make almost everything intelligent, in other words smart products, homes, and cities. The challenge in handling this data is that the traditional DBMS systems are too slow and non-scalable to make it feasible to analyze data in real time [12].

Unlike the earlier days in business analytics when the data is mainly static and analytics is usually done on the old data, nowadays the data is mainly dynamic. With newer, complex use cases like complex event processing, real-time processing, and emphasis of faster delivery of analytics to the business users, efficient ad hoc analysis, visual analytics, it became imperative that the underlying storage and analytical platform needs to run analytics at a far more faster and efficient and this is in conjuction with reducing memory costs and increasing speeds moving the data storage from disk-based systems to memory and using disk as persistent storage. By memory, we mean the DRAM-based main memory, not the NAND-based flash storage, even though there are some products which are based on flash storage yet marketed as in-memory databases. Some proponents even claim that in-memory systems are nothing fancy, they just store data in memory that's it. This argument is true to some extent but seriously flawed when we consider the fact that disk-based systems store data in blocks of pages which are loaded into the buffer pools of the memory. These buffers are swapped out of the memory as the newer data requested. And data is indexed and compressed as it is stored on the disk. This model works good disk-based database systems where the memory is assumed to be constrained. This model doesn't yield well with the memory-based system where the memory constraint is simply not there anymore. This changes the way data is accessed and managed in the system.

In-memory systems facilitate fast data query in ad hoc manner, i.e., randomly unlike disk-based systems where the ad hoc querying is simulated through sequential disk reads and some manipulation in the DBMs. Detailed data loading through multiple data sources is feasible in in memory, thereby helping businesses take faster and better decisions through analysis on multi-data sources. This helps in increasing the performance of such decision; analytical systems as the whole storage and processing are completely done in memory. This has brought a paradigm shift in data storage. Instead of storing data in form of table's aggregates of this data, and multidimensional cubes in case of analytical systems, here the creation of cubes and calculation of aggregates are completely avoided due to the faster query response capabilities [13].

It's been predicted that in memory is the way to go for the future. And in-memory databases are not limited to analytics domain. They are being used for transactional workloads as well as facilitating real-time transactions.

8.3.1   Architecture

The table below shows some of the prevalent in-memory analytical solutions [11] available in the market. Microsoft Excel has been a basic analytical tool for analysts and business users for a long time. One of the easiest ways to make in-memory analytics work without dependence on IT, much of knowledge of multidimensional techniques, etc. is to use in-memory add-in for Excel. This add-in helps in loading the large volumes of data into the memory from particular backend data management system. Once data is in memory, users can use Excel to run on the fly filtering, slice and dice, etc. on retrieving data sets. In-memory OLAP works in similar fashion; data is first loaded into in memory allowing for complicated computations to be done on demand with faster response times and support for what if analysis.

In-memory visual analytics integrates a high-performance visual analytical system with an in-memory database giving provision for the users to query data quickly and visualize the reports, forming interactive analytical systems. In-memory accelerator is yet another prominent way to work with traditional data warehouse yet provide benefits of in-memory analytical system. We will look into the modern enterprise data architecture which uses in memory for real-time analytics and complex event processing injunction with Hadoop, traditional data warehouse for predictive analytics, and exploratory analytics.

The goal of in-memory analytic system is simple to:

- Cater to the requirements of real-time analytics
- Perform faster analytics

Difference between traditional BI and INMA:

Categories of in-memory analytics (Table 8.1)

8.3.2 Benefits and Limitations

Some of the benefits in using in-memory system are noted as follows:

- With huge volumes of data and reading or moving data that becomes quite costly as we have noted in the previous sections. So instead of the moving the data, the computation engine simply returns the location of the stored data in shared memory.
- Improved decision-making and provides ease of use to allow business users build their own reports minimal technical expertise. Easy interactive analytics.
- Eliminating repetitive work reducing the burden of database.
- Offer finer performance and provision for ad hoc analytics.

These systems are hugely impacted by the memory in the system. So hardware support needs to be there to leverage this technology. Many major competitors are delivering there in-memory solutions with appliance. Appliances in simple terms are highly integrated hardware and software platforms.

In the next section, we will study some major solutions available in the market. Please note that the in-database processing and in-memory processing overlap in its goals. It is generally touted that a solution with in-database processing and in-memory processing clubbed together would be an ideal solution. Some of the solutions we study provide both in-memory and in-database processing capabilities which we will note separately.

Table 8.1 In-memory analytics categories

Category	Description	Pros	Cons	Systems
In-memory database-based solutions	The whole data is stored in memory	*Fast query and analysis*	Limited by physical space although we can use commodity machines to create in-memory database cluster	VoltDB, Microsoft SQL server 2014
		No modeling required		
		Reporting and analysis are simple		
In-memory spreadsheet	Spreadsheet like array loaded entirely into memory	Fast reporting, querying, and analysis since the entire spreadsheet is in memory	Limited by physical memory on a single system	Microsoft Power Pivot
		No modeling required		
		Reporting and analysis are as simple as sorting and filtering a spreadsheet		
In-memory OLAP. Classic MOLAP cube loaded entirely in memory		Fast reporting, querying, and analysts since the entire model and data are all in memory	Requires traditional multidimensional data modeling	IBM Cognos TM1, actuate BIRT
		Ability to write back	Limited to single physical memory space	
		Accessible by 3rd party MDX tools		
In-memory inverted index	Index (with data) loaded into memory	Fast reporting, querying, and analysts since the entire index is in memory	Limited by physical memory	SAP BusinessObjects (BI accelerator)
			Some index modeling still required	
		Less modeling required than an OLAP-based solution	Reporting and analysis limited to entity relationships built in index	

8.3.3   Representative Systems

8.3.3.1   SAP HANA Appliances

SAP HANA [14] is an in-memory database that is delivered as an appliance with partners like HP and Dell. This solution is tightly integrated with SAP BW [15]. This is the only database available in the market which claims to handle both transactional and analytical workloads simultaneously. This data is stored in both columnar and row wise tables making it capable to work efficiently with both type of workloads. Since its been delivered as an appliance, the software and hardware are tightly integrated, so deployment and management of the servers become a breeze. SAP HANA stores data in compressed format, thereby increasing the amount of data that can be stored in the database. The data loading is done through incremental updates only when the data is changed. Data can be partitioned to increase the performance and parallel capabilities. As we have noted down earlier, the database doesn't store any aggregates, as it can perform the calculations on the fly and respond very quickly. One advantage of the system which excels is that a single data store can be used for both transactional and analytical applications. There are use cases in the current organizations where the analytical decision is integrated with normal applications like recommendation engines or personalized news feeds, etc.

Going into the future, SAP is integrating its core offering ERP with HANA making way for real-time transactional applications. This, in the present day, eliminates usage of database specialized in transactional workloads to work on analytical processing, saving time and effort.

8.3.3.2 VoltDB

VoltDB is a New-SQL database built for developing data-intensive application working on streaming, fast data and also real-time analytics and feasibility to work with familiar tools like SQL and json. VoltDB applications developed in Java with SQL using JDBC and ODBC. Unlike many NoSQL databases which forgo durability for eventual consistency, VoltDB is durable and recovers transparently/gracefully from hardware and network failures. One of the striking features of VoltDB is that it

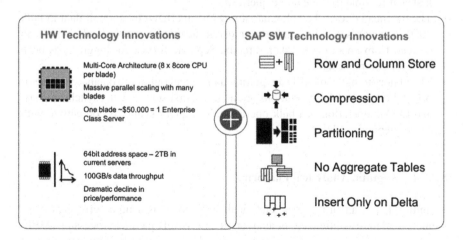

Fig. 8.6 SAP HANA features

provides full data consistency yet being elastically and linearly scalable. As a matter of fact, VoltDB is ACID compliant.

8.3.3.3 BLU for DB2

IBM DB2 with BLU Acceleration [16] utilizes dynamic in-memory columnar technologies. Memory-management decisions like which tables needs to be stored in memory etc are far too complex and dynamic for database administrators (DBAs) to make them manually. In most of the cases where manual decisions are taken by DBA leads to suboptimal memory settings leading to suboptimal performance. In-memory computing platforms should be as fast to boot as they are to query by eliminating memory configuration decisions at startup time.

These are two major points BLU focuses at, with dynamic management techniques ensuring equitable memory resources among transactional, analytical, and other type of workloads. BLU is part of IBM DB2 database which works like any other columnar database with a lot of optimizations while joining the tables, etc. IBM BLU is currently a single server solution limiting the scalability factor and is costly.

Some of the BLU technical highlights are:

- Query pipelining so that data scans can be shared between queries.
- Data skipping to reduce I/O burden and vectorization based on SIMD which works the same on Intel and Power processors.
- Probabilistic caching and automatic workload management which helps in storing more frequent data in memory and capping maximum number of queries per core to resolve contention problems.
- As with any other columnar database, it compresses with various strategies selected automatically. The order of data I preserved during the compression makes it feasible to issue range queries.
- The overhead due to the columnar storage is amortized by commit data in bulk 1000s of records at a time and since most of the queries are read only which can be read from uncommitted data directly. Separate format for logging has been used for columnar tables.
- The major strengths of BLU are getting data in and out of the database (in memory and on disk). SQL operations are memory first sent to disk asynchronously, and LOAD operation is a bulk operation. The query syntax is compatible with earlier versions of DB2.

8.3.3.4 Kognitio Analytical Platforms

Kognitio [17] is an in-memory analytical platform. It is a high-performance in-memory scalability optimized for analytic. It's massively parallel processing (MPP) architecture allows arrays of low cost, commodity servers to be aggregated into a single, powerful analytical engine with a very vast processing power. By keeping all the data of interest in memory, MPP architecture Kognitio can efficiently use every single core of every processor in the array, enabling it to answer individual and bundled within very less time to support "train of thought" processing, with Hadoop providing data ingestion and storage for huge volumes of data. Kognitio acts as a high-performance analytical cache. Data feeds are ingested from operational systems into Hadoop where the processing is done and data sets are made visible to Kognitio as external tables for analysis. High-speed data transport between tightly integrated technologies makes this platform highly suitable for interactive analysis. This technology goes in the opposite direction of in-database processing advocating separation between the data storage which is Hadoop and where data is analyzed (Fig. 8.7).

Other major products that fall under in-memory category are Oracle in-memory databases, Pivotal Gemfire, TIBCO, memsql, and Microsoft SQL server 2014. In fact IBM BLU and Microsoft in-memory technology is actually hybrid as they can still store some data on disks, moving the frequently accessed data to memory. SQL server writes changes to data logs which can be used to retrieve data if power goes down.

Gartner [4] coined the term HTAP in the beginning of 2014 to describe new age in-memory data systems that do both online analytical processing (OLAP) and online transaction processing (OLTP). HTAP relies on newer and much more

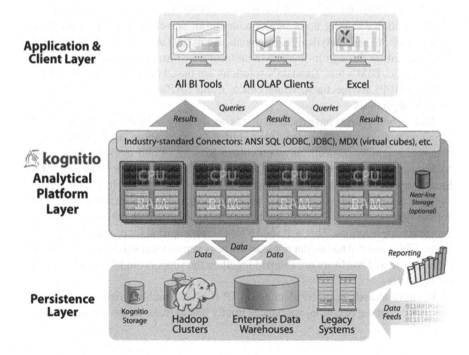

Fig. 8.7 Kognitio analytical platform architectural view

powerful, often distributed, processing: sometimes it involves a new hardware "appliance," and it almost always requires a new software platform. And thereby no more data replication and new transactional information become part of an analytical model and vice versa.

8.4 Analytical Appliances

As the size and complexity of workloads pose a huge concern for analytic applications even with the in-memory and in-database techniques available, hardware optimization becomes paramount to meet the present and future performance requirements. This optimization doesn't only improve the efficiency and performance; it also simplifies maintenance and scalability. This is the reason many companies are looking to augment their analytical infrastructure with effective mix of software and hardware. For example, Google uses search appliances to provide the Google search service to the millions of users. The appliances provide better performance due to the fact that the software, hardware, and operating systems are tightly integrated. Few notable analytical appliances in the market are Oracle Exadata, IBM Netezza, and Teradata Aster appliances. In order to understand the uptake of analytic appliances, it is important to note the paradigm shift that has shaped the information management needs of organizations. Why is there a need for appliances? To answer this question, we need to revisit the shift in user demands on IT. Conventional scaling up or newer scale out of servers is not quite keeping up with processing and analytical requirements. Analytical appliances offer higher performance either through in-memory architecture or through a parallel processing. For example, IBM's and Teradata's solutions are based on massively parallel processing (MPP) architectures, while Oracle's and SAP's are based on in-memory analytic appliances.

And secondly, firms have realized that faster delivery of business value is crucial. Using an analytic appliance, the time required to scope, setup, and optimize infrastructure is rapidly reduced. As of now there are a lot of mid-market solutions like Microsoft Parallel Data Warehouse (HP and DELL offer the hardware) and IBM Smart Analytic for all the budget constrained. So coming back, why should anyone consider investing in an analytical appliance other than the performance? First comes the ease of use and setup. Appliances are preconfigured, optimized hardware cum software solutions. This will shed a lot of time required for requirement gathering to deployment. And last but not least are easy support and troubleshooting; since the software and hardware are shipped together, the support model tends to be relatively simple.

We have already seen Teradata and SAP HANA which are delivered as appliances. We will see two more appliances briefly just to make things clearer.

8.4.1 Oracle Exalytics

Oracle Exalytics [19] is an in-memory analytical appliance from Oracle. This includes TimesTen in-memory database from Oracle and Oracle Business Intelligence foundation suite. This system has terabytes of memory and flash-based storage which is extended with usage of SAN. The system works on Oracle Enterprise Linux and Oracle Solaris. For the high availability servers, Exalytics machines are configured to work in active-active or active-passive modes.

Oracle TimesTen in-memory database is a relational database with persistence and provides SQL interfacing which doesn't need to change the legacy applications. This also supports columnar compression reducing the memory footprints. TimesTen database supports star join optimizations and hash indexes on non-primary key.

With whole set of management, visualization, automatic optimization of settings, and data read, the Oracle Exalytics can also be configured with Oracle Exadata machine which specializes in both analytical and transactional workloads.

8.4.2 IBM Netezza

IBM Netezza [18] integrates processing, storage, and database into a compact system which is optimized for analytical processing and scalability. Few of the principles Netezza follows are: bringing processing close to the data, massive parallel architecture, and flexible configurations and scalability.

Netezza is a data warehouse appliance. It utilizes asymmetric massively parallel processing (AMPP) architecture. AMPP architecture SMP front-end with a shared MPP backed processing queries. Another vital feature is that every processing element runs on multiple streams of data while filtering out superfluous data as early in the processing pipeline as possible.

Netezza has four major components:

Netezza Hosts These are the front-end SMP hosts which run high-performance Linux, in an active-passive configuration for high availability. The host in active state interfaces with external applications and tools, be it BI, dashboards, etc. These hosts receive SQL queries from client, which are compiled into executable code segments called snippets. Each snippet is made up of two elements: a set of FPGA parameters to configure FAST engines and compiled code executed by individual CPU cores. And then an optimized query plan is created which is then distributed to MPP nodes for execution (Fig. 8.8).

Field Programmable Gate Arrays (FPGA) The FPGA has an important role in reducing the data read. These filter out undesirable data as early in the data pipeline as possible. This process helps in reducing I/O load and frees up CPU, network, and memory which might've been occupied by superfluous data.

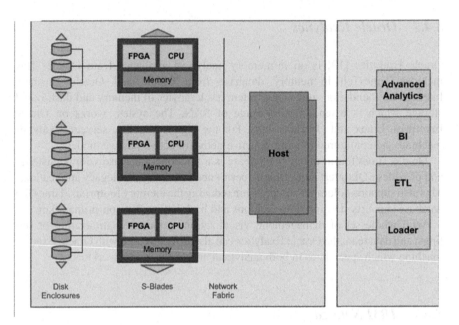

Fig. 8.8 IBM Netezza architecture

Each of these FPGA has embedded engines which perform data filtering and data transformation functions on the stream of data. These engines are called FAST engine. These engines can be reconfigured dynamically, making it feasible to modify them or extend them through software. These are customized for each snippet through the parameters provided in query execution. These engines act on the stream of data provided by a Direct Memory Access (DMA) module at extremely high speed.

Snippet Blades (S-Blades) S-Blades are the worker nodes or the intelligent processing nodes which form the MPP engine in the Netezza appliance. Every S-Blade is an independent server node which contains gigabytes of RAM, high-performance multicore CPUs, and multiengine FPGAs.

Disk Enclosures The disk enclosures are the persistent storage in the Netezza appliance. These contain high-performance and high-density disks. Each disk contains only a part of the database table data. Data distribution is done by the host using some randomized allocation or hash-based allocation. These enclosures are connected to S-engines through high-speed interconnects.

The data is compressed and cached in memory ensuring that the most frequently accessed data is served right from the memory instead from the disk. FAST engines which run in parallel inside the FPGAs un-compress and filter out 95–98 % of table data at physics speed, retaining only the data that is required to respond to a query. The remaining data in the stream is processed concurrently by CPU cores, also running in parallel. With these optimizations and clever use of FPGAs, Netezza offers higher performance and stands as one of the top players in analytical appliances market.

We have seen different technologies to solve the problems faced by organization nowadays in the analytical domain. Please head onto further reading session for further study.

8.5 Conclusions

In this chapter we have seen the difference between transactional and analytical workloads. Transactional workloads are short, discrete, and mostly atomic operations, whereas the analytical workloads require whole view of the data and the computations are generally more complex and data intensive. Then we studied in-database processing which is based on moving the processing close to the data. How can it be implemented as in SQL statements, user-defined functions, and embedded library functions? We have seen how Teradata, Fuzzy Logix, MonetDB, and some other products provide these processing capabilities.

Then we studied the limitations of this approach, namely, the real-time analysis and stream analysis. The motive of in-memory systems is to store all the data in memory and using some intelligent memory swapping and data loading techniques the in-memory databases are providing high performance. We studied the major contenders in this class of systems SAP HANA which supports both analytical and transactional workloads and VoltDB which is an ACID compliant NewSQL database. Kognitio in-memory analytical platform, its architecture.

Then we noted the challenges posed by the complex workloads on the infrastructure and user expectations. Appliances are pre-integrated software and hardware which reduce the deployment time and management efforts required, at the same time giving high performance to the users. IBM Netezza is one of the largest vendors in analytical appliance. The Netezza uses asymmetric massive parallel processing architecture. It is based on shared-nothing architecture and uses field programmable gate arrays for data filtering and processing at a very high speeds providing high-performance I/O and processing.

With this, we conclude this chapter. Head on to next section on learning resources which gives more details to study.

8.6 Exercises

1. Write about traditional analytical platforms?
2. Briefly explain the evolution of analytics?
3. Explain the difference between analytic workload and transactional workload? How do these differences translated to system architecture?

4. What are the problems/limitations associated with traditional analytical platform?
5. When does it make sense to use in-database processing?
6. What is in-database processing? What are the different ways in which it is implemented?
7. Write briefly about the architectural differences between conventional platform and in data-processing platform?
8. Write about a use case in which in-database processing is used.
9. What is in-memory analytics?
10. How is in-memory analytics different from in-database analytics?
11. What are the different ways of using in memory to speed up analytics?
12. What are the architectural features of an in-memory data store supporting analytics?
13. How is in-memory different from in-database analytics?
14. What are the factors that lead to in-memory analytics?
15. What are the advantages and limitations of in-memory analytics?
16. Write a use case where in-memory analytics can be used?
17. Write about the architecture of in-memory database program?

References

1. Chaudhuri S, Dayal U (1997) An overview of data warehousing and OLAP technology. ACM Sigmod Rec 26(1):65–74
2. Inmon WH (2005) Building the data warehouse. Wiley, New York
3. Chen H, Chiang RH, Storey VC (2012) Business intelligence and analytics: from big data to big impact. MIS Q 36(4):1165–1188
4. Russom P (2011) Big data analytics. TDWI Best Practices Report, Fourth Quarter
5. Taylor J (2013) In-database analytics
6. Nes SIFGN, Kersten SMSMM (2012) Monet DB: two decades of research in column-oriented database architectures. Data Eng 40
7. Chaudhuri S, Dayal U, Narasayya V (2011) An overview of BI technology. Commun ACM 54(8):88–98
8. Teradata. (n.d.) Retrieved January 5, 2015, from http://www.teradata.com
9. Dinsmore T (2012). Leverage the in-database capabilities of analytic software. Retrieved September 5, 2015, from http://thomaswdinsmore.com/2012/11/21/leverage-the-in-database-capabilities-ofanalytic-software/
10. Inchiosa M (2015) In-database analytics deep dive with teradata and revolution. Lecture conducted from Revolution Analytics, SAP Software & Solutions|Technology & Business Applications. Retrieved January 5, 2015
11. Plattner H, Zeier A (2012) In-memory data management: technology and applications. Springer Science & Business Media, Berlin
12. Plattner H (2009) A common database approach for OLTP and OLAP using an in-memory column database. In: Proceedings of the 2009 ACM SIGMOD international conference on management of data. ACM, New York, pp 1–2
13. Acker O, Gröne F, Blockus A, Bange C (2011) In-memory analytics–strategies for real-time CRM. J Database Market Cust Strateg Manage 18(2):129–136

14. Färber F, May N, Lehner W, Große P, Müller I, Rauhe H, Dees J (2012) The HANA database–an architecture overview. IEEE Data Eng Bull 35(1):28–33
15. SAP Software & Solutions I Technology & Business Applications. Retrieved January 5, 2015
16. Raman V, Attaluri G, Barber R, Chainani N, Kalmuk D, KulandaiSamy V, Lightstone S, Liu S, Schiefer B, Sharpe D, Storm A, Zhang L (2013) DB2 with BLU acceleration: so much more than just a column store. Proceedings of the VLDB Endowment 6(11):1080–1091
17. Konitio. Retrieved January 5, 2015.
18. Francisco P (2011) The Netezza data appliance architecture: a platform for high performance data warehousing and analytics. IBM Redbooks
19. GLIGOR G, Teodoru S (2011) Oracle Exalytics: engineered for speed-of-thought analytics. Database Syst J 2(4):3–8

Further Reading

Kimball R, Ross M (2002) The data warehouse toolkit: the complete guide to dimensional modelling. Wiley, [Nachdr]. New York [ua]
Nowak RM (2014) Polyglot programming in applications used for genetic data analysis. BioMed Research International, 2014

Chapter 9
High-Performance Integrated Systems, Databases, and Warehouses for Big and Fast Data Analytics

9.1 Introduction

The advancement of knowledge through discoveries (accidental or need-based deeper and collaborative investigations), fresh inventions, and data-driven insights has been a vital component in significantly and systematically enhancing the quality of human lives. The recognition of previously unknown linkages and relationships between occurrences, objects, and facts lays a stimulating and sustainable foundation for bringing in scores of praiseworthy advances in almost all the tangible domains ranging from life sciences, financial services, electronics and communication, homeland security, and government operations. Newer discoveries definitely bring in high value for individuals, institutions, and innovators along with enhanced care, choice, comfort, and convenience. One highly renowned factor is that discoveries ensure better security and safety for people and properties. For example, newer drugs for fatal diseases like cancer bring in billions of dollars for drug discovery companies as well as save many lives across the globe. Enterprising and inquisitive minds relentlessly explore for fresh avenues for increasing and sustaining their revenues. That is the incontrovertible reality in our society.

Recently, data has gained the distinction of being touted as the strategic asset and, for any organization to proceed with confidence and clarity, data-driven insights in place of intuitions are very much indispensable. Now the big and fast data era beckons us with the relentless accumulation and acclimatization of multi-structured data; the systematic extraction of actionable insights out of those data mountains gains immense momentum in order to derive in more decisive revelations and resolutions for the dreamt smarter world.

Discovery takes place when a researcher has a "Eureka!" moment, where a flash of insight leads to the formulation of a new idea that is being validated against certain observations in the real world. Data especially big and fast data with the help of data virtualization, analytical, mining, processing, and visualization platforms can assist in both of these phases. In short, applying data analytics and information

© Springer International Publishing Switzerland 2015 233
P. Raj et al., *High-Performance Big-Data Analytics*, Computer Communications
and Networks, DOI 10.1007/978-3-319-20744-5_9

visualization processes and products contributes for this notion of game-changing discoveries and their subsequent verification. However, making sense out of big and fast data is not an easy affair with the current data management technologies, platforms, and tools. In this chapter, we are to dig deep down to describe how the emerging converged and integrated systems in association with the latest stream of the traditional SQL databases and the recent NoSQL and NewSQL databases are to simplify the complicated task of generating timely and dependable insights. Precisely speaking, it is going to be the data-driven world. The major sources and types of data include:

- Business transactions, interactions, operations, and analytical data
- System and application infrastructures (compute, storage, network, application, Web and database servers, etc.) and log files
- Social and people data
- Customer, product, sales, and other business data
- Machine and sensor data
- Scientific experimentation and observation data (genetics, particle physics, climate modeling, drug discovery, etc.)

The advances being achieved in big and fast data analytics disciplines enable the IT team to design and deliver the following sophisticated and synchronized services for the total human society:

- Insight-driven, adaptive, real-time, and real-world services
- People-centric physical services
- Context-aware applications

In short, it is all about fulfilling the smarter planet vision. This chapter is mainly crafted in order to give a business-centric view of high-performance big data analytics. The readers can find the major application domains/use cases of high-performance big data analytics and the compelling needs and reasons for wholeheartedly embracing this new paradigm. The emerging use cases include the use of real-time data such as the sensor data to detect any abnormalities in plant and machinery and batch processing of sensor data collected over a period to conduct failure analysis of plant and machinery.

9.2   The Key Characteristics of Next-Generation IT Infrastructures and Platforms

The analytical workloads, platforms, and infrastructures are mandated to have some extra substance and stamina in order to be right and relevant for the emerging world of knowledge-filled services. As indicated above, analytics play an indispensable role in quickly pumping out insights out of a massive amount of multi-structured data. Such kinds of business-critical applications require infrastructures typically needed for hosting high-end transactional and operational systems. The major system parameters are availability, scalability, and performance. Analytical systems have to do more with less and ensure the same performance even if there is a fluctuation in user and data demands. As the data load is highly variable, the elasticity of system resources in order to meet up any kind of exigencies is paramount. There are auto-scaling methods being prescribed in order to satisfy this critical need. Not only infrastructures but also applications need to be designed and developed with the inherent capability of scalability in order to reap the originally envisaged benefits.

Cloud management software solutions in association with load balancers do the trick for auto-scaling. With the adoption of NoSQL databases, horizontal scalability of databases (scale-out) is seeing a nice and neat reality. Similarly, the availability of systems is very vital for extracting timely insights to act upon in time. Apart from the abovementioned quality of service (QoS) attributes/nonfunctional requirements (NFRs), instantaneously activating and running IT infrastructures; systematically empowering them to be proactive, preemptive, and adaptive in their operations and outputs; meticulously making them efficient in their deliveries towards the strategic goal of self-servicing IT; and controlling them via software to be extensible, sustainable, consumable, and composable are the critically acclaimed qualities expected out of futuristic IT infrastructures. IT is supposed to work from behind sagaciously yet silently in order to make things happening.

In the ensuing sections, we are to write on the state-of-the-art infrastructures and end-to-end platforms. In the latter part, we are to describe the delectable changes happening in the data management side. Predominantly, there are analytical, clustered, distributed, and parallel SQL databases apart from the recent NoSQL and NewSQL databases in order to streamline data storage. Let us start with a brief on integrated systems for the ensuing era of big data.

9.3 Integrated Systems for Big and Fast Data Analytics

There are several types of integrated systems towards big data analytics. There are converged infrastructure (CI) solutions, expertly integrated systems, data warehouse and big data appliances, and specially engineered systems. Let us start our discussion with a brief on the supercomputing-scale appliance for big data analytics.

9.3.1 The Urika-GD Appliance for Big Data Analytics

Traditional business intelligence (BI) tools, built on relational models, are highly optimized to generate defined reports from operational systems or data warehouses. They require the development of a data model that is designed to answer specific business questions but the problem is that the defined model limits the types of questions that can be asked. Discovery, however, is an iterative process, where a line of inquiry may result in previously unanticipated questions, which may also require new sources of data to be loaded. Accommodating these mandates a huge workload on IT professionals.

Graph analytics are ideally suited to meet these challenges. Graphs represent entities and the relationships between them explicitly, greatly simplifying the addition of new relationships and new data sources, and efficiently support ad hoc querying and analysis. Real-time response to complex queries against multi-terabyte graphs is also achievable. Graphs provide a flexible data model and hence the addition of new types of relationships and new data sources is greatly simplified. Any relationships extracted from multi-structured data can be readily represented in the same graph. Graphs have no fixed schema and hence there is no restriction on the types of queries that can be posed. Graphs also enable advanced analytics techniques such as community detection, path analysis, clustering, and others. In short, graph analytics can deliver predictable, real-time performance, as long as the hardware and software are appropriate to the task. Thus graph analytics come handy in unearthing new discoveries out of big data. The graph analytics database provides an extensive set of capabilities for defining and querying graphs using the industry standard RDF and SPARQL. These standards are widely used for storing graphs and performing analytics against them. Considering the vagaries of graphs, graph analytics requires a state-of-the-art appliance.

- *Discovery analytics [1] requires real-time response*—a multiprocessor solution is required for scale and performance.
- *Graphs are hard to partition*—a large and shared memory is required to avoid the need to partition graphs. Regardless of the schema used, partitioning the graph across a cluster will result in edges spanning cluster nodes. If the number of edges crossing cluster nodes is so large, then the network latency results in high data latency. Given the highly interconnected nature of graphs, users gain a significant processing advantage if the entire graph is held in sufficiently large shared memory.
- *Graphs are not predictable and therefore cache busting*—a custom graph processor is needed to deal with the mismatch between processor and memory speeds. Analyzing relationships in large graphs requires the examination of multiple and competing alternatives. These memory accesses are very much data dependent and eliminate the ability to apply traditional performance improvement techniques such as pre-fetching and caching. Given that even RAM memory is 100 times slower than processors and that graph analytics consists of exploring alternatives, the processor sits idle most of the time waiting for delivery of data. Cray developed hardware multithreading technology to help alleviate this problem. Threads can explore different alternatives, and each thread can have its own memory access. As long as the processor supports a sufficient number of hardware threads, it can be kept busy. Given the highly nondeterministic nature of graphs, a massively multithreaded architecture enables a tremendous performance advantage.

- *Graphs are highly dynamic*—a scalable and high-performance I/O system is required for fast loading. Graph analytics for discovery involves examining the relationships and correlations between multiple data sets and, consequently, requires loading many large and constantly changing data sets into memory. The sluggish speed of I/O systems (1000 times slower compared to the CPU) translates into graph load and modification times.

These requirements drove the design of the Urika-GD system's hardware and resulted in a hardware platform proven to deliver real-time performance for complex data discovery applications. The Cray's Urika-GD appliance is a heterogeneous system consisting of Urika-GD appliance service nodes and graph accelerator nodes linked by a high-performance interconnect fabric for data exchange. Graph accelerator nodes ("accelerator nodes") utilize a purpose-built Threadstorm processor capable of delivering several orders of magnitude better performance on graph analytics applications than a conventional microprocessor. Accelerator nodes share memory and run a single instance of a UNIX-based, compute-optimized OS named multithreaded kernel (MTK).

Urika-GD appliance services nodes ("service nodes"), based on x86 processors, provide I/O, appliance, and database management. As many I/O nodes may be added as desired, enabling the scaling of connectivity and management functions for larger Urika-GD appliances. Each service node runs a distinct instance of a fully featured Linux operating system. The interconnect fabric is designed for high-speed access to memory anywhere in the system from any processor, as well as scaling to large processor counts and memory capacity. The Urika-GD system architecture supports flexible scaling to 8192 graph accelerator processors and 512 TB of shared memory. Urika-GD systems can be incrementally expanded to this maximum size as data analytics needs and data set sizes grow.

The Cray's Urika-GD appliance is built to meet these requirements for smoothening discovery. With one of the world's most scalable shared memory architectures, the Urika-GD appliance employs graph analytics to surface unknown linkages and nonobvious patterns in big data, does it with speed and simplicity, and facilitates the kinds of breakthroughs. The Urika-GD appliance complements existing data warehouses and Hadoop clusters by offloading challenging data discovery applications.

9.3.2 IBM PureData System for Analytics (PDA)

IBM PureData System for Analytics is a high-performance, scalable, and massively parallel system that enables analytics on enormous data volumes. This system, powered by Netezza technology, is designed specifically for running complex analytics on very large data volumes, orders of magnitude faster than the traditional solutions. The PureData System for Analytics delivers the proven performance, scalability, sagacity, and simplicity your business needs. This appliance does analytics in parallel, on a massive scale, inside an easy-to-use data warehouse (DW) appliance. And it runs business intelligence (BI) and advanced analytics that were previously impossible or impractical. IBM PureData System for Analytics is a purpose-built and standards-based data warehouse and analytics appliance that architecturally and artistically integrates database, server, storage, and advanced analytic capabilities into a single and easy-to-manage system. It has been designed from the ground up for rapid and deeper analysis of data volumes scaling into the petabytes.

PureData System's orders-of-magnitude performance advantage over other analytic options comes from its unique asymmetric massively parallel processing (AMPP) architecture that combines open IBM blade servers and disk storage with IBM's patented data filtering using field-programmable gate arrays (FPGAs). This combination delivers blistering fast query performance on analytic workloads supporting tens of thousands of BI and data warehouse users, sophisticated analytics at the speed of thought, and petabyte scalability.

PureData System for Analytics dramatically simplifies analytics by consolidating all analytic activity in one place, right where the data resides. With the innate support for PMML 4.0 models, data modelers and quantitative teams can operate on the data directly inside the appliance instead of having to offload it to a separate infrastructure and deal with the associated data preprocessing, transformation, and movement. Data scientists can build their models using all the enterprise data and then iterate through different models much faster to find the best fit. Once the model is developed, it can be seamlessly executed against the relevant data in the appliance. Prediction and scoring can be done right where the data resides, in line with other processing, on an as-needed basis. Users can get their prediction scores in near real time, helping operationalize advanced analytics and making it available throughout the enterprise.

As an appliance, all of the integration of hardware, software, and storage is done for you, leading to shorter deployment cycles and industry-leading time to value for BI and analytic initiatives. The appliance is delivered ready to go for immediate data loading and query execution and integrates with leading ETL, BI, and analytics applications through standard ODBC, JDBC, and OLE DB interfaces. All components are internally redundant, and the failure of a processing node (S-Blade) causes no significant performance degradation for a robust, production-ready environment from the moment the appliance is plugged into your data center.

9.3.3   The Oracle Exadata Database Machine

The popularity of appliances is surging these days due to their unique capabilities and benefits. All the leading players in the IT hardware infrastructure solutions are jumping into the appliance bandwagon. As per the information provided in the Oracle website, this appliance with the recently released Exadata X5 is engineered to be the high-performing, cost-effective, and highly available platform for running the Oracle database. Exadata is a modern architecture featuring scale-out industry-standard database servers, scale-out intelligent storage servers, state-of-the-art PCI flash storage servers, and an extremely high-speed InfiniBand internal fabric that connects all servers and storage together. Unique software algorithms in Exadata implement database intelligence in storage, PCI-based flash, and InfiniBand networking to deliver the required high performance and capacity at lower costs. Exadata runs all types of database workloads including online transaction processing (OLTP), data warehousing (DW), in-memory analytics, and consolidation of mixed workloads.

The Exadata Database Machine is an easy-to-deploy system that includes all the hardware needed for running the Oracle database without any hitch or hurdle. The database servers, storage servers, and network are pre-configured, pre-tuned, and pretested by Oracle experts, eliminating weeks or months of efforts typically required to deploy any high-performance system. Extensive end-to-end testing ensures all the encapsulated components work as originally envisaged together and there are no performance bottlenecks or single points of failure that can potentially spread across to bring down the whole system. The appliance makers are typically tied up with software vendors to run their applications quickly. For example, SAS has a high-performance analytics application in its portfolio, and through the tie-up with Oracle products and solutions, SAS applications are easily deployed and delivered in a plug-and-play fashion. That is, SAS high-performance analytics runs efficiently on Oracle big data appliance and Exadata machine. Enterprises using SAS applications could gain a lot through this sort of tight integration. That is, high-performance business analytics is being achieved with less time on system configuration and administration. Time to value gets accelerated in an affordable and automated fashion.

9.3.4 The Teradata Data Warehouse and Big Data Appliances

Primarily there are two appliance offerings from Teradata. The first one is the data warehouse appliance and the other one is the integrated big data platform. Teradata is in the limelight through their high-performance appliances for different purposes through a host of sustained innovations by bringing forth newer solutions for solving business-critical problems. Teradata appliances are efficiently bestowed with sufficient analytic capabilities to realize big business value for particular workloads.

The Data Warehouse Appliance The data warehouse appliance is a fully integrated system that is purpose built for integrated data warehousing. This product features the Teradata database, a Teradata platform with the dual Intel twelve-core Ivy Bridge processors, SUSE Linux operating system, and enterprise-class storage—all preinstalled into a power-efficient unit. That means you can have the system up and running live in just a few hours for rapid time to value. This was designed to be easy to set up. Users will be submitting queries after only a few simple steps.

This delivers up to three times more system-wide performance improvement out of the box as compared to the previous one. This supports up to 512GB of memory per node and up to 4 TB of memory per cabinet. It uses Teradata Intelligent Memory to provide customers with fast access to their hottest data and to deliver the performance of in-memory in a way that makes sense for data warehousing. And for the highest performance and quickest query response times, the appliance leverages the Teradata columnar technology. With this enterprise-ready platform from Teradata, the customer can start building his integrated data warehouse and grow it as his needs expand. This appliance's innovative design is optimized for fast scans and deep-dive analytical analysis. Its software-based, shared-nothing architecture delivers always-on parallelism so even the toughest, most complex queries get completed quickly.

The Integrated Big Data Platform   The integrated big data platform is the premier platform for applying business analytics to massive amounts of detailed relational data at an affordable cost per data unit. As per the Teradata brochure published in the home page, this is an environment that enables agile analytics with incredibly fast parallel processing, scalability to process massive volumes of data, and rich in-database analytic capabilities. Teradata provides a comprehensive set of in-database analytics that leverages the database's speed while eliminating time-consuming and costly data movement. The analytics range from data exploration, geospatial, temporal, and predictive modeling to emerging open-source technology, big data integration, and development environments. This appliance delivers a best-in-class SQL engine at a breakthrough price per terabyte [TB], which is competitive with other big data technologies. It is purpose built to cost-effectively analyze extremely large amounts of detailed data—up to 234 petabytes uncompressed—to gain deep, strategic intelligence. Now customers are able to keep all of their data within the Teradata appliance—with the same format and schema—since there is no need to sample or discard data due to storage limitations. Customers can also choose to cost-effectively keep a second copy of their IDW [integrated data warehouse] for disaster recovery and offload some of its workload during peak periods. The appliance enables the Teradata database for analyzing massive sets of relational data and should be used for offloading colder data or specific workloads from IDWs. The appliance is ideal for organizations that are accustomed to all of the performance, support, features, ease of use, and powerful analytics that Teradata delivers. Hadoop is more suited for storing raw, multi-structured data, simple cleansing and transformations, and non-relational, non-SQL processing.

An analytics-optimized environment for rapid, iterative data exploration, this appliance combines big analytics technologies, such as Hadoop, MapReduce, graph, pattern, and path analysis, with ecosystem compatibility with BI and ETL tools, business-friendly ANSI-standard SQL, open-source R, pre-built MapReduce analytics, and mature, enterprise-grade system management solutions. It is a tightly coupled hardware and software solution that contains Teradata Aster Database and Apache Hadoop to process structured, unstructured, and semi-structured data.

9.4 Converged Infrastructure (CI) for Big Data Analytics

Converged infrastructure (CI) takes compute, network, and storage components and integrates them into a single yet cohesive system that is engineered, manufactured, and supported by the vendor. Thus the unification and synchronization enshrined in any CI make it very popular for businesses to cut costs and to accelerate time to value. In the ideal case, these fully integrated, pretested and tuned, and vendor-delivered CIs greatly reduce the administrative burden on IT managers and administrators. Converged infrastructures come as ready-made and turn-key IT solutions and can be up and running in minutes rather than hours and days. The much-anticipated convergence is being accomplished by completely changing how systems are designed, deployed, optimized, maintained, supported, and upgraded. By providing a standardized and vendor-delivered system, CI providers take care of many of the routine and repetitive administrative tasks that historically have been performed by IT teams. This calculated transition frees up time and resources for continued business innovation. The crucial distinctions include:

- *Design*—the system is engineered by the vendor as a single integrated pool for optimal performance, scalability, and availability and configured to meet customers' unique needs.
- *Deploy*—the complete system is manufactured and logically configured at the factory using standardized processes.
- *Maintain*—patches are preselected, pretested, and prepackaged by the vendor for interoperability and compatibility with installed configurations and are ready for immediate nondisruptive deployment.
- *Upgrade*—newer versions of components are preselected, pretested, and certified for interoperability and design integrity and are ready for immediate nondisruptive deployment.
- *Support*—there is a single point of ownership that is expert in all aspects of the system. All deployed system configurations are fully supported to accelerate problem resolution.
- *Evolve*—vendor engineers' next-generation system leveraging latest advances from each component while providing a migration path that interlocks roadmaps from each component.

Virtual Computing Environment (VCE) VCE is a leading CI solution emerged out of a joint venture formed by EMC, Cisco, and VMware. This enterprising endeavor brought together IT infrastructure from the three industry leaders and sought to deliver it to customers as a single entity. The venture named the CI product as the Vblock system. Vblock is suitable for those environments that are looking for easy-to-acquire, install, and deploy solutions. The major components are as follows:

- *Compute and network*—the Vblock's compute component is based on Cisco's unified computing system (UCS) product line and its network component is based on Cisco Nexus and MDS switches.

- *Storage*—all Vblocks use storage from EMC, the leading provider of external storage. Each Vblock series uses the EMC product that matches its target price, performance, and scalability parameters.
- *Virtualization*—VMware ESX is included in the solution package.
- *Management*—as a part of its package, VCE offers its Vision Intelligent Operations software. VCE Vision's features include virtualization optimization, converged operation, and an open API that enables users to use their own management tools of choice.

FlexPod Converged Infrastructure Solution   Similar to the Vblock product, there is another popular CI solution. FlexPod solution portfolio combines NetApp storage systems, Cisco UCS servers, and Cisco Nexus fabric into a single and flexible architecture. FlexPod solutions are designed and validated to reduce deployment time, project risk, and, above all, the cost of IT.

NetApp OnCommand management software and Cisco Unified Computing System Manager tools help you optimize your server and network environment, handling hundreds of resources for thousands of virtual machines. OnCommand controls and automates your data storage infrastructure. Cisco UCS Manager provides unified, embedded management of server and network components. It is possible to manage the FlexPod platform using common data center management tools. You can use Cisco UCS Director for centralized automation and orchestration of your FlexPod solution. FlexPod has been tested and documented with a range of cloud management platforms including CA, Cisco, Cloudstack, Microsoft, Openstack, and VMware. There are FlexPod Lifecycle Management tools and guidance to optimize performance. There are proven tools for FlexPod sizing, configuration, and support.

HP Converged Infrastructure Systems   HP has repackaged its homegrown and acquired components along with several software products into its current lineup of converged infrastructure offerings, which consists of the following 3 product families:

- *VirtualSystem*—VirtualSystem is HP's basic converged infrastructure offering. The family includes an x86 configuration that scales from 2 to 64 blades and one UNIX configuration that scales from 2 to 12 blades. For storage, VirtualSystem offers its midrange 3PAR storage.
- *CloudSystem*—for customers who need a more scalable system or who would simply prefer to use components or software other than those that come with VirtualSystem, HP offers CloudSystem. Unlike VirtualSystem, which offers standard configurations, CloudSystem is an open architecture that offers customers the ability to choose from a wide range of networking, storage, and other options or to forgo new top-of-rack networking and storage and connect to customers' existing components.
- *AppSystem*—AppSystem is a family of appliances that HP describes as "integrated systems optimized for dedicated business applications" such as SAP, Hadoop, data warehousing, and Microsoft Messaging.

Converged infrastructure (CI) solutions are being positioned as the most efficient and effective one for next-generation big and fast data analytics. Due to the coupling of all the hardware and software modules together, most of the administration tasks are taken care of by the machine so that the time to business value is very short.

9.5 High-Performance Analytics: Mainframes + Hadoop

Because of its unique capabilities, mainframe systems are still very popular in the business world. A significant amount of data transactions in banking, insurance, retail, telecommunications, utilities, and government from financial transactions to customer lists and personnel records to manufacturing reports are being accomplished via mainframes. As history shows, mainframe computers power many mission-critical applications throughout the enterprise by collecting, generating, and processing larger data sets. Without an iota of doubt, the mainframe is the undisputed king of transactional data. Since transactions are, by definition, highly repeatable entities, the past 50 years have seen a number of breakthrough improvements in the way the data underneath these transactions is being managed. Several statistics say that more than 60 % of the business-critical data are getting kept in mainframes. For the past couple of decades, the gold standard has been the relational database for storing transactional data.

The art of managing transactional data in relational databases has been perfected on the mainframe systems too. But in reality, the relational data only represents a fraction of all the data held on mainframes. Long-time mainframe shops almost certainly have significant data assets stored in record-oriented file management systems such as VSAM that predates the advent of the relational database. With the dawn of the era of analytics, the operational data are majorly put up in data warehouses, data marts, and cubes to efficiently extract data-driven insights. A significant amount of modern data is stored in XML and JSON formats and a largely untapped source of data comes in the form of unstructured or semi-structured data (tweets and sensor data, system, application and event logs, and similar data that is routinely generated by the day-to-day activities of operational systems). The big integrations, interactions, collaborations, transactions, and operations by systems, services, and people pour out a wider variety of voluminous, variable, and value-enabling data.

Neglecting this mammoth data stocked up in mainframes can result in missed business opportunities. However, while extremely fast, secure, and reliable, processing and analyzing data on the mainframe is a complex and costly affair. Therefore enterprise data warehouses (EDWs) came into picture strongly and the ETL tools are the main scheme for data integration and ingesting. The traditional ETL tools could not provide the scalability and performance required for processing massive quantity of data. As a result, organizations are nowadays increasingly adopting the Apache Hadoop framework as the potential mean to scale the collection and processing of data while substantially reducing costs. One of the Hadoop's greatest strengths is its ability to process and analyze vast amounts of data of all types. However, Hadoop does not reach its perceived potential unless it can connect to all kinds of data sources including mainframe systems.

IBM zEnterprise is the platform of choice for these industries because of its unparalleled quality of service and performance. For big data analytics, mainframes offer better solutions. It can process growing volumes of data quickly and in order to avoid any kind of data latency, today's mainframes are accordingly enhanced to have both transactional as well as analytical modules together. The data warehouse and transactional data systems can be accessed with a single connection or between layers if they are in separate subsystems. This reduces the path length and time from data to analysis by using internal memory speed that is not dependent on a physical network. The IBM zEnterprise analytics solution accelerates IBM DB2 for z/OS queries with in-memory processing, massively parallel architecture, row and columnar store technologies, highly compressed data, and compressed data operations. By combining System z and DB2 Analytics Accelerator.

Syncsort DMX-h, a high-performance ETL software that turns Hadoop into a more robust and feature-rich ETL solution, allows you to leverage all your data, including those stored in monolithic mainframes. With DMX-h, organizations are able to connect all of their data sources and target them to Hadoop with a single tool. The ingestion of data directly from mainframe without the need to install any additional software on it and translating and sampling the mainframe data on the fly without writing a single line of code are automated. Other noteworthy points include developing MapReduce ETL jobs visually without any coding and getting productivity quickly with a comprehensive library of accelerators to develop common ETL data flows and understand your mainframe data better with support for COBOL copybook.

SAS Applications and Mainframes The IBM DB2 Analytics Accelerator (IDAA) is designed to automatically and transparently offload analytic-type queries made by applications such as SAS. This dramatically changes the economics of performing analytics work on DB2 data hosted on mainframes. It gives organizations an opportunity to streamline some of their warehouse systems and data feeds as well as allow the simplification of some applications by removing data feeds for other applications that need access to the real-time transaction state. The IDAA allows for operational and analytical transactions to be performed within the same DB2 system or data sharing group. The IDAA may also remove the need for resource-hungry aggregation-type processing by being able to process the original queries in a timely manner. This has the potential to reduce costs.

The IDAA (as shown in the Fig. 9.1) is a workload-optimized appliance that can be added onto a zEnterprise mainframe system. The technology used to underpin the IDAA is a PureData System for Analytics appliance transparently integrated into the DB2 subsystem. The IDAA accelerates analytic queries with unprecedented response times. Once installed, it enables the efficient integration of business analytics into operational processes to drive better decision-making.

Once the tables have been loaded automatically into the IDAA, the DB2 optimizer uses a set of rules to determine whether a given query is better off being

Fig. 9.1 SAS applications
on IBM mainframes

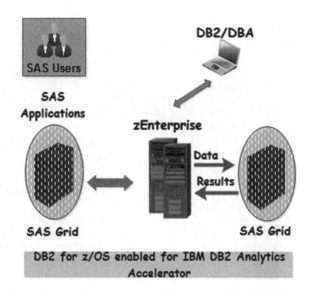

executed in DB2 core engine or needs to be routed to the accelerator. Generally, analytic-type queries will be recommended for offload processing and executed using minimal resources.

IBM InfoSphere System z Connector for Hadoop provides fast and seamless data connectivity between a variety of mainframe data sources and IBM InfoSphere BigInsights, the IBM's enterprise-grade Hadoop offering. Customers can easily extract data from z/OS sources including DB2, IMS, VSAM, and other file formats without the need for mainframe-based SQL queries, custom programming, or specialized skills. Once data is in Hadoop, clients can use the rich capabilities of InfoSphere BigInsights to quickly and cost-efficiently process and analyze data. Hadoop processing can take place on an external cluster connected to the zEnterprise mainframe or directly on mainframe Linux partitions using the System z Integrated Facility for Linux (IFL) for added security.

As indicated in the Fig. 9.2, by extending the capabilities of IBM System z with IBM InfoSphere BigInsights and the IBM InfoSphere System z Connector for Hadoop, customers enjoy the best of both worlds—a hybrid transaction and analytic processing platform capable of managing mixed workloads and coping with the unexpected.

Thus mainframes, tremendously famous for high scalability, availability, security, and dependability, host a lot of multi-structured data, and with the ready availability of integration, acceleration, and connection software solutions, business-critical applications are able to quickly gain the right and relevant insights out of the data heaps and mountains in mainframe computers to be extremely adaptive and adept in their operations and outputs. High-performance appliances are systematically and spontaneously attached with proven and potential mainframes to choose and deliver the best processing option for transaction, analytics, and interaction data.

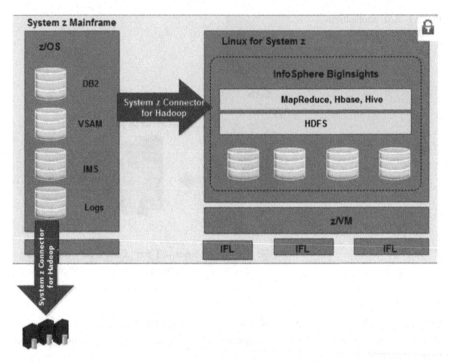

Fig. 9.2 IBM InfoSphere BigInsights on IBM mainframes

9.6   In-Memory Platforms for Fast Data Analytics

Although Hadoop's parallel architecture can accelerate analytics, when it comes to fast-changing data, Hadoop's batch processing and disk overheads are prohibitive. Therefore for real-time analytics, several viable and value-adding alternatives are being supplied. In-memory computing is one. Distributed caching is another prominent option for powering fast data analytics. Other approaches, such as complex event processing (CEP), use highly specialized programming models and require incremental investments in infrastructure, skills, training, and software. We are to discuss all the key approaches and solutions from different vendors in order to bring the much-needed clarity on real-time processing that in turn leads to real-time enterprises.

An in-memory platform is a single server or cluster of colocated servers whose main memory is used for fast data management and access. In practice, with this new arrangement, data accesses are being accelerated by a factor of 1000–10,000 times over the disk access. That means the ingestion and analysis of business data can happen instantaneously instead of taking longer time. The growing trend is that the value of data and data-driven insights goes down significantly if they are not captured and leveraged in time. The traditional batch processing steadily paves the way for fast processing as insights squeezed out in time bring in more value for organizations. Further on, real-time insights enable executives, decision-makers, data scientists, and IT managers to quickly consider important decisions with clarity and confidence. There are several praiseworthy advancements in the memory and its associated technologies. The recent advances in 64-bit and multicore systems have made it possible to store a large amount of data (in the range of terabytes) in RAM. Solid-state drive (SSD) is the most recent and powerful memory technology for RAM gaining higher market and mind shares. Though SSD price is a bit high at this point of time, with the faster maturity and stability of technologies, the manufacturing cost of SSD disks is to come down sharply. Also the network bandwidth is consistently on the upswing and the performance of network components is steadily increasing thereby combining several memory components and contents into a single large and logical memory unit is seeing the neat and nice reality. Thus the in-memory computing is being prepared and positioned systematically for the big data era.

In-Memory Databases (IMDB) This is all about hosting an entire database management system and data in the main memory of a server or server cluster to conduct rapid and radical analysis. Especially for analytics tasks, the inhibiting I/O operation is totally eliminated because no disks are involved. For storage purpose for posterior processing and analytics, disk-based storage can be recommended. A relational IMDB is the preferred solution if several independent applications access the data from different viewpoints and dynamically submit ad hoc queries for getting responses faster. IMDB is primarily spruced up for scale-up and not destined for scale-out as being achieved in Hadoop implementations. The data size is limited by the overall available main memory capacity of the server or the cluster. With the columnar databases, the compression factor comes to the rescue. That is, the total data size can go up between 10 to 50 times more.

Some IMDB products could embrace OLTP production data and interference-free OLAP queries in the same database instance. This facilitates an analysis of production data in real time. In such implementations, people typically use hybrid tables consisting of an optimized column store and a row store. Doing so, updates during transaction processing are deposited in the row store in order to avoid a permanent sort of the column store. With concurrent processing and analysis of all your historical and real-time data, IMDB enables businesses to react to opportunities as quickly as possible. SAP has championed and categorized its HANA platform as something that is capable of running all the business applications (mission-critical transactional systems such as ERP and CRM and analytical systems such as data warehouses and data marts on relational databases) of any company. Databases taking the game-changing advantage of in-memory processing really do deliver the fastest data-retrieval speeds available today. This is so enticing and encouraging companies to accomplish high-scale online transactions or timely forecasting and planning.

In-Memory Data Grid (IMDG) IMDGs store and load-balance data across an elastic cluster of commodity servers on which the grid is hosted. Because of the grid, data could be stored on multiple servers to ensure high availability. An IMDG's cluster can seamlessly scale its capacity by adding servers at runtime to handle growing workloads. These servers also provide the computational capacity needed for performing real-time analytics. This system primarily manages data as objects in memory avoiding expensive disk seeks. The focus here shifts from disk I/O optimization to optimizing for data management over a network. That is, a grid of servers is being leveraged for enabling real-time processing of memory-resident data. The much-anticipated scalability is being accomplished through a combination of proven and practical techniques such as replication (this is for accessing slowly changing yet very frequently requested data) and partitioning (this is tackling higher data volume). Data changes are synchronously managed across multiple nodes for protection against any kind of failures. Even advanced data grids support data getting asynchronously replicated over the WAN for disaster and data recovery.

Data grids can be equated to the proven and potential distributed caches with a variety of additional features. That is, data grids coexisting with relational databases are to bring up fresh advantages for the fast-changing business scenarios. IMDGs are intrinsically turning out to be a prominent solution for big data analytics. IMDGs can support hundreds of thousands of in-memory data updates per second and they can be clustered and scaled on demand in different ways to stock up large quantities of data efficiently. While an IMDB is optimally suited for ad hoc queries submitted by various applications, the main use case is for users with predefined queries. Applications are responsible for processing the data objects, whereas IMDG looks after the access to the data and applications need not know where the data resides. Additional functions for searching and indexing the data stored in an IMDG make the borders between an IMDG solution and a NoSQL database blur.

IMDGs have been widely deployed to host live and fast-changing data within operational systems. Because of the distinct capabilities such as low latency, scalable capacity, higher throughput, and high availability, there arises a stream of real-world and real-time application domains yearning for IMDG.

Integrating In-Memory Data Grid and Hadoop for Real-Time Big Data Analytics As indicated elsewhere, the integration of traditional systems with Hadoop implementations gains immense popularity as a way out for integrated systems to fulfill different needs via an integrated analytics. As told above, IMDGs automatically store and load-balance data across an elastic cluster of servers on which the grid is hosted. (They also redundantly store data on multiple servers to ensure high availability in case a server or network link fails.) An IMDG's cluster can seamlessly scale its capacity by adding servers to handle growing workloads. These servers also provide the computational capacity needed for performing real-time analytics.

There is a methodical movement towards a kind of positive empowerment by seamlessly clubbing in-memory data grid (IMDG) solutions with an integrated and stand-alone Hadoop MapReduce execution engine. This new technology delivers fast results for live data and also accelerates the analysis of large and static data sets. IMDGs need flexible storage mechanisms in order to handle widely varying demands on the data that they store because they host data as complex objects with additional semantics (metadata) to support features like property-centric query, dependencies, timeouts, pessimistic locking, and synchronized access from remote IMDGs. There are applications to store and analyze huge number of very small objects such as machine data or tweets.

The point here is that integrating a Hadoop MapReduce engine into an IMDG minimizes analysis time because it avoids data motion during processing by analyzing data in place. In contrast, hosting data in the Hadoop distributed file system (HDFS) requires data to be moved to and from disk, increasing both access latency and I/O overhead and significantly lengthening analysis time. Precisely speaking, in-memory databases (IMDBs) and in-memory data grids (IMDGs) are gaining lot of attention recently because of their support for dynamic scalability and high performance for data-intensive applications compared to the traditional databases. There is a host of open-source as well as commercial-grade Hadoop platforms getting gelled with other proven systems in order to provide advanced, accelerated, unified, and cost-effective analytics.

9.7 In-Database Platforms for Big Data Analytics

Analytics is all about the copious and cognitive leverage of a variety of proven and potential techniques, procedures and algorithms, well-defined policies, and formalized data for readily unearthing reliable and usable patterns, relationships, tips, alerts, opportunities, insights for spot as well as strategic decision-making, etc. Thus the art of analytics through highly synchronized IT platforms and sophisticated and state-of-the-art IT infrastructures is cruising at top speed within the industry circle. Every single organization specializing in one or more industry verticals across the globe is betting heavily on the leverage of the unique capabilities of analytical systems.

The traditional approaches to data analysis require data to be moved out of the database into a separate analytics environment for processing and then back to the database. Due to the massive data volume in the big data world, it is logical to restrict the data movement, whereas the processing and analytical logic can move to the location wherein data resides. That is, the need for a seamless integration between analytical and warehouse systems has emerged. In other words, both analytics and storage have to happen in a single place. Because these techniques are applied directly within the database, you eliminate data movement to and from other analytical servers, which accelerates information cycle times and reduces total cost of ownership (TCO). This is the crux of the fast-maturing concept of in-database analytics. Today use cases such as credit card fraud detection and investment bank risk management use this movement exceptionally well because it provides significant performance improvements over traditional methods.

At this point of time, the need for in-database analytics had become more pressing as the amount of data available to collect and analyze continues to grow exponentially. The speed of business has accelerated to the point wherein a performance gain of nanoseconds can make a significant difference in some industries. The introduction of the column-oriented database specifically designed for analytics, data warehousing, and reporting has helped make the technology possible. An in-database analytics system consists of an enterprise data warehouse (EDW) built on an analytic database platform. Such platforms provide parallel processing, partitioning, scalability, and optimization features geared towards analytic functionality. In-database processing makes data analysis more accessible and relevant for high-throughput, real-time applications including fraud detection, credit scoring, risk management, transaction processing, pricing and margin analysis, usage-based micro-segmenting, behavioral ad targeting, and recommendation engines, such as those used by customer service organizations to determine next-best actions.

Alteryx delivers data blending and advanced analytics that scale with the large databases analysts use everyday, without requiring handcrafted SQL coding. Using Alteryx Designer as the interface, in-database analytic workflows can be easily combined with existing workflows inside the same intuitive, drag-and-drop environment to allow analysts to take advantage of the large, rich data fabric they have access to.

SAS Analytics Accelerator for Teradata enables the execution of key SAS analytical, data discovery, and data summarization tasks within a Teradata database or data warehouse. This type of in-database processing reduces the time needed to build, execute, and deploy powerful predictive models. It also increases the utilization of the enterprise data warehouse or relational database to reduce costs and improve the data governance that is required for successful analytics applications. In-database analytics reduce, or eliminate, the need to move massive data sets between a data warehouse and the SAS environment or other analytical data marts for multi-pass data preparation and compute-intensive analytics.

- The massively parallel architecture of data warehouses is useful for processing larger, more complex information sets. Modelers can easily add new sets of variables if model performance degrades or changes are needed for business reasons.
- SAS Analytics Accelerator for Teradata enables analytical processing to be pushed down to the database or data warehouse, shortening the time needed to build and deploy predictive models. It also reduces the latency and complexity associated with the model development process. Analytics professionals have fast access to up-to-date, consistent data and increased processing power. This delivers faster time to results and provides better insights for improved business decision-making.
- In-database analytics helps modelers, data miners, and analysts focus on developing high-value modeling tasks instead of spending time consolidating and preparing data.

R is a popular open-source programming language for statistical analysis. Analysts, data scientists, researchers, and academics commonly use R, leading to a growing pool of R programmers. Once data has been loaded into the Oracle database, users can avail themselves of Oracle Advanced Analytics (OAA) to uncover hidden relationships in the data. Oracle Advanced Analytics offers a combination of powerful in-database algorithms and open-source R algorithms, accessible via SQL and R languages. It combines high-performance data mining functions with the open-source R language to enable predictive analytics, data mining, text mining, statistical analysis, advanced numerical computations, and interactive graphics all inside the database.

IBM Netezza is another interesting technology facilitating the in-database analytics and there is a solid asset document based on a proof of concept (PoC) experiment guaranteeing high-performance for big data analytics. In-database analytics is another promising phenomenon for the infrastructural challenges ahead for big data analytics.

9.8   The Cloud Infrastructures for High-Performance Big and Fast Data Analytics

As cloud computing has risen out of the "trough of disillusionment" into the mainstream, organizations across the globe are keenly embarking on the strategically sound cloud journey. IT service organizations are readying them to provide cloud integration, brokerage, and other client-enablement services. There are a few large public cloud service providers, such as AWS, IBM, Microsoft, HP, Google, etc., to rent a sufficient number of IT resources (servers, storage, and networking components) to the world. Then there are incredibly inventive platform and software developers jumping into the cloud bandwagon to feverishly explore fresh avenues for extra revenues. Communication service providers are too pitching vehemently to play a highly visible and valuable role in the cloud revolution, which is incidentally sweeping the entire world at this point of time. Similarly, there are other purpose-specific and agnostic service providers such as service auditing, security, and procurement professionals in order to sagaciously strengthen the cloud idea. There are cloud advisory, consulting, and brokerage service providers in the highly competitive market in order to facilitate worldwide clients, consumers, and customers to get hooked to the raging cloud paradigm to enhance their relevance and to sustain their offerings for the extremely interconnected society. Independent software vendors (ISVs) are doing the right and relevant modernization on their software solutions in order to empower them to get quickly and securely hosted and delivered comfortably to cloud users.

In short, the cloud marketplace is fast-growing with the continued and calculated addition of web, sense and respond (S & R), mobile, social, embedded, desktop, wearable, transaction, IoT, and analytical applications and the service registry repository is finding its feet strongly. Both software and hardware are being positioned as elegantly subscribable services so that any institution, individual, and innovator across the breadth and length of the world could publicly discover and choose the right services at right amount at right time and price.

Cloud infrastructures are therefore centralized, converged, mixed (virtualized, containerized, and bare metal), orchestrated, and shared, monitored, measured, and managed via a host of standards-compliant tools and programmable entities empowering business operations. In short, through the technology-sponsored cloudification, IT infrastructures are being continuously automated, simplified, streamlined, rationalized, and transformed to be highly optimized and organized. To bring in more decisive flexibility and sustainability, the powerful technique of abstraction and virtualization go deeper down into every module in the IT stack. The role of software in infrastructure activation, acceleration, and augmentation is on the climb. That is, there are articulations and accomplishments on software-defined IT infrastructures (software-defined compute (SDC), software-defined storage (SDS), and software-defined networking (SDN)). Software-defined data centers are going to be the core and critical IT component of every kind of enterprising business.

There are many allied technologies supporting the evolution and revolution of the cloud idea. For speeding up the data transfer among distributed and different cloud systems especially with the dawning of big data era, there are innovative WAN optimization technologies and solutions. IBM Aspera is one such popular solution for faster file transfer. Another point insisted here is that high-performance platforms are being deployed in cloud infrastructures for fulfilling high-performance needs. Clouds can be federated through standards and cloud infrastructures are clustered seamlessly for high scalability and availability. The high-performance technologies enable clouds to be touted as the cheap supercomputers. Precisely speaking, clouds come handy in realizing the high-performance computing capabilities.

The Cloudification Way

- Virtualized, bare-metal servers and containerized
- Software defined to have commoditized infrastructures
- Policy based and orchestration enabled
- Programmable, secure, sharable, consumable, etc.
- Accessible and autonomic
- Federated yet converged
- Distributed deployed yet centrally governed and managed

Next-Generation Clouds for Big and Fast Data Analytics

- *A mixed environment with choices*—bare-metal servers and virtual machines, dedicated and shared, full of choices and conveniences.
- *A high-performance cloud*—provides high-performance/high-throughput and contemporary computing at an affordable cost.
- *A wider variety of appliances*—data warehouse (DW), Hadoop-based batch processing, real-time analytics, etc.
- *Wider storage options*—enables multiple storage technology options including the famous object storage.
- *Hosting enterprise workloads*—clouds deliver a bevy of enterprise-class operational, transactional, interactive, and analytical software as a service.

- *Big data analytics (BDA) as a service*—BDA solutioning is accelerated through BDA platforms (open and commercial grade), parallel file systems, and NoSQL and NewSQL databases.
- *Auto-scaling* is facilitated for concurrent provisioning of multiple VMs, containers, and bare-metal servers.
- *High-performance analytics* through natively available in-memory and in-database analytical platforms (IBM Netezza, SAP HANA, VoltDB, etc.).
- *Impenetrable security environment*—compliant to most of the security-related standards in order to give unbreakable security and safety for customer assets.
- *Standards compliant*—fully compliant to industry-strength and open standards to avoid any kind of vendor lock-in.
- *Fully automated environment*—a bevy of automated tools to accelerate and augment the cloud center operations and for enabling clients' onboarding.
- *Policy-based* management, configuration, customization, and standardization mechanisms are in place.
- *Faster data transmission*—WAN-optimized transfer of large-scale data for cloud-based data analytics.

Why Big and Fast Data Analytics at Clouds?

- *Agility and affordability*—no capital investment of a large size of infrastructures. Just use and pay.
- *Hadoop platforms in clouds*—deploying and using any Hadoop platforms (generic or specific, open or commercial grade, etc.) are fast.
- *A variety of analytical platforms* for operational, machine, performance, security, predictive, prescriptive, and personalized analytics are strategically innovated and installed in clouds.
- *Databases in clouds*—all kinds of clustered, parallel, analytical, and distributed SQL databases and NoSQL and NewSQL databases are made available in clouds.
- *WAN optimization technologies*—there are WAN optimization products and platforms for efficiently transmitting data over the Internet infrastructure.
- *Web 2.0 social networking sites* are already running in cloud environments for enabling social media and networking analytics, customer and sentiment analytics, etc.
- *Business-critical applications in clouds*—enterprise-scale and business-critical applications, such as ERP, CRM, SCM, e-commerce, etc. are already successfully running on public clouds.
- *Specific clouds* such as sensor, device, mobile, knowledge, storage, and science clouds are becoming popular. Apart from social sites, digital communities and knowledge centers are increasingly found in their residence in clouds.
- *Operational, transactional, and analytical workloads* in clouds.
- *Cloud integrators, brokers, and orchestrators*—there are products and platforms for seamless interoperability among different and distributed systems, services, and data.
- *Multi-cloud environments*—clouds come in public, private, hybrid, and community formats.

Hadoop as a Service (HaaS)   As indicated elsewhere, the cloud paradigm is to enable service computing. That is, everything in and around IT is bestowed and destined to be given as a service. Cloud infrastructures are the most appropriate one for enabling this strategic transition. In that journey, nowadays there are providers offering "Hadoop as a service" especially for small and medium businesses. All the capacity planning, data collection, processing, analysis, visualization tasks, job scheduling, load balancing, etc. are being accomplished by HaaS providers by taking away all the IT-related worries from customers. The operational aspects, administration, configuration, monitoring, measurement, management, and maintenance are being taken care of well by Hadoop experts. The dynamic elasticity of data nodes in cloud-based clusters is being automated thereby the cost optimization can be achieved through the advancements in cloud management, orchestration, and integration arena. Similarly, the performance of the cluster is ensured in order to give an enhanced comfort for customers and their users. The HaaS concept includes the full integration with the Hadoop ecosystem, including MapReduce, Hive, Pig, Oozie, Sqoop, Spark, and Presto. Connectors for data integration and creating data pipelines provide a complete solution. Qubole (http://www.qubole.com/) is one key player in this fresh space. Their Hadoop-based cluster is eliminating the need for extra time and resources devoted to managing nodes, setting up clusters, and scaling infrastructure. Hadoop in the cloud environments requires no upfront investment for Hadoop cluster or for the associated IT support. Spot instant pricing reduces costs up to 90 % compared to on-demand instances.

MapR teams up with industry-leading cloud service providers to bring the flexibility, agility, and massive scalability of the cloud to Hadoop users. The MapR platform's fully distributed metadata architecture, POSIX-compliant file system, and high performance allow cloud users to build homogeneous clusters that scale up and down easily, ingest data into the cluster using standard interfaces, and get the best ROI from ephemeral instances. https://www.xplenty.com and https://www.altiscale.com/ are the other well-known HaaS providers.

Data Warehouse as a Service (DWaaS)   Database is an essential ingredient of any enterprise system these days. However, the trend is to move databases to remote cloud environments in order to deliver database as a service (DBaaS). There are specially databases for both big and fast data world. IBM Cloudant is one such solution delivering DBaaS. Thus the combination of databases is to bring forth a flurry of advancements for businesses as well as database developers. Not only SQL databases but also databases more pertinent for the big data world such as NoSQL and NewSQL databases are being modernized and migrated to clouds in order to fulfill the long-drawn goal of DBaaS. We have talked extensively about various databases for cloud and big data applications in the sections below.

Data warehouse (DW) is a crucial IT need for any growing organization. With the onset of the big data era, the need for DWs for their data analytics is bound to grow up in the days to unfold. However, DW appliances or enterprise DW solutions are not getting cheaper. At this critical juncture, the cloud-based DW is coming out as good news for those small- and medium-scale enterprises. There are end-to-end platforms for collecting and crunching data to come out with actionable insights for executives and decision-makers.

IBM dashDB is a fully managed data warehouse (DW) service in the cloud and it is an analytics powerhouse. dashDB allows you to break free from all your infrastructural constraints and all your business expectations are fully met with dashDB, which can help extend your existing infrastructure into the cloud seamlessly or help you start new data warehousing self-service capabilities. It is powered by high-performance in-memory and in-database technology that delivers answers as fast as you can think. dashDB provides the simplicity of an appliance with the elasticity and agility of the cloud for any size organization. The key stumbling block of security is being addressed by the dashDB solution.

Use dashDB to store relational data, including special types such as geospatial data. Then analyze that data with SQL or advanced built-in analytics like predictive analytics and data mining, analytics with R, and geospatial analytics. You can leverage the in-memory database technology to use both columnar and row-based tables. IBM BLU Acceleration is fast and simple. It uses the dynamic in-memory columnar technology and innovations such as actionable compression to rapidly scan and return relevant data. In-database analytic algorithms integrated from Netezza bring simplicity and performance to advanced analytics. dashDB is built to connect easily to all of your services and applications. You can start analyzing your data right away with familiar tools.

The Snowflake Elastic Data Warehouse uniquely delivers the following capabilities:

- *Data warehousing as a service*—Snowflake eliminates the pains associated with managing and tuning a database. That enables self-service access to data so that analysts can focus on getting value from data rather than on managing hardware and software.
- *Multidimensional elasticity*—Snowflake's elastic scaling technology makes it possible to independently scale users, data, and workloads, delivering optimal performance at any scale. Elastic scaling makes it possible to simultaneously load and query data because every user and workload can have exactly the resources needed, without contention.
- *Single service for all business data*—Snowflake brings native storage of semi-structured data into a relational database that understands and fully optimizes querying of that data. Analysts can query structured and semi-structured data in a single system without compromise.

Treasure Data is another cloud-based and managed service for data collection, storage, and analysis. That means that they are operating a massive cloud environment for end-to-end data processing, where they do all the infrastructure management and monitoring. Treasure Agent facilitates data collection, Treasure Plazma is for data storage, and data analysis is accomplished via SQL and Treasure query accelerators. Thus data warehouse as a service (DWaaS) is all set to flourish with clouds emerging as the one-stop solution for all our IT needs. Data warehouse is a costly system entailing both huge capital and operational costs. With DW being supplied as a service, businesses based on the needs can turn to these service providers to fulfill their DW needs instantly at a fraction of the cost.

The Cloud Summary   The noteworthy optimizations being brought in the IT arena through cloud technologies and tools are inspiring many to ponder about the leverage of software-defined cloud centers for high-performance computing especially big data analytics. The public, open, and cheap Internet is the principal communication infrastructure for public clouds. All kinds of IT services (infrastructures and platforms) are being availed from clouds. Mission-critical business applications (packaged, homegrown, etc.) are accordingly manipulated, deployed, delivered, orchestrated, maintained, and managed in cloud platforms. It is therefore not an exaggeration to infer that clouds are turning out as the central and cognitive IT environment for every kind of personal, professional, and social application.

9.9   Big File Systems for the Big Data World

File systems are very critical for the grand success of big data analytics. There are multi-structured data coming from different and distributed sources. File systems are the essential modules for big data storage, indexing, searching, and retrieval. Having realized the significance, the Hadoop framework designers have incorporated the Hadoop distributed file system (HDFS).

Hadoop Distributed File System (HDFS)   The key point of Hadoop is to form an elastic cluster of commonly available, cheaper, and commodity servers to process data in parallel. Each server internally has a set of inexpensive set of disk storages. External storages such as SAN and NAS are not suitable for Hadoop style of data processing. The data latency will rise in case of external storages; the extra network communication and security got eliminated with the leverage of internal disks. HDFS is a Java-based file system that provides scalable and reliable data storage. HDFS is designed to span large clusters of commodity servers. As per the Hortonworks site, in production clusters, HDFS has demonstrated the much-needed scalability of up to 200 PB of storage and a single cluster of 4500 servers, supporting close to a billion files and blocks.

By distributing storage and computation across many servers within a cluster, the combined storage capacity can raise on demand. These features ensure that the Hadoop clusters are highly functional and highly available. At the macro-level, the primary components of a HDFS cluster are one or two NameNodes which manage the cluster metadata and hundreds of DataNodes that store the data. Files and directories are represented on the NameNode by inodes. Inodes record attributes like permissions, modification and access times, or namespace and disk space quotas. The file content is split into large blocks (typically 128 megabytes), and each block of the file is independently replicated at three DataNodes. The blocks are stored on the local file system on the DataNodes. The NameNode actively monitors the number of replicas of a block. If there is a loss of a replica due to a DataNode failure or disk failure, the NameNode creates another replica of the block in another DataNode. The NameNode maintains the namespace tree and the mapping of blocks to DataNodes keeping the entire namespace image in RAM. The replication technique here ensures higher availability as the frequency of commodity hardware failure is on the higher side. Apart from the higher availability, this replication-induced redundancy offers multiple benefits. This redundancy allows the Hadoop cluster to break work up into smaller chunks and run those jobs on all the servers in the cluster for better scalability. Finally, you get the benefit of data locality, which is critical when working with large data sets.

Lustre File System   Lustre is a massively global and parallel distributed file system, generally used for large-scale cluster computing. Lustre is emerging as a high-performance file system solution for not only small but also for big compute clusters. There are two main Lustre server components of a Lustre file system: Object Storage Server (OSS) nodes and Metadata Server (MDS) nodes. File system metadata is stored on the Lustre MDS nodes and file data is stored on the Object Storage Servers. The data for the MDS server is stored on a Metadata Target (MDT), which essentially corresponds to any LUN being used to store the actual metadata. The data for the OSS servers are stored on hardware LUNs called Object Storage Targets (OSTs). The big data storage chapter has a lot of information about this powerful and pervasive file system. Most of the cluster and supercomputing solutions in the market leverage this powerful file system to do justice for large-scale storage and processing.

Quantcast File System (QFS)   The Hadoop-prescribed file system is the Hadoop distributed file system (HDFS), which is being supported by almost all the Hadoop distributions. Newer and powerful file systems are being crafted in order to attain the much-needed efficiency in data storage and access. In this section, we are to discuss the leading high-performance Quantcast File System (QFS). QFS written in C++ is plugin compatible with Hadoop MapReduce and offers several efficiency improvements compared to HDFS. It is proved that around 50 % disk space savings is being achieved through erasure coding instead of replication. The write throughput is just doubled. Further on, QFS has faster name node and supports for faster sorting and logging through a concurrent append feature. QFS has a native command line client that is faster than the Hadoop file system and global feedback-directed I/O device management. As QFS works out of the box with Hadoop, the task of migrating data from HDFS to QFS gets simplified by simply executing hadoop distcp.

The real differentiator of Hadoop is that the data processing logic traverses to the location wherein data resides. As data size is typically very huge, the code movement is more beneficial in ensuring resource efficiency. The network bandwidth gets saved and the data latency is almost zero. To achieve the mandatory fault tolerance, HDFS adopts the replication technique. That is, it stores one copy of the data in the machine itself, another copy on the same rack, and the third copy on a distant rack. These arrangements clearly tell HDFS is network efficient but not particularly storage efficient. Therefore, the storage cost is bound to shoot up significantly.

However, by smartly leveraging the hardware engineering advancements, QFS takes an altogether different route for bringing down the storage expenses. Cluster racks are getting chattier and today 10 Gbps networks are becoming commonplace. Affordable core network switches can now deliver bandwidth between racks to match disk I/O throughput so other racks are no longer distant. Quantcast has leveraged these noteworthy developments to come out with an efficient file system. The designers simply abandoned the aspect of data locality and instead relied upon faster networks to deliver the data where it is needed. This way QFS could achieve storage efficiency. QFS employs Reed-Solomon erasure coding instead of the three-way replication. To store one petabyte of data, QFS actually uses 1.5 petabytes of raw storage, 50 % less than HDFS, and therefore saves half the associated costs. In addition, QFS writes large amounts of data twice as fast as it needs to write 50 % less raw data than HDFS.

In summary, QFS has the same design goal as HDFS to provide an appropriate file system interface to a distributed and petabyte-scale data store built on a cluster of commodity servers. It is intended for efficient Hadoop- style processing wherein files are written once and read multiple times by batch processes rather than for random access or update operations.

9.10   Databases and Warehouses for Big and Fast Data Analytics

Today the overwhelming trend and transition is that every kind of tangible object in our places is being systematically digitized with the faster maturity and stability of edge technologies. The digitalization enables them to be connected and service enabled empowering them to integrate and interact with one another seamlessly and purposefully. The interactions result in a tremendous amount of data getting generated. Thus technologies and their adoptions are the key ingredients and instigators for the big data era. The pursuit for tackling the well-known big data challenges has given rise to a plethora of data management systems characterized by high scalability, simplicity and availability. On the infrastructure side, there are generic and specific, scale-up as well as scale-out systems. There are powerful, high-end, and dedicated appliances and supercomputers. The other and growing possibility is to leverage clusters made out of common, cheap, and commodity servers. In short, the big data discipline is laying a stimulating foundation for fresh possibilities and opportunities for immensely benefiting the total human society.

Today, there is no doubt that every kind of enterprise confronts a highly complicated and rapidly changing IT landscape. The application domains and categories are on the growth trajectory. Predominantly, there are new stand-alone and composite cloud, enterprise, embedded, and social applications. On the date front, as indicated before, there are different classes and categories of data getting generated, captured, and crunched for extracting actionable insights. There are elegant and exemplary data virtualization tools for data integration and transformation. Business intelligence (BI), reporting, and information visualization platforms are being leveraged in order to complete the full life cycle of data becoming information and then knowledge. The knowledge discovery process starts with data collection; proceeds with data ingestion, preprocessing, processing, mining, etc.; and ends with knowledge discovery and dissemination. There are sophisticated algorithms for doing deeper and decisive investigation on data heaps to squeeze out pragmatic insights in time. Distributed file systems, such as HDFS, can cope up with large-scale data volumes of various types. However, compared with a file system, a database allows a far better and more efficient access to the data primarily due to the query language included. Fine-grained querying is the renowned hallmark about the relational databases.

On the database side, there are improvisations at different dimensions. SQL databases are a pretty suited to transaction processing of structured data of a limited size. They are exceptionally optimized for a record-wise parallel access by many users as well as for inserting, updating, and deleting records. However, querying involves a lot of work. Big data exceeds the size limits, includes a lot of data which is not structured, and is about analyzing data which includes frequent queries. All these clearly demonstrate that the traditional SQL databases might face some practical difficulties. Therefore, the traditional SQL database vendors have embarked on accordingly enhancing their products to suit for the extreme requirements of big and fast data. That is why, we often hear, read, and even experience parallelized, analytical, clustered, and distributed SQL databases.

9.10.1 NoSQL Databases for Big Data Analytics

Then there is a notable phenomenon called "NoSQL databases" emerging and equipping big data applications. NoSQL systems are typically simplified and highly scalable systems fulfilling the properties and priorities such as schema-free, simple APIs, horizontal scalability, and eventual consistency. That is, NoSQL databases are not sticking to a rigid schema and flexible enough to easily cope up with new data types. They implicitly allow format changes without disrupting applications. As we know SQL databases are general purpose, whereas NoSQL databases are developed and destined to address some special use cases in a simplified manner. NoSQL databases are designed to be distributed across the nodes of a server cluster and for scale-out, allowing basically an almost linear and unlimited scalability. Replication of data to several server nodes enables fault tolerance and an automatic recovery after failure. Considering the demands for accelerated data access and processing, advanced NoSQL implementations comprise an integrated caching function to keep frequently used data in RAM. NoSQL systems provide the much-needed simplicity in complex data environments and higher throughput for the data volumes leveraging commodity hardware.

The Different Data Models of NoSQL Databases Primarily there are four types of data models optimized for different problems in the NoSQL world:

Key-Value Stores These stores typically consist of a large number of key-value pairs. The value is accessed using the key which uniquely references the value. The application decides the structure of the values. The key-value model is suitable for representing and processing the Web data such as click streams in online shopping applications quickly. Each record has two fields: key and value. The type of value is string/binary and the type of key can be integer or string/binary. There are many implementations of the key-value store approach. The recent ones include in-memory based and disk persistent. In-memory-based key-value store is often used for caching data and disk-persistent key-value store is used for storing data permanently in file system. When the number of items in database increases to millions, the performance is steadily going down. That is, both read and write operations slow down sharply. It is therefore important to conceive and concretize a simple and high-performance persistent key-value store, which has to perform better than the existing key-value stores. Especially the memory consumption has to be minimum, whereas the speed of data access and retrieval on the higher side. With IT infrastructures being software defined and cloud enabled for several business, technical, and user advantages, key-value stores are bound to move towards clouds as cloud-based big data storage. Next-generation data and process-intensive applications need high-performance key-value stores.

Having realized the need for a high-performance key-value store, Thanh Trung Nguyen and Minh Hieu Nguyen have together designed and developed a new powerful key-value store. The details are found in their research paper titled as "Zing Database: High-Performance Key-Value Store for Large-Scale Storage Service" published in the *Vietnam Journal of Computing Science* (2015). They have named it as the Zing Database (ZDB), which is a high-performance persistent key-value store designed for optimizing reading and writing operations. This key-value store supports sequential write, single disk seek random write, and single disk seek for read operations. This new store is verified and validated using a sample scenario and is found to be blessed with high performance.

Document Stores The IT infrastructure optimization being ensured through the sublime and subtle cloud technologies has brought down deployment and storage costs dramatically. However, data ought to be divided and spread across multiple servers easily without any disruption to enjoy the benefits. In a complex SQL database, this is difficult because many queries require multiple large tables to be joined together to provide a response. On the other hand, executing distributed joins is also beset with a very complex problem in relational databases. The need to store a large amount of unstructured data such as social media posts and multimedia has grown rapidly. SQL databases are extremely efficient at storing structured information. However, we need appropriate workarounds or compromises for storing and querying unstructured data. Another brewing trend is that the database schema needs to change rapidly as demands evolve. SQL databases mandate their structure to be specified well in advance. Schema evolution in RDBMSs is accomplished by expensive alter-table statements. Altering tables requires manual DBA intervention and blocks application teams from iterating quickly.

These needs put the stimulating foundation for the NoSQL space and document store is one such efficient NoSQL data representing model. In a document database, such as MongoDB, everything related to a database object is encapsulated together. MongoDB is a document database that provides high performance, high availability, and easy scalability. It is high performing because embedded documents and arrays reduce need for joins, embedding makes reads and writes fast, and indexes can include keys from embedded documents and arrays and optional streaming writes (i.e., no acknowledgments). MongoDB ensures high availability through replicated servers with automatic failover capability. It also supports the scalability feature through automatic sharding, which is the most sought-after technique for runtime distribution of collected data to spread across multiple machines in the cluster.

In this model, data is stored in documents. Here the documents are the values that are being referenced via unique names (keys). Every document is free to have its own schema to be used by the application. New fields may be added on need basis, whereas existing fields can be replaced or removed. The applications have to have everything to purposefully process data stored in documents. Document stores are used for storing contiguous data in a document. HTML pages are one prime example. The serialized object structure represented in JSON format is another one recommended for document stores. Twitter uses document stores for managing their user profiles while considering followers and tweets.

Columnar Stores Typically shared-nothing databases (NoSQL) partition data horizontally by distributing the rows of each table across both multiple nodes and multiple disks on each node. There is a twist here, that is, partitioning data vertically so that different columns in a table are stored in different files. While still providing an SQL interface to users, the "column-oriented" databases empowered with horizontal partitioning in a shared-nothing architecture offer tremendous performance advantages. We have explained the key advantages of column stores versus row stores. A data warehouse query generally accesses only a few columns from each table, whereas in a row-oriented database, the query must read all columns. This means that a column store reads 10–100 times less data from disk. Thus data compression plays a very vital role as the disk I/O speed is not progressing compared to other improvements such as the disk and memory sizes and network speed are growing steadily, the computation speed is going up with the pervasive nature of multicore processors, etc.

In the NoSQL space, the columnar or column-oriented database is very popular due to the unprecedented efficiency. The surging popularity for this data model is due to the fact that it is possible to store large amounts of structured database that cannot be fluently accessed and processed in a typical row-oriented SQL database. Imagine there are large tables with billions of rows representing the data records. If the number of columns per record is small and due to the fact, in a row-oriented data store, all rows have to be read for every query, the productivity goes down significantly as many queries could even relate to a smaller number of columns. Therefore, storing data in columns goes a long way in enhancing the efficiency trait. Further on, the access can be restricted to certain columns that are of interest for the query. Due to the limited number of columns per record, usually an entire column can be accessed in one read. This minimizes the amount of data to be read dramatically. Also a column can be split into multiple sections for simple parallelized processing in order to accelerate analytics.

Column-oriented databases are self-indexing. While providing the same performance benefit as indices, no extra space is required for indexing. As a certain column contains only one type of data and quite often there are only a few distinct values per column, it is possible to store only these distinct values and references to these values. This ensures high compression. On the other hand, more CPU cycles are needed when inserting or updating data records. This column-oriented DBMS brings distinct advantages for data warehouses, customer relationship management (CRM) systems, and library card catalogs and other ad hoc inquiry systems where aggregates are computed over large numbers of similar data items.

One of the most popular columnar databases is the Apache HBase, which is recommended when you need random, real-time read/write access to your big data. The goal here is the hosting of very large tables involving billions of rows × millions of columns atop clusters of commodity hardware. Apache HBase is an open-source, distributed, versioned, non-relational database modeled after Google Bigtable. Just as Bigtable leverages the distributed data storage provided by the Google File System (GFS), Apache HBase provides Bigtable-like capabilities on top of Hadoop and HDFS. The vital characteristics of HBase include:

- *Consistency*—although it does not fully support all the "ACID" requirements, HBase offers strongly consistent reads and writes and is far better than the eventually consistent model.
- *Sharding*—because the data is distributed by the supporting file system, HBase offers transparent and automatic splitting and redistribution of its content.
- *High availability*—the HBase cluster architecture comprises a master server and scores of regional servers in order to ensure faster recovery if there is a failure. The master server is responsible for monitoring the region servers and all metadata for the cluster.

The HBase implementations are best suited for:

- High-volume and incremental data gathering and processing
- Real-time information exchange (e.g., messaging)
- Frequently changing content serving

Graph Databases Neo4j is a leading graph database (http://neo4j.com/). In this section, we are to discuss why graph database is indispensable for the big data world. As mentioned elsewhere, we live in an intrinsically and interestingly connected world. All tangibles, pieces of information, and domains in and around us are cognitively interrelated in one or other ways and they can be hierarchically partitioned and presented. Therefore, only a database that embraces such relationships as a core aspect of its data model is efficiently able to store, process, and query connections. Other databases actually create relationships expensively at query time. However, a graph database stores connections as first-class citizens, making them readily available for any "join-like" navigation operation.

Thus graphs are turning out to be an excellent mechanism for representing information and their relationships via vertices and edges. Accessing those already persistent connections is an efficient and constant-time operation and allows you to quickly traverse millions of connections per second per core. The prominent use cases are schedule optimization, geographical information systems (GIS), Web hyperlink structures, and determining relationships between people in social networks. If the number of vertices and edges becomes too large for a single server, the graph has to be partitioned to enable the scale-out.

9.10.2   NewSQL Databases for Big and Fast Data Analytics

Especially with the big and fast data era, traditional databases are constricted to deliver capacity on demand. So application development is most of the time hindered by all the works to make the database scale. Thus there are famous hybrid versions (NewSQL databases) of SQL as well as NoSQL systems. The primary aim of NewSQL systems is to achieve the high scalability and availability of NoSQL systems while preserving the ACID properties for transactions and complex functionality of SQL databases. NewSQL database systems are widely recommended for applications where traditional RDBMS is being used but they require automated scalability and high performance. NewSQL DBs are emerging as the highly scalable relational databases for online transaction processing (OLTP). That is, they are destined to provide the proven scalable performance of NoSQL systems for read-write workloads as well as maintaining the ACID capabilities of traditional relational DBs. NoSQL systems achieve the needed breakthroughs over the conventional RDBMS performance limits by employing the NoSQL-style features such as column-oriented data storage and distributed architectures. Other venerable alternatives such as in-memory and in-database processing methods, symmetric multiprocessing (SMP), or massively parallel processing (MPP) come handy in effectively handling the big data characteristics (huge volume, greater varieties, and unpredictable velocity).

In general, the nonfunctional requirement "scalability" occupying the top slot in the hybrid cloud arena is being achieved in two major ways: scale-up and scale-out. The standout scale-out techniques are partitioning, sharding and clustering especially for database systems. For scale-up, the common approach is to employ bigger machines at more cost. The brewing business trends yearn for data systems with the innate scalability. That means, new data nodes can be readily added with the running DB machine dynamically without affecting the functioning of applications. With the aspect of commoditization is glowing, distributed computing is the most appropriate approach for such kinds of scale-out options in a cost-effective manner. These databases have to leverage distributed architecture copiously. We have shared more details on this crucial concept in the following sections. As indicated above, SQL is the primary interface for NewSQL databases. The applications targeted by NewSQL systems are characterized as having a greater number of transactions.

NuoDB is a NewSQL (scale-out SQL) database for the cloud centers. It is the NewSQL solution designed to meet the needs of cloud-scale applications and over 50 billion connected devices in use worldwide. NuoDB's three-tier distributed database architecture is the foundation for just that kind of scale-out performance. It's a true cloud database. NuoDB is a multi-tenant database. That is, with a single install of NuoDB, you can run any number of distinct databases serving distinct clients. Each database maintains its own physically separate archives and runs with its own set of security credentials. Hybrid transaction/analytical processing (HTAP) is a very recent capability being insisted for database systems. A single database should be capable of performing both online transaction processing and real-time operational intelligence processing. The underlying architectures for transactional and analytical databases have traditionally been separate and distinct with each offering optimized to perform only their own specific and distinct functions. However, NuoDB's peer-to-peer (P2P) architecture overcomes this hurdle by allowing you to dedicate database and hardware resources to perform either function. Today cloud-native and enabled applications require local performance, data consistency, and resilience to datacenter failure. NuoDB resolves these challenges by enabling you to distribute a single, logical database across multiple geographies with multiple master copies and true transactional consistency. Rubato DB is another highly scalable NewSQL database system running on a collection of commodity servers that supports various consistency guarantees including the traditional ACID and BASE and a novel consistency level in between and conforms to the SQL2003 standard.

Clustrix is also a powerful NewSQL solution. Clustrix was founded with the aim of bringing the benefits of NewSQL to transactional and big data applications by providing a competent technology that:

- Delivers linear scale to accommodate unlimited numbers of users, transactions, and data by leveraging the power of massively parallel processing
- Offers a full relational database implementation that protects information with full ACID capabilities thereby ensuring transactional integrity and consistency
- Supplies automatic fault tolerance freeing developers and administrators to concentrate on fulfilling their primary responsibilities

These are natively provided without the complex and challenging workarounds such as sharding. This solution is being offered as an on-premise appliance as well as in public, private, and hybrid cloud configurations, Clustrix's technology strategy provides the following technical advantages:

- *Data distribution*—the Clustrix platform implements a shared-nothing architecture and is constructed using industry-standard building blocks such as extremely fast solid-state disk drives (SSD). Clustrix automatically distributes information across nodes to provide the best possible performance without the need for any administrator intervention or specialized application logic.
- *Massively parallel query processing*—Clustrix's distributed relational database architecture provides linear transactional performance. Nodes can be added as needed and there is no upper limit on the number of nodes that can be deployed.

Clustrix also provides a single-query interface that lets users submit queries across all nodes without needing to know where data resides. This patented query evaluation approach brings all query types to the data and runs them in parallel. Complex queries are broken into query fragments and routed to relevant nodes for parallel processing. This unique approach eliminates data movement, reduces interconnect traffic, and dramatically increases performance. Thus database scaling is fairly a business and technical impediment to application development. An ideal DBMS should scale elastically, allowing new machines to be introduced to a running database and become effective immediately. NewSQL databases are bound to play a very stellar role in shaping up the emerging expectations for big data analytics and applications.

9.10.3 High-Performance Data Warehouses for Big Data Analytics

A data warehouse is a multidimensional and purpose-built database built for data analysis and knowledge discovery. Data warehousing has become a vast field today and data warehouses are being built and sustained to encompass a variety of applications from large-scale advanced analytical data stores supporting dozens of sophisticated analysts to pre-built business intelligence applications for supporting tens of thousands of users. There are enterprise-scale data warehouses (EDWs) and departmental data marts/cubes. Every corporate has a data warehouse infrastructure and platform, the mainstay of IT infrastructure for the ensuing knowledge era. Data warehouses are enabling executives and decision-makers to indulge and involve in long-term as well as short-term planning to steer the organization in the right direction. Data analytics platforms such as data warehouses come handy in extracting all kinds of actionable insights in time to empower people with authority to take perfect decisions with all the confidence and clarity. The mainstream and allied technologies towards data warehousing are already matured and are being leveraged with keenness to be ahead of their competitors in the knowledge-driven and market-oriented economy.

Now with big data, the role and responsibility of data warehousing is bound to grow further. Generally big data and data warehousing share the same goals at the macro-level. It is all about enhancing business productivity and value through deeper data analytics. However, there are some crucial differences between data warehousing and big data platforms. Data warehousing is to analyze an organization's data sourced from other databases within the organization. That is, an enterprise's data warehouse contains data from its operational systems (ERP, CRM, SCM, etc.), transactional systems (B2C e-commerce, B2B e-commerce, C2C e-auction, etc.), billing and point-of-sales (PoS) systems, etc.

The era of big data beckons us now. Not only big data but also fast data is also dawning upon us triggering a variety of applications. That is, without an iota of doubt, data, whether big or fast, is laying a stimulating foundation for fresh possibilities and opportunities for businesses. The real reasons and motivations for big data include the technological maturity and adoption, multiplicity and heterogeneity of newer data sources, process excellence, infrastructure optimization, architecture assimilation, etc. The IT team in charge of every enterprise is putting up big data analytical systems in place to harness the new sources of data effectively and allow enterprises to analyze and extract business value from these massive data sets. There are competent technologies (Hadoop (MapReduce, YARN, and HDFS), NoSQL, and NewSQL databases) emerging and evolving fast to work with big data. There are similarities as much as deviations between data warehouses and big data systems. Hence, this needs a careful view. Data warehousing solution providers are therefore preparing to enhance data warehouses to accommodate big data so that with a single and integrated system, both traditional and big data analytics can be achieved.

Oracle has indicated in its home page that the data warehouse systems will be accordingly augmented by a big data system, which literally functions as a "data reservoir." This will be the repository for the new types and sources of large volumes of data: machine-generated log files, social data, videos, and images as well as a repository for more granular transactional data. Data flows between the big data system and the data warehouse to create and present a unified foundation for data analytics. In the days ahead, the majority of business users will access the data in this new integrated information architecture from the data warehouse using SQL-based environments. With Oracle Big Data SQL, a feature of the Oracle Big Data Appliance, Oracle offers unified SQL access across both the database and the big data environment.

Apache Tajo: A Big Data Warehouse System on Hadoop Apache Tajo is a robust big data relational and distributed data warehouse system for Apache Hadoop. Tajo is designed for low-latency and scalable ad hoc queries, online aggregation, and ETL (extract-transform-load process) on large data sets stored on HDFS (Hadoop distributed file system) and other data sources. By supporting SQL standards and leveraging advanced database techniques, Tajo allows direct control of distributed execution and data flow across a variety of query evaluation strategies and optimization opportunities.

Tajo does not use MapReduce and has its own distributed processing framework which is flexible and specialized to relational processing. Since its storage manager is pluggable, Tajo can access data sets stored in various storages such as HDFS, Amazon S3, Openstack Swift, or local file system. Tajo team also has developed its own query optimizer which is similar to those of RDBMSs but is specialized to Hadoop-scale distributed environments. The Apache Tajo architecture is as the Fig. 9.3.

Basically, a Tajo cluster instance consists of one Tajo Master and a number of Tajo Workers. Tajo Master coordinates cluster membership and their resources, and it also provides a gateway for clients. Tajo Worker actually processes data sets stored in storages. When a user submits a SQL query, Tajo Master decides whether the query is immediately executed in only Tajo Master or the query is executed across a number of Tajo Workers. Depending on the decision, Tajo Master either forwards the query to workers or does not. Tajo has its own distributed execution framework. Figure 9.4 shows an example of distributed execution plan. A distributed execution plan is a direct acyclic graph (DAG). In the figure, each rounded box indicates a processing stage, and each line between each rounded boxes indicates a data flow. A data flow can be specified with shuffle methods. Basically, groupby,

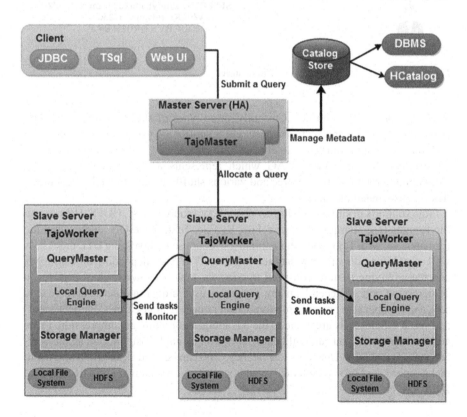

Fig. 9.3 The Apache Tajo reference architecture

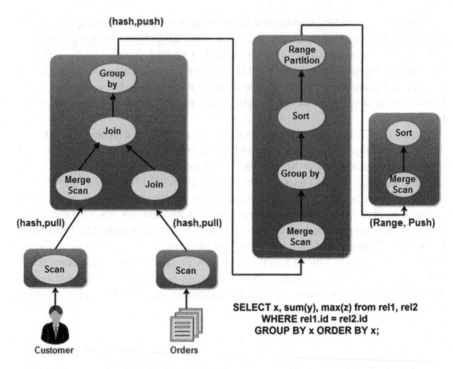

Fig. 9.4 The macro-level architecture of Tajo cluster

join, and sort require shuffles. Currently, three types of shuffle methods are supported: hash, range, and scattered hash. Hash shuffle are usually used for groupby and join, and range shuffle is usually used for sort. Also, a stage (rounded box) can be specified by an internal DAG which represents a relational operator tree. Combining a relation operator tree and various shuffle methods enables generating flexible distributed plans.

Tajo supports in situ processing on various data sources (e.g., HDFS, HBase) and file formats (e.g., Parquet, SequenceFile, RCFile, Text, flat JSON, and custom file formats). So, with Tajo, you can maintain a warehouse by involving ETL process as well as archiving directly raw data sets without ETL. Also, depending on workloads and the archiving period, you need to consider table partitions, file formats, and compression policy. Recently, many Tajo users use Parquet in order to archive data sets, and Parquet also provides relatively faster query response times. Parquet's storage space efficiency is great due to the advantages of columnar compression. From archived data sets, you can build data marts which enable faster access against certain subject data sets. Due to its low latency, Tajo can be used as an OLAP engine to make reports and process interactive ad hoc queries on data marts via BI tools and JDBC driver.

9.11 Streaming Analytics

Typically data are at different states. Data is at rest/persistence or in motion/transit or could be leveraged by business applications. Data processing has to happen on the fly while it is being transited over any networks. On the other hand, data processing happens by retrieving data from local as well as remote storages. We have extensively studied how data gets subjected to a flurry of investigations while at rest. That is, the activities such as retrieval, preprocessing, analysis, and mining of data are exemplified on data stocked on disks or in memory. Now due to the extremely dynamic growth of data sources and resources and the data velocity, data needs to be gleaned and processed while on the move itself in order to extract real-world and real-time insights. There are several proven formalisms for expressing data. For the "request and reply" pattern, data are massaged into data messages that in turn internally comprise input and output parameters, the method signature, etc. Further on, documents are also encapsulated inside messages and communicated to the recipients. On the other side, messages are unwrapped and understood without any ambiguity and the correct action gets initiated and accomplished. However, live data is being covered and communicated as event messages. In the recent days, it is being annotated as data streams.

An event is something that happens. Events are emitting one or more implications and insights. Decision-enabling and value-adding events are very frequently happening all around us all the time. A price change in the securities market is an event. A business transaction is an event. An airplane taking off is an event. Further on, there are nonevents. That is, something that should have happened in time does not happen. A nonevent could be a car part that misses a step in the assembly line or an inventory item that does not make it from the delivery truck to the warehouse. Any state change, a threshold overshoot, a noteworthy incident or accident, a positive or negative abnormality, etc. can be considered as events.

With the unprecedented growth of connected machines, appliances, sensors/actuators, social media, smart phones, cameras, etc., any event data compactly gets well encapsulated inside standardized messages and are being poured in as data streams at a very high speed. These streams need to be quickly collected, ingested, and analyzed on the fly in order to extract actionable insights. Events are filtered and correlated and corroborated for all kinds of usable patterns and tips. A sample event application is an automated trading application that scans massive amounts of incoming market data to spot trading opportunities, where the trigger to trade has to be instantaneous or the opportunity is missed.

(continued)

Event processing is the best for applications that require near-real-time responses to dynamic, multifaceted, and rapidly changing business situations such as algorithmic trading and transaction surveillance. Event processing can also be used to manage and interpret events in a wide variety of business processes. For example, one insurance company uses an event processing engine to monitor the actions of eternal business partners so that it can react if these actions delay the progress of deals. Event processing solutions are used for:

- Detect, inform, and act applications
- Detect and act applications
- Real-time and real-world applications
- Integrated business processes
- Event-driven data analysis
- Spotting patterns or trends that represent opportunities or threats, as they happen, so that businesses can respond immediately
- Combining data from multiple sources and continuously computing aggregate high-level values so that businesses know their positions (or exposure) at all times
- Constantly monitoring the interaction of data so that businesses can adjust to changing conditions
- Automated decision-making that takes into account current conditions
- Dashboards that give the information help to make effective and timely decisions

This kind of real-time analytics is based on a set of predefined rules that include a condition and an action. If the condition (which may be a correlation of logical and timely aspects) is fulfilled, then an appropriate action will be triggered in real time. That is, event processing has been a crucial requirement for several industry verticals in order to be relevant to their constituents and customers.

The underlying IT infrastructure has to be exceptionally nimble enough to cope up with tens of thousands of events per second. Another critical parameter is latency. The time elapsed between the event input and the knowledge output determines whether the business could achieve the expected success or not. For these reasons, any event processing engine has to be really quick and scalable. In order to avoid the time-consuming I/O processing, the collecting tank for event streams is typically organized in the memory itself. If the load caused by event streams cannot be managed by a single server, then the extra loads will be distributed across colocated multiple servers. Each of the participating and contributing servers is being equipped with an event process engine. Incoming events are processed and sometimes get forwarded to other servers for deeper investigations. In short, event processing software has to continuously collect, process, and analyze data in real time, producing results without delay, even when the data arrives at very high rates.

If certain rules require large memory capacity for processing long-window-time events, an IMDG solution comes handy as any IMDG implementation inherently enables the load distribution across several servers. Data losses can be avoided due to the high availability features in the IMDG solution. That is, IMDG facilitates the automatic data replication to another server or to a persistent storage in case of any outage. Thus the event processing complexity is consistently on the rise due to the unprecedented data growth. Depending on the use case, results of any event processing engine can be forwarded to HDFS, NoSQL databases, in-memory databases, or in-memory data grids to be used for further purposes such as analytics, visualization, or reporting.

Forrester's report states that complex event processing (CEP) platform is a software infrastructure that can detect patterns of events and expected events that did not occur by filtering, correlating, contextualizing, and analyzing data captured from disparate live data sources to respond as defined using the platform's development tools. CEP is one of a collection of product categories that have event processing features. Others include business activity monitoring (BAM), business process management (BPM), systems and operations management, active databases, operational business intelligence (BI), business rule management systems (BRMS), messaging middleware, etc.

Event processing is the analysis of event data in real time to generate immediate and immaculate insights and enable instant responses to changing conditions. It is all about proactively and intelligently capturing and real-time processing of streams of business events to come out with actionable insights in the form of tips, trends, associations, patterns, etc. The reference architecture for event processing is as depicted in the Fig. 9.5.

Solace (http://www.solacesystems.com/) has taken an innovative approach to addressing the challenges of real-time data movement by handling the routing of information with hardware. Solace message routers efficiently move information between all kinds of applications, users, and devices anywhere in the world over all kinds of networks. This gives Solace customers an application-aware network for their enterprise with elastic capacity and unmatched performance, robustness, and TCO. This offers bottom-line business value and lets them focus on seizing business opportunities instead of solving data movement problems. The architectural representation is being given through the Fig. 9.6.

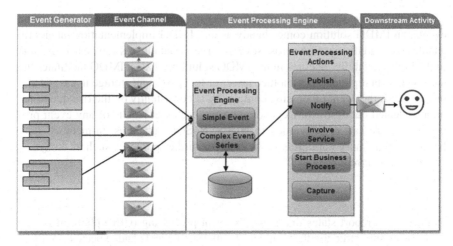

Fig. 9.5 The high-level event processing architecture

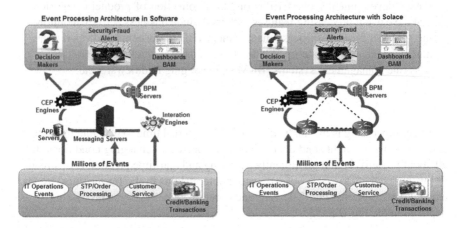

Fig. 9.6 Two different event processing architectures

IBM InfoSphere Streams for Streaming Analytics

The Streams solution is IBM's flagship and high-performance stream processing system. Its unique design and implementation enable it to ingest streaming and real-time data at a large scale and process it at line rate. As a result, it has found applications in a diverse array of domains including transportation, speech analysis, DNA sequencing, radio astronomy, weather forecasting, and telecommunications. The Stream Processing Language (SPL) atop Streams enables practitioners to define complex applications as a series of discrete transformations in the form of operators over potentially multiple

(continued)

data streams, which flow from "sources" to "sinks" while abstracting away the intricacies of distributed execution. With a built-in library and assorted toolkit of common stream processing constructs and domain-specific utilities, an application can be up and running in a matter of minutes. Along with SPL itself, users have the option of defining their operators in C++ and Java or other languages that can be wrapped into these two programming languages, such as Fortran and scripting languages. In addition, Streams Studio is an all-encompassing development and management environment that streamlines development to drag-and-drop placement of existing components while exposing a central portal for cluster management and monitoring. Architecturally, Streams consists of management services that take care of different aspects of distributed state management, such as authentication, scheduling, and synchronization. Streams jobs are executed within processing elements, which can further be fused together to optimize for low latency. Furthermore, the standard TCP-based queuing mechanism can be replaced with a built-in high-performance low-latency messaging (LLM) to further optimize applications in certain environments. The details are in https://developer.ibm.com/streamsdev/wp-content/uploads/sites/15/2014/04/Streams-and-Storm-April-2014-Final.pdf.

Apache Storm is an open-source stream processing framework. A Storm application, called a topology, can be written in any programming language with Java as the predominant language of choice. Users are free to stitch together a directed graph of execution, with spouts (data sources) and bolts (operators). Architecturally, it consists of a central job and node management entity dubbed the Nimbus node and a set of per-node managers called Supervisors. The Nimbus node is in charge of work distribution, job orchestration, communication, fault tolerance, and state management. The parallelism of a topology can be controlled at 3 different levels: number of workers (cluster wide processes), executors (number of threads per worker), and tasks (number of bolts/spouts executed per thread). Intra-worker communication in Storm is enabled by the LMAX Disruptor, while ZeroMQ1 is employed for inter-worker communication. Moreover, tuple distribution across tasks is decided by groupings, with shuffle grouping, which does random distribution, being the default option. The software solutions being used include ZooKeeper for cluster management, ZeroMQ for multicast messaging, and Kafka for queued messaging.

Thus the discipline of streaming analytics (the technology-supported real-time analysis of distributed and different data streams for real-time insights) is gaining momentum due to the multiplication of streaming sources. Also analytics, which has been primarily done on historical data for tactical as well as strategic decisions, is being increasingly accomplished on real-world, real-time, and live data streams.

Considering the need for instant decisions and actions for attracting new customers and for retaining existing customers by providing premium and delightful services in plenty, the highly sophisticated streaming analytics is turning out to be an excellent and elegant tool for worldwide organizations. Real-time analytics is the hot requirement today and everyone is working on fulfilling this critical need.

9.12   Conclusions

We all know that data has incredible power to transform your business. Whether it is process optimization, fine-tuning supply chains, monitoring shop floor operations, gauging consumer sentiment, etc., a systematic capture and analysis of all kinds of data being generated due to these activities in the respective environments is the need of the hour. Big data analytics is now moving beyond the realm of intellectual curiosity and propensity to make tangible and trendsetting impacts on business operations, offerings, and outlooks. It is no longer hype or a buzzword and is all set to become a core requirement for every sort of business enterprises to be relevant and rightful to their stakeholders and end users.

In this chapter, we have clearly articulated the compelling IT infrastructures for accelerating big and fast data analytics. In the recent past, there are integrated and converged IT systems to sagaciously speed up data analytics. Appliances are being touted as the hardware-centric advanced IT solution for big data analytics. Besides, we have covered a lot about an array of file systems, databases, and data warehouses for big and fast data storage and processing. Big data analytics on big infrastructure lead to big insights (knowledge discovery). We have allocated a special chapter for knowledge dissemination, information visualization, report generation, and dashboards.

9.13   Exercises

1. Write a short note on converged infrastructure for big data analytics.
2. Explain IMDG.
3. Write short notes on the following:

   - Hadoop as a service
   - Data warehouse as a service

4. Explain the different data models of NoSQL databases.
5. Explain the Apache Tajo reference architecture.
6. Describe event processing architecture and its variants.

Chapter 10
High-Performance Grids and Clusters

10.1 Introduction

The data is building up in the warehouses exponentially day by day. We will be producing zettabytes of data by the end of 2014. The consumer data from the multinational shopping chains like Walmart and online Web services like Google, Facebook, and Amazon is meganormous. Adding fuel to this trend is the growing interest in Internet of Things promoted as Internet of Everything by Cisco. The IoT makes it possible to collect data from everyday machines and analyze them for optimizing processes. The data is not restricted to the transactional data which mostly falls under relational database domain (data records have a fixed structure) but also our social feeds; our everyday diet, health, and exercise details; our Internet searches; and even maybe our interaction with everyday things like refrigerator and air conditioner (due to IoT and smart appliances) which may not have a fixed structure.

All the data collected about a particular person can be used to classify his or her behaviors into predefined classes and group together people with similar interests and tastes to form clusters. This analysis can be used to recommend products and increase the customer experience, for example, the recommendation engine from e-commerce websites, the Facebook ads which target users with similar interests, and spam filtering in network security. This is not limited to our digital lives, the data can be analyzed to build a contextual picture of the world we are living which can be used to reshape the world. The data can be used to predict the outbreak of a flu or to visualize the water scarcity among the world nations.

But to realize the benefits and unlock the promise held by data, the data must be crunched, search for familiar patterns, discover unknown patterns, and find relationships between objects and their behaviors. The data first needs to be preprocessed to remove the noise and select relevant data; the analysis must be visualized in a simple understandable manner so that it can be put to work to make better decisions.

© Springer International Publishing Switzerland 2015
P. Raj et al., *High-Performance Big-Data Analytics*, Computer Communications and Networks, DOI 10.1007/978-3-319-20744-5_10

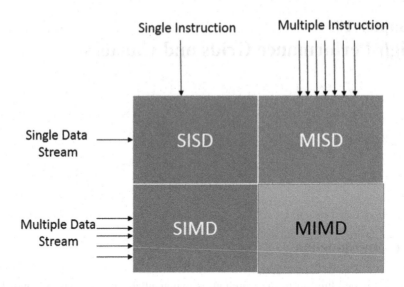

Fig. 10.1 Parallel programming models

Processing platforms should enable data crunching for large volumes of data with highly disparate velocities and varities (The cahracteristic 3 Vs of Big Data). The processing systems should be able to store both structured and non-structured data. This type of processing is termed as data-intensive computing. This kind of computation when done on a single system generally takes lots of time to complete as a system might not provide enough data storage and I/O capabilities or doesn't have enough processing power. To solve the problem, we can use the principle of "divide and conquer" whereby we divide the task into smaller tasks (task parallelization) and execute them in parallel or divide the huge data into manageable sets of data and work on the data in parallel (data parallelization). These parallel processing techniques are generally classified as either data intensive or compute intensive (Gorton et al. 2008; Johnston 1998, Skillicorn and Talia 1998). Once the smaller tasks are executed on different systems the results can be aggregated to give the final output (Fig. 10.1).

Compute-intensive processing refers to the application programs that are compute bound. In these applications most of the execution time is devoted to processing instead of I/O. These typically work on small volumes of data. Parallel processing of compute-intensive applications comprises parallelizing individual algorithms and dividing the overall application process into separate tasks to execute in parallel to achieve overall higher performance than sequential processing. In task parallel applications, multiple operations are executed simultaneously, with each operation addressing a particular part of the problem (Abbas 2004). Supercomputers, vector computers, come under this class of systems. These systems address complex computational requirements and support applications with weighty processing time requirements. Supercomputers have commonly been associated with compute-intensive types of problems and scientific research, but this is slowly changing as data-intensive applications are also programmed. Supercomputers utilize a high

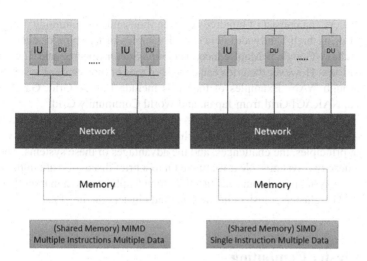

Fig. 10.2 Task parallel (MIMD) vs. data parallel (SIMD)

degree of internal parallelism and characteristically use specialized multiprocessors with custom memory architectures which have been highly optimized for numerical calculations [1]. Supercomputers also require special parallel programming techniques to take advantage of its performance potential. Most research and engineering organizations generally used these systems to solve the problems like weather forecast, vehicle collision modeling, genome research, etc. High-performance computing (HPC) is used to describe computing environments which utilize supercomputers and computer clusters (Fig. 10.2).

Data-intensive computing encompasses scalable parallel processing which allows government, commercial organizations, and research environments to process substantial amounts of data and develop applications which were infeasible earlier. The fundamental challenges of data-intensive computing are managing and processing exponentially growing data volumes; significantly reducing associated data analysis cycles to support practical, timely applications; and developing new algorithms which can scale to search and process massive amounts of data. Relational database technologies are good for transactional data, but as we have seen the data that's been generated doesn't always fit in the relational realm. The RDBMS solutions have problems scaling up, giving the high performance required for the analytic workloads, and processing that required for Web scale organizations. This resulted in several organizations developing technologies to utilize large clusters of commodity servers for providing high-performance computing capabilities to process and analyze massive data sets. The other phenomenon that started in the late 1990s is something called grid computing (earlier referred to as metacomputing). This system architecture helped in aggregating idle resources across the organizational or geographical boundaries. While the clusters made it possible to share computing power at organizational level, grids provided the means to collaborate between various different organizations with a lot more secure features.

The clusters can consist of hundreds or even thousands of commodity machines connected using high-bandwidth networks. Examples of this type of cluster technology include Google's MapReduce, Hadoop, Sector/Sphere, and LexisNexis HPCC platform. However the grids can consist of tens of thousands of systems connected through WAN. Examples of the grids include Europe Grid, Garuda Grid from India, NARAGI Grid from Japan, and World Community Grid.

In the following sections, we will learn more about these two powerful computing platforms. We will study the basic architectures of the cluster and grid systems, the design principles, the challenges, and the advantages of these systems. Then we compare these two systems. Next we move on to a brief discussion about the future of processing systems and some advanced systems/applications in market like GPU clusters, FPGA clusters, clusters inside grid, and clusters on the cloud.

10.2   Cluster Computing

According to the Moore law, the processing power of the processors doubles every 18 months. The computing power of today's workstations is more than that of the supercomputers in late 1980s and early 1990s. This has led to a new trend in supercomputer design for high-performance computing: using clusters of independent processors interconnected in parallel. Algorithms for many computing problems can be parallelized where often problem can be divided in a manner that each independent processing node can work on a portion of the problem in parallel.

10.2.1   Motivation for Cluster Computing

Every organizations look for IT solutions to be scalable to keep up with the increasing data stored, and complex workloads at the same time should be cost-effective to make sense for the businesses. The architecture as such should be extensible and should give high performance with economies of scale. With these requirements, Cluster computing forms a viable and effective solution for enterprices.

Traditional enterprise architecture design is based on the assumption that there are three main types of hardware resources to manage: the servers enclosing thousands of cores of processors and main memory that should never be idle; the storage arrays enclosing types of storage technologies with different costs per GB ranging from tapes, SATA, to SSDs; and storage area network connecting a set servers to a set of storage arrays. One of the beauties of this architecture is that the servers and storage are decoupled which can upgrade, repair, or retire independent of each other. The SAN enables applications run on any of the servers to have access to any of the data stored on any of the storage arrays as long as they have access with write privileges. In enterprise setting all the components are designed to be robust, and to ensure high availability, these components don't fail often and are replaced as soon

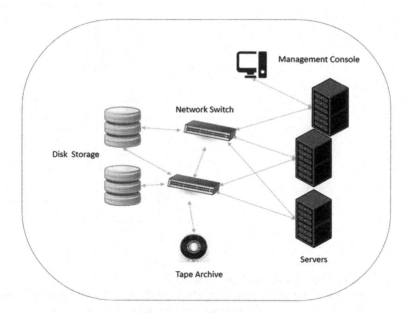

Fig. 10.3 Illustration of enterprise IT architecture with SAN

as this failure happens. However this very property drives the value up and demands a premium price. This mainly used computing-intensive applications with a lot of processing cycles on just a minimal subset of data. This data is copied from storage arrays through SAN and is processed and written back through SAN (Fig. 10.3).

Consider, for example, Walmart runs statistics and analytics at the end of day on the daily consumption of milk across the United States, given the portfolio of Walmart milk is a very small subset of the data. Now imagine you actually need to do similar processing on big data. In order to process similar query, the entire data set needs to be processed. While the servers don't store the data, it has to be moved from SAN to servers for processing which not only takes a lot of time but also causes huge overload on SAN. This surely is a data-intensive job. So we need to understand the architecture which can handle big data workloads, deliver performance requirements of a business, and still be economical. This is what drives us to cluster computing.

10.2.2 Cluster Computing Architecture

Basic design principles that cluster computing architecture are based on the following:

1. Use commercial of the shelf components for processing cores, storage, and network interconnects to leverage economies of scale and cut costs.

Fig. 10.4 High-
performance cluster

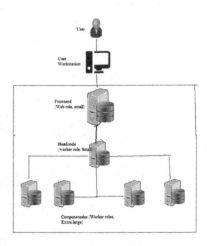

2. Enabling data-intensive applications to scale Web scale and beyond.
3. Two of the major characteristics of big data are the velocity and variety, so the
   system should support high-throughput and preferably real-time performance.

High-performance computing clusters not only have their benefits in data mining
or research. Design engineering teams leverage these technologies to run simulations at a faster rate giving more collaboration time and effective IT resource utilization. Clusters are built to enable this programming paradigm. Today, many
engineering and data mining applications such as CAE, CAD, and Mathematica
have cluster-ready versions ("parallelized") to take advantage of parallel architecture available in a computer and the clustered computing architecture. These parallelized applications take advantage of the multiple cores in the nodes of a cluster.
Cluster systems allow cost-effective use of classroom systems. Some of the high-
performance cluster systems easily compete with supercomputers in the market.

A high-performance computing (HPC) cluster refers to a group of servers built
from off-the-shelf components that are connected via high-speed interconnect technologies. A cluster can deliver aggregated computing power from its many processors in which many cores can scale so as to meet the processing demands of more
complex workloads. Clusters built on commodity processors and other widely
available components can deliver a superior price/performance advantage over
alternative solutions such as custom-built systems or supercomputers (Fig. 10.4).

A cluster architecture is modular in the sense that it is made up of simple and
basic components which can be assembled together easily. Every computing
resource part of the cluster is called a node. Nodes are connected through interconnect such as InfiniBand and Ethernet.

Each node consists of commodity processing cores with main memory attached
to commodity storage. These nodes can be a single processor system or multiple
processors like a PC or workstation or even an SMP. A stack of nodes form a rack.

And a set of racks form a cluster. Vendors these days offer preconfigured cluster solutions that package multiple nodes into a cabinet, or clusters can be created by linking together existing computer hardware.

The architecture is highly modular and scalable; keep adding nodes and racks and the capacity increases; this is also called as horizontal scaling as opposed to vertical scaling, i.e., replace the processor/memory with more powerful ones in enterprise architecture. Data locality is yet another design principle which most of the modern-day clusters follow. It says that the data is processed on the same nodes where data has been collocated in the disk, eliminating or reducing the data transfer through networking, making the network no longer a bottleneck. This hugely helps in parallelization of activities and tasks of massive parallel processing nature. The parallelization of disk I/O also increases the number of I/O operations while at the same time retaining the same cost per GB. For example, an SSD costs $1.20/GB and gives about 5000 write I/O ops and 30,000 read I/O ops, while the SATA costs around $0.04/GB giving only 250 I/O ops. Now consider we have 120 nodes in a cluster with SATA disks, that is, 120*250 I/O ops are possible = 30,000 I/O ops, the same performance of an SSD with the cost of SSDs. Another important characteristic is that the system provides a single system image for the user. For example, if the user submits a program to 100 cluster systems and 1000 cluster systems, the user need not manipulate the program for different size of clusters and is abstracted from the management of the cluster.

Outlining the design goals and characteristics of the clusters as we have studied in the earlier sections, the cluster computing architecture is as follows:

- Use of commercial machines and networks as individual components to drive economies of scale
- Scalability so as to serve ever-increasing processing load
- High availability to be more fault resilient and responsive to errors
- High performance so as to serve the complex workloads and give faster responses
- Single system image allowing the users and developers abstracted from the intricacies in the cluster management and focused more on the applications
- Load balancing for effective utilization of unused or underused resources

This being said cluster computing also has some potential caveats, e.g., the cluster is based on commodity hardware which will fail, so the software managing the cluster and applications running on the cluster need to detect and respond to failures which increases the complexity. Second typically to cope with the data loss, the data is replicated to many nodes at a time which increases the amount of storage required. Another potential caveat is that in order to achieve the performance, the data needs to be distributed evenly across the cluster. The application needs to be designed in MPP style and careful management is required.

In the early 1990s, researchers connected systems in the laboratories and classrooms, making the initial cluster systems like Beowulf and network of workstations software libraries like MPI and PVM.

10.2.2.1   Beowulf Cluster

The name Beowulf originally referred to a specific computer built in 1994 by Thomas Sterling and Donald Becker at NASA. A Beowulf cluster allows the processing to be shared among the computer connected through LAN. This is done with support of program and libraries such as MPI and PVM. In the end what we get is high-performance parallel computing cluster formed from inexpensive components.

Beowulf clusters normally run Linux system built up using open-source libraries. Using the parallel processing libraries such as MPI and PVM, a programmer can divide the task into subtasks and assign them to computers in the cluster, and after processing is done, results are sent back to the user. The major distinction between the University of Berkeley's Network of Workstations (NOW) and Beowulf is the single system image it portrays.

Some of the Linux distributions designed for building Beowulf clusters are MOSIX, ClusterKnoppix, and Ubuntu. Software tools like Open Source Cluster Application Resources (OSCAR) can be used to automate the provisioning of resources on the cluster.

10.2.3   Software Libraries and Programming Models

10.2.3.1   Message Passing Interface (MPI)

MPI [2] stands for message passing interface providing means for passing data between nodes in support of distributed execution. This library provides routines to initialize, configure, and send and receive data and supports point to point and point to multiple data transfer like broadcast and multicast. In the MPI model, a set of processes are started at program start-up. There is one process for each processor, which might execute different processes. This implies MPI falls under the multiple instruction, multiple data (MIMD) category of parallelism. The number of processes of an MPI program is fixed and each process is named. The one-to-one communications use the process names, while the broadcast or synchronization uses process group which is simply grouping of processes. MPI provides the communication context on message exchange and feasibility to use both synchronous and asynchronous message passing. The MPI standard defines message passing semantics, functions, and some primitives for reusable libraries. MPI doesn't provide infrastructure for program development and task management. This is left to the MPI implementations and developers. MPICH2 and OpenMPI are two popular implementations of MPI.

There are various implementations of MPI, such as the high-performance implementation MPICH2. The program can be made fault tolerant, adaptable to the network disturbances and disruptions. While this can be used to coordinate and execute distributed algorithms in parallel, the internal parallelization using threads can be utilized using the libraries like pthreads and OpenMP. These libraries greatly

```
/* C Example */
#include <stdio.h>
#include <mpi.h>


int main (argc, argv)
     int argc;
     char *argv[];
{
  int rank, size;

  MPI_Init (&argc, &argv);        /* starts MPI */
  MPI_Comm_rank (MPI_COMM_WORLD, &rank);        /* get current process id */
  MPI_Comm_size (MPI_COMM_WORLD, &size);        /* get number of processes */
  printf( "Hello world from process %d of %d\n", rank, size );
  MPI_Finalize();
  return 0;
}
```

Fig. 10.5 Hello world program using MPI

simplify the parallelization constructs. The combination of MPI and OpenMP can be used to envelop more powerful system with distributed parallel processing and thread parallel processing as well (Fig. 10.5).

The above program shows a simple hello world program using OpenMPI. Next let's look at one of the simple yet crucial computations in statistical language processing called word frequency. Word frequency is one of the basic steps to be done to calculate term frequency. It denotes the number of times a particular word appears in a document. Inverse document frequency gives the number of times a particular word appears in a set of documents. Term frequency and inverse document frequency are used for keyword-based searching statistical techniques. The code excerpt in Fig. 10.6 shows the calculation of word frequency in simple C.

Now the problem arises when the string size is too big to fit in the buffer of a single system, for example, when you are building a simple software which shows all the files which contain a particular word and when the number of files is of the range of 10 million or so.

Present-day search engines index much more than 100 m pages. Situations like this are when distributed computing comes in. Now we want to extend the above program such that even if a file is too big to fit in buffer, we can process it and return the results as quickly as possible. Using MPI the master system reads the file and distributes the data (as in Figs. 10.7 and 10.8), the worker systems receive part of the original data, process the data using the code in Fig. 10.6, and give back results to master.

10.2.3.2   Parallel Virtual Machine

Another parallel processing library that enables data processing in cluster is Parallel Virtual Machine (PVM). There would be one controlling machine and multiple worker machines in the cluster. And this library allows controlling machine to

```
void insert_word (word *words, int *n, char *s) {
        int     i;

        /* linear search for the word */
        for (i=0; i<*n; i++) if (strcmp (s, words[i].s) == 0) {

                /* found it?  increment and return. */

                words[i].count++;
                return;
        }

        /* error conditions... */

        if (strlen (s) >= MAXSTRING) {
                fprintf (stderr, "word too long!\n");
                exit (1);
        }
        if (*n >= MAXWORDS) {
                fprintf (stderr, "too many words!\n");
                exit (1);
        }

        /* copy the word into the structure at the first available slot,
         * i.e., *n
         */

        strcpy (words[*n].s, s);

        /* this word has occured once up to now, so count = 1 */

        words[*n].count = 1;

        /* one more word */

        (*n)++;
}
```

Fig. 10.6 Word frequency in MPI and C

```
MPI_Send(void* data, int count, MPI_Datatype datatype, int destination,
         int tag, MPI_Comm communicator)
```

```
MPI_Recv(void* data, int count, MPI_Datatype datatype, int source,
         int tag, MPI_Comm communicator, MPI_Status* status)
```

Fig. 10.7 Send and receive functions using MPI; data is the data buffer while the count is the number of records sent or received at most and data type denotes the data type of the object and destination, and source gives the address of the sender and receivers

Virtual Datacenter

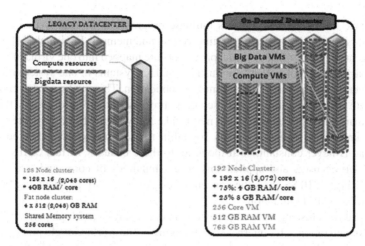

Fig. 10.8 On-demand SMP using vSMP product forms ScaleMP

process on other nodes and allows creation of encapsulated environment for running parallel programs even on heterogeneous systems.

The Parallel Virtual Machine (PVM) [3] has daemon processes which run on all cluster nodes and an application programming library. PVM in a way virtualizes the cluster and represents the heterogeneous resources as a homogeneous cluster environment to a program. The PVM daemon process can run on machines with widely differing computational capabilities, from notebooks to supercomputers. PVM offers language bindings to C and C++ as a set of API functions and a binding to Fortran as a series of subroutines.

Using PVM is pretty upfront. First, the user starts up the PVM daemons on the cluster nodes to combine them into the shared cluster resource. Next, the user codes serial programs making calls to PVM API. One user executes a "master" program on one machine. The master program will spawn slave programs as needed on other nodes using PVM API. The execution of the slave programs comes to an end with the finish of master program. Code for each slave program must be available to the PVM daemon before the master program starts. Basically in all nodes, running program in PVM instance is done as task executed on host operating system. PVM tasks are identified by a task ID which forms the basis for inter-task communication. A PVM task can belong to one or more task groups which are dynamic, i.e., a task can join or leave a task group at any time without any notification. Task groups can be used for multi-case communications and PVM also supports broadcast communications.

10.2.3.3   Virtual Symmetric Multiprocessing

Symmetric multiprocessing allows multiple programs to be run by two or more processors sharing a common operating system and memory. In virtual SMP two or more (generally 10s to 100s) virtual processors are mapped into one virtual machine. Due to aggregation of powerful industry, standard systems in one system user can access very large amount of data from any application. This can be used in conjunction with multithreading where separate processes run on different threads. On-demand SMP provisioning is a major take away from vSMP software. As we already know, SMP is highly suitable for online transaction processing systems. The user load is never constant, so responding to these changes, virtual SMPs can be created letting users and applications access hundreds of cores and terabytes of memory. Figure 10.8 shows the concept of on-demand SMP provisioning through ScaleMP's vSMP Foundation.

These days' clusters are used for extensive data analysis and high performance at a large organization. The Internet search engine of the world Google pioneered the distributed parallel programming for Web scale data using commercial off-the-shelf

Google the Internet search engine which handles 67 % of the PC search market and 83 % of the search queries as released by comScore on August 2014, is as we have seen the pioneer of MapReduce programming, and is based on cluster computing systems. A single Google query has to crunch 100s of MBs of data. Given the average number of queries is close to 4.5 million queries per second, the data and processing requirements are huge. Google uses clusters due to better price to performance trade-off. Two important design goals are high throughput and reliability. With high replication, load balancing, and parallel execution, the clusters of more than millions of commodity PCs distributed across the globe, the design goals are realized.

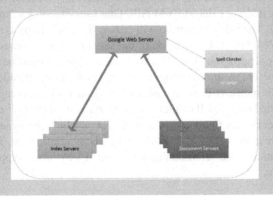

(continued)

The above figures show the work of the Google search engine in a simplest manner. Index servers have the inverted index through which the search query is mapped to a set of documents. Scores are calculated based on how relevant a particular document is to the user and results are returned in the order of this score. Once the document has been found, then the file is read and the keyword-in-context portion of the document is retrieved in addition to that the spell checker and the ad server are also activated. The main source of revenue for Google is through ads. The ad servers send out relevant ads based on the queries and context of the user. While the spell checker corrects the spellings in the keywords in the search query.

components. It created a highly available and highly reliable distributed file system, Google File System, and distributed processing framework called MapReduce. This has been used for machine learning, analytics, and basis for a lot of other applications for Google. A notable open-source implementation is Hadoop. Hadoop [4] has been used for various Internet companies like Facebook, Yahoo, Twitter, LinkedIn, etc., and several other systems based on Hadoop are built.

Hadoop also has distributed file system called HDFS and processing framework called Map-Reduce. Today the latest version is Hadoop 2.4.1. In the following paragraph, we study Hadoop architecture briefly and write a basic MapReduce program to count the word frequency of a text.

Hadoop is a top level Apache Project which is an open-source implementation of Google's MapReduce and Google File System. The Hadoop Ecosystem also includes Apache Mahout a large-scale machine learning library, Apache Zookeeper a coordination service for distributed systems, and Apache Hbase inspired from Google BigTable. The Hadoop has two main components.

Hadoop distributed file system supports high-throughput access to application data.

1. MapReduce, a system for parallel processing of large data sets
2. Hadoop YARN, a framework for job scheduling and resource manager

10.2.3.4 MapReduce

MapReduce is a parallel programming model which can be executed on large clusters on a huge data set. The model is simplistically made up of two functions called map and reduce [5]. In a way the map function can be seen as preprocessing of data and reduce as the actual computation and aggregation. Not all problems can be fitted into MapReduce paradigm, while for some problems, we can use iterative MapReduce to solve. In the iterative MapReduce, there exists a sequential component which launches iterations of MapReduce job. A MapReduce job usually splits the input data set into independent chunks which are in parallel processed by map tasks. Then the framework sorts the outputs of the map tasks and sends the sorted output to reduce tasks. To solve the problem of intermediate failures, intermediate outputs and inputs are written to disk. The reduce phase picks up the intermediate key value pairs and produces the output < key, value > pairs that can be understood by the user [5], the basic framework of MapReduce programming model.

For now let's look into a simple problem counting the word frequency. We take an example of counting the number of words in a file as the basic example that gives more insight into understanding of MapReduce model. Consider two files with any number of lines. For simplicity sake, here we have taken only one line per file.

The input lines are given to the map function which extracts each word in the line that are separated by space and assigned a value of one. A set of (word, 1) < key, value > pairs are generated from map function which is sorted in the sort phase as intermediate (word, {1, 1...}) < key, value > pairs. These intermediate key value pairs are passed to the reduce function that sums up the number of times the word has appeared in the file producing (word, count) < key, value > pairs as the output. The different phases for this sample example are given below.

Another realistic example of MapReduce can be "finding number of users who were logged in for all the dates present in the log file."

HDFS is a distributed file system which is designed to run on commodity hardware. The main characteristics of HDFS are high fault tolerance, high-throughput access, large data sets, data local computations, support for heterogeneous hardware, and a simpler coherence mode. HDFS has a master-slave architecture. The master server is called NameNode and this system manages the file site namespace and regulates the file access. And the DataNodes manage the data stored in them. The file is divided into blocks of storage typically 64 MB (to 512 MB which can be configured) to enable storing very large files that are hundreds of megabytes, gigabytes, and petabytes in size.

The data local computations are supported through the DataNodes. These DataNodes act on the data they have locally, thereby decreasing the data movement through the network. The data blocks are replicated so as to prevent data loss due to system failures or network failures as well as provide means for parallel processing and load balancing. However the NameNode is the central machine in the cluster. It creates the vulnerability of single point of failure due to which the cluster can go offline even though the DataNodes are still functioning. Some ways to solve the problem is to keep multiple copies of metadata. But as of now the Hadoop implementation doesn't include automatic failover.

In the earlier versions of Hadoop, the MapReduce execution environment also had master-slave architecture where the master node is called jobtracker which typically runs on NameNode of HDFS. The jobtracker monitors various MapReduce jobs running in the cluster. The jobtracker also takes care of load balancing and rescheduling of task in case of any failures. The jobtracker poses a risk of single point of failure. This has been taken care in form of YARN.

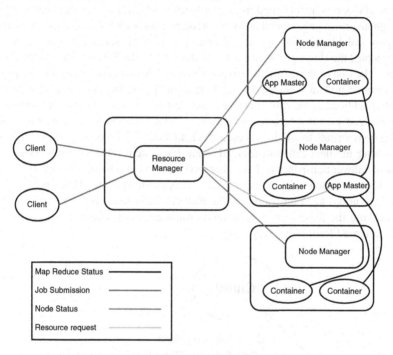

The fundamental idea of YARN is to split up the two major functionalities of the jobtracker, resource management, and job monitoring into separate daemons. There would be a global resource manager and per-application application master. The resource manager and per-node node manager form computation framework. The resource manager arbitrates resources among all the applications in the system. The per-application application master negotiates resources with resources manager and works with the node managers to execute and monitor the tasks. The resource manager is responsible for allocating resources to applications based on some constraints and job queue and also responsible for accepting job submissions, creating application master, and restarting application master in case of failure.

Zookeeper is a centralized coordination service for distributed applications. This exposes common services such as configurations, synchronization, management, and naming in a simple interface. The coordination of different processes is through a shared hierarchical namespace. Unlike file systems the data is kept in-memory giving high-throughput and lower latencies. The servers that make up zookeeper service must all know about each other. They maintain an in-memory image of state with transaction logs and snapshots in persistent store. It is ordered and fast. The main capabilities that enhance the Hadoop cluster are process synchronization, self-election of leader, reliable messaging, and configuration management.

The Hadoop is mainly used in case of batch workloads as it is designed for high-throughput processing rather than lower latencies. Facebook [6] needed a system which is highly scalable and can support real-time concurrent yet serial access to the data. So they adopted the Hadoop system and made changes to HDFS to provide more real-time access. The first of those modifications is the use of Avatar node [7] which is typically a wrapper around the NameNode, and there would be another hot standby avatar node which quickly takes the role of primary node in case of failure. These two servers are synchronized such that both have the most recent system image to support these new transactions written to edit log on each block allocation. The second modification is to use a layer in client called distributed avatar file system (DAFS) which handles the cases of failover transparently. Few other modifications to achieve real-time system are RPC time-out which is set to fail fast and retry opposite to default Hadoop.

Where nodes keep on waiting if the NameNode is still alive is a behavior done by revoking the lease to the file quickly. Another import enhancement is that the client can read from local copy of data.

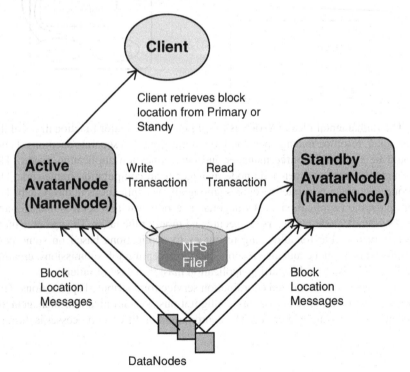

Graph Processing Using Map Reduce

Graph processing doesn't quite fit in MapReduce paradigm of programming because of recursive nature of graph processing algorithms. One way to make graph processing algorithms fit in MapReduce framework is to launch MapReduce jobs for each iteration. General graphs of Web scale have 1000s to millions of nodes linking each other. Representing graph through linked edges won't work for iterative applications, so another way of representing graph is adjacency matrix which denotes if an edge exists between the current node in the row and nodes in columns. Yet again large portion of matrix would be zero, so unnecessary network load increases. Another approach is to use sparse matrices, which just denotes the list of node pairs which has an edge for each node. Now since we have represented the graph, let's look at a basic problem in graph processing, finding shortest path between two nodes. Using Dijistra algorithm is as follows.

Input: Graph $G = (V, E)$, directed or undirected; positive edge lengths $\{l_e : e \in E\}$; vertex $s \in V$

Output: For all vertices u reachable from s, $dist(u)$ is set to the distance from s to u.

procedure DIJKSTRA(G, l, s)

    for all $u \in V$ **do**
        $dist(u) = \infty$
        $prev(u) = \texttt{nil}$
    $dist(s) = 0$

    $H = $ MAKEQUEUE(V) ▷ using dist-values as keys
    while H is not empty **do**
        $u = $ DELETEMIN(H)
        for all edges $(u, v) \in E$ **do**
            if $dist(v) > dist(u) + l(u, v)$ **then**
                $dist(v) = dist(u) + l(u, v)$
                $prev(v) = u$
                DECREASEKEY(H, v)

(continued)

Shortest path using MapReduce is as follows:

```
1: class MAPPER
2:     method MAP(nid n, node N)
3:         d ← N.DISTANCE
4:         EMIT(nid n, N)                          ▷ Pass along graph structure
5:         for all nodeid m ∈ N.ADJACENCYLIST do
6:             EMIT(nid m, d + 1)                  ▷ Emit distances to reachable nodes

1: class REDUCER
2:     method REDUCE(nid m, [d₁, d₂, ...])
3:         d_min ← ∞
4:         M ← ∅
5:         for all d ∈ counts [d₁, d₂, ...] do
6:             if ISNODE(d) then
7:                 M ← d                           ▷ Recover graph structure
8:             else if d < d_min then              ▷ Look for shorter distance
9:                 d_min ← d
10:        M.DISTANCE ← d_min                      ▷ Update shortest distance
11:        EMIT(nid m, node M)
```

For each iteration of one MapReduce job, the graph hops one unit further. The point to be considered is the termination of MapReduce algorithm, for a simple termination condition can be a number of iterations.

There are a lot of other alternatives to Hadoop MapReduce implementation, Disco open-source platform originated from Nokia, HPCC platform from LexisNexis, DyradLinq from Microsoft, and Sector/Sphere, another contender for high-performance distributed computing.

Whether turnkey or homegrown, the basic idea behind a cluster is the same: take a complex computing problem and divide it into smaller pieces that the cluster's many cores can solve in parallel, resulting in shortened runtimes. Developing programs for distributed environment and debugging them can be a daunting task. To help solve the problems, various debugging tools like XMPI for MPI and XPVM for PVM and resource management tools like Condor are also available. OSCAR is one such tool available for managing cluster. Cluster management forms the primary function to utilize the functions; some of the software available in the market are platform HPC, Windows HPC server, Altair Gridworks, Oracle Grid Engine, and a lot of other open-source software.

10.2.4 Advanced Cluster Computing Systems

10.2.4.1 GPU Clusters for High-Performance Computing

A GPU cluster is a computer cluster where each node has a graphics processing unit (GPU), leveraging the massively parallel computational power in the GPUs for more general processing. The data analysis is done in a cluster with GPU as accelerators. Higher-level language constructs like CUDA from NVIDIA and OpenCL from AMD also helped a long way in bringing general computing onto the GPUs. CUDA and OpenCL are c-based languages with programming contracts very similar to that of OpenMP [8].

Another major step is through virtualization of GPUs, where in the cluster only few nodes are equipped with GPU and these nodes are connected to each other; RCUDA middleware [9] lets the machines of the clusters access the GPU as if it's on the host system. There are a lot of works towards virtual GPUs in virtual machines. Cloud providers like Amazon and Nimbix provide GPU on demand for high-performance applications.

10.2.4.2 FPGA Clusters

There have been an increasing number of accelerator products for FPGA accelerator-based high-performance solutions. The advantage the FPGA has is that the hardware circuit inside the chip can be rewired and used as per our need which is the case with CPUs and GPUs. While this has still a long way to go, mainstream financial companies and researcher across the globe are using these products leveraging the raw processing to boost the applications multifold. For example, research groups like CASPER have been providing client libraries and open-source circuit design plug-ins for MATLAB. This group's focus is mainly in RADIO astronomy and electronics engineering. Open-source compilers or language constructs like CUDA as in GPUs for converting the program in any general high-level language to HDL to run on FPGA are needed to be developed to make the FPGA clusters more market ready.

10.2.4.3 Clusters on Cloud

Cluster computing generally involves in connecting two or more physical machines together, whereas the clusters in cloud are virtual, i.e., a virtual cluster. A virtual cluster is a collection of VMs deployed on a single server. Each VM can be deployed on a physical cluster as a matter of fact. These virtual machines are connected through virtual network interface controllers and allowed to communicate with each other. Amazon Web services and Windows Azure allow for the creation of virtual clusters on their cloud environments. Organizations are leveraging the cloud computing for reducing the computing costs for high-performance jobs which only last for a few hours. For example, a cluster with 128 TB of storage and 1000 cores of processing power takes something around $1000 in AWS.

10.2.5 Difference Between Grid and Cluster

Difference lies in the structure, range, and use of applications. Cluster was traditionally used to provide redundancy, availability, and high performance. Beowulf cluster is a precursor to modern-day cluster computing. Two similar systems form a single entity and work on a bigger problem by coordinating with each other. They provide single system image, generally scaled to around 100s of servers in the current generation. Petascale clusters are being scaled to 1000s of servers and some clusters are also supporting inter-data center load distribution. Grid is mainly to run high resource-intensive applications. Earlier this was limited to science and engineering applications. They can be seen as a resource sharing platform, with multiple owners and highly dynamic heterogeneous system. The few notable grids are Eurogrid, Japan Grid, and Indian Garuda Grid. Grids have distributed load balancing and scheduling and support computation across administrative sets or domains. They can be computational grids and data grids, the controlled sharing and management of large amounts of distributed data, and can be seen as crude form of on-demand computing we see in the present-day cloud computing. Grid can make use of spare computing power on a machine, while the systems in the cluster are dedicated to work as a single unit. In a grid the resources are generally distributed across the geography, whereas in a cluster the machines are relatively closer mainly in the same data center or so.

10.3   Grid Computing

Grid computing [10] can be seen as a utility or infrastructure for complex and huge resource-intensive tasks where the remote resources are available through Internet from a workstation, a laptop, and a mobile device. The vision of grid computing [10] is similar to that of power grid where user doesn't know where the electricity is generated. Analogous to electricity in electricity grid, we have computing resources in grid computing. Imagine millions of computers, clusters, and supercomputers are owned by individuals or institutes from various countries dispersed across the world connected to form a single huge supercomputer. And the users can leverage these computing resources by paying for their usage. That is too far-stretched possibility of the grid. You can perceive this as a grid of grids. Albeit not so popular, there exist some grid economic models.

Grid computing has been going through a long journey along the path of integrating various diverse technologies and platforms. The key values of this paradigm lie in the underlying distributed computing infrastructure that is evolving in support of cross-organizational resource and application sharing, in other terms virtualized or transparent access to resources; this virtualized access is across organizations, technologies, and platforms. This sort of virtualization is highly impossible without the use of open standards. Open standards help ensure that applications can transparently take advantage of apt resources available to them, providing interoperability between heterogeneous platforms. Such an environment not only provides the ability to share and access resources across a distributed and heterogeneous environment but also needs to provide technologies and standards in the areas of authorization, scheduling, task coordination, security, and so on.

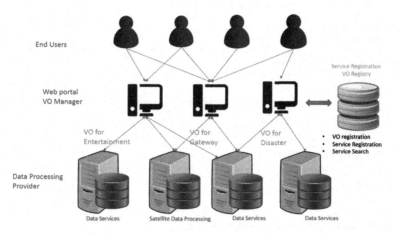

Fig. 10.9 Virtual organization

Most of the grids present now are distinct in the sense that the resources are shared just in a single organization or resource sharing is across organization. These distinctions between intraorganizational grids and interorganizational grids are not solely based on technological differences. Instead, they are mainly based on configuration choices like security domains, type of policies and their scope, degrees of isolation desired, and contractual obligations between providers of the infrastructures and users. Grid computing involves an evolving set of open standards for Web services and interfaces that make services, or computing resources, available over the Internet (Fig. 10.9).

A virtual organization (or company) [14] is one whose members are geographically apart, usually working by computer messaging, while appearing to others to be a single, unified organization with a real physical locate. The authorizations of the shared resource and the possible ways the resource will be used (memory, computing power, etc.) are some of the factors to be considered in virtual organization.

Very often grid technologies are used on homogeneous clusters, and they can add value on those clusters by assisting, for example, with scheduling or provisioning of the resources in the cluster. The term grid, and its related technologies, applies across this entire spectrum.

10.3.1   Motivation for Grid Computing

High-end computer applications are, e.g., simulation of nuclear reactor accidents, drug discovery, and weather forecast. Even though the CPU power, storage, and network speeds continue to increase, these resources are falling short of satisfying ever-increasing ever complex user demands.

RANK	SITE	SYSTEM	CORES	RMAX (TFLOP/S)	RPEAK (TFLOP/S)	POWER (KW)
1	National Super Computer Center in Guangzhou China	Tianhe-2 [MilkyWay-2] - TH-IVB-FEP Cluster, Intel Xeon E5-2692 12C 2.200GHz, TH Express-2, Intel Xeon Phi 3151P NUDT	3,120,000	33,862.7	54,902.4	17,808
2	DOE/SC/Oak Ridge National Laboratory United States	Titan - Cray XK7 , Opteron 6274 16C 2.200GHz, Cray Gemini interconnect, NVIDIA K20x Cray Inc.	560,640	17,590.0	27,112.5	8,209
3	DOE/NNSA/LLNL United States	Sequoia - BlueGene/Q, Power BQC 16C 1.60 GHz, Custom IBM	1,572,864	17,173.2	20,132.7	7,890
4	RIKEN Advanced Institute for Computational Science (AICS) Japan	K computer, SPARC64 VIIIfx 2.0GHz, Tofu interconnect Fujitsu	705,024	10,510.0	11,280.4	12,660
5	DOE/SC/Argonne National Laboratory United States	Mira - BlueGene/Q, Power BQC 16C 1.60GHz, Custom IBM	786,432	8,586.6	10,066.3	3,945
6	Swiss National Supercomputing Centre (CSCS)	Piz Daint - Cray XC30, Xeon E5-2670 8C 2.600GHz, Aries interconnect , NVIDIA K20x Cray Inc.	115,984	6,271.0	7,788.9	2,325

Fig. 10.10 Top 6 supercomputers from top500.org

The logical components of a typical high-performance computing looks as in the following figure.

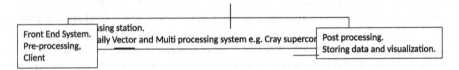

The user submits the job through the front-end client, the processing station which is generally a vector system or SMP system (Milkyway2, Stampead, etc.) which easily crosses 1 Tflop within today's limits. Programming on this system requires special tools and languages. After the processing the processed data is sent to post-processing stations for visualization and storing. But this supercomputer setup is ridiculously expensive. The cost factor is the main reason for the evolution of grid computer. The idea of utilizing the unused resources is another motivation behind the start of the cluster and grid computing models (Fig. 10.10).

Yet another reason for the increased growth and adoption of grid computing is the potential for an organization to lessen the capital and operating cost of its IT resources, while still maintaining the computing capabilities it requires. This is because the computing resources of most organizations are greatly underutilized, but are essential for certain operations for brief periods. Thus the ROI on IT investments can increase through participation in grid computing even though networking and service costs may increase slightly. This is also a leading factor why companies are looking towards clouds for these sporadic requirements (Fig. 10.11).

The characteristics of grid computing are slightly explained through the above figure; the users in the grid are a very large and dynamic population; the users can join and leave the grid at any point. The users have their own privileges and authorizations based on the roles in their respective organizations and have their own confidential data. The sites implicitly tell about the distributed nature of resources

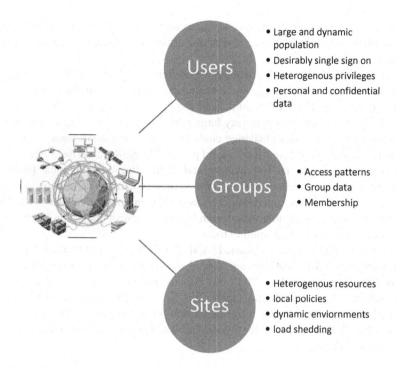

Users
- Large and dynamic population
- Desirably single sign on
- Heterogenous privileges
- Personal and confidential data

Groups
- Access patterns
- Group data
- Membership

Sites
- Heterogenous resources
- local policies
- dynamic enviornments
- load shedding

Fig. 10.11 Characteristics of grid computing

in the grid. These sites might have different usage policies and potentially different types of resources. The load is to be balanced between different sites in the grid given the high workload or optimal processing requirements [11].

10.3.2   Evolution of Grid Computing

Over the last 3 decades, processing powers of PCs have gone up significantly (100 MHz to several GHz) and with fast and cheap networks; with built-in storage the utilization of personal computers have gone up exponentially. Free, open-source software and operating systems like Linux have emerged as a robust efficient OS with plenty of applications. Many a times Linux clusters have been used in academic research institutes given the low cost and high performance.

The ideas of grid computing are not new. The idea of "shared computing power" came from 1960s and 1970s, when computing was dominated by huge mainframe computers shared by whole organizations. And the idea of "computing as a utility" is first suggested by the developers of an operating system called Multics (an ancestor of UNIX, which is an ancestor of Linux) in 1965.

Grid computing's direct ancestor is "metacomputing," which dates back to early 1990s. Metacomputing was used to describe efforts to connect US supercomputing centers.

FAFNER (Factoring via Network-Enabled Recursion) and I-WAY (Information Wide Area Year) were cutting-edge metacomputing projects in the United States, both conceived in 1995. Each influenced the evolution of key grid technologies. FAFNER's aim was to factorize very large numbers, a challenge highly relevant to digital security. Since this challenge could be broken into small parts, even fairly modest computers could contribute useful power. FAFNER's contribution to today's grid is that the techniques for dividing and distributing computational problems were forerunners of technology used for various volunteer computing projects. I-WAY's aim was to link supercomputers using existing networks. One of I-WAY's innovations was a computational resource broker, conceptually similar to those being developed for grid computing today.

In 1996, Globus project was started (ANL & USC). In 2002, Open Grid Services Architecture (OGSA) was first announced during the Global Grid Forum (now Open Grid Forum). In July 2003 the Globus Toolkit using a service-oriented approach based on OGSA and Open Grid Services Infrastructure (OGSI) was released. In 2004 Web service resource framework was released and the following year Globus Toolkit supported the WSRF. In 2006, Global Grid Forum was renamed to Open Grid Forum.

10.3.3   Design Principles and Goals of a Grid System

The idealized design goals of a grid system [12] to provide users a seamless computing environment are as follows:

- Heterogeneity. A grid involves an array of resources which are highly heterogeneous and encompasses a vast range of technologies.
- Multiple administrative domains and autonomies. Grid resources might not only be distributed geographically but can easily span multiple administrative domains and possibly owned by different organizations. The autonomy of resource owners has to be observed alongside their local resource management and usage policies.
- Scalability. A grid can have few integrated resources to millions. While this is desirable, the performance might degrade as the size of the grid increases. Accordingly, applications requiring a great deal of geographically located resources have to be designed taking into consideration the latency and bandwidth tolerance. Today's largest grid has more than 435 Tflops of processing power and more than 2 million hosts (BOINC Stats World Community Grid).
- Dynamicity or adaptability or fault resilience. In a grid, resource failure is the rule rather than the exception. With a very high number of resources in a grid, the probability of some resource failing is pretty high. Resource managers or

applications must adapt their behavior dynamically and use the available resources and services efficiently and effectively.

Reduce computing costs, increase computing resource utilization, reduce job turnaround time, and reduce complexity to users are some of the other goals in designing a grid environment.

An ideal grid environment will therefore provide access to the available resources in a seamless manner such that physical discontinuities, such as the differences between platforms, network protocols, and administrative boundaries, become completely transparent. In essence, the grid middleware turns a radically heterogeneous environment into a virtual homogeneous one.

The following are the main design features that should be provided by a grid environment:

- Communication services: Different applications have different modes of communication ranging from point to point to multicast messaging. These services are also required for machine to machine interaction and task coordination between distributed resources. The grid should provide flexibility for the applications to choose the communication mode taking into consideration the important QoS parameters such as fault tolerance, bandwidth, latency, reliability, and jitter control.
- Information services: Given the dynamic nature of grid environment, it is necessary to make all resources accessible to any process in the system, without regard to the relative location of the resource user and also the information about the grid structure, resources, services, and status.
- Naming services: The naming service provides a uniform namespace across the complete grid environment. In a grid, names refer to various objects like processing stations, services, and data objects.
- Distributed file systems: Most of the time distributed applications require access to files distributed among many servers.
- Security and authorization: Any system has to provide security following the CIA principle confidentiality, integrity, and authentication. But the security within a grid environment is complex as it requires diverse resources to be autonomously administered and interacts in a manner that does not impact the usability of the resources or creates security flaws in the overall system.
- System status and fault tolerance: Tools provide a reliable and robust environment, including utilities to monitor resources and applications.
- Resource management and scheduling: The overall aim is to provide efficient and optimum usage of resources to process the applications on the grid computing environment. From a user's point of view, resource management and scheduling is completely transparent from the users. The grid schedulers should be able to coordinate with local management techniques as the grid may involve different organizations with different usage policies.
- Programming tools and paradigms: The most important part of the grid is to provide means to develop grid applications. A grid should provide interfaces, APIs, tools, and utilities to provide a rich development environment. Most

Fig. 10.12 Grid
architecture

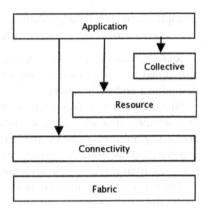

common grid programming languages C, C++, Java, and Fortran should be available, as should application-level interfaces such as MPI, DSM, and PVM. The grid should also support various debugging tools, profilers, and user libraries to make programming simpler.

User and administrative GUI need to be simpler and intuitive; the interface may also be a Web-based interface for easier administration and usage. Computational economy and resource trading not only incentivize resource owners but also provide a means of keeping up with supply and demand. Administrative hierarchy determines how administrative information flows through the grid.

10.3.4   Grid System Architecture

The key distinction between grids and other technologies like network computing models lies in the resource management and discovery. The grid middleware interfaces applications and resources. This grid middleware can be perceived as core middleware and user middleware. While the core middleware provides the basic services like secure and effective access to resources, the user middleware provides services for job execution and monitoring, authentication, and transferring results back to user (Fig. 10.12).

Grid architecture [11] can be seen in terms of different layers with each layer having a predefined function. The higher layers are generally user-centric, whereas lower layers are more hardware-centric, focused on various resources:

- The lowest layer is network layer which forms the basic backbone for any grid connecting various grid resources to each other, for example, National Knowledge Network in India.
- Right above the network layer lies the resource layer which has the actual grid resources connected to the network. These resources can be workstations, PCs, sensors, telescopes, and even data catalogues.

- Next is the middleware layer which provides various tools to enable the various resources to participate in a grid.
- The highest layer is the application layer. This includes grid applications and development toolkits for supporting the applications. Grid users interface with this layer and also provide general management functions and auditing functions.

Different applications can be processed on grids and different organizations use grids for various use cases. Some organizations might use grid for high-performance computations or aggregation of resources, or they might be using grid for distributed data storage and access. Different types of grid architectures are designed to meet these requirements; the grid can be classified as follows:

10.3.4.1 Computational Grid

Computational grid [17] is used in organizations looking to expand abilities and aggregate and share existing resources to maximize the utilization or require more processing capability than what is available. These organizations may be solving the global warming problem, forecasting the weather, or doing cutting-edge research in basic sciences, financial data, distributed data mining, or high-performance web serving. Whatever the reason may be, all these problems have one pretty serious similarity: availability and reachability of processing resources. This is the main goal for this class of grids. Note that not all algorithms are able to leverage parallel processing and data-intensive and high-throughput computing.

Computational grids can be recognized by these primary characteristics: instant access to resources on demand, clusters or supercomputers, the computational power to process large-scale jobs, and CPU scavenging to utilize resources effectively.

The primary benefits of computational grids are a reduced total cost of ownership (TCO) and shorter deployment life cycles. The World Community Grid, the Distributed Petascale Facility (TeraGrid), European Grid Infrastructure, and Garuda Grid from India are all different examples of deployed computational grids.

10.3.4.2 Data Grid

While computational grids are more suitable for resource aggregation and remote resource access, the data grids [17] tend their focus towards providing secure access to distributed and heterogeneous pools of data transparently to the user. These data grids can also include resources such as a distributed file system or even a federated database or any other distributed data stores. Data grids also harness storage, network, and data located in different administrative domains with respect to the local and global policies on data usage and efficient scheduling of resources given the constraints (both local and global) and provide high-speed and reliable data access. One of the use cases that bring interest to the data grids is when organizations take

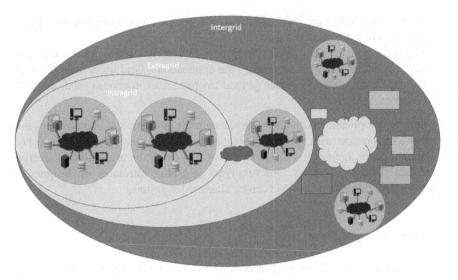

Fig. 10.13 Grid topology

initiatives to expand data mining abilities with maximum utilization of existing storage infrastructure investment and thereby reduce data management complexity.

10.3.4.3   Grid Topology

The more the number of partners, geographical parameters, and constraints, the more complex the grid. Upon resource discovery, availability and nonfunctional requirements such as security and performance become more complex. The resource sharing is not primarily a mere file exchange; it is direct access to computational resources and data. This requires a range of collaborative problem-solving and resource-brokering strategies from the grid environment. This sharing should be highly secure and auditable. So, the grid computing topology is classified as the following as per the complexity and involving partners: Intragrids are formed within single organizations and have a single cluster. The Extragrids are formed by bringing together multiple Intragrids. This usually involves more than one organization and the management complexity increases security concerns. The security is dispersed, and the resources are more dynamic. An Intergrid is formed through dynamic integration of resources, applications, and services and the users obtain access through WAN/Internet (Fig. 10.13).

10.3.4.4   Work of a Grid Computing System

The user first submits the job (the task which user wants to run in the grid). The grid puts the job on the queue and schedules the job when the job is to be run. The grid first finds appropriate resources required for the job and organizes efficient access

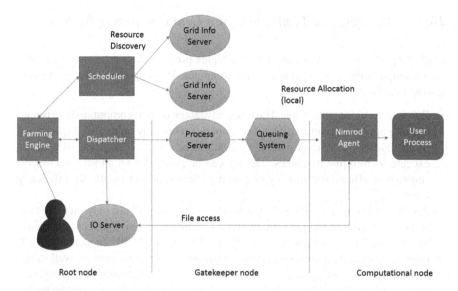

Fig. 10.14 Processing of grid job

to data and deals with the authentication, interfaces to local site's resource allocation mechanism and policies, runs the job, monitors progress, recovers execution in case failure occurs, and informs back once job is done. Another way a grid can function is in the form of services. With the advent of Web 2.0 and SOA, most of the grid middleware is adapted or designed around grid services. A grid service is the service interface related to a grid resource. In the grid environment resources and its state are monitored and controlled through grid services (Fig. 10.14).

The above figure processes execution using Nimrod scheduler. Computational nodes are those in which the job runs. Scheduler takes the scheduling decision of which resources are to be allocated in the grid. These resources can be in the grid or it has to access resources from external grid system. Root node is where the user submits the jobs and gatekeeper node takes care of job queuing.

Though powerful, these computing frameworks require a high degree of knowledge capital to successfully deploy and exploit. This limitation can represent a barrier to the entry of sorts for individuals or groups who wish to experiment with grid computing. For new programmers, this is like trying to use Struts for your first Web application, rather than writing your own servlets from scratch.

Yet many grid middleware provides highly abstracted mechanisms for developing grid applications. These middleware supports a version of MPI to develop applications and also provide user libraries and grid API to leverage the grid infrastructure. Please refer to further reading section for more information on programming for grid infrastructure.

10.3.5 Benefits and Limitations of a Grid Computing System

Grid computing is all about attacking a complex problem with an army of computers running parallels rather than a single computer. This approach gives us the following benefits:

- Efficient resource utilization: The basic advantage of grid computing is to run an existing application on a different machine(s). This may be due to the overload on the earlier machine or even the job might be resource intensive so it has to execute on multiple machines. The job can be processed on an idle machine(s) somewhere else on the grid. By putting the idle resources to work, the efficiency increases.
- Parallel CPU capacity: By aggregating resources, the grid not only increases the resource utilization but also accumulates potentially massive processing capacity. The world grid forum has more than 435 Tflops of CPU capacity in 2014. Grid environments like many parallel programming environments are well suited to execute applications which can be parallelized. Using library and programming models like MPI and PVM, it is possible to pass data and coordinate the processing between distributed resources.
- Virtual resources and virtual organizations [14]: Dynamically organizing grid users into a number of virtual organizations with different policies. When we talk about resource sharing, it is not limited to just files; it can involve many specialized resources, appliances, services, software licenses, and so on. All these resources are virtualized so that there is more uniform, interoperable, and reliable access among all grid participants.
- Access to additional resources and scalability: Most of the time a particular application or services can have average load, but occasionally the load may peak. Especially in those occasional peak times, many organizations look for additional resources. Or sometimes the organization crunches data for periodic analysis which may need additional resources for processing the analysis.
- Fault resilience: Generally modular structure in grid environments and no single points of failure make the grid to be more fault resilient and jobs are automatically restarted or transferred when the failure occurs.
- Reliability: Due to the distributed nature of the grid, the failure at any one location doesn't affect the functioning of other areas of grid. The multiple copies of data and jobs are kept so as to serve the QoS and critical application constraints
- Resource management and maintenance: Due to the aggregation of resources and monitoring them in the grid, the scheduling and management of these distributed resources becomes simpler.

As with every other paradigms, grid computing has some disadvantages or limitations:

- Memory-intensive applications which cannot be distributed are not suitable for grid environment.
- High-performance interconnects may be required for high-performance distributed applications.

Fig. 10.15 Grid vs. cluster
vs. cloud

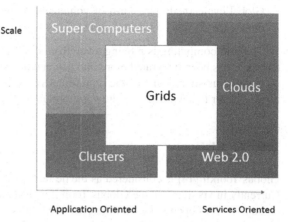

- Synchronization in large-scale grid environment with several administrative domains is challenging.
- Reluctance of organizations to share the resources, so necessary policies must be entrusted.
- Some of the other challenges might be performance analysis, network protocols, security, programming models, and tools.

10.3.6   Grid Systems and Applications

Grid computing is not only useful in resource-intensive applications; any repetitive work is a good candidate. It doesn't matter whether an organization is hugely multinational or medium-sized company grid can be utilized to increase the efficiency and resource utilization. Grid initiated on-demand computing model, and with the proliferation of cloud computing, the on-demand computing approached a new level. Grid computing is almost a decade older to cloud computing and it overlaps with the cloud computing model. For grid computing to go mainstream, compelling business use cases giving high business value are essential. The first such use case might be of distributed data mining. Data mining is a way in which interesting relationships and patterns are identified from business data. A grocer could use data mining to study buying patterns and strategically decide how stock of a particular product needs to be kept in store or any other recommendation engines e-commerce or advertising sites are using. The second use case might be data-driven decision making and risk analysis.

The most common approaches through which the grid computing environment is architected are as follows (Fig. 10.15):

- Dedicated machines just for the usage in grid workloads
- Network cycle stealing through which the idle computers in an organization are repurposed they can run grid jobs

- Global cycle stealing: a form of volunteer computing in which the volunteers donate CPU cycles over the Internet

The grid computing is moving away from the niche high-performance applications and has been integrated more into day and day systems [13].

Now let us study some of the representative grid environments available in the market. After this we will look at two important grid computing projects.

10.3.6.1   Globus

Globus Toolkit [14] is considered as the de facto standard for current state of grid. Currently in version 5.0, the Globus Toolkit is designed by the Globus Alliance. It contains a set of open-source utilities, services, APIs, and protocols. This is the most widely used middleware for the construction of grids. Globus modules such as resource management or information infrastructure can be used independently, without using the Globus communication libraries. The Globus Toolkit supports the following:

- Grid Security Infrastructure (GSI)
- GridFTP
- Globus Resource Allocation Manager (GRAM)
- Metacomputing Directory Service (MDS-2)
- Global Access to Secondary Storage (GASS)
- Data Catalogue and Replica Management
- Advanced Resource Reservation and Allocation (GARA) (Fig. 10.16)

Globus is a seen as a set of APIs for accessing underlying services of a grid environment. Globus Toolkit gives a logical view for the application developers to create grid-enabled applications. With Globus, developers can offer secure and robust file transfer, as well as identity, profile, and group management to their user communities. Globus allows end users to create and manage a unique identity which can be linked to external identities for authentication. End users can also transfer files across wide area networks faster and more easily, whatever their location.

Legion is an object-based grid system developed at the University of Virginia. In the Legion system, every resource, either software or hardware resource, is represented as an object. Every object interacts through method invocation. Legion defines an API for object interaction.

10.3.6.2   BOINC

BOINC [15] is originally designed for volunteer computing like SETI@HOME and Folding@Home. Yet it also works for grid computing environment. World Community Grid is one such grid which is based on BOINC. Scientist uses this to create volunteer computing, while universities use this to create virtual supercomputer and companies use this to create desktop grid computing. Some major

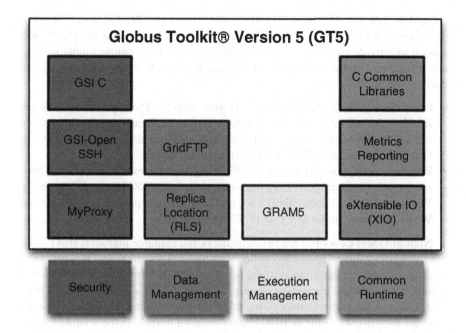

Fig. 10.16 Globus Toolkit modules

differences in desktop grids and volunteer computing are that in desktop grids computing resources are mostly trusted and screensaver graphics is not required.

The overall flow of BOINC is as follows:

- When a BOINC client is a free resource, it coordinates with resource scheduler for tasks. In the process client states its platform and other parameters.
- The schedulers find the unprocessed jobs and pass them to the client.
- Now the client downloads the files associated with the application versions and work units and executes the programs.
- After the completion of job, the results are uploaded from the client.

This process goes on indefinitely.

SZTAKI desktop grid and Jarifa are based on BOINC and are developed for sharing resources in hierarchical organizations, forming computational grid.

10.3.6.3 OGSA

The Open Grid Services Architecture (OGSA) [16] represents an evolution towards a grid system architecture based on Web service concepts and technologies. A grid service addresses the issue of a virtual resource and its state management. A grid is a dynamic environment. Hence, a grid service can be transient rather than persistent. A grid service can be dynamically created and destroyed, unlike a Web service, which is often presumed available if its corresponding WSDL file is accessible to its client. Web services also typically outlive all their clients. The following are some of the key capabilities in that the OGSA Service Model requires a compliant Grid service to provide creations on new instances of resources, unique global naming and references, lifetime management, registration and discovery of services, and client notifications:

- Open Grid Services Interface (OGSI) grid service: The Open Grid Services Interface defines rules about how OGSA can be implemented using grid services that are Web service extensions. Grid services are defined via Grid Web Services Definition Language (GWSDL), an extension of WSDL.
- Web Services Resource Framework (WSRF) grid services: These are set of Web service specifications describing the implementation of OGSA capabilities using Web services. The Globus Toolkit 4.0 and later versions provide an open-source WSRF development kit and a set of WSRF services.

Nimrod-G and Condor-G are two schedulers and resource managers that can be used alongside Globus Toolkit to confine with the QoS requirements. It is generally possible to integrate multiple systems we discussed to form a far more powerful system. One such grid computing project is Lattice. It is based on BOINC we have seen earlier. It integrates Condor-G for scheduling and Globus Toolkit as the backbone for the grid, while the BOINC clients are used to include the volunteer computing resources as well.

Few of the scientific grids currently in function are as follows:

European Data Grid

The European Data Grid is a European Union funded project which aims to create a huge grid system for computation and data sharing. It is aimed at projects in high energy physics, led by CERN, biology and medical image processing, and astronomy.

Worldwide LHC Computing Grid

The Worldwide LHC Computing Grid (*WLCG*) project is an international collaboration in 40 countries and 170 computing centers connecting various national and international grids with 2 million jobs run every day. The mission of the WLCG project is to provide global computing resources to store, distribute, and analyze the ~30 petabytes (30 million gigabytes) of data annually generated by the Large Hadron Collider (LHC) at CERN on the Franco–Swiss border.

10.3.6.4   In-Memory Grid Computing

In-memory grid [17] is a completely different kind of data store unlike NoSQL, RDBMS, and in-memory databases. The data fabric is a distribution of multiple data storage servers at a single location or across multiple locations. This distributed data model is known as shared-nothing architecture. The data is stored in memory of the servers. More memory can be added by adding more servers nondisruptively. The data model is non-relational and is object based. Distributed applications written on the .NET and Java application platforms are supported. The data fabric is resilient, allowing nondisruptive automated detection and recovery of a single server or multiple servers. Some of the in-memory grid products available in the market are as follows:

Name of product	Platform	Open source	Commercial
VMware Gemfire	Java	No	Yes
Oracle Coherence	Java	No	Yes
Alachisoft Ncache	Dot Net		
GridGain		No	Available
Hazelcast	Java	Yes	Available

Utilization of in-memory data grid enables organizations to achieve the following characteristics in their IT environment:

- Scale-out computing: Every node adds their resources to the cluster which can be used by all nodes.
- Fast big data: It enables very large data sets to be manipulated in memory.
- Resilience: Minimizing impact on applications, while the nodes fail randomly without data loss.
- Programming model: A simpler single system image for the programmer.
- Dynamic scalability: Nodes can join or leave the grid dynamically.
- Elastic main memory: Every node adds their ram to grid's memory pool.

In-memory data grids are often used with databases; given its distributed, resilient load sharing features, it improves the performance of applications with huge data and enables high throughput of data ingestion as well. The obvious push in performance is due to lesser disk reads and all data is being present in the memory. One limitation of in-memory data grids is that it usually lacks full ANSI SQL support; on the bright side, it provides massive parallel processing capabilities. Key/ value access, MapReduce, and a limited distributed SQL querying and indexing capabilities are the key data access patterns. The limited distributed SQL query is going away with companies like GridGain are providing pretty serious and constantly growing support for SQL including pluggable indexing, distributed joins using a key/value store allows greater flexibility for the application developer. The data model and application code are inextricably linked, more so than a relational structure.

In-Memory Data Grid and Business Benefits

The competitive advantages businesses gain using IMDG [18] are that businesses are now able to make better decisions faster and at the same time businesses can improve decision-making quality.

By making more data available for the users, the business efficiency increases and so does the profitability. Providing the basis for a faster, reliable Web service for the users vastly improves the user satisfactions.

It paves the way for solving big data problems that involve transactional, analytical, or hybrid capabilities and enables various types of data—structured, unstructured, real time, and historical—to be leveraged in concert within the same applications, while providing unprecedented gains in speed and scale. Due to high load sharing and distributed data, IMDG can be used for high-performance transactions which are dominated mostly by mainframe computers even nowadays. Another major use case for IMDG is real-time analytics; the huge memory availability, integration of various types of data stores, and access patterns enable organizations to perform analysis on huge data on the fly.

Another use case of IMDG is utilizing IMDG as a distributed caching mechanism. The key idea is to provide nondisruptive application for businesses even in the face of machine failures, thereby reducing the IT risk to businesses. Due to replication of data in distributed environment, a tough trade-off between consistency of data and performance has to be taken. SQL joins cannot be efficiently performed in distributed environment. This is the key reason between horizontal scalability (scale-out architecture) of IMDG following the MPP-based approach and vertical scalability (scale-up architecture) of RDBMS.

A major consideration in using IMDG is that IMDG sits in between application layer and data layer in conventional processing. Although IMDG always works with all databases, the applications then rely on this layer for superfast data access and processing. But the developers have to make some changes to the application to benefit from these new performance capabilities which also includes MPP data access pattern in addition to SQL data access.

In the following section, we will study one of the products available in the market GridGain.

GridGain In-Memory Data Fabric

GridGain [19] is one of the important players in the market of In Memory data grid. Here we briefly discuss the architecture of GridGain Data Fabric and how it can be used to accelerate applications.

Data Grid

The data grid is designed for horizontal scalability with comprehensive semantics for data locality and affinity-based data routing. This supports local, replicated, and partitioned data sets and allows to freely cross-query between these data sets using SQL syntax. The main features of data grid are as follows: off-heap memory support, SQL-syntax support, load balancing, fault tolerance, remote connectivity, support for distributed joins, support for full ACID transactions, and advanced security.

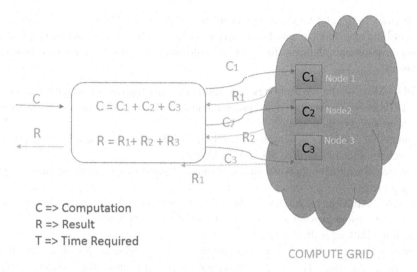

C => Computation
R => Result
T => Time Required

Fig. 10.17 GridGain Data Fabric for Hadoop acceleration

The above diagram shows the data transfer between application, grid, and database layer.

Clustering and Compute Grid

In-memory clustering and compute grids utilize the high-performance distributed memory systems to perform computations and transactions on Tera-scale data sets in real time with orders of magnitude faster than what is possible with traditional systems. GridGain In-Memory Data Fabric provides users with APIs to distribute computations and data processing across multiple computers in a cluster in order to gain high performance and low latency.

Hadoop Acceleration

One interesting use case for GridGain memory fabric is to accelerate Hadoop which is limited to batch jobs mainly due to heavy read and writes to the disk. The GridGain in-memory file system (GGFS) can work as a stand-alone primary file system in the Hadoop cluster, or in conjunction with HDFS, serving as an HDFS intelligent caching layer. As a caching layer, it provides highly tenable read-through and write-through logic and users can freely select which files or directories to be cached and how (Fig. 10.17).

10.3.7 Future of Grid Computing

Till now we have seen grid computing environments mainly for desktops, SMPs, and clusters. The advent of mobile phones has created exciting opportunities and possibilities in the potential development of grid/distributed computing techniques, especially in the current era of powerful smartphones and tablet devices. With over ten million smartphones out there today and expected to grow further, smartphones pose a potential platform for grid or distributed computing for the following reasons:

CPU—Most of the smartphones (and tablet devices likewise) today have at least 1 GHz of processor speed and greater than 256 MB of RAM, and these specifications are ever increasing.

Connectivity—Wider geographical reach of mobile networks and advancements in technologies like GPRS, 3G, 4G, and Wi-Fi.

Storage—Significant increase in the storage capabilities of running into a few gigabytes.

Sensors—Attachment of sensors like GPS, accelerometer, compasses, camera, etc. These sensors provide a context for the distributed application.

The four challenges that need to be taken care of are:

Power—There is only a limited amount of power available on a mobile device at any given time. Heavy computational tasks will drain the battery almost rapidly.

Platform—Distributed applications targeted at mobile platforms have to run on heterogeneous systems using a variety of hardware, OS, and libraries. Popular platforms like Android are heavily fragmented, further adding a level of complexity.

Network—A mobile device is often intermittently connected to a network and connects to a variety of networks including cellular, data, Wi-Fi, etc.

Social—Mobile device owners may not be compelled to have their devices participate as their primary concern would be battery drainage and connectivity charges that they may incur, although contributing towards the bigger goal of solving a large problem may be encouraging:

BONIC Mobile is The Berkeley Open Infrastructure for Network Computing (BOINC) is an open source middleware system for volunteer and grid computing which uses idle time on personal computers to run computational problems. BOINC Mobile, aimed at BOINC developers attempts to the BOINC platform and its projects (SETI@Home, etc.) to ARM platform based mobile devices. BOINCOID is a project that attempts to port BOINC to Android device

Cloud altered supply of computing resources to users. Leveraging advances in commodity computer technologies, companies (like EBay, Twitter, Google, Facebook) met the huge demands cost-effectively either with enormous data centers themselves or outsourced infrastructure needs to IaaS vendors. The commoditization of virtualization fuelled this change, making it easier to allocate computing resources on demand. As we have seen earlier, there is much overlap in the portions of grid and cloud computing. The enterprise grids in the earlier days are now analogous to the private grid with a major distinction in the usage of virtualization for dynamic provisioning of resources. Major emphasis has shifted towards service-oriented architecture of grids, making it feasible for deploying real-time applications.

10.4 Conclusion

In this chapter we have learned how distributed computing is playing role in big data analytics. Task parallelization is dividing tasks onto multiple processing stations, whereas data parallelization is dividing the data and processing with the same program in multiple processors.

Clustering computing is a way of connecting multiple systems on the local network together to make a more powerful computer system. This has started in the early 1990s with NoWs in the science labs. MPI, PvM, and the new Hadoop MapReduce are some of the ways of building a cluster computer for ourselves. Newer generation clusters are not limited to CPUs; they are moving towards GPU clusters and FPGA clusters which can give huge jump in performance for highly parallel scenarios.

The basic difference between clusters and grids is that computer clusters are mostly used on a local network and grids are more distributed. Grid computing can be seen as a utilitarian form of computing.

Unused resources can be used by those with the requirements in the grid system. Grids which mainly share data storage resources are classified as data grids, while those who share processing powers are classified as computation grids. Globus is the de facto standard for grid computing. In-memory data grid is a new form of data grid where the whole data is stored in primary memory.

10.5 Exercises

1. What is grid computing?
2. What is cluster computing?
3. Explain benefits of using grid computing.
4. Explain the benefits and potential of cluster computing.
5. What is difference between grid computing and cloud and cluster computing?
6. Explain the architecture of grid computing.
7. Explain the architecture of cluster computing.
8. Elaborate on architectural principles and design goals of cluster system.
9. Elaborate on architectural principles and design goals of grid system.
10. Write about Globus Toolkit.
11. Explain the programming for cluster computer.
12. Write about MPI vs. PVM vs. MapReduce programming.
13. Elaborate graph processing using MapReduce programming.
14. Install a sample grid and explain the procedure.
15. What are the different ways to program application for grids?
16. How do you think grid computing impacts modern-day life?
17. What are the problems associated with resource sharing and access in grids?
18. Explain one critical usage of grid computing.
19. What are the advances of cluster computing?

20. How do you run distributed data mining algorithm on grids?
21. How do grids help in analytics processing?
22. Imagine you created a grid system to utilize the unused computing resources among those with you.

  – What are the design goals of such a system?
  – How do you intend to use such a system?

Now a friend of you stays nearby who also wants to share resources with you; he has a cluster of 10 systems.

23. What are the advantages and potential caveats for such sharing?

After knowing about your arrangements, all your friends want to contribute their resources and so you created a grid with more than 1000 systems and with many partners.

24. What are the challenges at this scale?
25. What are the expectations from such a system?

After this you understood there are many resources that still lay idle and you want to sell resources.

26. What do you think is the potential for such an economy?

References

1. Udoh E (ed) (2011) Cloud, grid and high performance computing: emerging applications. IGI Global, Hershey
2. Open MPI: open source high performance computing. Retrieved August 14, 2014, from http://www.open-mpi.org
3. Sunderam VS (1990) PVM: a framework for parallel distributed computing [Journal]. Concurrency Exp 2(4):315–339
4. Apache Hadoop Introduction (2013) Retrieved October 5, 2014, from http://www.hadoop.apache.org
5. Dean J, Ghemawat S (2004) MapReduce: simplified data processing on large clusters [Conference]. In: Symposium on operating systems design and implementation
6. Facebook Engineering Blog. Retrieved September 5, 2014, from https://code.facebook.com/posts/
7. Borthakur D, Gray J (2011) Apache hadoop goes real-time at facebook [Conference], SIGMOD. ACM, Athens
8. Kindratenko VV et al (2009) GPU clusters for high-performance computing [Conference]. In: IEEE cluster computing and workshops. IEEE, New Orleans
9. RCUDA Documentation. Retrieved September 5, 2014, from http://www.rcuda.net/
10. Magoulès F, Pan J, Tan KA, Kumar A (2009) Introduction to grid computing. CRC Press, Boca Raton
11. Foster I, Kesselman C. The grid 2: blueprint for a new computing infrastructure [Book]. [s.l.]. Elsevier
12. Baker M, Buyya R, Laforenza D (2002) Grids and grid technologies for wide-area distributed computing. Softw Pract Exper 32(15):1437–1466

13. Pallmann D (2009) Grid computing on the Azure cloud computing platform, part 1. Retrieved September 5, 2014, from http://www.infoq.com/articles/Grid-Azure-David-Pallmann
14. Foster I, Kesselman C, Steven T (2001) The anatomy of the grid: enabling scalable virtual organizations [Conference]. In: First IEEE/ACM international symposium on cluster computing and the grid. [s.l.] IEEE
15. Anderson DP (2004) BOINC: A System for public resource computing and storage [Conference]. In: 5th IEEE/ACM international workshop on grid computing, Pittsburgh, USA [s.n.]
16. Globus (2014) Open grid services architecture Globus Toolkit Documentation. Retrieved September 5, 2014, from http://toolkit.globus.org/toolkit/docs/6.0/
17. Preve N (2011) Computational and data grids: principles, applications and design [Book]. [s.l.]. IGI Global
18. Out Scale (2014) In-memory data grid technology [Online]. Scaleout software: in memory data grids for the enterprise
19. Grid Gain Hadoop Accelarator. (2014). Retrieved September 5, 2014. http://gridgain.com/

Further Reading

Pearce SE, Venters W (2012) How particle physicists constructed the world's largest grid: a case study in participatory cultures. The Routledge Handbook of Participatory Cultures
Wilkinson B (2011) Grid computing: techniques and applications. CRC Press, Boca Raton
Kirk DB, Wen-mei WH (2012) Programming massively parallel processors: a hands-on approach. Newnes
Kahanwal D, Singh DT (2013) The distributed computing paradigms: P2P, grid, cluster, cloud, and jungle. arXiv preprint arXiv:1311.3070

Chapter 11
High-Performance Peer-to-Peer Systems

11.1 Introduction

Earlier, in the age of mainframe computers, most of the computation is done on the central systems which are super powerful and quite expensive. This central super muscular computer is accessed through computer points. Then came the era of the Internet, the era in which the information was becoming digital and the processing power of the clients is gradually increased. And still the computational loads or storage loads of the systems are not sufficient for a client to access so they relied mainly on servers. This started a movement to use the unused resources of all the systems connected to the same network. The more the processing power of the individual systems raised, the more computation is done on local systems instead of the servers. The usage of computer as a personal system also increased the number of people having access to more computational power that's being underutilized. The more the personal usage increased, the more data and computations are transferred from one place to another. This increased the bandwidth demand making it feasible for faster networks. The faster the networks, the powerful the computers, the expensive the servers, and better the collaboration. This marked the change from centralized computation to more and more collaborative computation between relatively less powerful computers. The collaboration increased the availability of resources to find solutions for bigger and complex problems that were not initially solvable. This trend also is widely capitalized by SETI@Home [16] giving rise to various other similar projects. This has been called voluntary computing.

This progress also tempted the users to share files from client to client reducing the load on servers. Earlier, the most common usage of P2P technology was to distribute digital content. Sometimes illegal/copyrighted content is also transmitted. The notorious Napster [29] is of this kind. However, nowadays increasing number of media companies and other businesses are using this paradigm for their commercial applications.

© Springer International Publishing Switzerland 2015
P. Raj et al., *High-Performance Big-Data Analytics*, Computer Communications
and Networks, DOI 10.1007/978-3-319-20744-5_11

In the earlier days the information was mostly dispersed through hand written letters, radio, and television. But if you fast forward the scenario to present day, the complete presence of the information is digital, and the communications are done through e-mails, websites, blogs, tweets, Facebook posts, and cloud storage, and it can easily be distributed to the whole world in a matter of seconds. Not only the world of information exploded, the format of information has also transformed. With this overabundance of data, people have to filter loads of junk data to finally come across information they are interested in. With advent of new age communications, tools, knowledge forums, learning systems like MOOCs, webinars, and real-time messaging, physical presence is no longer a limiting factor.

Peer-to-peer computing paradigm can be seen as perfect form of collaboration between different peers. In P2P, different systems with diverse computing powers come together, sharing their resources like bandwidth, storage, compute cycles, and common set of responsibilities. There would be no master, but there may be a central server for coordination between peers. This is in line with the current form of teams where collaboration is emphasized more. P2P paradigm completely relies on contributions from peers. This contribution may be of the content itself, or of bandwidth for distributing content to other users, storage, and compute cycles.

Unlike traditional client server model, p2p computing model supports ad hoc collaboration and communication. The cost of ownership is distributed to peers. The anonymity of peers is assured. Due to the fact that there is no central server implying no single point of failures, P2Ps can be more scalable than conventional client-server systems. The peers in the P2P systems can be anything for sensor nodes to mobile devices to workstations. Due to decentralized nature of P2P systems, which implies fewer bottlenecks and no single points of failure, P2P systems offer higher fault tolerance, higher fault resilience, and higher combined performance.

Even though P2P systems have a lot of merits, there are several limitations associated with them as well. There is an inherent trust factor between peers; sufficient guarantees must be established. For a non-trusted environment, centralized systems are a better option in terms of security and access control.

But today's systems have far moved to a paradigm where the users are ready to give a part of their computing resources to have a better experience or to solve most complex problems. And even the research institutes and multinational organizations like Facebook, Amazon, and Google are developing their own P2P-based systems to efficiently utilize and cater their massive computing and petascale data retrieval.

The structure of the chapter is as follows: in Sect. 11.2, we will be studying design goals and characteristics of P2P systems. In Sect. 11.3, we will study the different architectures of P2P systems and we will also discuss some techniques of searching for resources in corresponding architectures. We are going to see advanced peer-to-peer architectures based on mobile ad hoc and other frameworks. In Sect. 11.4, we will do some case studies on high-performance systems like Cassandra [17, 18], Cassandra file system, SETI@Home [16], and bitcoin.

11.2   Design Principles and Characteristics

The primary goal while designing P2P systems is to support high-performance applications and competing and complex user demands. The major goals of any P2P system are as follows:

Heterogeneity, resource aggregation, and interoperability: Participating nodes in distributed system are varying in capacity like computing power, network bandwidth, and storage. As different systems with different capabilities are coming together, interoperability becomes more important as to aggregate of these varied resources.

Cost sharing: In centralized systems, most of the cost bearer is the server which caters the demands of the clients, while on the other hand the peers share equal responsibility in computation and bandwidth load, thereby distributing the cost to all nodes. This cost reduction comes from utilization of unused resources.

Improved scalability, increased autonomy, and reliability: Without central server giving commands and more autonomy among the peers gives more reliance towards failures and making it feasible more scalability in the high-end systems. And most of the work is done locally or on the near neighbors.

Anonymity/privacy: Another major unique selling point of these peer-to-peer systems to normal users has been anonymity, i.e., the user doesn't want their service providers to track his or her activity. In case of client-server systems, it is quite difficult to keep our privacy, whereas in P2P systems identifying users can be complex and difficult [25].

Dynamism and ad hoc collaboration: P2P systems assume the computing environment to be highly dynamic. The dynamism can be of (A) population dynamism in which the transient population of nodes mandates the routing mechanism to be adaptive to failures or (B) content dynamism in which as network size increases as well as the contents in systems also increases rapidly and so is the relocation of contents making ad hoc collaborations more feasible and desirable.

To achieve the above goals, P2P systems tend show the following characteristics:

Decentralization: The centralized system is well suited for tasks with high security requirements but at the cost of potential bottlenecks, inefficiencies, and elevated costs, whereas in a fully decentralized system, every peer is an equal participant with equal responsibilities and share costs among them.

Self-organization: The organization or the structure of the system changes as a response to external or internal events. Since the dynamism is inherent to P2P systems, the structure of the system has to be adapted without any manual intervention [28, 34].

Lesser cost of ownership: This refers to the cost of setting up the system plus the maintenance costs. P2P computing works from the paradigm of shared ownership. This implies that cost is shared among the peers and overall cost of ownership is greatly reduced. For example, SETI@Home [30] has more than 5 PFlops of processing power at only a fraction of cost−1 % of a supercomputer with similar processing power.

High performance: Aggregation of computing cycles (e.g., SETI@Home) and distributed storage capacity (e.g., Gnutella, BitTorrent) of systems across the networks helps in achieving high performance in P2P systems. Given the decentralized nature, networking can easily become a limiting factor for performance. The performance can be improved by having replicas of the data on multiple systems. Caching reduces the path length necessary for fetching object/file. Communication latency is a serious bottleneck of the system. Intelligent routing and network organization can be another technique to improve the performance.

Highly scalable: We can call a system scalable when we can achieve more performance by adding more number of systems to the network. Number of serial operations, parallelizability of an application, and amount of state data to be maintained are often some of the limiting factors for scalability.

Other characteristics displayed and supported by P2P systems are ad hoc connectivity, security in P2P systems which depends upon trust chains between peers, encryption, transparency and usability, fault resilience, and interoperability owing to the fact that each peer can have different processor and can be based on different platforms and operating systems.

11.3 Peer-to-Peer System Architectures

11.3.1 Centralized Peer-to-Peer Systems

Systems belonging to this category can be seen as having architecture midway between purely decentralized systems and purely client-server systems. The centrals in these systems are used to locate resources relevant to the request and to coordinate peers unlike in client-server systems where servers do most of the processing. Peer first sends a query to the central server requesting certain resources, central server in turn returns the addresses of the requested resource (e.g., BitTorrent [1]), and from then on the peers communicate with other peers directly. In case of SETI@Home [15] and BOINC [2], the peers coordinate with the central server for fetching the work units directly. The major advantage with these systems is that there is time bound on locating resources and response times, and organizing and maintaining become easier at the cost of potential bottleneck and scalability.

The peers of the peer-to-peer community connect to a central directory where they can publish information about the content they will offer to others. When the central directory gets a search request from a peer, it will match the request with the peer in the directory and return the result. The BestPeer could be the closest (though this could be hard to determine), the fastest, the cheapest, or the most available. When a peer has been selected, the transaction will follow directly between the two peers. This algorithm requires a central server which is a drawback in peer-to-peer systems. It is a single point of failure, and it can produce scalability problems.

Fig. 11.1 Centralized
peer-to-peer system

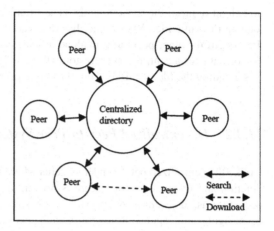

However, history shows that this model is quite strong and efficient even in larger systems (Fig. 11.1).

Since systems in this centralized architecture employ server(s) for major functioning of the system, it can be a bottleneck for the whole system. The scalability of these systems might be restricted.

This architecture has similar problems of P2P systems like the malware, distribution of outdated resources. Other than these, centralized P2P systems have a vulnerability of Denial of Service attack and Man in the Middle attacks which are quite possible in client-server architecture space.

11.3.1.1 Case Studies

Napster

Napster was a phenomenon that drew a lot of discussion into P2P computing. It is a Web application which allows users to swap MP3 files directly just like messages in instant messaging. Napster is an example of a centralized P2P architecture, where a group of servers perform the lookup function needed by the other peers. A peer must first establish an account with the Napster server and provide the list of music files available. Subsequently, it can send search requests to the Napster server and receive a list of peers who offer the desired music file. Then, the requester can select any of these peers to directly download the file [22].

BitTorrent

BitTorrent [1] is a centralized unstructured peer-to-peer network for file sharing. A central server called tracker keeps track of all peers who have the file. Each file has a corresponding torrent file stored in the tracker which contains the information about the file such as its length, name, and hashing information. When receiving a download request, the tracker sends back a random list of peers which are downloading the same file. When a peer has received the complete file, it should stay in the system for other peers to download at least one copy of the file from it. Since BitTorrent uses a central server to store all the information about the file and peers downloading the file, it suffers from the single point of failure.

11.3.2 Decentralized Peer-to-Peer Systems

Unlike the centralized peer-to-peer systems where there is a central server for coordination and resource finding, there is no central server in decentralized peer-to-peer systems. In decentralized peer-to-peer systems, every peer in the system is with equal rights and responsibilities, since each peer has information of only part of the whole systems. No central index structure is available, implying that request routing is done in a distributed manner. Peers typically send requests to its neighbors; this goes on till the request can be fulfilled by a peer. Locating peers with relevant data or resources quickly becomes a perplexing issue. There is a need of trust among the peers as there is no central authority. And yet these systems are highly immune to single point of failure as in case of centralized systems, since all the tasks and services are distributed through the network and no peer is dominant to the system. Thus, the system has strong immunity to censorship, partial network failures, network partitions, and malicious attacks. These pure P2P systems possibly enjoy higher scalability, performance, and other desirable issues.

These systems can be further categorized according to the structure of the network and topology (the overlay network). The network structure can be a flat (single tier) or hierarchical (multi-tier). In the flat structure, the peers share the load and functionality uniformly. Hierarchical systems unsurprisingly offer certain advantages like security, bandwidth utilization, and fault isolation.

The topology is concerned whether the system is structured or unstructured. The fundamental difference between these two systems lies in the mapping of resources to that of peers. In unstructured systems, each peer is responsible for its own resources, and it keeps track of a set of its neighbors. This implies that locating resources is daunting; there is no completeness of answers until the whole network is queried and no assurance on response time. Query routing is done through message broadcasting with time to live (TTL) value attached to each message to avoid network flooding. The TTL value decreases for each message hop, and once the value reaches zero, the message is no longer forwarded. Examples of decentralized systems are Freenet [7] and Gnutella [10]. On the other side, in a structured P2P system, data placement is predetermined (e.g., Distributed Hash Table or DHT). There is an upper bound on search cost (either precise or probabilistic). But this is achieved by maintaining certain metadata about the topology. Most of the structured P2P systems adopt a key-based routing strategy for locating relevant resources. CAN [27] and Chord [13] use this routing strategy. Since the data location is tightly controlled, the cost of ownership and maintenance is relatively higher especially when the churn rate is higher. To elevate this limitation, hybrid topology can be utilized, still offering autonomy at a lesser maintenance costs.

The system is highly decentralized, self-organizing, and symmetric. There is an approach Canon [3] to turn flat DHT into a hierarchical DHT taking advantage of both flat ad hierarchical structures. Hierarchical structures can be advantageous in case of fault isolation. Using DHT helps in even distribution of objects over the peers. The limitation with DHT-based systems due to the usage of hashing function is that the search is efficient over exact key lookup and these systems generally don't support complex queries like range queries and k-near neighbors.

Scalability

Scalability poses an existential concern for any P2P system aiming to be of web-scale. In DHT-based systems, the namespace chosen for the peers determines the maximum number of peers that can be participating and sharing resources in the system, while the unstructured systems are not highly scalable due to heavy message flooding. Skip graph-based systems (e.g., SkipNet) are highly scalable.

Locating Resources

Locating resources is one of the critical tasks for making the peer-to-peer system functional. Here we will see two of those models:

Flooded Request Model Each query is flooded throughout the network. Each peer forwards the request to its directly connected neighbors until the request is answered or a preset maximum number of flooding steps has been reached. This model consumes a lot of bandwidth and has very low scalability, and in case of smaller networks, this model works fine. To increase the scalability, one can look at using super peers for resource location or even caching at peers which also increase the availability of the data requested.

In the document routing model, the data is assigned an ID which is a hash based on the data itself, and peers are also assigned a random ID. Each peer has an information of a number of other peers. Data is forwarded to peer which has the same ID or the one similar to it. This process goes on till the data ID is the same as the peer ID or the closest one. When a request for data comes from a peer, the request is routed in the same manner; it will be forwarded to the peer with the ID of the requested data. Each peer in this route keeps a local copy. The major plus point for this model is scalability is higher. And the major limitation comes from the complexity of search compared to flooding model.

11.3.2.1 Case Studies

Freenet

Freenet [7] is designed to make it feasible to distribute informations through the Internet freely without any censorship. Freenet is designed based on decentralized P2P architecture. Any computer connected to the Internet can be a part of the system by just installing either the Freenet Daemon or Freenet Server. As the peer interaction goes on, every peer accumulates knowledge of other peers which is then used to assist in the resource discovery process. Since every peer doesn't have the full picture of the whole P2P system, every peer is considered equal. The discovery and messaging between peers is one-to-one based. These mechanisms can be efficient in terms of bandwidth consumption but are rather inefficient in terms of response time.

Gnutella

Gnutella [8] is another classic example of a pure p2p application. Gnutella allows anonymous file sharing, fault tolerant, and adaptability and supports the formation of virtual network system. There would be specialized servers, and the message routing is done in a constrained broadcast in a breadth-first mechanism limiting the number of hops. The response from a peer in case of a match to the request follows the same path as the request traverses. The flooding message passing affects the system scalability. And there is also a possibility of DoS attack where the attacker might take advantage of this lookup mechanism and issue some request for some nonexistent resource.

Chord

In Chord [13], the peers are structured in a form of a circle. This circle structure is named a Chord ring with each peer having a unique ID. The peers are inserted in the order of their IDs along the ring. Successor and predecessor are the two neighbors every peer in the Chord has. A new peer is inserted based on the ID order, and the pointers of successor and the predecessor will be changed to reflect the insertion. The correctness of the peers is so critical for the functioning of the system. So as to ensure the correctness of these pointers, each peer keeps a successor list holding the peer's first r successors. Each data item is given an ID. This data item is stored on the owner peer and its immediate successor. Request is routed along the Chord. Each peer maintains a finger table, which has a set of pointers to peers at a certain distance called fingers.

11.3.3   Hybrid Peer-to-Peer Systems

The hybrid P2P systems take advantage of quick and reliable resource located in centralized systems and higher scalability in decentralized systems. But there are no servers; instead, there are peer nodes called super peers which are more powerful and assigned more responsibility than other peers. Two major points which differentiates central servers and super peers are that (a) super peers are not as highly capable as central servers and super peers are in charge of subset of peers and

(b) super peers not only coordinate normal peers but also contribute its resources as any other normal peer. The major advantages with hybrid P2P architecture are optimization of network topology, improving response time, and no single point of failure.

Some of the systems developed with this architecture are BestPeer, PeerDB (reference), PeerIS (reference), CQBuddy (reference), and Spotify (reference).

Finding peers with relevant resources can be a two-step process in which the peer issuing query can send request to the same subnetwork it is part of; if the resource is not found, then the query or the message is routed to super peers which in turn search among themselves and forward request to the subnetworks they coordinate.

These systems are still vulnerable to churn rate in the super peers level that form higher level of the systems. They can achieve higher scalability compared to other peer-to-peer systems.

These systems are vulnerable to malware that might be present in the system. There is lesser possibility of DoS attack on the system, while man in the middle attack can be executed.

11.3.3.1 Case Studies

Hybrid P2P System

In this paper [21], a hybrid P2P system is proposed which is made up of two parts: one part is the core-transit network in which peers are placed on a ring-like structure very much similar to a Chord and the second a stub-network (s-network) which has a structure similar to Gnutella, and this s-network is attached to a t-peer. The basic thought behind using two different types of networks is that the t-network (transit network) for efficient service and s-network for flexibility. The lookup request in s-network is passed through flooding-based routing which we saw earlier. While the routing in the t-network is done by passing through the ring, message flood doesn't have any major implications in s-network because the message is limited to smaller number of peers. And flooding simplifies the joining and leaving of peers, while the t-network faces problem in cases of high churn rates. And yet any s-peer can replace a t-peer connecting both t-network and s-network so the effect of churn can be minimized. There is a possibility to have a BitTorrent-type architecture instead of a Gnutella-based architecture in s-network. And there is a tunable parameter which can decide how many nodes will be in t-network and s-network correspondingly (Fig. 11.2).

BestPeer

BestPeer [23] has a small set of global name lookup servers (called LIGLOs) forming the higher level system. These servers generate a unique ID for the peers under its managing. The LIGLOs don't assist in locating resources instead they help in

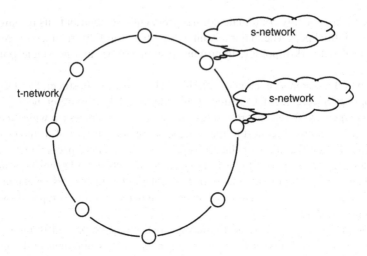

Fig. 11.2 Hybrid peer-to-peer architecture with Chord ring like t-network and Gnutella like s-network

recognizing peer's neighbors even in face of dynamic IP and making it feasible for the peers to reconfigure neighbors dynamically. BestPeer supports local computation of the data; there is a possibility to extend the computation and share the resources. BestPeer helps in keeping the peers with high potential to answer queries nearby, thereby reducing the response times.

A peer when joining the system registers with the LIGLO server which gives the peer a unique identifier BPID. LIGLO server also returns a set of peers with their BPID and Ips so as to bootstrap the peer. The peers which are unreachable are simply removed from the list. When an old peer wants to join the network, the LIGLO server plainly updates the peer's IP address. This doesn't effect the data that is stored before leaving since it is still intact.

The newer BestPeer [23] supports actor-based concurrent programming model to achieve both high-efficiency and heterogeneous data processing. It also supports DHT-based indexing and searching with a possibility to use MapReduce [9] framework to run batch analytics.

11.3.4 Advanced Peer-to-Peer Architecture Communication Protocols and Frameworks

In their paper, Traintafillow et al. [32] propose a system based on document classification and cluster of peers, thereby decreasing load on most of the peers during the resource locating. The documents are grouped together by their keywords, and they are classified into semantic categories. The peers are clustered together based on the semantic categories of the documents. The load balancing is achieved in two steps: first the load is balanced between peer clusters by assigning document categories to different clusters and second way of balancing load is by sharing load among the peers of the same cluster. The routing indices or the metadata is exploited relating semantic categories and peer clusters.

The normal network protocols like TCP and UDP don't work well with peer-to-peer systems; even the standardized protocols like STCP and DCCP don't offer sufficient modularity required to reach an optimal granularity and performance in context of P2P and HPC. To elevate this limitation, a new P2P self-adaptive communication protocol [5] has been introduced which is based on Cactus framework [12, 33]. This protocol depends on micro-protocols and automatically chooses apt communication mode based on application layer level choices, e.g., synchronous communication/asynchronous communication and topology of network. This model is completely different to other middleware-like BOINC (reference) where there is no need for the peers to communicate with each other. The major extension to the Cactus framework that has been done is that instead of copying message between layers in network model, just a pointer to the message is made. A simple Socket API-like programming interface is developed. Through this API, we can send, receive, open, and close connections, get session state, state change, etc.

The architecture high-performance P2P distributed computing [24] that has been developed has a user Daemon which interfaces application and the environment, a topology manager to organize peers into clusters and to maintain mapping between peers and clusters, a task manager to distribute sub-tasks and aggregate results, and a load balancer to estimate workload of peer and transfer workload from overloaded peer to non-overloaded peer. The architecture has been applied to obstacle problem [31]. And one of the interesting application of this architecture is to segregate user requests based on the location coordinates. Location-based services like hotel recommendations, etc. suit perfectly with this kind of location-based overlay architecture. In Geodemlia [11], the idea of the architecture is that the peers are located on a sphere and each peer is able to locate itself by the GPS locations (longitude, latitude coordinates). Every peer has a random ID, the objects are associated with a particular location, and the objects have a unique random ID. When a request is put for any object, it corresponds to a particular location. The probability of peer q in the routing table of p is inversely proportional to the distance between them. Routing structure maintenance is done when a node querying cannot access it's peer or when node queries at a random location.

In Fig. 11.3, we can see the routing table structure of Geodemlia which divides the whole sphere into set of directions. Geodemlia is compared to Globase [17], a hierarchical tree-based model, and it gave about 46 % more success rate. It's well suited for geo-location-based services.

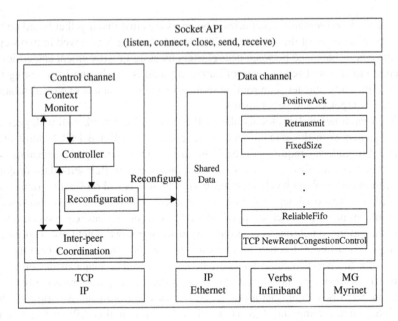

Fig. 11.3 HPC P2P self-adaptive communication protocol architecture

11.4   High-Performance Peer-to-Peer Applications

All the P2P applications can be categorized into four groups: edge services which involves pushing relevant content to clients which helps in balancing load on servers and networks, increasing storage space with reduction of maintenance and bandwidth costs. An example of such service is Intel Share and Learn Software (SLS) [14]; collaboration P2P can be used to revitalize individual and team communications and collaborations in real time.[4]. Few ways in which collaboration helped are in communication (ICQ, IRC, instant messaging), content delivery, and Internet search; file sharing has been an important focus point for P2P applications; and distributed computing P2P can be used to solve large-scale problems for industry. Upon aggregating the resources, the unused computational resources will easily be more than generally available. Volunteer computing also comes under this group where the clients donate their computational resources for solving a particular problem. Overall the cost is drastically reduced. One of such major example which uses this model is SETI@Home [16].

   We have briefly touched the areas of applications of P2P model. We will briefly study about some of the high-performance applications and systems based on peer-to-peer technologies.

11.4.1   Cassandra

Cassandra [18, 19] is a distributed database built to handle petabytes of data spanning across several clusters with high availability as its unique selling points. Cassandra achieves high availability through peer-to-peer interactions and replication. Cassandra was initially developed to solve the inbox search problem at Facebook. It takes cues from Google Bigtable's column-oriented data model with Amazon Dynamo's fully distributed design. At this point of time, Cassandra is deployed at stalwarts such as Cisco, Netflix, Rackspace, and Twitter.

An instance of Cassandra is just a collection of independent nodes that are configured into a cluster. In Cassandra, every node is equal, shares equal responsibilities, and is called a peer. Implying no master or any other central server coordinating between peers in Cassandra. This is a pure P2P system. The topology of the Cassandra is a circular space or a ring. As we have seen in the taxonomy, this is a structured decentralized peer-to-peer system.

The peer-to-peer communications are done through gossip protocol. State information and peer discovery are passed on through this protocol. If Cassandra finds any failed node, then the requests are diverted. Peer joins the cluster first by referring to configuration files and contacting seed nodes in the cluster it belongs to. Data is written to commit logs as well as to an in-memory structure, called a memtable. This memtable resembles a write-back cache. Once this memtable is full, the data is written to a persistent storage in an SSTable data file. All the data files written are partitioned and replicated throughout the Cassandra cluster. From time to time, SSTables are consolidated, and columns marked as deleted (tombstones) are discarded. Cassandra is a row-oriented database. The data can be accessed through CQL (Cassandra Query Language) which is similar to SQL. Asynchronous responses are supported through CQL. The read or write requests from a client can be routed through any nodes in the cluster. When a request is placed by the client to a node, this node acts as a coordinator for this request (see Fig. 11.4).

There is support for tunable consistency where we can tune the level of consistency from "consistent writes" to "readable replicas" or somewhere in between. Cassandra integrates with HadoopMapReduce [9] for batch analytics (Fig. 11.5).

The core characteristics of Cassandra are decentralization, scalability, fault tolerance, data partition and replication. There is a feasibility to choose how the data is partitioned across the cluster. Based on the row key, the column family data is splitted across the nodes. Cassandra offers a wide variety of partitioners. The default partitioning strategy is random partitioner which uses MD5 hashing to determine the node storing a particular row. The other partitioner which is mainly supported by the second version is ordered partitioner which warrants that the row keys are stored in sorted order.

One of the major measures to ensure high availability of data is replication. Replication by name suggests the replica of data item a row is stored in some other node which can be used in case of a failure of original node or to share the load. The simplest mechanism of replication is to store the replica on the successor node

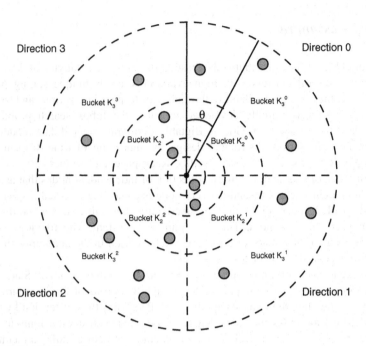

Fig. 11.4 Geodemlia routing structure

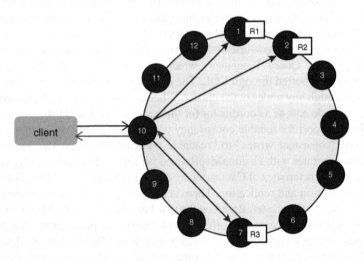

Fig. 11.5 Client request to a node. Node acts as request coordinator

without any consideration of data center location or rack awareness. A more sophisticated yet recommended replication strategy is to use the network topology to store the replica. This is done through placing the replicas on the nodes which are on different rack and through moving in clockwise. The primary index is based on the row keys, while the secondary index is also supported on the column values.

In paper [26] comparison of Cassandra with other NoSQL databases and sharded MySQL is done. Cassandra achieves the highest throughput for maximum number of nodes, and the performance is highest for high insertion rates.

11.4.1.1 CassandraFile System

An interesting application of Cassandra is Cassandra file system (CFS) from Datastax [20]. The main aim of the CFS is to replace the HDFS from Hadoop. This CFS tries to solve the problem single point of failure in HDFS (i.e., the NameNode which stores the metadata of files). Another design goal for CFS is easy Hadoop integration for the Cassandra users. While Hadoop can be considered a centralized peer-to-peer system, we will study more about it in the chapter on high-performance clusters.

For supporting storage massive files in Cassandra, CFS has been designed as a keyspace with two column families. The difference between HDFS and CFS is that per-file replication cannot be set in CFS. These two column families represent two vital HDFS services. The NameNode service which keeps a track of files, metadata, and location of the blocks is replaced by the "inode" column family. The DataNode service in HDFS, storing file blocks, is replaced by the "sblocks" column family. These changes brought scalability and fault tolerance to the file system.

The metadata stored in the inode column family includes filename, file type, parent path, user, group, and permissions. The block IDs are based on timestamp and are ordered sequentially. The "sblocks" column family has the actual file blocks where each row represents a block of data that corresponds with an inode record. The columns are sub-blocks which are compressed and ordered in time. These blocks when combined will be equal to one HDFS block. So for Hadoop, the block from columns of a single row in sblocks looks like a single block, and so there is no change to job split in MapReduce.

11.4.2 SETI@Home

The scientific projects require tremendous computational powers. Traditionally, this requirement is fulfilled through high-performance supercomputers, but the cost of maintenance and ownership was too high. Search for Extraterrestrial Intelligence at Home (SETI@Home) is a forerunner in using the computational resources attached at the tip of the Internet and a very marginal cost, starting a wave of other voluntary computing projects like Einstien@Home, Folding@Home, and Genome@Home. SETI@Home has a big ambition to detect intelligent life outside the earth. SETI@Home splits the complex computational task into convenient work units and distributes that work unit to peers (volunteers' computers participating in SETI@Home). Once these work units are processed, they are sent back to the central server, and the peer can fetch some other work unit. With large number of volunteers signing up, SETI@Home has evolved into one of the world's most powerful computers [15].

SETI@Home was launched on May 17, 1999. It has over five million participants. In fact, SETI@Home is one of the biggest supercomputers in the world, with an average processing power at 3.5 PFLOPs. Users are from more than 200 countries. The University of California at Berkeley developed a general purpose distributed computing project—BOINC [6].

SETI@Home has four components: screensaver (SETI@Home client), user database, data collectors, data server, and Science database. Data collector is a radio telescope or antenna system which receives the data in form of radio signals from outer space and records the received signals into Digital Linear Tapes (DLT). Data splitters divide these signals into manageable work units which are transferred to temporary storage (which typically can hold about 470,000 units). The data server handles distribution of work units and storage of returned results. These work units then will be dispersed to the clients (the computers that installed the screensaver). This screensaver can easily be downloaded onto the client which need not be a desktop PC; it can also be a mobile phone with the client app. This client application runs on free CPU cycles. A typical work unit requires 2.8 to 3.8 Tflop which takes about 4–6 h on a 2 GHz home computer. The science database contains information on the time, frequencies, sky coordinates, as well as information about how many times a work unit is sent to SETI@Home users and how many times results have been received. User database is a relational database that tracks SETI@Home user information, work units, tapes, results, etc. When the processing at the client's end is done, the client returns a few potential signals per work unit. Errors made in the processing are fought upon by validating signal with permitted values, and the same work unit is sent to multiple volunteers whose results are cross-verified (Fig. 11.6).

SETI@home is a high-performance system but still it is vulnerable to single point of failure due to usage of central server(s). The bottleneck for SETI@home lies in providing more connections, storage space for results, and work units. And due to limited capability of server(s), SETI@home cannot achieve higher scalabil-

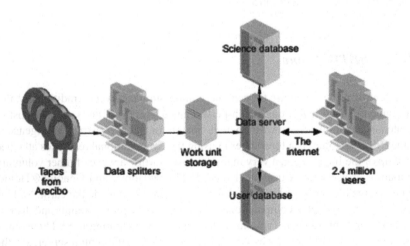

Fig. 11.6 SETI@Home architecture

ity. For the validation of work unit result, a threshold timespan is defined if the result is returned in more time than threshold; then the result is scraped and work unit is assigned to some other peer.

11.4.3 Bitcoin: Peer-to-Peer-Based Digital Currency

Bitcoin is a digital currency system based on peer-to-peer currency coin creation and validation. It is introduced as an open-source software by Satoshi Nakamoto in 2009. Every payment is recorded in a public ledger with its own currency called bitcoin. All the payments are done in peer-to-peer fashion without any central repository.

Bitcoins are made as a compensation for payment processing work. This work involves in users expending their computational resources for verifying and recording transactions in public ledger. This processing is called mining and is done in exchange for transaction fees or for newly generated bitcoins. Moreover, bitcoins can also be received in exchange for services, products, or even money. Users can send and receive bitcoins electronically for an optional transaction fee.

The bitcoin is defined as a chain of digital signatures. The transfer is done by digitally signing the hash of the previous transaction and the public key of the following client to whom coins are transferred. The problem that arises is that the payer might be double spending the coin. In the case of centralized money transfers, the central authority verifies that the payer is not double spending. This problem is solved by using a timestamp server. The timestamp server takes the hash of a block of transactions to be time stamped are published including the previous timestamp forming a chain. But to make this work on peer-to-peer-type system, there should be some proof of work. This proof of work involves scanning for a value which once hashed, the hash value with a number of zero bits. So once the CPU resources are consumed to satisfy proof-of-work, the block of transactions cannot be changed without redoing the whole work. This work increases exponentially as the chain of blocks increases (Fig. 11.7).

Nodes consider the longest chain to be the right one and keep on working to extend this chain. Nodes broadcast transactions to all nodes. Each node aggregates these new transactions into a block and tries to find a proof of work for this block which is broadcasted once found. Nodes accept this block only when all the transactions are spent, which once accepted will be working the accepted block as the previous hash.

The basic point of any currency system is to prevent unauthorized currency transfers. As bitcoin transaction transfers ownership to a new address and the obligation to proclaim all transactions publicly looks bad on privacy part, use of public-private key-based hashing scheme can anonymize the users corresponding to the transactions. Since every transaction is signed with payer's private key, it is absolute that the private key must be kept safe. Otherwise, the transactions with all common private key can be tracked, and all bitcoins associated with it even spent. Using

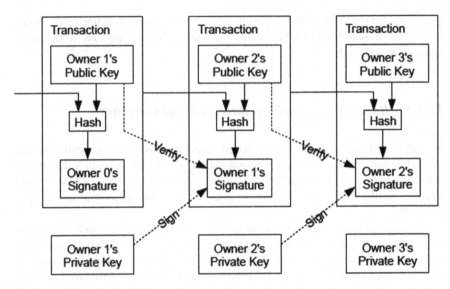

Fig. 11.7 Chain of ownership in bitcoin

different key pairs can solve this problem to some extent but still some related incidence is unavoidable.

While the security of bitcoin is debated with some reported incidents, the idea of using peer-to-peer computing resources to form a virtual currency might pave way for next generation of innovations.

11.5   Conclusions

We have learned the importance of peer-to-peer systems and compared them with client-server systems. We introduced the design goals and characteristics of the system like anonymity, security, etc. We learned about different architectures of peer-to-peer systems like centralized systems, decentralized systems, and hybrid systems.

In centralized architecture, we studied about BitTorrent and Napster and analyzed the security aspects of the systems like single point of failure and DoS attacks. We have seen how this kind of architecture scales less compared to other architectures. We also studied SETI@Home which comes under centralized architecture and how SETI@Home distributes the work among the volunteer computers and developed one of the fastest computers on the planet.

In decentralized architecture, we again classified the systems based on the network topology into structured and unstructured overlays. We studied various systems like Chord, Freenet, and Gnutella and how they are architected. In the case study, we studied Cassandra and Cassandra-based file systems and how high-performance applications are deployed on Cassandra.

In hybrid systems, we studied how super-peer-based systems combine advantages of both decentralized and centralized architectures. We studied BestPeer and other hybrid systems how they are different from the above architectures.

We also studied some advanced architectures like the one with attaching semantic meaning to nodes and clusters. We have studied Geodemlia where the data is dispersed across the globe forming location-based services, and then, we saw Cactus framework-based high-performance systems with micro-protocols.

We tried to get the feel of the high-performance peer-to-peer system through study of bitcoin, the virtual currency based on peer-to-peer architecture.

11.6 Exercises

1. What are the differences between client server systems and peer-to-peer systems?
2. Explain the peer-to-peer system?
3. What are the advantages of using a peer-to-peer system?
4. Explain the disadvantages of peer-to-peer system?
5. What is the importance of peer-to-peer system?
6. What are the few characteristics of peer-to-peer systems?
7. What are the design principles behind peer-to-peer systems?
8. Explain different architectures of peer-to-peer architectures?
9. Explain the security aspects of decentralized systems?
10. Explain various facets of hybrid peer-to-peer systems?
11. Compare peer-to-peer systems with client-server-based systems?
12. How can you classify decentralized system?
13. Write about the structured decentralized system?
14. Explain any hybrid peer-to-peer system discussed in the chapter?
15. Write about the transaction processing in bitcoins?
16. Write about Cassandra?
17. What do you know about P2P file systems?
18. What are the challenges with P2P systems?
19. Try out the Cassandra and brief your experiences?
20. Develop application based on BitTorrent protocol?

References

1. BitTorrent Protocol. Retrieved July 5, 2014, from http://bittorrent.org
2. Anderson DP (2004) BOINC: a system for public-resource computing and storage. In: 5th IEEE/ACM international workshop on grid computing. Pittsburgh, USA
3. Vu QH, Lupu M, Ooi BC (2010) Architecture of peer-to-peer systems. In: Peerto-peer computing. Springer, Berlin/Heidelberg, pp 11–37

4. Barkai.D. (2002). *Peer to Peer computing: Technologies for sharing and collaborating on the net.* Intel Press.
5. Baz DE, Nguyen T (2010) A self-adaptive communication protocol with application to high-performance peer to peer distributed computing. In: The 18th Euromicro international conference on parallel, distributed and network-based computing, Pisa
6. *BOINC* (2014). Retrieved from BOINC: http://boinc.berkeley.edu/
7. Clarke I, Sandberg O, Wiley B, Hong T (2000) Freenet: a distributed anonymous information storage and retrieval. In: ICSI workshop on design issues in anonymity and unobservability. Berkley, California
8. Crespo A, Garcia-Molina H (2002) Routing indices for peer-to-peer systems. In: Proceedings of the 22nd international conference on distributed computing systems. IEEE, pp 23–32
9. Dean J, Ghemawat S (2008) Map reduce: simplified data processing on large clusters. Commun ACM 51(1):107–113
10. Gnutella (n.d.) Development home page. Retrieved from http://gnutella.wego.com
11. Gross C, Stingl D, Richerzhagen B, Hemel A, Steinmetz R, Hausheer D (2012) Geodemlia: a robust peer-to-peer overlay supporting location-based search. In: Peer-to-peer computing (P2P), 2012 IEEE 12th international conference on. IEEE, pp 25–36
12. Hiltunnen MA (2000) The catcus approach to building configurable middleware services. DSMGC2000, Germany
13. Stocia I, Morris R (2003) Chord: a scalable peer-to-peer lookup protocol for internet applications. IEEE/ACM Trans Netw 11(1):17–32
14. Intel Ltd (2001) Peer to peer computing, p2p file sharing at work in the enterprise. USA. Retrieved from http://www.intel.com/eBusiness/pdf/prod/peertopeer/p2p_edgesvcs.pdf
15. Korpela EJ, Anderson DP, Bankay R, Cobb J, Howard A, Lebofsky M, ... Werthimer D (2011) Status of the UC-Berkeley SETI efforts. In: SPIE optical engineering+applications. International Society for Optics and Photonics, p 815212
16. Korpela E, Werthimer D, Anderson D, Cobb J, Lebofsky M (2001) SETI@Home-massively distributed computing for SETI. SETI – University of Berkeley. Retrieved from http://seti-athome.berkeley.edu/sah_papers/CISE.pdf
17. Kovacevic A (2010) Peer-to-peer location-based search: engineering a novel peer-to-peer overlay network. ACM SIGMultimed Rec 2(1):16–17
18. Lakshman A, Malik P (2010) Cassandra: a decentralized structured storage system. ACM SIGOPS Oper Syst Rev 44(2):35–40
19. Lakshman A, Malik P (2009) Cassandra – a decentralized structured storage system. LADIS
20. Luciani J (2012) Cassandra file system design. Retrieved from Datastax: http://www.datastax.com/dev/blog/cassandra-file-system-design
21. Yang M, Yang Y (2010) An efficient hybrid peer-to-peer system for distributed data sharing. Comput IEEE Trans 59(9):1158–1171
22. Napster (n.d.) Napster: protocol specification. Retrieved from opennap: opennap.sourceforge.net/napster.txt
23. Ng WS, Ooi BC, Tan K-L (2002) BestPeer: a self-configurable peer-to-peer system. Data Engineering. IEEE, San Jose
24. Nguyen T, Baz DE, Spiteri P, Jourjon G, Chua M (2010) High performance peer-to-peer distributed computing with application to obstacle problem
25. Pfitzmann AW (1987) Networks without user observability. Comput Secur 6:158–166
26. Rabl T, Sadoghi M, Jacobsen H-A, Villamor SG, Mulero VM, Mankovskii S (2012) Solving big data challenges for enterprise application performance management. VLDB Endowment, Vol. 5, No. 12, Istanbul, Turkey
27. Ratnasamy S, Francis P, Handley M, Karp R, Shenker S (2001) A scalable content-addressable network, vol 31, No. 4. ACM, pp 161–172
28. Rhea SWC (2001) Maintenance free global data storage. Internet comput 5(4):40–49
29. Saroiu S, Gummadi KP, Gribble SD (2003) Measuring and Analyzing the characteristics of Napster and Gnutella hosts. Multimedia Syst 1(2):170–184
30. Introduction to SETI. Retrieved May 5, 2014, from http://setiathome.ssl.berkeley.edu/

31. Spiteri P, Chau M (2002) Parallel asynchronous Richardson method for the solution of obstacle problem. In: 16th Annual International Symposium on High Performance Computing Systems and Applications, pp 133–138
32. Triantafillow P, Xiruhaki C, Koubarakis M, Ntamos N (n.d.) Towards high performance peer to peer content and resource sharing system, Greece
33. Wong G, Hiltunen M, Schlichting R (2001) A configurable and extensible transport protocol. IEEE INFOCOM '01. Achorage, pp 319–328
34. Zhao BK (2001) Tapestry: an infrastructure for fault tolerant wide area localization and routing. Computer Science Division, Berkeley

Further Reading

Asaduzzaman S, Bochmann G (2009) GeoP2P: an adaptive and fault-tolerant peer-to-peer overlay for location-based search, ICDCS, 2009

Boxun Zhang, Kreitz G, Isaksson M, Ubillos J, Urdaneta G, Pouwelse JA, Epema D (2013) Understanding user behavior in Spotify, INFOCOM. In: Proceedings of the IEEE, On page(s), pp 220–224

Dominik Stingl, Christian Gross, Sebastian Kaune, Ralf Steinmetz (2012) Benchmarking decentralized monitoring mechanisms in peer-to-peer systems ICPE'12, April 22–25, 2012, Boston

Tran D, Nguyen T (2008) Hierarchia multidimensional search in peer-to-peer networks. Comput Commun 31(2):346–357

Mihai Capota, Johan Pouwelse, Dick Epema (2014) Towards a peer-to-peer bandwidth marketplace. Distributed computing and networking ICDCN 2014, LNCS 8314, pp 302–316

Meulpolder M, Meester LE, Epema DHJ (2012) The problem of upload competition in peer-to-peer systems with incentive mechanisms. Article first published online: 2 MAY 2012 doi:10.1002/cpe.2856

Viswanath B, Post A, Gummadi KP, Mislove A (2010) An analysis of social network-based sybil defenses. In: Proceedings of the ACM SIGCOMM 2010 conference applications, technologies, architectures, and protocols for computer communication. ACM, New York, pp 363–374.

doi:http://doi.acm.org/10.1145/1851182.1851226

Chapter 12
Visualization Dimensions for High-Performance Big Data Analytics

12.1 Introduction

Data are simply a collection of facts. These facts can be observations, words, measurements, numbers, or even description of things. What makes these data so important is that data are the basis of everything we monitor and that we want to analyze to find answers to complex questions. Another interesting aspect of the data is that within a particular context the information it implies does not change with interpretation. For example, if the total number of views of a particular blog post is X, it remains X for the blogger or visitor or for the software that ranks the blogs. Data, when processed, give us information that when further analyzed leads to understanding and knowledge of the ways the market is moving, how people interact with each other, and many other factors.

'Big data' is happening now: it is no longer a future trend. What is new here is that companies and organizations are realizing the benefits of collecting and storing data that can be used to offer better products and services, making interactions more personalized and secure. With sophisticated data collection and storage, we have generated and recorded more than a zettabyte of data. And that is not all: experts predict that soon we will be generating 50 times as many data as in a current day now. That is *huge*. But, collecting and storing data does not mean much unless we can draw some insights from the stored data. Another important aspect of big data is the extremely fast speed. Unless we can analyze, visualize, and strategize at the speed of data, the benefits will be limited in certain scenarios. This Big Data revolution is not about the quantity of data. Rather, it is about the insights and the actions we take based on those insights from the data. Improved storage, analytical tools, advanced visualizations, and automatic actions are at the crux of this revolution.

The one step that must come between analysis and taking actions on the insights is how we interpret and understand the results. For example, consider three

© Springer International Publishing Switzerland 2015
P. Raj et al., *High-Performance Big-Data Analytics*, Computer Communications
and Networks, DOI 10.1007/978-3-319-20744-5_12

Table 12.1 Monthly sales of representatives

Person	Sale area	Sales amount
A	100	40
B	50	30
C	100	30

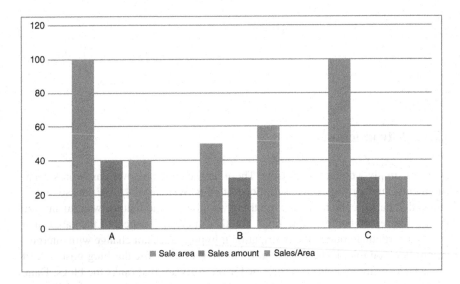

Fig. 12.1 Monthly sales of representatives: bar graph

salespersons: A, B, and C. Their sales in their corresponding sales area are shown in Table 12.1 and Fig. 12.1.

Now, suppose their company has a program to decide who is the best performing salesperson. How will we know which is the best performance? If we go by total sales, then we will award 'A,' but if we go by total sale per square meters, then 'B' gets the award. If we store the data in a bar chart in which each bar represents sales per square meters, we can easily pick the top performer, even if there are hundreds of salespersons.

We understand visual things far better than analytical numbers. This understanding further helps in taking profitable actions. This realization is simply what information visualization is all about, that is, representing information in a way that we can understand easily and which allows us to take strategic actions.

If we are able to understand and engage with the never-ending information with which we are bombarded, the more likely we can make decision about what information we can take a deeper view and what is irrelevant to us. So, visualization is about providing actionable knowledge. This ability quickly becomes important as we constantly handle information at a scale that we can no longer comprehend easily.

Table 12.2 Monthly sales of representatives for a period of 12 months

Person	Jan	Feb	Mar	Apr	May	Jun	Jul	Aug	Sep	Oct	Nov	Dec
A	10	20	30	15	23	31	17	25	33	20	29	40
B	25	24	26	25	25	60	24	26	25	25	25	25

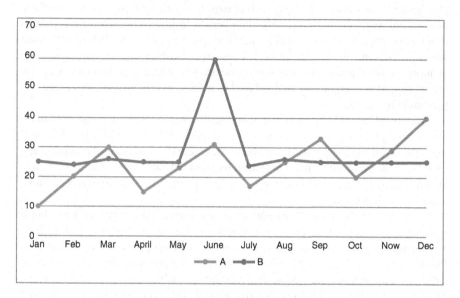

Fig. 12.2 Monthly sales of representatives for a period of 12 months

Data visualization [6] is graphical or visual representation of information, with the simple goal of providing qualitative understanding of the information it is representing. This information can be simple numbers, processes, relationships, or concepts. Visualization may involve manipulating graphical entities (points, circles, lines, shapes, text) and visual attributes (intensity, color, size, hue, position, shape).

Information visualization is graphical or visual display of abstract information done basically for two reasons: one, to understand the data, and second, to communicate the same understanding or interpretation.

As the saying goes, "A picture is worth a thousand words," which is often more so with the right context and the right picture. The obvious pattern if represented with the correct visual technique might be hard to find if we are looking at the table of sales numbers. For example, we can take the case of salespersons for whom we have the sales records for 12 months (Table 12.2 and Fig. 12.2).

Representing data in this table is advantageous because of the accuracy of the sales data. But if we want to understand the scenario or story of these sales figures, this representation has serious drawbacks. Now, if we represent the same data in the form of a line graph, we discover some patterns: the sales of salesperson A plummet at the start of the quarter, gradually outperforming those of B by the end of the quarter, whereas the sales of B remained consistent, except with a steep spike of sales in the month of June 2014.

For these data, in which we could not see the patterns when the data were represented as a table, when represented visually we were able to understand the patterns and make sense of the data. This is the advantage of visualization.

Information visualization not only depicts relationships between quantitative values, it can also display relationships between prescriptive data as well. For example, for the followers on Twitter, each person is represented as a node, and there exists a link with another person this first person follows. This type of representation can be used to answer simple analytical questions such as "Who's following whom?" "Whom might you know?" These relationships can be enhanced with quantitative information, such as how close are you with the person to whom you are related. This strength can be displayed as a thickness in the line connecting two persons (Fig. 12.3).

The advantages [15] being stated, it is equally vital to visualize in the right manner. A wrong technique or overcrowded dashboard can hurt the ease of understanding. Visualization can only be successful to the extent that it encodes the information such that it is easier for us to comprehend and understand. The goal of a good visualization is to represent information in such a way that it can be easily, accurately, and efficiently decoded.

People have been representing data in tabular format for a very long time, but it was Rene Descartes that gave us two-dimensional graphs with x and y axes. Visualization of data was brought to its dawn in the eighteenth century by William Playfair, the pioneer for many of the graphs, and the first to display time-series of data, etc. Through his book *Semiologie Graphique* (*The Semiology of Graphics*), Jacques Bertin (1967) laid down the principles of visual perception that can be used to visualize information intuitively, accurately, and efficiently. Then, John Tukey of Princeton gave us exploratory data analysis.

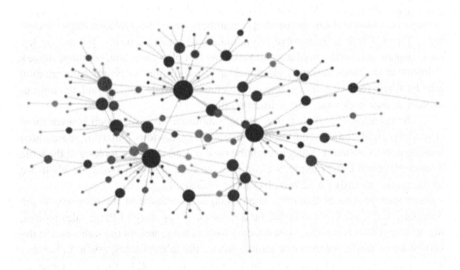

Fig. 12.3 Social network visualization

With the entry into the twenty-first century, data visualization has been main-streamed with many products, helping to make sense of data and at the same time creating beautiful visualizations. Of course, data visualization is one such means to convert big data into actionable insights. Data analysis tools such as SAS generate descriptive, predictive, and prescriptive data analysis giving meaning to data. Even in this case visualization makes it simpler to represent descriptive data, as well as prescriptive data (best alternative solutions) and predictive analytics (reflecting rela-tionships among data).

So, what makes a good visualization? A good visualization will be as follows:

- Effective, in the sense that it is easy for the user to interpret
- Accurate, so as to represent data for further analysis
- Efficient, in that every visualization is designed to convey a clear message or goal. Visualization should not stray from this ideal and should represent the goal in a straightforward message without any sacrifice of relevant complexity, with-out burdening the user with irrelevant or extraneous data.
- Aesthetics, implying appropriate usage of several visual elements such as axis, colors, shapes, and lines as essential for delivering the intended message, highlighting conclusions, and revealing relationships, and at the same time add-ing to visual appeal
- Adaptable, in that visual can adjust to serve multiple needs that might arise
- Informative, so that the visual may provide knowledgeable information to its user. When designing a visual, several considerations are involved, but the most important factor that is relevant to us right now is the delivery of the intended message (Fig. 12.4).

Mendeleev's Periodic Table of elements

A hugely popular visualization showing the chemical elements and their properties. These properties recur periodically and organization of elements into rows and columns to reflect this periodicity. The structure of the table is given by the data, allowing quick access to the properties of the given elements and predict the properties of undiscovered elements. This visualization is unquestionably informative, efficient.

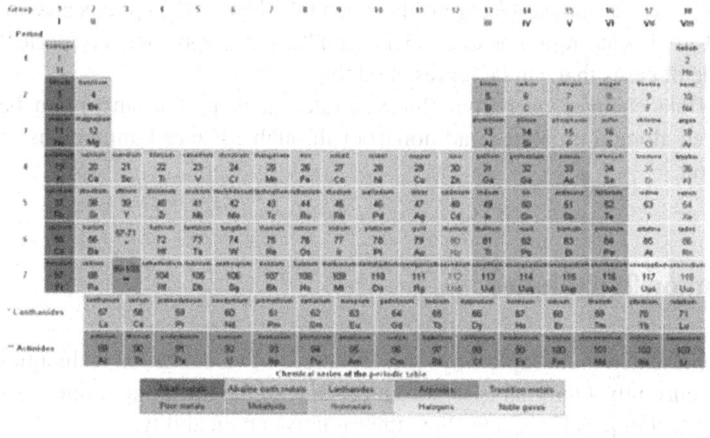

Fig. 12.4 Periodic table of elements

One of the important aspects of information visualization is that, with the right context, it helps in narrating better stories. Within the right context, utilizing data as a part of the story helps make a lasting impact on the viewers [17]. Not every visualization requires stories. Some visualizations are simply a work of art. The process of visualization is done through following key steps.

1. Formulate the question: The question drives the story. This approach helps while gathering and filtering data. It would be helpful to focus on data-centric questions for the purpose of visualization. Questions beginning with "what," "where," and "how much/how often" allow us to focus while searching for data. Questions beginning with "Why" are a good signal that you are moving into data analysis.

2. Gathering the data: Searching for the data can be exhaustive, taking much time and effort. Instead, our governments are providing open data catalogues, and census data are also freely available. If you have some business questions to answer then most probably you must acquire the necessary data. Make sure you have the right format of data so that the data in the data set are relevant.

3. Apply visual representation: Now, we know what question(s) needs to be answered and on what data these questions are to be answered. At this stage, portrayal of data is needed. So, we need to pick up a visual representation of the data, which is simple, some kind of visual dimension that can correspond with the data.

   (a) Size: This is the most commonly used representation because of its extreme usefulness and intuitive representation: it is easier to differentiate two objects based on their size. For example, when comparing the GDP of two countries, say China and Afghanistan, it is more effective to see the relative sizes of the GDPs of these two countries than to see the numbers. This representation is also often misused.

   (b) Color: This is an awesome visual representation method for huge sets of data. It is easy to identify many shades of color, in a gradient, so color is a natural choice for representing high-level trends, distribution, etc.

   (c) Location: This visual representation links data to some form of map or visual element corresponding to a location.

   (d) Networks: These show connections between two distinct data points and are helpful in viewing relationships. Social graphs, job graphs, etc. are perfect example of cases that can be represented thus.

   (e) Time: Data changes over time (literacy rate, stock performance) can be portrayed along a timeline (traditional) or through advanced animations of some sort.

12.2 Common Techniques

Data can be represented in multiple ways [5]. Hundreds of visualization techniques are being used currently. Our goal is to introduce some of the most important types of visualization techniques [2, 4] and show their relative applicability.

Before going into the techniques [16], let us briefly look at the data. The values in the data can be a single variable, for example, histograms, or sales figures, or multiple variables as in a website view count and churn rate. Data can be quantitative: data that can be counted or measured as numerical values. Data can be discrete: numerical data that can only have a finite number of possible values. Data can be continuous: data with a value within a range, for example, temperature in a year. Data can also be sorted and grouped together as a single category as in groups of users of categories of products sold. Whatever data visualization technique we choose, it should be able to represent the type of data efficiently.

12.2.1   Charts

Charts are used to represent single variable data effectively, such as a pie chart or a bar chart.

12.2.1.1   Bar Chart

Bar charts are very versatile, using a horizontal data marker to represent data. These charts can be used to show trends over time or to compare discrete data. The bar graph can be represented either horizontally or vertically. A version of the bar chart in which different categories are compared as part-to-whole relationships is called a stacked bar chart. Keep in mind that the color needs to be consistent and users should be able to view the data without much difficulty (Fig. 12.5).

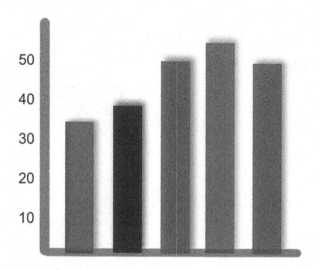

Fig. 12.5 Bar chart

12.2.1.2 Pie Chart

This is one of the most popular chart types, although some opponents of this technique argue that not everyone is able to interpret angles consistently. This type is used to represent parts of a whole relationship. The more stylish version of the bar chart has a donut shape wherein total value or some graphic is embedded in the center. It is always better not to use multiple pie charts to compare different categories; instead, it is better to use a stacked bar chart in this scenario. To ensure all the data add up to 100 %, the sections are ordered in such a way that the largest section is at 12'o clock as this increases readability. These representations are considered to be very dangerous charts unless we can differentiate small differences in angles consistently. Instead, stacked bar charts are used to show parts of a whole in relationships (Figs. 12.6 and 12.7).

Fig. 12.6 Pie chart

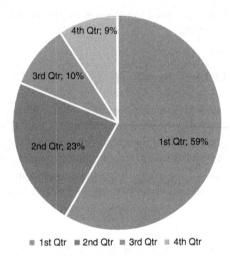

Fig. 12.7 Donut chart

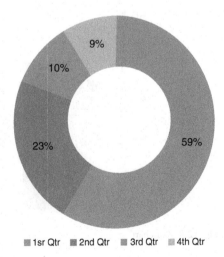

12.2.1.3 Line Chart

Line charts plot data at regular intervals, which are connected by lines. These charts can be used to represent data over time-series relationships with continuous data. These visuals help in showing trends, acceleration, volatility, etc. If more than four lines are plotted in a single chart it becomes clumsy and difficult to understand; instead, use multiple plots for a better comparison (Fig. 12.8).

12.2.1.4 Stacked Area Chart

Area charts depict a time-series relationships as does the line chart, but area charts can also represent volume. A stacked area chart can be used to represent parts of a whole relationship, which can be used to help show how each category contributes to the cumulative total. These charts can also be used to emphasize magnitude change over time. Ensure that less volatile data are placed at the bottom and vice versa, do not display discrete data as the connected lines imply intermediate values, and never use more than four data categories to make it simpler for the users to understand (Fig. 12.9).

12.2.2 Scatter Plot

Scatter plots are used to show relationships between items based on two sets of variables. Data points are used to plot two measures along the scale. We can use more variables such as the size and color of the dot to encode additional data variables. Use trend lines to help draw correlation between variables showing a trend (Fig. 12.10).

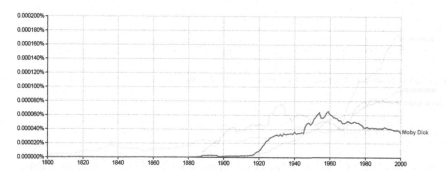

Fig. 12.8 Line chart showing the number of mentions of a character made in books published in that year

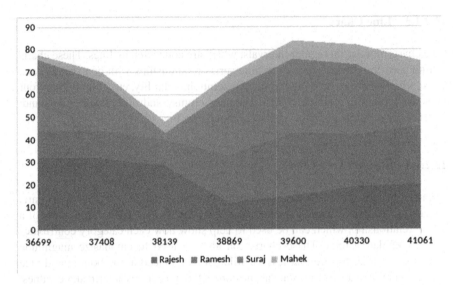

Fig. 12.9   Salary figures of four persons during 10 years

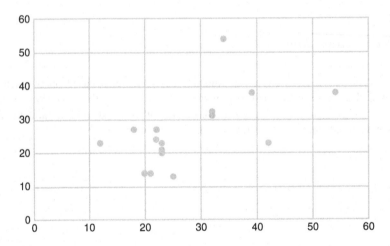

Fig. 12.10   Scatter plot depicting food intake versus weight

12.2.3   Treemap

A treemap is used for representing large amounts of hierarchically structured data. The visualization is split into rectangles. The size and color of these rectangles represents quantitative variables. The levels in the hierarchy can be displayed as rectangles within rectangles; the rectangles in the visualization are ordered as the

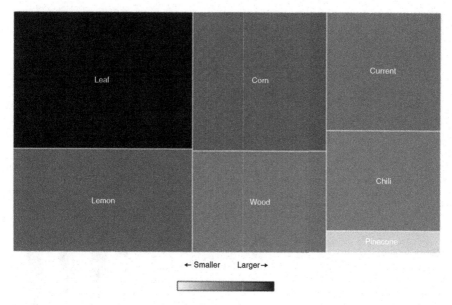

Fig. 12.11 Treemap showing the biggest space

largest rectangle is displayed in the top-left coroner and the smallest rectangle in the bottom-right portion. This order is valid at all levels of hierarchy, and can be made interactive with the option to drill down (Fig. 12.11).

12.2.4   Box Plot

A box plot separates the data into quantiles. These box plots are useful to show the statistical distribution of data values such as the median, lower and upper quartiles, and outliers. The outliers are plotted as separate points in the chart. They are used to get a better understanding of how values are spaced out in different sets of data. These can be used to track the consistency of the result of an experiment over multiple trails, and also used to compare data separated into different categories (Fig. 12.12).

12.2.5   Infographics

Infographics (information graphics) are data visualization techniques that can present complex information clearly and quickly. These are data-rich visualizations of a story and can also been seen as a form of storytelling. These graphics can contain other visualizations and can be overlaid with a story. These are highly useful to

Fig. 12.12 An example of
a box plot

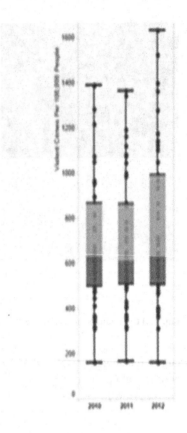

present simple overviews of a complicated concept and help in the communication of ideas and message.

Infographics are essentially changing the ways people experience stories. Infographics make it easier to present information more neatly and in a way suitable to a general audience. Some of the tools that provide these visualization techniques are Protovis, D3.js, and piktochart.com (an online service).

A well-designed infographic can tone down a complicated topic into a simpler version that otherwise would have been a boring experience (Fig. 12.13).

12.2.6 Heat Maps

A heat map is a two-dimensional representation of data. The values in the data are represented by colors and in some cases by size as well, providing an immediate summary of information in a visual format. Even more elaborate heat maps assist users in understanding complex data sets.

Heat maps can be represented in a box map or even overlaid on Map or a webpage, or any picture for that matter. For example, you use a heat map to understand what features in an application are hot and what have not been used in a while, or to

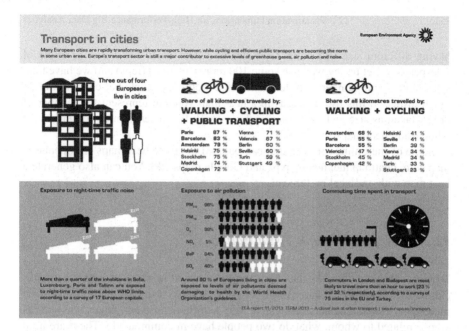

Fig. 12.13 Infographic related to transport in the European Union

Fig. 12.14 Heat map

check which state has more weight in the number of parliament seats. Another example is a list of stocks: those that are traded often can be displayed to have more heat (Fig. 12.14).

The heat map is one of the powerful and most useful data analysis tools available. Multiple rows of data can easily understood by representing each row as having different size and color. Consider an extension to the earlier example of salespersons. Let us say we have some 100 representatives (reps) and we have total sales figures and number of orders taken in a month. A simple bar chart would do much justice to this use, whereas in a heat map you can represent the number of orders taken as size and total sales as the color. It far easier to interpret the results while using heat maps.

Some of the online services that can be used to create heat maps are openheatmap.com, heatmap.me, heatmap.js, and Google maps API. You can also generate a heat map with an Excel or Tableau.

12.2.7   Network/Graph Visualization

To visualize more complex data that simply do not fit in a tree structure, networks can be used to denote relationships between persons, or things or events, or even molecules. Visualizing networks can be very helpful in answering questions such as who is related to whom, what do two people have in common, etc. These are used to perform exploratory data analysis.

The visualization of your social network can be used to understand how diversified or focused your reach is and how influential is any person in your network. For example, you create a professional social graph where people's skills are also denoted; in this case, you can explore and find people with the skill you want to learn or reach out to people who can be beneficial to you career wise. Following is a visualization of LinkedIn created using socilab.com (Fig. 12.15).

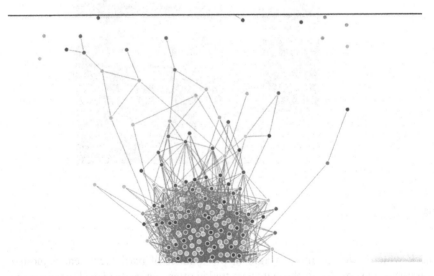

Fig. 12.15 Network visualization of professional social network [3] where each color denotes people belonging to a different sector

Fig. 12.16 Word cloud representation of Mr. Prime Minister's speech

Some Opensource tools that can be used to create these networks are Gephi, Cytoscope, and Socilab.com.

12.2.8   Word Cloud/Tag Cloud

This is an effective visualization tool for analyzing textual data and easy communication of tools: this is easy to use and an inexpensive visualization technique that gives more prominence to the frequency rather than the importance of the words. These visuals do not denote any context, and the best way to use this technique is in pre-processing and filtering data. Nevertheless, this is a good exploratory text analysis tool. It can have quite an impact when given the right context and shape in which words are displayed that are relevant to the theme.

In this technique, the word's size is directly proportional to the frequency of the word. This helps in quickly understanding and observing patterns that might have been lost in the paragraph. These visuals started appearing as Tag Cloud in the 1990s. Tools such as Wordle and Tagxedo make it simpler for users to generate these visual quickly without much effort. Following is the Tag cloud representation of Mr. Prime Minister's speech (Fig. 12.16).

12.3   Data Visualization Tools and Systems

12.3.1   Tableau

Tableau [7] is an easy-to-use business intelligence and analytics tool. Tableau's supercharged business intelligence offers an easy and fast way to make visual analytics. Tableau caters to a user's need, whether these are data visualization, data discovery,

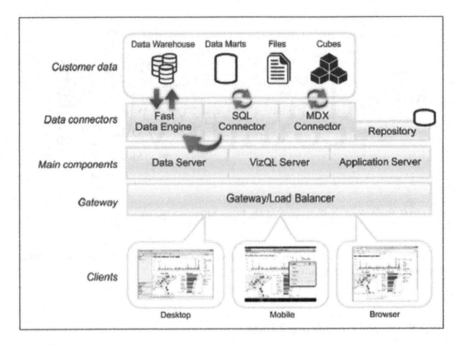

Fig. 12.17 Tableau server components

or to create beautiful dashboards. This tool features creation of interactive data visualization, eliminating the need for creating several variations. Complex reports can easily be designed even by people who are not IT experts. Tableau Server can be used to share enterprise visualization among colleagues.

Tableau Desktop is the main application through which workbooks are created. One can create, publish, and consume visualizations of any types of data producing highly interactive reports in a matter of minutes. Generally there would be one super-user who has a license to Desktop who creates the visualization and publishes it to a Tableau server through which users can view the visualization. Tableau Server is a repository of workbooks created using Tableau Desktop. No special expertise is required to interact with the workbooks on the server.

The merits to be considered in Tableau are ease of creation of dashboards, easy data importing, and with help of data-blending features, data from different sources can be utilized to build an analysis. It has a very active forum (Fig. 12.17).

Customer data are stored in a heterogeneous data environment that consists of a data layer. Tableau leverages in-memory data storage, but there is no compulsion to bring all the data into memory. Existing data platforms can be leveraged to answer questions.

Optimized data connectors exists for databases ranging from Oracle to Cloudera Hadoop and for those systems without a native connector or JDBC connector. The data can be interacted through either a live connection or an in-memory data storage engine. Through live connection Tableau can leverage existing data infra-structure by dynamic SQL and MDX queries directly to the database. Through the in-memory data engine, Tableau achieves fast query response. It first extracts all the data into memory and then processes the queries.

The job of the Tableau server is divided into four components.

Application Server: This service manages permissions and browsing visualizations on Tableau mobile and web interfaces.

VizQL Server: Once the user checks are done and the view is opened, VizQL server receives a request from the client. The VizQL process on behalf of the client sends queries to the data source and returns results back to the client after render-ing data as images. VizQL is a patented query language that converts visual, drag-and-drop actions into database queries and then renders the response graphically.

Data Server: This process centrally manages and stores data sources, and maintains metadata such as calculations and definitions from Tableau Desktop.

Gateway/Load Balancer: This is the primary component that routes the request to other components. In the distributed environment, this also acts a load balancer.

Tableau Server can be used to host workbooks created using Tableau Desktop. Although Tableau tops almost every survey in data visualization tools, some major problems are that it does not provide ETL capabilities; in some cases performance penalties are observed while using Tableau with Large data sets; and finally, there is no way to extend the SDKs, which restricts customizing of the environment (Fig. 12.18).

Tableau Public is a free service that publicly hosts the workbooks created using Tableau Desktop. The foregoing figure (Fig. 12.18) was created using Tableau Public, which shows adult obesity rates by different states as a colored heat map and the relationship between obesity and smoking; exercise versus diet is shown in scat-ter plots.

12.3.2 BIRST

Birst [12] is a cloud-based business intelligence (BI) suite. Even though it does not provide powerful features for data transformation, it is simple and easier to develop. With Birst we can create a data warehouse in the cloud and display reports and dashboards with relative ease.

Birst compartmentalizes each deployment, allowing different departments of a company to access and analysis shared data repositories. Each space provides a data warehouse repository, dashboard settings, and user access rights. Flat files can be uploaded in the browser. Birst connects can be used to upload from a desktop, and cloud-based extractors can be used to pull data from cloud repositories.

Burst provides custom charting, dashboards based in a browser, and scheduling reports. The report designer tab can be used to design reports through a guided

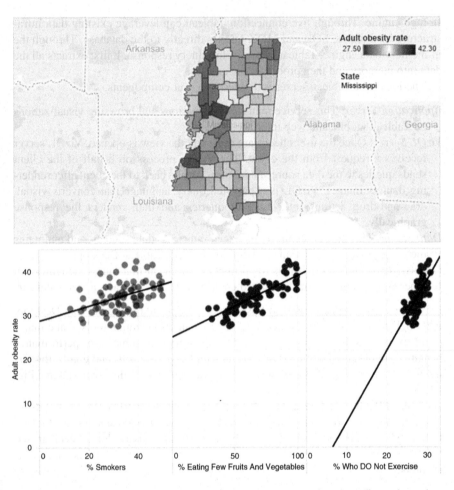

Fig. 12.18 Adult obesity rate by state and comparison of percentage of smokers, diet, and exercise. Created using Tableau Public

selection of chart types and various other parameters. This tab has a predefined measure for business data that can make dashboard design a breeze, which is already simple through a drag-and-drop interface. Birst offers various chart templates such as gauge, funnel chart, and mapping options in which you can also use Bing maps for displaying data on the map.

The few demerits of Burst are that the visualizations are somewhat static and there is no provision to do what-if analysis or ad hoc visualizations. SQL is abstracted, so complex queries are definitely not possible, although it provides its own Birst query language to allow time-series analysis.

12.3.3   Roambi

Roambi [11] is a leading mobile reporting and analytics application, a completely mobile centric BI tool that differs from many others. Some of the great features of this tool are multi-touch centric UI, easy visualization creation with stunning templates, integration with other analytical solutions, access control, localization, integration with multitudes of data sources, automatic refresh and integration with active directory, and advanced security features as well.

A few examples in which this application can be perfect is for executive reports and dashboards, sales representatives who are constantly on the move, and customer interactions.

RoamBI is a completely mobile information visualization tool. RoamBI can be used to present your data in a beautiful visualization on mobile devices. Creating a visualization is as simple as uploading your data, in either Excel, CSV, Salesforce crm data, SAP business objects, or other sources. Select the 'how want to view the data,' customize the view, and publish. The next time you open RoamBI the visualizations are automatically downloaded. It is not just a static presentation: you can drill down the data and discover patterns (Figs. 12.19 and 12.20).

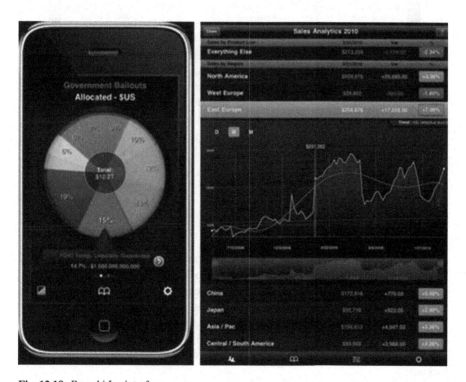

Fig. 12.19 Roambi Ios interface

Fig. 12.20 Roambi flow story

RoamBI Flow lets the users embed visualizations in documents and create a specialized enterprise publishing platform for mobile devices. This application uses an on-premise RoamBk Es server that can be integrated with a range of Bio servers such as IBM Cognos, SAP Business Objects, etc. Web-based RoamBI flow publisher gives us templates into which you can place text and images, explain your analysis, or tell a compelling story. The RoamBI Flow system provides advanced security features from user access control to remote wiping of data and device lockout.

12.3.4   QlikView

Qlikview [10] is one of the major shareholders in the visualization market. Qlikview generates interactive visualizations, making it easier for business users to get answers to multiple questions in a few applications. All the visualizations are mobile supported. The users can access the visualization on Qlikview server with download-free Ajax clients. Users can collaborate in real time, and in-app threaded discussions are also provided. Qlikview Desktop can be used to create secure apps. Qlikview Desktop is a Windows application through which developers can create SQL-like scripts for collection and transformation of data. There is a plug-in for a visual studio as well. Data can be sourced using ODBC connectors for standard sources, XML, or Qlikview data exchange for importing from nonstandard sources such as Google BigQuery. It has connectors for SAP ERP systems and Saleforce.com as well. As a matter of fact, data can be imported from any SQl-compliant data sources.

Qlikview uses in-memory storage to achieve higher performance. If the data cannot be stored in memory, it directly queries the data source. Holding shared data in memory for multiple users helps in reducing the wait time. It also calculates aggregates on the fly and automatically maintains associations in the data. It compresses in-memory data, significantly reducing the size of the in-memory data used for analysis. The drill-down paths are not predefined as in other visualization tools. It follows what it quotes, as "start anywhere, go anywhere" (Fig. 12.21).

Qlikview Sense is a self-service data visualization application. With drag-and-drop visualizations, it is simpler to create visualization and data exploration.

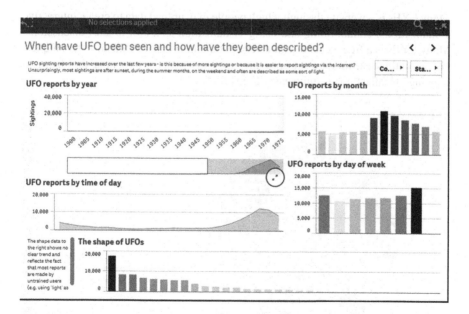

Fig. 12.21   QlikView sample dashboard: UFO sightings across states

The data used in a single app can be sourced from different sources: this provides standard APIs to be integrated in a website and to extend the standard feature set to meet a customer's requirements.

12.3.5   IBM Cognos

IBM Cognos [9] is a traditional enterprise-level business intelligence (BI) suite that has multiple components including database administration tools, query and analysis tools, dashboard creation, ETL, and report creation and distribution, which is useful for large enterprises where the deployment is governed and overseen by an information technology (IT) department. The major merits of this platform are that it is highly scalable, has a broad feature set, and a mature and enterprise-level BI platform. Its demerits are that it is not very intuitive for the users, who need expertise and training. The visualizations are somewhat old and flat.

Historically speaking, the aesthetics of IBM Cognos is not particularly a strong point although it is that which earned it praise. But with the release of Cognos 10+ this has changed. With the arrival of RAVE (Rapid Adaptive Visualization Engine), interactive visualizations at least as beautiful and powerful as those in other visualization tools can be created.

12.3.5.1   Many EYEs

Many EYEs is a website through which people may upload data to create interactive visualizations, collaborating and using visualization as a tool to start discussions. Many EYEs is a free website with a very good number of visualization techniques. For an enthusiast, this website provides a great service. Uploading the data and creating visualizations is quite easy (Fig. 12.22).

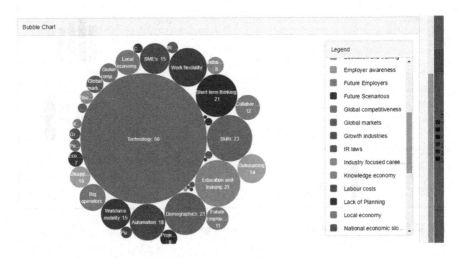

Fig. 12.22 Packed bubble chart using Many Eyes

12.3.6   Google Charts and Fusion Tables

Google Charts [13] is one simple charting library available that supports multiple chart types, which are exposed as JavaScript classes. These charts can be customized and shared on websites. These charts are highly interactive and support events that can be used to create complex dashboards. The data are populated using the DataTable class, which provides methods for sorting and filtering data, supporting any database or data providing Chart Tools data source protocol such as Google spreadsheets, Google Fusion tables, Salesforce, etc.

Although this is a wonderful way to integrate visualization into a website, website access can be controlled by existing security infrastructure, which requires expertise in JavaScript, and thus integration with enterprise data sources or pure analytical platforms or analytical databases such as Vertica is not possible. Moreover, this is not a prime offering or open source so the availability of this library is at the discretion of Google, which makes it not so viable a contender for information visualization for enterprises (Fig. 12.23).

12.3.7   Data-Driven Documents (D3.js)

D3.js [14] is relatively new, but trending libraries use this for data visualization on the Internet. Using D3 you can bind arbitrary data to Document Object Model (DOM) and then you can apply any transformations to the documents based on the data. Emphasizing web standards and leveraging the full capabilities of modern browsers, using HTML, SVG, and CSS D3, brings life to data. D3 follows the declarative style of programming and functional style, allowing code reuse through components and plug-ins. D3 has minimal overhead, and it is extremely fast, supporting dynamic behaviors and large datasets for interaction and animation.

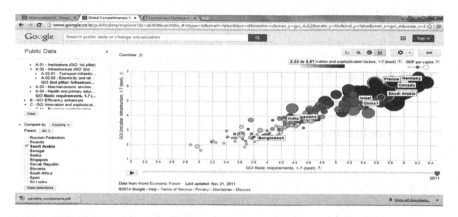

Fig. 12.23 Innovation index: visualization in Google public data and Google charts

Fig. 12.24 Chord diagram using D3.js. Chord diagrams show directed relationships among a group of entities. See https://github.com/ mbostock/d3/wiki/ Chord-Layout for instructions on creating chord using D3

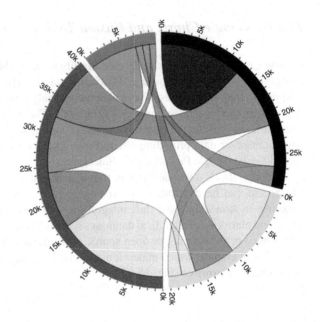

The community is very active, but a few demerits associated with D3.js are that the visualizations are mainly developed by software developers and designers. It can be rather hard for the novice business user to develop a visualization. Interactive analysis and data exploration can be provided using events, but while building complex animations with D3, the code can become clumsy (Fig. 12.24).

12.3.8   Sisense

Sisense [8] is a one-of-a-kind full-stack BI product differing from many other competitors, such as Tableau. It is based on Elasticube, which is simply an in-memory columnar database. Sisense bridges the gap between expensive traditional full-stack tools, which are cumbersome, and more modern business-friendly visualization tools that lack the power on the backend to crunch big data. Using Sisense, users can join multiple independent data sets, then analyze and visualize them (Fig. 12.25).

12.4   Conclusions

Data visualization is the representation of data visually using visual characteristics such as size, shape, color, and length. As humans, we understand data better if these are presented in visual format. With Big Data, the amount of data to be comprehended has increased beyond our limits. One of the best ways to make sense of this

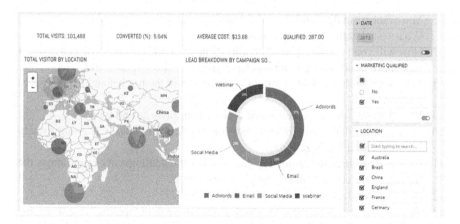

Fig. 12.25 Dashboard displaying number of users and number of conversions according to location. Sisense Demo dashboard can be accessed at http://www.sisense.com/demo/

is using data visualization, which is effective in the sense that it is easy for the user to interpret.

To make a data visualization beautiful, it should be informative, giving some knowledge to the viewer, accurate, and efficient: the ink-to-data ratio should be less, and the visualization should have aesthetic value and be adaptable.

The process of visualization starts with forming the question or objective that needs to be fulfilled by the visualization. The next step is to gather relevant data, and finally to represent the data visually.

A few important visualization techniques are bar chart, line chart, scatter plot, area chart, heat map, network map, word cloud, location map, and Infographics; there are many more visualization techniques.

A few of the visualization tools on the market are Tableau, IBM Cognos, Sisense, Birst, D3.js, and Google Charts.

12.5 Exercises

1. What is information visualization? And why is it vital for a successful BI implementation?
2. What makes a beautiful visualization? Explain your argument.
3. How does information visualization assist our understanding of complex information?
4. What is the process of creating a successful visualization? Is it science or art? Explain with an example.
5. What design principles are employed while creating information visualization?

6. You want to understand how the housing prices in a city change over time. What visualization will you use and why?

7. How will you visualize your LinkedIn social network such that you can connect with more interesting people and have meaningful conversations?

8. Survey the tools available for data visualization in the market and list their pros and cons.

9. Which among the aforementioned tools is your favorite and why?

10. What impact does visualization have on big data and how is it going to help businesses and organizations?

11. Create a visualization using Tableau to show the adult obesity rates across the states in your country and share your experience.

12. Build a visualization for a mobile using RoamBI.

13. Where does data visualization stand in the whole data pipeline? Are there any tools that focus on full-stack analytics instead of just frontend or backend analytical tools? Elaborate on this idea and why it is useful.

14. Imagine you are working for a company, datum.org, and your job is to create reports and visualizations to assist the sales and marketing departments.

    A. You were given sales figures across five categories, and your objective is to compare sales figures across these categories. What visualization technique will you use and why?

    B. Now you are given profit margins as well. How will you compare across categories now? And why did you make this particular choice?

    C. Now you are given a task to make a visualization so that an easy comparison can be made between sales across different locations. How will you visualize this?

    D. Now the shipping department asks you to create a simple visualization for understanding the shipping routes for delivery of orders. How will you use the shipping log data and sales distribution across locations to realize this requirement?

References

1. Fayyad UM, Wierse A, Grinstein GG (eds) (2002) Information visualization in data mining and knowledge discovery. Kaufmann, San Francisco
2. Few S (2009) Introduction to geographical data visualization. Visual Business Intelligence Newsletter, pp 1–11
3. Lieberman M (2014) Visualizing big data: social network analysis. In: Digital research conference
4. Friedman V (2007) Data visualization: modern approaches. Smashing Magazine, 2
5. Chi EH (2000) A taxonomy of visualization techniques using the data state reference model. In: IEEE symposium on information visualization, 2000. InfoVis 2000. IEEE, New York, pp 69–75
6. Yau N (2012) Visualize this! Wiley, Hoboken

7. Tableau 9.0: Smart Meets Fast. Retrieved March 1, 2015, from http://www.tableau.com/new-features/9.0
8. Sisense Business Analytics Software Built for Complex Data. (n.d.). Retrieved February 13, 2015, from http://www.sisense.com/features/
9. Cognos software. Retrieved February 18, 2015, from http://www-01.ibm.com/software/in/analytics/cognos/
10. Qlik Sense Architecture Overview. Retrieved January 5, 2015, from http://www.qlik.com
11. Roambi Mobile Analytics. Retrieved February 5, 2015, from http://roambi.com/
12. Cloud BI and Analytics|Birst. Retrieved February 5, 2015, from http://www.birst.com/
13. Google Charts. Retrieved February 5, 2015, from https://developers.google.com/chart/
14. D3.js – Data-Driven Documents. (n.d.). Retrieved September 5, 2015, from http://d3js.org/
15. McCandless D (2010) The beauty of data visualization. TED website. http://bit.ly/sHXvKc
16. Soukup T, Davidson I (2002) Visual data mining techniques and tools for data visualization and mining. Wiley, New York
17. Visualising Data. Retrieved February 5, 2015, from http://www.visualisingdata.com

Further Reading

Bertin J (1983) Semiology of graphics: diagrams, networks, maps
Few S (2004) Show me the numbers. Analytics Press, Oakland
Steele J, Iliinsky N (2010) Beautiful visualization: looking at data through the eyes of experts. O'Reilly Media, Sebastapol
Ware C (2012) Information visualization: perception for design. Elsevier, Amsterdam

Chapter 13
Social Media Analytics for Organization Empowerment

13.1 Introduction

The use of analytics provides a lot of business value for present-day organizations. The evidence has been seen since the era of business intelligence which was prevalent in the early 1980s which was mainly based on the decision support which was generated using the data which was collected from various databases/warehouses of the organization. Today, analytics has progressed to several stages of maturity from the business intelligence phase. It encompasses several aspects of an organization like governance, enterprise performance management (EPM), and risk and compliance. Organizations which have the capability to smartly use their data to derive business insights have progressed much farther in their business than the others who lack the capability. The two noteworthy trends in analytics which are worth mentioning are the following:

- The evolution of the new *big data* era where several types of data in diverse formats, sizes, and varieties from diverse sources get assimilated in the organization.
- The *social revolution* due to the proliferation of social media and other social collaborations in various forms like blogs, wikis, and other communities of knowledge. Customers nowadays want their opinion to be considered seriously by the organizations. This has led to the emergence of a new stream of analytics which exclusively focuses on the analysis of social data. This stream of analytics is referred to as social media analytics. The different dimensions of social media analytics are summarized in the diagram which follows:

© Springer International Publishing Switzerland 2015
P. Raj et al., *High-Performance Big-Data Analytics*, Computer Communications and Networks, DOI 10.1007/978-3-319-20744-5_13

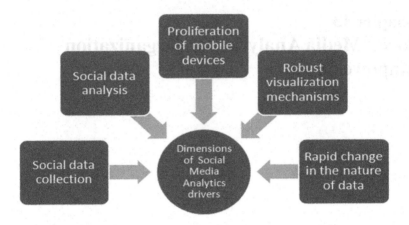

13.1.1   Social Data Collection

Social media discussions and conversations should be tracked carefully by organizations to understand the sentiments and concerns of customers towards their brand. Apart from social media, there are several forums that exist both within and outside the organization like blogs, forums, and wikis. Social collaborations and discussions that happen within these forums will provide wealth of information and insights for the organization. There is also a growing trend towards the concept of social media call centers. These call centers have listening platforms which listen to the discussions about the organization/brand of products, and in case of a concern, they try to resolve the issue and address the concern. This will go a long way in retaining customer loyalty with the help of social media analytics. Many organizations like Salesforce.com already have their full-fledged social media call centers in place which track and respond to the concerns of the customers instantaneously.

13.1.2   Social Data Analysis

All types of relevant information should be made available and accessible to all employees. This will help to bring together employees who belong to diverse business units together and facilitate democratization of thoughts across the organization. Such democratization will go a long way in inducing innovation into the work culture. It is estimated that in a traditional enterprise, only 25 % of employees will have access to relevant information. However, in the concept of social enterprises, 100 % of employees will have access to the information which is relevant to them. This will empower them with additional information which will make their job easier.

In a social enterprise, the employees will be encouraged to share their knowledge which in turn will help to facilitate effective collaboration across the organization silos.

Effective analytics in a social enterprise goes much beyond the analysis of customer data alone. It fosters collaboration among the various business units of an organization using the data which is derived from budgets, key performance indicators, and several other parameters which could be beneficial for the overall growth of the organization.

Data when shared across organizations can help to identify root causes of specific issues. For example, consider a business unit in an organization which consistently shows high rate of visa rejections which in turn impacts the revenue of that business unit due to the cancelation of important business travel. Analytics could reveal that high number of cases of visa rejection could be because of poor sales planning of the sales team which always manages to fix up a client meeting only in the peak of the moment which gives very less time to plan and prepare adequately for travel and visa processing which in turn leads to high rate of visa rejection and travel cancelation.

13.1.3 Proliferation of Mobile Devices

With many organizations taking strides towards the implementation of bring your own device (BYOD) concept, mobile devices and smart phones have become inevitable for the growth of organizations. Every year, on an average, the mobile device subscriber base is increasing by more than a million worldwide. Roughly a billion new mobile subscribers were added in the last 4 years, and this number is expected to increase further in the years to come. This has laid out a strong growth trajectory and innovation space using mobile devices and the plethora of other technologies that form a part of mobile devices. Analytical tools no longer personal computers/servers with high-end configuration, many robust analytical tools with sophisticated capabilities are already available as mobile applications. These mobile applications which have the capability to run on mobile devices and tablets are highly intuitive with powerful analytical capabilities. The availability of analytical capabilities on mobile devices has opened a new era for data analysis more so for social media data analysis on account of the availability of several social media applications on the mobile devices.

13.1.4 Robust Visualization Mechanisms

In the early era, analytical results were displayed mainly using complicated spreadsheets. Visualization tools and technologies have undergone revolutionizing changes in the recent times. Now gone are those era of spreadsheets; the present-day visualization tools represent the results of analysis using several techniques like graphs, visuals, and interactive simulations. Many visualization tools also provide a dashboard view of analysis results which in turn can be drilled down further to perform deeper analyses of data.

Another important advent in the field of visualization is the emergence of tools which can provide visualization capabilities to mobile devices. As per 2012 predictions by Gartner, mobile devices will be the key focus area for business intelligence and analytics to the extent that more than one-third of BI and analytics functionality will be taken over by mobile devices within the next couple of years. Some of the prominent mobile business Intelligence visualization tools which are available in the market are Roambi, Tableau, and Cognos BI.

13.1.5   Rapid Change in the Nature of Data

Business ecosystem is changing rapidly. Hence, it is very important to capture data in real time and make it available for decision making. If analytics has to be successful in the present context, it is necessary to ensure that real-time data is captured and made available to the analytical tools to perform real-time analytics and provide timely insights for the business executives. Rapid advances in the field of real-time data capture and the availability of high-speed networks for real-time data transfer are great enablers for real-time data analytics.

In the context of social media, there are social media listening platforms which are very robust and have the capability to track and capture references about a specific brand or product in social media networks in real time. The organizations can be alerted about these references so that they can take quick actions to remediate the concern which is discussed in the social media forums by the customers. This will go a long way in retaining the customer loyalty and customer satisfaction.

Providing right insights to the right people using appropriate devices is also very critical for the success of real-time data analytics. Mobile devices act as a key enabler by facilitating 24/7 access to real-time data insights. The availability of mobile BI visualization tools has opened a new era in the field of business value which is offered by real-time data analytics. In this context, it is very important to quote about a Motorola study which revealed that when equipped with mobile technology, 75 % of retail associates report providing a better in-store shopping experience. The same study indicated that 67 % of shoppers cite a better experience in a store where associates and managers use the latest mobile technology to present real-time data insights [1].

13.2   Getting Started with Social Media Analytics

The amount of social data generated is increasing exponentially. As per the most recent statistics, Twitter users produce 100,000 tweets per minute. To add on, during every minute of every day, 48 h worth of content is getting uploaded to YouTube. Some other amazing statistics about social media networks are:

- 47,000 apps are getting downloaded from Apple.
- 684,478 items are getting shared on Facebook.
- 100,000 new posts appear on Twitter.
- Two million search queries are sent to Google every minute.

These massive amounts of social media data demand a lot of thoughts on how they can be managed and exploited for the benefit of business. The amount of social data which flows into an organization is forcing the present-day organizations to break the existing boundaries and go beyond the existing *information era.* It is very critical for organizations to take the next step towards *networked intelligence.* The whole idea of networked intelligence is about using the power of human brains to collaborate, share, and derive insights by using the social networks judiciously. Research studies indicate that organizations which have transformed themselves into social enterprises/social organizations are more competitive when compared to the organizations which have not adopted the *social* way of business. All these aspects are the key drivers for the evolution of a separate branch of analytics which is dedicated for analyzing and deriving insights from social data. This branch of analytics is called social media analytics. In other words, social media analytics is defined as an analytics discipline which equips an organization to analyze and measure the impact of social media data on its brand value by examining data from various internal and external forums which are listed in the diagram given below:

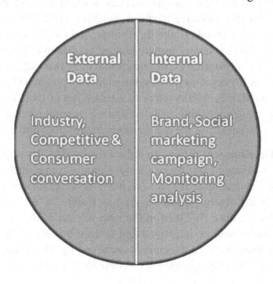

Social media analytics can offer a lot of business value for various functional units of an organization. They are:

Marketing Using social media analytics, marketing teams will have the ability to respond in real time to customer sentiments. Let us first consider the example of a new product launch. When a new product is launched in the market, its impact in the market can be immediately assessed based on social media conversations about that product. Various valuable insights can be captured using social media analytical tools about various aspects like:

- Product reviews/feedback
- Amount of discussions about the product in various social media forums
- Percentage of customers who have expressed favorable opinion about the product features
- The features of the product which require improvement/change

All these insights will help the marketing team to assess if the product needs to be rebranded, tweaked, or discontinued. Nowadays, the marketing teams of most of the organizations use analytics for their decision making.

How Walmart Marketing Team Uses Analytics to Predict Sales of Beer
The Walmart marketing team discovered through analyzing customer data that the demand for beer and Pop-Tarts spike in areas where hurricanes are expected. They were able to adjust the prices of beer accordingly to increase their profits.

Customer Service The sentiments reflected by the customers about a specific product or brand will help the customer service team to thank them for a positive feedback or address their negative feedback quickly. Analysis of conversations on social networks like Facebook, LinkedIn, Twitter, and Google+ acts as a real-time barometer for the customer service team to understand customer sentiment. The main concern with regard to customer experience is that there is no single version of truth or codified customer history. One quick solution for this problem is the use of master data management (MDM). MDM refers to a collection of tools and processes for collecting, aggregating, managing, and distributing corporate data within an organization to ensure consistency in the maintenance of customer information.

Research and Development They can reduce the product development cycles by analyzing the conversations that happen about a product or product feature in social media networks. For example, if there are many discussions in social media networks about difficulty of using a specific product feature "a" and about the absence of another product feature "b," then in the next release of the product, feature a is something which could be improved and feature b is something which could be added. More than 70 % of executives surveyed by McKinsey said that they regularly generate value through their Web communities and social media network conversations.

Human Resource They can understand employee sentiments and employer brand by listening to employee conversations on specific professional networks like Vault. com, Glassdoor.com, and employee alumni networks. Social media networks can provide a wealth of information for managers about the sentiments of employees towards the organization. This will help the managers to devise appropriate retention strategies to retain critical employees.

Finance They can understand and plan strategies for the decision making of organizations by using the data which is gathered from social media networks. Several parameters can be derived from social media networks like factors that affect the cash outflow of organizations, factors which may impact the sales of various products offered by an organization, and so on.

13.2.1 Chapter Organization

This chapter is divided into two sections as outlined in the diagram which is given below:

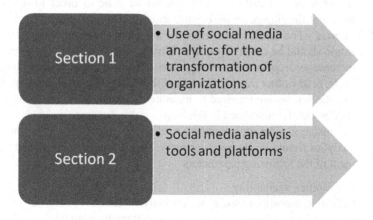

13.3 Building a Framework for the Use of Social Media Analytics for Business

The benefits offered by social media analytics to an organization are immense. However, it is not possible for all organizations to derive benefits from social media analytics. Adoption of social media analytics by organizations should imply realization of immediate business benefits for an organization. The framework given below specifies the steps which need to be followed by an organization in order to realize immediate business benefits.

Step 1	• Define business objectives • Identify required insights
Step 2	• Define success • Recommend actions
Step 3	• Identify required resources • Identify barriers
Step 4	• Identify tools based on strategy, metrics and organization

Step 1   Strategy – This is the key step in which the organization's expectations of using social media analytics should be clearly laid out. If there are any changes required in the existing processes in order to attain organization's expectations, a feasibility study should be done in order to assess the impact of the change on the organization's existing business.

Step 2   Metrics – The metrics to measure the impact of social media on an organization should be clearly specified. Whether it is to drive brand awareness, increase awareness about competitors, improve sales, generate business leads, or any other aspect of that kind should be defined in this step. If any specific actions are required to measure the metrics, those actions should also be clearly mentioned in this step.

Step 3   Organization – An organization's readiness to adopt and use social media analytics should be assessed correctly. This is done by performing assessment of the following parameters:

- Resource availability
- Skill availability in social media analytics tools
- Availability of tools/processes for social media analytics

Step 4   Technology – Once all the previous steps are completed, there will be a clear direction in terms of strategy, metrics, and skill availability. In this last step, the tools which are required for performing analytics on social media data are selected. While selecting, it is important to assess various parameters like cost, success rate of the product, training curve, and license maintenance process for renewal/upgrades.

13.4   Social Media Content Metrics

The key aspect with regard to the use of social media by organizations is the type of content which is posted in the social media. Development of content for social media needs to done carefully and should be governed by a set of metrics so that effective content development strategies can be devised for various types of social media networks. This in turn allows companies to leverage social media marketing to fetch optimal return on investment. The four different types of metrics available for measuring the effectiveness of content are:

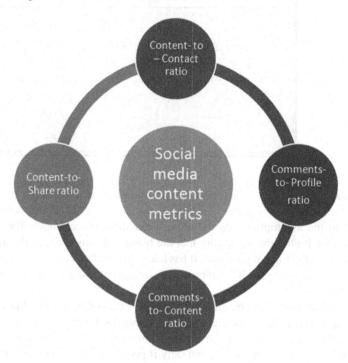

Content-to-contact ratio: This measures the ability of an organization to publish engaging content which in turn helps them to generate new social profiles in social media networks. On average, it has been observed that for an average organization, the content-to-contact ratio has been roughly about 8:1 (this means that for every 8 pieces of content which is published, a new social profile is created). For best companies, content-to-contact ratio could be as high as 1:1. In this context, usage of terms average and best refers to the experience of the company in the social media marketing domain. So initially for all organizations, the response using social media marketing could be dull which in turn will pick up over time as organizations gain more experience in the field of social media marketing.

Comments-to-content ratio: This measures the impact of an organization's content campaign. Comments-to-content ratio can be measured with the help of various social media parameters like likes and comments. Comments-to-content ratio also measures the capability of an organization's campaign to create successful social profile engagements. More number of comments and likes denotes higher degree of engagement. Organizations which are veterans in social media marketing have a comments-to-content ratio which is much higher than the organizations which are new entry into the field of social media marketing.

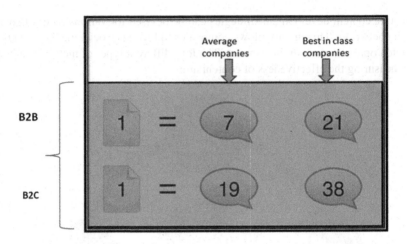

Comments-to-profile ratio: This measures an organization's capability to connect with its existing social profiles with the passage of time. This ratio is measured based on the assumption that the more the number of comments for existing profiles, the higher the possibility that the brand will stay fresh in the minds of customers at the time of purchase. It has been observed that comments-to-profile ratio for best-in-class B2C companies is significantly higher when compared B2B companies.

Content-to-share ratio: This measures the content's capability to extend beyond the reach of social media boundaries into other networks, forums, or communities of people. The higher the ratio, the higher is the success rate of the content. This assumption is based on the fact that only if people like some content, they will take that extra mile to register for the content and share it with others who are outside the network. High values for content-to-share ratio also denote new social prospects for an organization's brand and products.

13.5   Predictive Analytic Techniques for Social Media Analytics

Of late, predictive analytical techniques are used extensively on social media data to generate valuable insights. There are several APIs and tools to access data from social media networks. There are also several service providers which access the social media data and convert it into a form where analytics can be performed.

Text mining is the technique which is used to perform sentiment analysis on data. Text mining uses the textual content which is posted in the social media sites to judge whether the sentiment towards a product/brand or any other organization under consideration is positive or negative. With the availability of several powerful text mining techniques like tag cloud, the use of text mining for sentiment analysis has become very widespread.

Sentiment analysis works on the basis of an appropriate subjectivity lexicon which has the capability to understand the relative positive, neutral, or negative context of a word or expression. This understanding is based on both language and context. An excellent example is given below:

I find it very good and comfortable to work in organization X, though the salary is a bit less.

In the sentence which is given above, there are three words which express sentiments. They are:

- Good
- Comfortable
- Less

But the overall sentiment of the sentence is rated as positive as the sentence has two positive words and one negative word. In addition to the words, there is a qualifier which is used to enhance the positive word (very) and the negative word is put into perspective using the qualifier a bit. Lexicons can have varying levels of complexity and accuracy. The results produced by the lexicons are also based on these parameters which are associated with a lexicon. The availability of several tested algorithms and tools for text mining makes sentiment analysis using text mining a powerful tool which can be used by the organizations to perform social media analytics.

Another predictive analytic technique which is very commonly used in social media analytics is network analysis. Network analysis is a technique which uses communication between various individuals on specific topics to establish various connections among them and detect various aspects like the strong followers of a brand/organization and their impact in specific topics/discussions. All other existing predictive analytic techniques, such as clustering, modeling, and scoring, can be used for social media analytics only if the input data can be converted into a specific format which is required by these techniques.

13.6 Architecture for Sentiment Analysis Using Text Mining

Underlying assumptions about the type of data which is considered in this architecture are given below:

- An article is an initial contribution made to a social media network.
- An article may have comments and notes which may be considered as replies to the article.
- An article with all the comments and notes added as a response to it is considered as a single-user document.
- The architecture will have various components which will analyze each document and decide whether its sentiment is positive or negative.

As discussed before, a word can be considered as positive or negative based on itself or on the context in which it is used. The frequency of occurrence of negative and positive words throughout a document is used as a basis for classifying the attitude of the document. Similarly, the frequency of negative and positive words, used by specific users across all documents, is used as a basis for classifying the attitude of the user. The greater the number of negative words used by a specific user, the more negatively the attitude of the user is considered. In contrast, the more positive words a user uses, the more positively the attitude of the user is considered.

An architecture model for sentiment analysis using text mining is depicted in the diagram which is given below. The various components of the architecture are:

- Bank of words (BoW) node
- Term frequency node
- Tags to string node
- Document scoring node and user scoring node

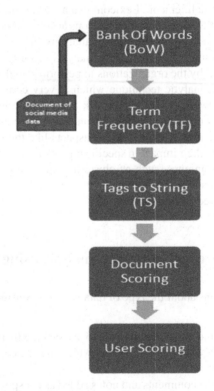

The roles of the various nodes are explained below:

BoW: Documents which are created from social media data generated by users are given as inputs to the bank of words node. The BoW node creates a bag of words for each document input. BoW consists of at least two columns: one which lists the documents that are given as input and the other column which contains the terms that are occurring in each document.

Term frequency (TF): This node calculates the relative term frequency of each term in each document. TF is calculated by dividing the absolute frequency of a term occurring in a document by the sum total of all the terms that are present in that document.

Tags to string (TS): This node determines the nature of sentiments present in each document based on the calculated TF and assigns tags to the document based on the number of positive and negative words that is present in the document.

Document scoring: This node assigns a score to the document based on the comparison of the number of positive and negative words which is present in the document.

User scoring: This node assigns a score to each user based on the positive and negative words used by a user in each document.

13.7 Network Analysis on Social Media Data

Network analysis of social media data which is one of the prominent predictive analytic techniques represents the social media relationships in terms of network theory. The main components of the network are nodes which depict actors within the network and links between the nodes which depict relationships between the individuals, such as Facebook friendships, followers, responses, and so on. Network analysis is a widespread technique which has diverse applications in almost all business domains and it delivers a wealth of invaluable data about various parameters which can be used to boost business.

Let us take an example of how a sample output of network analysis in a retail outlet and how it can be used by the retail organization to boost its business.

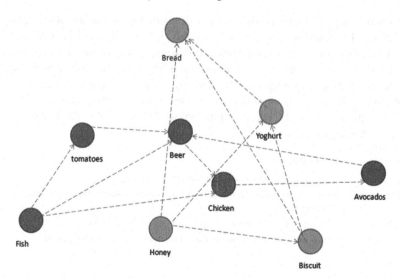

In the above network diagram, the colored circles denote the products which are purchased together and the connector lines denote the number of transactions.

How can the retail organization derive benefits using this output?

Retail organizations can predict the sales of individual products and also predict buying patterns of customers which can be used to devise promotional offers on specific products with less sales, reduce the rate of certain items to boost their sales, and change the shelf arrangement of products in the outlet in such a way that certain groups/combinations of products can sell better.

13.7.1 Getting Started with Network Analysis of Social Media Data

What are the leading sources of social media data for performing network analysis? The leading sources are listed below:

Network maps of social media data provide useful insights of social media topics which may be of importance for each individual. Network maps provide an easy way to analyze the social communication structure which has evolved around specific topics which were discussed in social media networks. Network maps also provide an easy way to interpret different ways in which groups in specific social media networks use URLs, hashtags, words, @usernames, and phrases.

Following are some of the key terminologies used in social media in the context of network analysis: [1]

Term	Explanation
Degree	How many people can reach this person directly?
Betweenness	How likely is this person to be the most direct route between two people in the network?
Closeness	How fast can this person reach everyone in the network?
Eigenvector	How well is this person connected to other well-connected people?

13.7.2   Network Analysis Using Twitter

One of the most important use cases of network analysis is to mine social media data which is generated in Twitter. Network analysis is done on Twitter data to measure the conversations about the following aspects:

- About a specific hashtag
- Twitter account
- Brand
- Public policy and so on

There are six basic types of Twitter social network analysis maps. They are: [1]

- Polarized network map: Two dense clusters with little interconnection
- In group: Few disconnected isolates with many connections between them
- Brand/public topic: Many disconnected isolates and some small groups
- Bazaar: Many medium-sized groups, some isolates
- Broadcast: A hub which is retweeted by many disconnected users
- Support: A hub which replies to many disconnected users

13.7.3   Polarized Network Map

These types of network maps are formed commonly during the discussion of political issues. One important point to be noted is that these types of maps are formed . due to huge difference in opinion which exists among multiple groups with regard to their opinion on any specific issue.

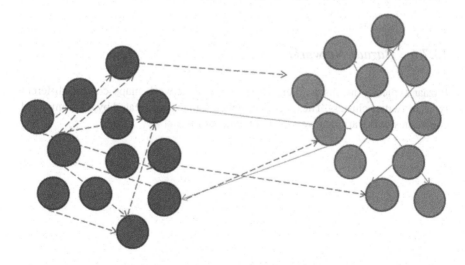

13.7.4   In-Group Map

These types of maps are often seen to evolve at conference groups and during communications among tightly knit groups of people who may be a part of a group or community. The speciality of this type of map is that the members of a network do not venture outside their membership. From a marketing perspective, these types of maps are useful to track conversations about technical products over Twitter. This map gives flexibility to the organizations to create hashtags for their products and then use the hashtags to track conversations and follow comments about those products with the help of twitter maps. In short, these types of maps are very useful and a must to have for specific organizations/brands which have technical products in their arena.

13.7.5   The Twitter Brand Map

These types of Twitter maps provide very good visualization and data interpretation capabilities. The following are some of the features offered by these types of maps:

- Track conversations about a specific brand
- Track major influencers and connectors for a brand/product (a connector is a social media user who has the capability to create a large number of followers/conversations)

It gives options for organizations to contact the connectors for their feedback and also makes an attempt to try and use their feedback about a missing feature/functionality in the next release of their product.

13.7.6   Bazaar Networks

Bazaar typically means market. These types of network maps contain different types of twitter clusters. These types of network maps are created by medium-sized companies with various levels of involvement of users.

13.7.7   Broadcast Map

These kinds of maps are typically dominated by specific individuals/groups. These specific individuals could belong to the category of *most influential people/group*. These individuals or groups like football teams, cricket teams, and so on can measure their brand value based on their broadcast maps.

13.7.8   Support Network Maps

These types of maps are used by some organizations for providing customer support service using social media networks. These categories of maps are the rarest among the different types of network maps.

> **Dell's Social Media Listening Command Center**
> Dell operates under the philosophy that "Everyone is listening" and created a social media listening command center in December 2010. While Dell is organized in the holistic model for social media, it uses a hybrid holistic/coordinated model for listening. The goal is to embrace social media as an organization and as an integral part of the workday, while supporting all employees with social media "air cover." While the social media listening command center includes a ground control team, it is not the only location in which employees listen. A significant number of the more than 100,000 Dell employees—beyond the command center and social media team—listen to social channels as part of their daily responsibilities.

13.8   Different Dimensions of Social Media Analytics for Organizations

Organizations can utilize social media analytics in various ways in order to derive business benefits. The various possible use cases for social media analytics are given in the diagram which is given below:

Brand advocacy and health management: Nowadays, organizations focus a lot on brand value and are continuously on the lookout for steps to enhance brand value. Social media contains valuable information which will help organizations to keep track of their brand value in the market. Some Twitter mechanisms to track brand value were discussed in the previous section on network analysis. Brand health tracking and monitoring typically involves tracking social media conversations about specific organizations/products using specific keywords and hashtags.

The following are some of the business benefits which brand health monitoring can offer to organizations:

- Capability to track and monitor the region or location which has maximum brand penetration and design product launch or pilot accordingly.
- Assess the strength of a specific brand versus similar brands by competitors.
- Understand highest performing brands in specific domains.
- Track and maintain a database of influencers of specific brands.

- Analyze the sentiment of people towards a specific brand (this is measured by means of the number of likes or positive comments).

One of the key parameters which is used for determining the brand loyalty of customers is the Net Promoter Score. The fundamental assumption behind the Net Promoter Score is that all the customers can be grouped in one of the following three categories:

- Promoters
- Passives
- Detractors

Promoters   These are the category of customers who are supposed to be most loyal to an organization's brand. They typically have a score of 9 or 10 in a 10-point scale. Promoters are considered to be very important for fuelling the growth of an organization's brand. Organizations should take steps to retain them at any cost.

Passives   These are the category of satisfied customers. However, they are always susceptible to be carried away by a competitor's brand. They generally have a score of 7–8 in a 10-point scale. Organizations should handle this category of customers carefully and should try to retain them by providing them customized discount offers and prepackaged deals which will keep them away from competitor brands.

Detractors   These are the category of unsatisfied customers. It can also be predicted that they could even propagate negative aspects about a specific brand. They have a score of 0–6 in a 10-point scale. Organizations should take special care about this category of customers. They should try to understand the reason for the dissatisfaction of these customers and take appropriate steps to correct them; otherwise, this category of customers could turn out to be a major threat for the organization's brand value.

The Net Promoter Score can be calculated in several ways like tracking the likes and positive comments about a brand and number of followers of a brand and by hosting surveys.

Optimize Marketing Communication Programs   Present-day organizations invest heavily on marketing communication programs and other marketing campaigns. So it is very important for them to assess and understand the effectiveness of their marketing campaign so that they focus more on one particular mode of campaign instead of investing in all different forms of campaigns. Social media responses and surveys can be used as a very effective tool to track the effectiveness of campaigns.

In addition to using the social media to measure the effectiveness of marketing campaigns, social media itself can be used as a medium for marketing communication programs. This concept which is gaining a lot of popularity nowadays is called social marketing. A concept which is very prominent in the context of social marketing is engagement analysis. Engagement analysis helps to measure the impact of marketing campaigns on different social media platforms. The various steps in engagement analysis are summarized in the diagram which is given below:

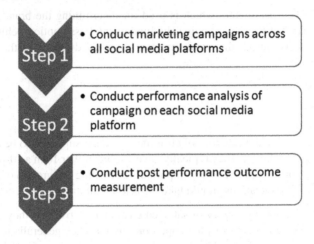

Following are some of the applications of engagement analysis in business:

- Monitor and track people who liked the content used in the marketing campaign.
- Analyze the sentiments of people towards the campaign and the product which was marketed in the campaign.
- Track the effectiveness of the campaign.
- Understand appropriate time of the year/month/day to host promotional campaigns for different types of products.
- Analyze the most effective type of campaign for each geographical region.

13.8.1 Revenue and Sales Lead Generation

Social media cannot be directly used for generating revenues. However, they can be used as a means for lead generation and conversion. In order to achieve complete success in this process, it is important to understand the importance of social media in the buying process of the customers and then tune it to influence the customers towards a specific brand/product.

It is often a tough task to quantify the impact of social media on the lead generation process and to track the number of leads which are generated using social media. One high-level formula which could be used to track lead generation using social media is given below:

Lead generation effectiveness of social media = number of leads generated using social media/total number of leads

Another metric which is very useful in measuring lead generation effectiveness is content-to-contact ratio.

Some specific applications of this use case are the following:

- Track leads which are generated by each social media channel
- Track lead conversions using each social media channel
- Track impact of social media marketing on search results and search engine optimization
- Assess impact of social media marketing on customer loyalty

13.8.2 Customer Relationship and Customer Experience Management

Customer experience management which in turn forms the foundation of customer relationship management has heavy dependency on social media networks. Social media can create long-lasting impact in managing customer experience which in turn can provide a lot of benefits to organizations in terms of enhancing its brand value.

There could be different levels of expectations from customers while using different types of social media channels of organizations. For example, when it comes to specific channels like technical communities or forums, customers are willing to share their concerns and sort them out using the inputs of other members of the community.

Following are some of the use cases of customer experience management for organizations:

- Monitor the intensity of specific product features/issues.
- Assess the weak points in terms of customer relationship management for an organization.
- Monitor the time taken by organization to respond to the concerns of the customers which are expressed through social media.

13.8.3 Innovation

It has become a trend nowadays for many organizations to use communities and websites to collect crowd sources and innovative product feature ideas and product ideas. One prominent example of this organizational behavior is the website which is maintained by Starbucks (http://mystarbucksidea.force.com). But some organizations which do not have the capability to maintain such dedicated websites for innovative idea collection resort to the usage of social media websites to collect innovative product ideas and product feature ideas pertaining to their domain. But for collection of such innovative ideas from social media, it is important for organizations to constantly listen to social media networks using social media listening tools and platforms. We will discuss more about social media tools and listening platforms in the next section.

13.9   Social Media Tools

Some of the leading social media tools are discussed in this section. Social media tools can be broadly classified into two categories:

Social media monitoring/listening tools
Social media analytics tools

13.9.1   Social Media Monitoring Tools

These tools mainly use text analytics to refer to usage of specific terms in selected social media networks and other forums. Most of the social media listening tools listen to words/phrases and track and report them. In most of the cases, these tools provide just monitoring capabilities and they do not have the features which are required to support robust social media analytics using the data generated from social media networks. Some examples of social media listening tools are discussed below:

Hootsuite: This is a very popular social media listening tool which can monitor multiple social media networks like Twitter, Facebook, LinkedIn, WordPress, Foursquare, and Google+. This tool has the capability to manage online brands and submit messages to social media services which are offered by Twitter, Facebook, LinkedIn, WordPress, Foursquare, and Google+. This tool also provides limited social media analytical capabilities by generating weekly analytical reports.

TweetReach: This tool has the capability to assess the impact and implications of tweets by measuring how far the tweets travel. It has features that help to track the most influential followers of a specific organization/brand. These influential followers can be used at later stages as brand ambassadors to promote and propagate specific brands.

Klout: This tool measures the impact or influence created in social media by a specific brand or person and then assigns a score called Klout score based on the amount of influence created. Influence in this context refers to the response of the people towards the content which is posted in social media networks and other online forums, the number of followers for the social media content, and so on.

Social Mention: This is a free social media listening tool and monitors more than a hundred social media sites. This tool has the capability to analyze data from social media sites in four different dimensions:

- Strength
- Sentiment
- Passion
- Reach

HowSociable: This tool measures a brand's social media presence and also has the feature to compare it with a competitor brand's social media presence. There are two types of account options which are offered by this tool:

- Free account: With a free account, it is possible to track 1
- 2 social media sites.
- Paid account: With a paid account, it is possible to track 24 additional websites.

This tool also has the capability to assign scores for a brand based on the brand's responses on different social media platforms. This will provide insights to the organization on which social media platform is the best for brand advocacy.

13.9.2 Social Media Analytics Tools

Social media analytics tools have the capability to measure the baseline social media parameters and provide deep analytical insights and patterns. Patterns are predicted for present and future scenarios. These predictions sometimes are made available as reports. In short, the main differentiating factor of the social media analytics tool is the ability to apply analytics to social media data for deep insights. Some of the major players in the market are Insight by Adobe, Radian 6 by Salesforce, Cognos Consumer Insights by IBM, and Brandwatch.

13.10 Conclusions

In this chapter, the importance of social media analytics and the key drivers for the proliferation of social media analytics was discussed. The different use cases of social media analytics for present-day organizations were also discussed at length in the first section of this chapter. One new variant of social media analytics called sentiment analysis is gaining a lot of prominence nowadays. The various aspects of sentiment analysis were also discussed in this chapter. The second section of this chapter focuses on the various tools which are available to perform social media analytics.

13.11   Exercises

1. Explain the different dimensions of social media analytics.
2. Explain different types of social media content metrics with examples.
3. Describe the different use cases of social media analytics for organizations.
4. Write a short note on social media analytical tools.
5. Explain the concept of network analysis in the context of social media analysis.

Reference

1. 75 percent of Retail Associates Report Latest Mobile Technology Leads to Better Customer Experience, Motorola Solutions Survey (2011) Motorola Solutions, Inc., Dec 20, 2011

Chapter 14
Big Data Analytics for Healthcare

14.1 Introduction

There is a lot of data in the world today and one of the sectors contributing to this huge data is healthcare.

Data is growing at an uncontrollable rate. Making effective use of data is very important and analytics is required for the same. Data analytics is not something new; it has been practiced for a very long time even before the right use of analytics was known to people. With the advances in technology and the change in medical practices, the way people see data has transformed. Analytics has changed the way healthcare is practiced altogether, giving a new meaning to health. Large population, increase in unhealthy population, technology innovations, and evidence-based medicine approaches are some of the sources contributing to huge data that the world has ever seen. Big data is discovering bigger opportunities in the field of healthcare. Getting value from the vast amount of data is the expected job from big data analytics. Turning data into useful insights is big data analytics. The below figure shows the various sources contributing to the huge volume of data in healthcare (Fig. 14.1).

Another biggest challenge of healthcare is about looking into ways on how data can be processed in an efficient and secure manner. Big data analytics has different dimensions in healthcare—making use of the so-called "big" data into useful insights, improving healthcare to provide better care to patients, using high-performance computing for healthcare, and reducing healthcare cost.

In this chapter, we will talk about big data in healthcare, the challenges involved, benefits of big data analytics, and the need for high-performance computing in healthcare. There are few interesting activities. So enjoy reading this space!

Activity Section
Let's begin with a fun activity!

© Springer International Publishing Switzerland 2015
P. Raj et al., *High-Performance Big-Data Analytics*, Computer Communications and Networks, DOI 10.1007/978-3-319-20744-5_14

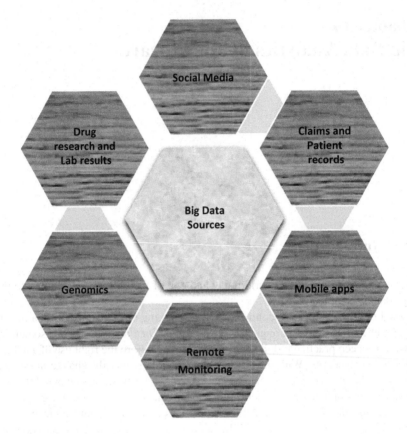

Fig. 14.1 Big data sources

Activity No. 1 :

Take a chart and draw a tree with many branches, each having leaves and fruits.

Now on each branch, specify one source which contributes healthcare data, mark the leaves with the devices which transmit data from that particular source, and mark the fruits which the data coming out of the devices. Name the tree trunk as big datasources (Fig. 14.2).

Example of a source can be home monitoring (have this in a branch), where devices can be sensors (write in on a leaf coming from the same branch) and the data coming from the sensors can be blood glucose, blood pressure, weight, etc. (write this on a fruit from that particular branch).

Fill up the tree with details like this. Try to identify as many healthcare sources that can be possible.

Pictorial representation makes the data capture more lively and it is easy to understand the same.

Fig. 14.2 Big data sources

14.2   Market Factors Affecting Healthcare

There are a lot of market factors influencing healthcare. The significant rise in aged population, growing lifestyle-related health problems, and chronic illness have opened the door for a lot of healthcare opportunities (Fig. 14.3).

With increase in patients visiting hospitals, there is a rise in competition between consumers offering various health solutions. Increased healthcare costs are urging for better reimbursement policies. Healthcare is looking forward for a more integrated delivery system where providers and suppliers go hand in hand.

Technology-based approaches are looked into as a hope for business development in the healthcare sector. The healthcare industry is going mobile with a lot of doctors and nurses using mobile devices to keep pace with their patients and also with the advances in medical practices.

Innovation is the key to growth. Health organizations have to look for innovative solutions that will help reduce cost and provide better quality care to its members thereby increasing transparency.

With all these new changes coming in, how is the healthcare industry going to sustain its quality and lower its costs? That is where big data analytics is seen as a ray of hope.

> **Did You Know?**
> *There is a lot of data in the world and 90 % of the world's data has come in the last two years.*
>   *The volume of medical data doubles every five years.*
>   *81 % of physicians can't even spare 5 hours per month to keep up with the growing data.*
>   *By 2020, doctors will face 200× the amount of medical data and facts that a human could possibly process.*
>   Source: http://www-03.ibm.com/systems/in/power/solutions/watson/

Fig. 14.3 Market factors driving healthcare

14.3 Different Shareholders Envisaging Different Objectives

Different shareholders have different objectives and hopes for big data analytics:

- *Providers* are looking forward for big data analytics to help them take better informed decisions. They want technology to be a great support of help to improve quality care to their patients. For big data analytics to work, providers need real-time access to patient medical records and other clinical data. Big data can help providers take decisions based on an evidence-based approach.

- *Patients* want technology to be an enhancer in their day-to-day routine. They are looking for healthcare that is simple to understand, user friendly, and a one-stop shop and has better care coordination between the patients, providers, and health organizations.
- *Pharmaceutical companies* want to better understand the disease causes and get the right patient to perform the clinical trial. They are looking for more successful clinical trials that will help them market safer and also help them to set up more effective pharmaceuticals.
- *Payers* are moving from to a new business model from fee for service to pay for performance. They are looking into big data as an opportunity that will help them choose a better business model which will include wellness management and other data analytics.
- *Medical device* companies are collecting data from various medical sources like sensors that collect data about patients at regular intervals thereby ensuring prediction of problems at an early stage. But the main concern of these companies is what should be done with this huge data that is getting collected every day as there are large investments that go in storing the data.
- *Researchers* are looking for new tools that will help them improve the outcome of experiments with the help of new tools. It will provide a better insight of developing new treatment solutions that would successfully meet the regulatory approvals and market process.
- *Government* is looking forward to reduce healthcare costs by mandating laws that will ensure everyone is provided with better quality healthcare. There is a lot of burden on the government to provide patient-centric care that is best in quality and also ensured low cost.
- *IT team* is hoping for better opportunities to serve the new market that is huge and growing constantly. The software development team is pretty excited as innovation is the key here and everyone is looking for innovative products that respond quicker to the massive amount of data and new technology improvements.

14.4 Big Data Benefits to Healthcare

By effectively using big data, there are a lot of advantages that can be benefitted to health organizations that range from single provider organization to multi-provider organization, large hospital providers, and care organizations. The benefits include but are not limited to improving the efficiency and quality of healthcare delivery, managing specific health population and individuals, detecting diseases at an early stage, providing evidence-based treatment options to patients, and detecting early fraud in the healthcare system. Some of the big data benefits includes:

Big Data Benefits
Healthcare efficiency and quality
Earlier disease detection
Fraud detection
Population health management

14.4.1 Healthcare Efficiency and Quality

Healthcare costs are rising exponentially where members are not able to cope up with the sudden rise in costs. One of the top priorities for health organizations is to bring down costs in order to have a satisfied member experience for the patients. On the other hand, chronic diseases like diabetes are growing at a rate that is uncontrollable. This is a reason why a great percentage of health resources are getting utilized thereby increasing cost.

The implementation of electronic health records (EHRs) along with good big data analytical tools will open the door for a lot of opportunities for health members (Fig. 14.4).

The below is an example of how data flows in an EHR-centric world where patient care is of utmost importance, thereby improving efficiency and healthcare quality.

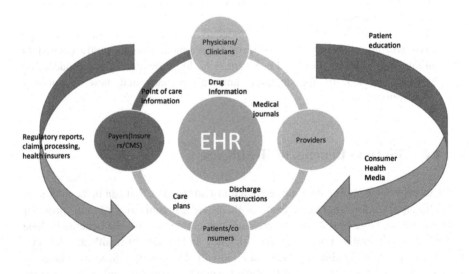

Fig. 14.4 Market factors driving Healthcare

14.4.2 Earlier Disease Detection

Today, there are a lot of sensors that are used to track patients' daily routine checks where change in blood pressure, in blood glucose, and in heartbeat rate can be transmitted to a clinician's office for a patient resting at home. There is a lot of data that is hoarded by these types of sensors.

A lot of researches have come up in this area where the data transmitted from these devices can be used for early detection of diseases thereby saving lives. Analytics can also be used to detect side effects from medicine and any development of allergy or infections.

This kind of remote sensing surprises the patient about the care that he is provided from the health organization thereby delivering quality care to patients.

14.4.3 Fraud Detection

Big data is expected to change the claim payment systems where there is manual verification of claims that are paid under the traditional fee-for-service method. Using big data tools and techniques, the manual process can be transformed, thereby preventing wrong claims being keyed in the system. Big data analytics can help detect fraud thereby improving the quality of the US healthcare system (Fig. 14.5).

The above is a typical fraud model where claims come from input systems like outpatient, pharmacy, hospital, etc. The validity of the claims has been justified

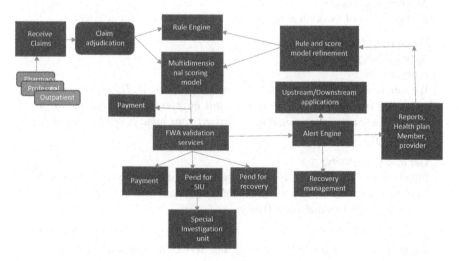

Fig. 14.5 Fraud detection

by predefined rules in the rule engine. The valid claims are pushed to payment. The claims which are incorrect or suspended in the first step of validation are sent for further investigation. The information is also sent to the alert engine along with the specific reasons for claim being suspected. The suspected claims are further sent to the first step of validation where processing happens and new formulas and trends are calculated based on data analytics which is used for refinement of the rule engine which keeps evolving with every new data entered. These details can be used to make smarter decisions about the amount financial risk due to fraud and error.

14.4.4   Population Health Management

With influential big data tools and techniques, big data analytics can be applied to population health management. Chronic diseases like diabetes, heart disease, cancer, stroke, and arthritis are among the most common diseases. There are a lot of people's deaths that are recorded due to these chronic diseases. Big data analytics will help physicians take informed decisions in preventing this disease occurrence. Regular health checkups for population where these chronic diseases are common would help detect the diseases earlier and prevent them. Also focusing on wellness programs also helps to educate people on the importance of having a healthy lifestyle (Fig. 14.6).

Activity Section
It's been a lot of theoretical study; now let's get into a small activity.

Population Health Management
Activity No. 2 :
Introduction:
We saw few areas wherebig dataanalytics can be used. These are only few areas that are focused. You all reading this have experienced the healthcare system, and many ideas would have crossed your mind about the use of big data analytics.

Get into the activity:
Identify other areas wherebig dataanalytics can be used in healthcare. Jot the same as points and also show a pictorial representation of the same. The same can be done on a board using Post-its.

Tip:
Think of ideas that relate to one particular service area of healthcare.
Example: provider, patient, pharmaceutical companies, etc.

Fig. 14.6 Population
health management

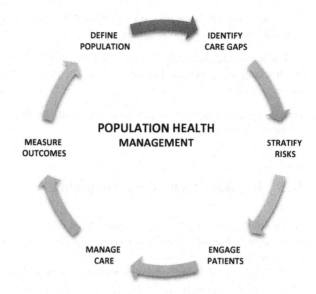

Example Idea Here's a small example just for you!

Whenever you visit a provider for a particular symptom, the provider analyzes your symptom and gives a prescription for the same. A lot of prescription details lie in the patient database. With this huge data of symptoms and prescriptions, can we do something? Yes, big data analytics is about bringing value from data that you feel might not be useful at all.

14.4.4.1 Big Data Idea

Load all the symptoms and their corresponding prescription data into a database for a particular hospital network. Compare the symptoms and see if there are similar symptoms. If you find similar symptoms, do the ones below:

- Analyze the medication that is given by different physicians for the same symptom.
- If the medications are the same, check the dosage of the medicine given. This can actually help identify overdosage or underdosage for a particular medicine.
- Less dosage can be a reason for readmission of the patient. On the other hand, overdosage can be a risk.
- Approach the physicians and question them about the dosage level and the reason for giving the same.
- Another perspective is, if different physicians have given different medications for the same medicine, do an analysis on why this is done.

- Propose a medication plan for physicians which will help them choose the best medicine which is high in quality and low in cost.

The above idea has helped reduce readmission by tracking the medicine dosage and tracking any problems before hand and helped provide high-quality medicines to the patients.

This is just an example, and similar to this, you can bring in good ideas that favor the use of big data analytics.

14.5 Big Data Technology Adoptions: A New Amelioration!

Technology is often called the enabler; on the other hand, technology is the barrier. In the area of big data analytics, technology has seen to be an enabler opening up new road maps for innovation.

The advent of information technology solutions such as electronic health records, where we are moving from the era of hard copies to data digitalization, and clinical decision support systems is driving the adoption of clinical and business intelligence applications.

Today, there are a lot of amazingly new technology solutions that healthcare is seeing which is looked as a sunshine in a dark cold place.

Let's look at few of the technology enablers that are used in the healthcare industry.

14.5.1 IBM Watson

After many decades of programmatic computing, finally we are in an epoch where a machine can understand human speech and respond back to questions by digesting voluminous amount of data and has the capability to learn and think from its experiences. It is a game-changing machine which can do things we never ever thought. IBM Watson was introduced to this world through the quiz show Jeopardy. IBM Watson defeated Jeopardy's all-time champions! From then on, Watson has evolved from a quiz show winner to an innovation system capable of providing best cognitive solutions.

To summarize:

- IBM Watson is a *supercomputer* which can answer questions put up in natural language.
- Watson can read *unstructured data* and also support *open domain questions.*
- Watson can process data at the *rate of 80 teraflops* which is equal to trillion floating point operations per second.
- Watson can access over *200 million pages of information.*

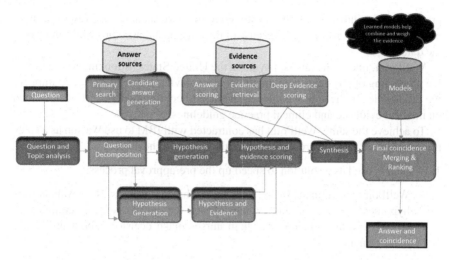

Fig. 14.7 IBM Watson architecture

14.5.2 IBM Watson Architecture (Fig. 14.7)

Watson works on the principle that uses deep content analysis and evidence-based reasoning. It uses advanced natural language processing, analysis and information retrieval, automated reasoning, and machine learning using parallel hypothesis generation. It is not about asking a question and getting an answer; rather it is a system that performs diagnosis by generating a wide range of possibilities with a confidence level attached to the answers. The confidence level is achieved by gathering, analyzing, and assessing evidence based on available data.

For each question or a case, Watson first builds a representation of the user's information needs and through search generates many possible responses. For each possible find, Watson looks into independent threads that combine different types of answers from structured and unstructured sources. It delivers a set of possible answers ranked based on evidence profile describing the supporting evidence.

14.6 Watson in Healthcare

14.6.1 WellPoint and IBM

According to the Institute of Medicine, 30 % of the amount spent annually on healthcare in the United States is wasted. While there are so many reasons for the same, one of the major reasons is utilization management (UM). The UM process takes care of the pre-approval process of health insurance coverage for any medical procedure. The industry has always strived to improve accuracy and response time, but this has been a difficult task because of the huge data that comes while analyzing the data.

WellPoint, one of the largest payers in the United States, is looking to accelerate the processing of physician's treatment requests, saving members' time and improving efficiencies in the approval process while still continuing to take UM decisions on medical evidence and clinical practice guidelines.

To achieve the same, WellPoint has contracted with IBM to use Watson as a solution to improve patient care and improve the quality of healthcare:

1. Watson is used as a solution to speed up the pre-approval process.

   – WellPoint has trained Watson with 18,000 historical cases. Now Watson uses hypothesis generation and evidence-based learning to generate confidence-scored recommendations that help nurses make decisions about utilization management.

2. Watson is helping physicians take informed decisions using an evidence-based approach.

   – Watson is used in Sloan Kettering Cancer Center.
     Here Watson is helping an oncologist to take informed decisions and identify the best treatment options for cancer patients.

14.7 EHR Technology

An EHR refers to as electronic health record. An EHR is a systematic collection of health records for a particular patient or population.

The advantage of EHR is that it is in digital format and can be shared across various other healthcare centers.

EHR may include a variety of data that includes demographics, medical history, laboratory data, radiology images, vital signs, and personal data of a patient like height, age, weight, and billing information.

EHR technology is designed in such a way to capture accurate data about a patient at any point in time. It allows the entire patient history to be viewed for any medical purpose.

Shown below is a typical diagram showing how data flows in an EHR. Please follow the diagram for stepwise details on the same.

Did You Know?
Artificial intelligence is not something new to IBM. IBM has its own history of artificial intelligence starting with Arthur Samuel's checkers players in the 1950s and the Deep Blue chess computer (1990s), and now we have Watson!

14.7.1   EHR Data Flow (Fig. 14.8)

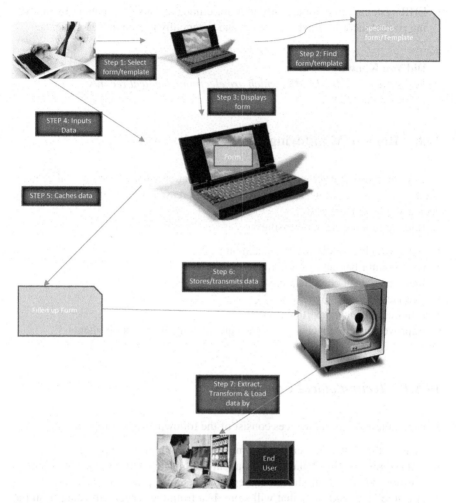

Fig. 14.8 EHR data flow

14.7.2   Advantages of EHR

- It requires significantly less space compared to paper-based records.
- The patient information is available at a single place which makes data retrieval very easy.
- EHR improves overall efficiency.
- EHR data can be used for statistical reporting in areas of quality improvement, resource management, etc.

- EHR data enables information to be used and shared over secure networks.
- EHR data can be read on any workstation and also mobile devices
- EHR systems can automatically monitor clinical events for a patient by analyzing patient records which can detect and potentially prevent adverse events.

Did You Know?
EHRs are also called EMRs which are electronic medical records.

14.8   Remote Monitoring and Sensing

Remote monitoring refers to the monitoring of patients outside of clinical centers, maybe at home. Remote monitoring allows increased access to patient care by decreasing healthcare costs.

Remote monitoring and sensing:

- Improves chronic disease management
- Can monitor patient reaction to medicines
- Reduce medical complications
- Reduce inpatient stays
- Limit emergency department visits
- Improves the effectiveness of home care and outpatient appointments

14.8.1   Technological Components

Most remote monitoring devices consist of the following four components:

- Sensors that is wireless enabled to measure physiological parameters
- Data storage at a local place at the patient's site which will interface between the sensors and other centralized data repository and the provider destination
- A centralized repository that will store data from the sensors, the data from the local storage, and data from the provider destination
- Diagnostic application which creates the treatment recommendation and other alerts to keep the patient in pace with what is happening with respect to his/her health

The sensors that are installed depend on the patient's problem. It might vary for different patients (Fig. 14.9).

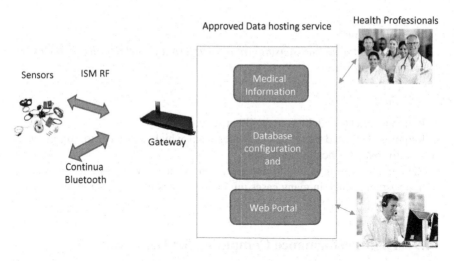

Fig. 14.9 Remote monitoring and sensing

14.8.2   Healthcare Areas Where Remote Monitoring Is Applied

- Diabetes: To manage diabetes control for a patient, the data required would be blood pressure, weight, and blood glucose. The real-time data of blood glucose and blood pressure will help create alerts for patients and healthcare providers to intervene when required. This has proven very effective in many cases.
- Heart failure: There are a lot of medical devices with sensors available to monitor heartbeat rate and the functioning of the heart. The home monitoring of heart failure patients has helped to improve their quality of life and provider-patient relationship, reduced stays in hospitals, and reduced healthcare cost.
- Dementia: For patients with dementia who are at a great risk to fall, sensors are installed to the individual or to their mobility devices like walkers and canes. The sensors usually monitor patient's location, gait, linear acceleration, and angular velocity and utilize a mathematical algorithm that would predict the likelihood for falls and alert the caregivers if the individual has fallen.
- Infertility: There are a lot of sensing devices that are used to monitor infertility in many patients who have chosen the in vitro fertilization (IVF) treatment, and this can prove effective in many cases.

14.8.3   Limitations of Remote Monitoring

- Remote monitoring is dependent on the individual interest to be monitored.
- Cost is a barrier for remote monitoring as the devices and peripherals are expensive.

> **Did You Know?**
> *Remote monitoring and sensing are often referred as RPM which is remote patient monitoring.*

- Reimbursement guidelines are still not set properly.
- Requires dedicated healthcare provider team which will have to continuously monitor patient's health condition.
- Remote monitoring is highly dependent on extensive wireless telecommunication systems which in many cases might not be feasible to install in rural areas.

14.9   High-Performance Computing for Healthcare

Researches around the globe are not only finding solutions to cure a patient but are looking to improve the diagnosis and treatment methods with different big data tools.

One such method is using high-performance computing techniques which can improve the quality of life for those having medical problems and also improve patient experience during diagnosis and treatments. High-performance computing is all about parallel processing where the data can be processed faster in a limited amount of time.

High-performance computing techniques are looked upon a new innovation driving platform which can reduce healthcare costs.

Let's now look at few areas where high-performance computing is used in healthcare.

14.10   Real-Time Analysis of Human Brain Networks

An important tool that is used in the diagnosis of neural disorders is functional magnetic resonance imaging (fMRI). But fMRI is an expensive option and it takes almost a week for the data to be analyzed. The current process requires multiple scan to be taken to achieve proper results.

The use of high-performance computing may result in achieving faster results, more accurate diagnosis, better outputs, and use of less expensive scanner time. The brain scanning through HPC allows the test to be intervened and it can be adjusted as required while the scanning is in progress. This potential has allowed diagnosing various brain disorders that include schizophrenia, autism, Alzheimer's, and ADHD. High-performance computing helps the analysis process to be automated in such a way that the analysis can be broken down into simple models.

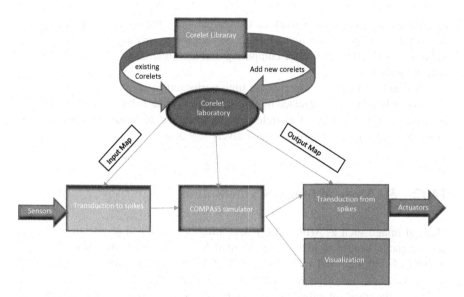

Fig. 14.10 Real time analytics of human brain networks

Described below is an architecture showing the process of developing neural networks that can process and respond to sensor input (Fig. 14.10).

The above consists of:

1. Spiking (digital) neuron-type circuit.
2. SDK—programmatic units of the fundamental units, map unit interactions, and maps I/O to network.
3. Simulator to predict what your neural network code will do.
4. Example library—holds premade corelet examples; real-time actuator and sensor examples are included.

The above example uses cognitive computing by utilizing less space and power but yielding faster results.

14.11   Detection of Cancer

Cancer rates are increasing globally. Various researchers are putting a lot of potential to find medicines that would cure and also prevent cancer occurring in the society. Major cancer includes lung cancer and head and neck cancers.

A lot of analysis goes in to develop algorithms that would identify common signatures in cancer, the advancement in diagnosis, the course of the medical condition, and treatment capabilities.

High-performance computing helps verify if the cancer drugs used on patients are really working or not. For example, patient's genetic conditions are analyzed to determine what drugs really work on the patient and what do not work. Such kind of analysis is not possible with traditional computing, comparing the data that needs to be analyzed. HPC aids faster computing and less time taken for analyzing huge volume of data.

Also another field in cancer where high-performance computing is used is for leukemia where drugs are created by examining molecular behavior. HPC platforms are used for the selection of modules for the treatment of leukemia. This enables faster drug development with a comparatively less cost.

14.12   3D Medical Image Segmentation

Medical image such as MIR and CT scan images has helped physicians examine and diagnose health problems at a detailed level. But the barrier was the huge amount of data that had to be processed. A lot of high-performance computing architectures are now used to treat the huge volume of data.

One of the most important advancement that is seen today is the emergence of 3D images. The advantage of the same being, data can be viewed at various dimensions to bring out accurate health decisions. This has resulted in a huge amount of data that is transmitted. Therefore, processing huge data brings down the execution time from several hours to a few minutes. Now researchers are coming up with solutions of parallel processing that would deliver faster output in a limited amount of time.

Did You Know?
Intel collaborates with companies to drive high-performance computing that dramatically lowers the cost and shortens the DNA sequencing and indexing time so researchers can advance the fight against cancer and other difficult problems.
99.5 % of genome data has been generated in the last 5 years.
  Source:http://www.intel.com/content/www/us/en/healthcare-it/computing-for-next-generation-of-medical-therapies-video.html

14.13   New Medical Therapies

High-performance computing is used for the next generation of medical therapies. Predictive sciences and modulation and simulation will be a key part of the next generation. Genomics is the most researched topic today. Previously, we were not able to see the DNA data in our human body, but today it's all possible. A single cell in a human body has 6 gigabytes of data and 100 trillion base pairs in the human body which is 14 times of 6 gigabytes. Therefore, a massive amount of computer power is required to analyze and diagnose the data.

Fig. 14.11 Big data use cases

Personalized medicines are incredibly difficult to understand. Use of genomics profile to bring in possible therapy that would treat us now or would treat us in the next 20 years is very important. And all this requires parallel processing using high-performance computing that can help analyze data at a much faster rate.

14.14   Use Cases for BDA in Healthcare

There are a lot of use cases that can be quoted for big data analytics. The below figure shows some of the use cases for BDA (Fig. 14.11).

We will see in detail a few use cases of big data in healthcare.

14.15   Population Health Control

Provided below is one approach for population health control in which big data tools and techniques can be used (Fig. 14.12).

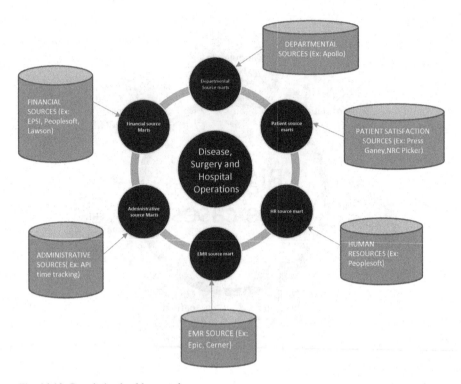

Fig. 14.12 Population health control

Steps to be followed to maintain population health control:

1. Load all critical data that is required for analysis.
2. Analyze data and segregate data that are really important especially those which consume high resource and are considered opportunities for improvement.
3. Once the data of focus is decided, the next step is to discover the right patient population using analytical applications that define population using a variety of administrative and clinical criteria.

14.16 Care Process Management

Given below is one of IBM's care process management which meets the needs of clinics, hospitals, and accountable care organizations for evidence-based medicine. The CPM architecture can be even deployed in state, provincial, or government level (Fig. 14.13).

The CPM reference architecture has the following key value propositions:

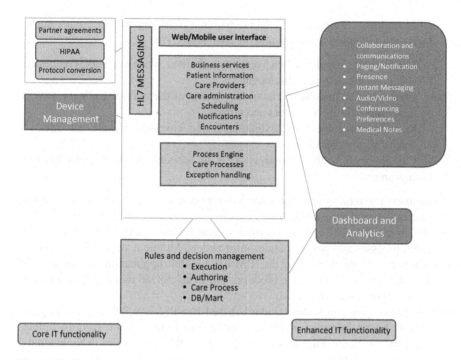

Fig. 14.13 Care process management

- Has flexibility to provide core and enhanced IT functionality
- Follows architectural best practices for separation of user, business, and information concerns
- Is based on established reference architectures that embrace the intersection of SOA, BPM, and decision management
- Is secured

    - Integrates with enterprise directory and security infrastructure
    - Provides role-based access customizable to enterprise roles

14.16.1   Core IT Functionality

While CPM can be implemented using a broad portfolio of IT services, just four functional components are needed to provide the minimum required IT functionality. Additional services (plus security) can be layered into the solution as requirements evolve:

- *BPM engine*—care processes execute within a BPM engine. The engine implements the following functions that are critical to CPM:

    – Notifies care providers when a patient is admitted, when a consult is requested, and when the patient is discharged
    – Creates and maintains an electronic version of the multidisciplinary activity plan on behalf of the doctors and nurses
    – Manages assignments, reassignments, and coverage of care activities on behalf of care providers
    – Can integrate with external systems to schedule medical procedures or equipment

- *Business services*—implements services for access to CPM functions by the user interface and by external applications.
- *Web or mobileuser interface*—provides a way for care providers to participate in care processes and access patient information. Mobile access from iPads® or tablets can be provided using the IBM BPM mobile application. However, BPM also supports Safari® mobile browsers and a customized user experience can be implemented using Dojo.
- *HL7 messaging*—provides standards-based Health Level 7 (HL7) exchange of patient, health information, clinical orders and results, health records, billing, and reimbursement. HL7 messages allow the CPM environment to be integrated with other IT systems such that:

    – Creation of a patient MDAP begins with check-in or admission.
    – The MDAP is updated as care activities progress.
    – The MDAP is suspended or terminated when the patient is discharged or their visit is completed.

IBM has implemented the core capabilities of CPM using IBM Business Process Manager and WebSphere Message Broker.

14.17 Hadoop Use Cases

While we continue to talk about big data use cases, we will see how many health organizations use Apache Hadoop to overcome the healthcare challenge with respect to big data.

Some of the Hadoop use cases include:

Predictive Analysis	Real Time Monitoring	Historical EMR analysis
• Heart patient weigh themselves at home using scales that transmit data wirelessly to the health centre • Algorithms analyse data that indicates a high risk of readmission alerting a physician	• Patient statistics are transmitted using wireless sensors every minute • If the vital signs exceed thresolds,the staff can attend to the patient imeediately	• Hadoop reduces the cost to store data on clinical operations allowing longer retention of data on staffing decisions and clinical outcomes. • Analysis of this data allows administrators to promote individuals and practises that achieve the best results

Medical device management	Research Cohort Selection
• For biomedical device maintanence,sensor data can be used to manage medical equipments.The team can know where all the equipment is without wasting much time • Data can be used to make decisions about when to repair or replace eqipment	• Researchers at teaching hospitals can access patient data in Hadoop for cohort discovery and then present the sample to internal review board

Given below is the architecture diagram for Hadoop (Fig. 14.14).

How Data Analysis Works with Hadoop

1. Source data comes from different sources as shown in the diagram above.
2. Apache SQOOP is included in the data platform which transfers data between external structured data stores (such as Teradata, Netezza, MySQL, or Oracle) into HDFS or related systems like Hive or HBase.
3. Depending in the use case, data is processed in batch (using HadoopMapReduce and Apache Pig), interactively (with Apache Hive), online (with Apache HBase), or by streaming (with Apache Storm).
4. Once data is stored and processed, it can be analyzed either in a cluster or exported to relational data stores for analysis there. These data stores might include:

   (a) Enterprise data warehouse
   (b) Quality data mart
   (c) Surgical data mart
   (d) Clinical data mart
   (e) Diagnosis data mart
   (f) Neo4j database

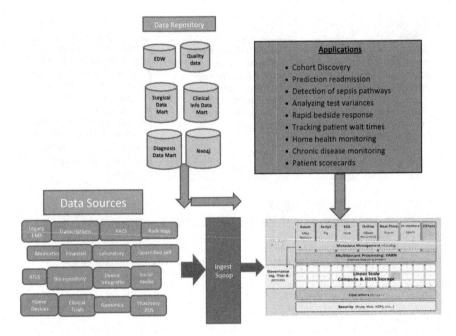

Fig. 14.14 HADOOP

Activity Section

Let's take a small activity to learn more about big data use cases.
The Internet is flooded with a lot of areas where big data is put into practice
in the field of healthcare.

Activity No. 3 :

Using a pictorial representation, list out as many use cases you see in the
Internet regarding big data that have come up from different companies.
The takeaway from this activity is to learn practically happening things in the
field of healthcare big data analytics.
Happy Interneting!

14.18 Big Data Analytics: Success Stories

Below are few success stories about the value that big data has delivered to
healthcare.

- The University of Ontario's Institute of Technology partnered with a prominent
  technology firm—IBM—to develop Project Artemis, a highly flexible platform
  that leverages streaming analytics to monitor newborns in the neonatal intensive
  care unit of a hospital. Using these technologies, the hospital was able to predict

the onset of nosocomial infections 24 h before symptoms appeared. The hospital also tagged all time-series data that had been modified by software algorithms. In case of a lawsuit or medical inquiry, the hospital felt that it had to produce both the original and modified readings. Plus, the hospital established policies around safeguarding protected health information.

- A recent *New Yorker* magazine article, by Atul Gawande, MD, described how orthopedic surgeons at Brigham and Women's Hospital in Boston, relying on their own experience combined with data gleaned from research on a host of factors critical to the success of joint-replacement surgery, systematically standardized knee joint-replacement surgery, with a resultant increase in more successful outcomes and reduced costs. Similarly, the University of Michigan Health System standardized the administration of blood transfusions, reducing the need for transfusions by 31 % and expenses by $200,000 a month.

- The Department of Veterans Affairs (VA) in the United States has successfully demonstrated several healthcare information technology (HIT) and remote patient monitoring programs. The VA health system generally outperforms the private sector in following recommended processes for patient care, adhering to clinical guidelines, and achieving greater rates of evidence-based drug therapy. These achievements are largely possible because of the VA's performance-based accountability framework and disease-management practices enabled by electronic medical records (EMR) and HIT.

- The California-based integrated managed-care consortium Kaiser Permanente connected clinical and cost data to provide a crucial data set that led to the discovery of adverse drug effects and subsequent withdrawal of the drug Vioxx from the market.

- Researchers at the Johns Hopkins School of Medicine found that they could use data from Google Flu Trends (a free, publicly available aggregator of relevant search terms) to predict surges in flu-related emergency room visits a week before warnings came from the Centers for Disease Control and Prevention. Similarly, Twitter updates were as accurate as official reports at tracking the spread of cholera in Haiti after the January 2010 earthquake; they were also 2 weeks earlier.

- Researchers at IBM have devised a prototype program that predicts the likely outcomes of diabetes patients, based on the patients' longitudinal health data and association with particular physicians, management protocols, and relationship to population health management averages.

Activity Section: **It's Time to Get Creative!**
Take any of the above success stories from the above list and create a model. The model should depict the process flow of the success story. I am calling each success story as a project.
Below are the points to be incorporated:

1. *Input to the project*
2. *Process flow—depiction of how big data is used*
3. *Output—the benefits received from the project*

Activity No.4:
Prerequisites:
Before starting with the model creation, gather all the input you need for the project chosen. Draw a rough figure in a paper to come up with a flow diagram on how the model will look. You can use any material—thermocole, Post-its, plastic toys, color papers, etc.
By just seeing your model, any laymen should be able to understand the flow. You can take a maximum of 15 days to create the model.

14.19   Opportunities for BDA in Healthcare

Big data is said to be the future of healthcare. Big data with analytics is a perfect combination. The continuous increase in the health record digitalization along with electronic health records presents new opportunities where big data can be leveraged to take clinically important decisions and answers questions that seemed extremely unanswerable.

Few areas where big data is seeing a lot of opportunities include *clinicaldecision support* where big data is used to provide better treatment recommendations and decisions, *personalized care* to highlight the best possible treatment for a disease using genomics, and *population healthcontrol* where social media and Web-based data can be used to determine diseases that are likely to occur in a particular population.

Now let's talk about few BDA opportunities in detail.

14.20   Member 360

Employers are facing exasperation due to the huge rise in healthcare costs and are looking for ways to lower the burden. As a result, healthcare costs are more likely shifted to the employees. The employees who have added burden of healthcare costs look for value added service and personalization.

The Member 360 provides a member-centric solution that gives a personalized view of the members across all service areas. It is a single solution which can provide an architecture that would reduce the expense of data integration and provide a single enterprise view of the business and member data. With the data that is maintained as part of the Member 360, health plans can help their members better manage their plans by reducing healthcare cost and increasing customer satisfaction.

Member 360 will help in achieving the below targets.

Providing latest data that is accurate

Online services help improve member interaction

Manage complete member view including claim,provider and product information

Providing easy access to information by ensuring the data is secure in all aspects

Delivering right informtaion at the right time to the right people

Getting efficient benefits from member information to provide better care

14.21   Genomics

Genomics is about relating a disease with the genetic factors of a human being. It is a unique way of looking in depth to find out what diseases can be affected to a particular person or the right medication that needs to be given to a person suffering from a particular disease. Genomics can help identify what medicines really work for the person and what do not work. This can help prevent any side effects that can occur due to the medicine. A lot of big data analytical tools are used to research on genomics to improve personalized care.

Genomics includes sequencing, mapping, and analyzing a wide of DNA codes to identify their behavior to either prevent or cure a disease.

Now let's see the factors that encourage genomics (Fig. 14.15).

A lot of companies are working on many approaches to make effective use of genomics in order for the patient to meet the right doctor at the right time with the right treatment options.

Below is a data flow on how genomics happens (Fig. 14.16).

The figure above illustrates our approach for jointly modeling the haplotype data and the gene expression data. The *haplotype model* is a statistical model of correlations within the haplotype data. SNP variants that are closely linked in the genome are in nonrandom association with neighboring SNPs, leading to a block-like structure in the haplotypes, where blocks are conserved between different individuals. We aim to use a haplotype model that will capture correlated structures in the data to compactly represent the entire observed haplotype sequences. SNPs can affect

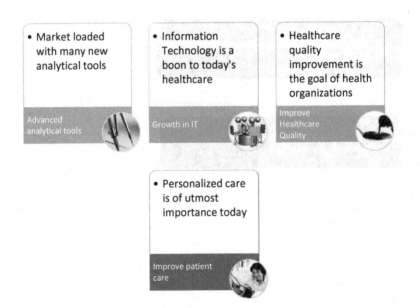

Fig. 14.15 Factors driving genomics

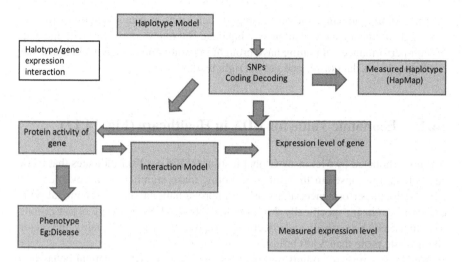

Fig. 14.16 Factors driving genomics

the functionality of genes in two main ways; SNPs in the coding regions of a gene affect the protein that the gene codes for while SNPs in the regulatory region affect how much gene is expressed.

Our framework separates out these two pathways so that direct and indirect effects on gene expression can be modeled in different ways. Genes are often co-regulated or co-expressed, leading to strong correlations in expression levels between different genes. These have been examined in previous gene expression models. As we have information from coding SNPs, we plan to extend such models to a richer *interaction model* that also models the intracellular relationship between levels of protein activity and levels of gene expression. The final stage of our analysis will be to identify correlations between our haplotype and interaction models and the phenotypes or diseases of the individuals that the samples come from. This will identify relationships between genetic variation and gene expression and hence lead to improved understanding of the genetic causes of human disease.

14.22 Clinical Monitoring

Devices that can measure physiological activity on or inside a human being through various sensors or medical devices are called clinical monitoring. There are a lot of smartphone applications in the market today that capture data which is used to monitor the behavior of patients by accessing data like blood glucose, heart rate, etc. This can help prevent an adverse situation which can create problems to the patient. The quality of care is improved as the patient receives personalized care.

The capture, indexing, and processing of such kinds of data which differ in size, type, and volume are a big challenge to big data. But many companies with the help of high-performance computing have brought in parallel processing techniques that can help process data faster and get the right results.

14.23 Economic Value for BDA in Healthcare (Fig. 14.17)

A study conducted by Mckinsey Global Institute (MGI) in 2011 indicates that BDA can potentially transform the global economy, make significant improvements to organizational performance, and work to improve national and international policies. For healthcare specifically, MGI predicted that if US healthcare organizations were to use BDA creatively and effectively to drive efficiency and quality, the sector could create more than $300 billion in value annually.

McKinsey's research points out that valuable insights such as patient behaviors, along with demands and efficiencies about the environment surrounding the patient, are buried in unstructured or highly varied data sources. The report cites successful pilot projects in the United States and internationally that have used BDA to find efficiencies in clinical operations, analyze data from remotely monitored patients, assess clinical and cost efficiencies of new treatments, and use analytics in public health surveillance and disease response.

Fig. 14.17 Healthcare affecting global economy

A significant component of the $300 billion in forecasted value in the MGI report comes from clinical operations and how BDA may affect the way clinical care is provided. Examples include:

- Outcomes-based research to determine which treatments will work best for specific patients ("optimal treatment pathways") by analyzing comprehensive patient and outcome data to compare the effectiveness of various interventions
- Pre-diagnosis that automatically mines medical literature to create a medical expertise database capable of suggesting treatment options to clinicians based on patients' health records
- Remote patient monitoring for chronically ill patients and analyzing the resulting data to monitor treatment adherence, reduce patient in-hospital bed days, cut emergency department visits, improve the targeting of nursing home care and outpatient physician appointments, and reduce long-term health complications

14.24 Big Data Challenges for Healthcare

It is an accepted fact that there are a lot of big data uses that help transform our healthcare operations, improve quality of care, and provide personalized patient care. But big data has a lot of challenges which when eradicated would make life easier. It is easy to use the word eradicate but it is not as easy to implement the same. The below listing shows about a few big data challenges that we face today (Fig. 14.18).

14.25 Future of Big Data in Healthcare

There is no doubt in saying big data is the future of healthcare. Big data analytics is really important to answer many healthcare-related business questions and to make the world a healthy place to live in. Below are some areas which have been seen as an area of improvement for healthcare in the near future (Fig. 14.19).

14.26 Conclusions

Big data is the potential of healthcare. Big data has a big role to play in transforming data into health information. By investing more on research, health organizations can look into better ways to improve care for its members. Out-of-the-box thinking is today's requirement. Seeing innovation in every aspect aids not only to a better healthcare but to a healthcare that none of us have visualized. Proper analytics and innovative solutions can make the earth a healthy place to live.

Data security and Privacy

- Disclosure of Personal Health Information is a major risk
- Existing policies have to revisited to ensure that PHI data is handled with utmost care

Skilled Resource set

- There is a need to have Data scientist and Data analyst to perform big data analysis.
- There is already a huge shortage in the required skillset for BDA.

Data Ownership

- There is a lot of big data flowing which includes genomics,remote sensing,social media,mobile app and many other data types.
- Who is going to own and govern this data is a BIG QUESTION???

Healthcare Models

- There is a need to have sufficient business case evidence in health to measure investment return
- Do we have all required evidences at this point in time??

Funding Types

- Funding models have to be revisited to ensure better care.
- There should be differentiation of incentives to physicians who provide quality care services and to those to fall below standards.

Governace

- Big data analytics will impact the Governance policies.
- Existing legislation,governance and information management process are highly impacted.

Fig. 14.18 Big data challenges

Research - Genomics and beyond

Transform Data into useful insights

Ensure personalized care

Help providers take informed decisions through evidence based approach

Increase awareness about diseases and their treatment methods

Early disease detection

Fig. 14.19 Future of big data in healthcare

14.27 Exercises

Objective Type

1. What is the approximate data that would be accumulated by 2015?

   (a) 2 billion terabytes
   (b) 8.5 million terabytes
   (c) 8.5 billion terabytes

2. By 2020, physicians should face _____ amount of medical data and facts that a human could possibly process.

   (a) 100×
   (b) 200×
   (c) 250×

3. _____ refers to the different type of data coming from different sources.

   (a) Volume
   (b) Variety
   (c) Veracity

4. What are the data types that IBM Watson can process?

   (a) Structured
   (b) Unstructured
   (c) Both a and b

5. US healthcare can create _____ if big data was used effectively and efficiently.

   (a) $300 billion
   (b) $400 billion
   (c) $500 billion

Detailed Type

1. What are the different market factors driving healthcare?
2. What are the different healthcare types? Explain each component in detail.
3. Why is high-performance computing required for healthcare?
4. Explain big data challenges with respect to healthcare?
5. What is IBM Watson? Explain IBM Watson and its benefits?
6. Explain use cases of big data analysis?
7. What is genomics? Why it is genomics data very important?

Index

© Springer International Publishing Switzerland 2015   425
P. Raj et al., *High-Performance Big-Data Analytics*, Computer Communications
and Networks, DOI 10.1007/978-3-319-20744-5

Printed in the United States
By Bookmasters